More praise from across the nation for the JobBank series:

"One of the better publishers of employment almanacs is Adams Media Corporation ... publisher of *The Metropolitan New York JobBank* and similarly named directories of employers in Texas, Boston, Chicago, Northern and Southern California, and Washington DC. A good buy...."

> **-Wall Street Journal's**
> **National Business Employment Weekly**

"*JobBank* books are all devoted to specific job markets. This is helpful if you are thinking about working in cities like San Antonio, Washington, Boston, or states such as Tennessee or the Carolinas. You can use them for research, and a particularly useful feature is the inclusion of the type of positions that are commonly offered at the companies listed."

> **-Karen Ronald, Library Director**
> **Wilton Library, Wilton, CT**

"If you are looking for a job ... before you go to the newspapers and the help-wanted ads, listen to Bob Adams, publisher *of The Metropolitan New York JobBank.*"

> **-Tom Brokaw, NBC**

"Since 1985 the Adams *JobBank Series* has proven to be the consummate tool for the efficient job search."

> **-Mel Rappleyea, Human Resources Director**
> **Starbucks Coffee Company**

"Having worked in the Career Services field for 10 years, I know the quality of Adams publications."

> **-Philip Meade, Director of Graduate Career Services**
> **Baruch School of Business (New York NY)**

"I read through the 'Basics of Job Winning' and 'Resumes' sections [in *The Dallas-Fort Worth JobBank*] and found them to be very informative, with some positive tips for the job searcher. I believe the strategies outlined will bring success to any determined candidate."

> **-Camilla Norder, Professional Recruiter**
> **Presbyterian Hospital of Dallas**

"The ultimate in a superior series of job hunt directories."

> **-Cornell University Career Center's**
> *Where to Start*

"Help on the job hunt ... Anyone who is job-hunting in the New York area can find a lot of useful ideas in a new paperback called *The Metropolitan New York JobBank*...."

-Angela Taylor, *New York Times*

"A timely book for Chicago job hunters follows books from the same publisher that were well received in New York and Boston ... [*The Chicago JobBank* is] a fine tool for job hunters...."

-Clarence Peterson, *Chicago Tribune*

"Because our listing is seen by people across the nation, it generates lots for resumes for us. We encourage unsolicited resumes. We'll always be listed [in *The Chicago JobBank*] as long as I'm in this career."

-Tom Fitzpatrick, Director of Human Resources
Merchandise Mart Properties, Inc.

"Job hunting is never fun, but this book can ease the ordeal ...*[The Los Angeles JobBank*] will help allay fears, build confidence, and avoid wheel-spinning."

-Robert W. Ross, *Los Angeles Times*

"*The Seattle JobBank* is an essential resource for job hunters."

-Gil Lopez, Staffing Team Manager
Battelle Pacific Northwest Laboratories

"*The Phoenix JobBank* is a first-class publication. The information provided is useful and current."

-Lyndon Denton
Director of Human Resources and Materials Management
Apache Nitrogen Products, Inc.

"*The Florida JobBank* is an invaluable job-search reference tool. It provides the most up-to-date information and contact names available for companies in Florida. I should know – it worked for me!"

-Rhonda Cody, Human Resources Consultant
Aetna Life and Casualty

"I read through the 'Basics of Job Winning' and 'Resumes' sections [in *The Dallas-Fort Worth JobBank*] and found them to be very informative, with some positive tips for the job searcher. I believe the strategies outlined will bring success to any determined candidate."

-Camilla Norder, Professional Recruiter
Presbyterian Hospital of Dallas

"Through *The Dallas-Fort Worth JobBank,* we've been able to attract high-quality candidates for several positions."

-Rob Bertino, Southern States Sales Manager
CompuServe

What makes the JobBank series the nation's premier line of employment guides?

With vital employment information on thousands of employers across the nation, the JobBank series is the most comprehensive and authoritative set of career directories available today.

Each book in the series provides information on **dozens of different industries** in a given city or area, with the primary employer listings providing contact information, telephone and fax numbers, e-mail addresses, Websites, a summary of the firm's business, internships, and in many cases descriptions of the firm's typical professional job categories.

All of the reference information in the JobBank series is as up-to-date and accurate as possible. Every year, the entire database is thoroughly researched and verified by mail and by telephone. Adams Media Corporation publishes **more local employment guides more often** than any other publisher of career directories.

The JobBank series offers **20 regional titles**, from Boston to San Francisco. All of the information is organized geographically, because most people look for jobs in specific areas of the country.

A condensed, but thorough, review of the entire job search process is presented in the chapter **The Basics of Job Winning**, a feature that has received many compliments from career counselors. In addition, each JobBank directory includes a section on **resumes and cover letters** the *New York Times* has acclaimed as "excellent."

The JobBank series gives job hunters the most comprehensive, timely, and accurate career information, organized and indexed to facilitate your job search. An entire career reference library, JobBank books are designed to help you find optimal employment in any market.

Top career publications from Adams Media Corporation

The JobBank Series:
each JobBank book is $17.95

The Atlanta JobBank, 15th Ed.
The Austin/San Antonio JobBank, 4th Ed.
The Boston JobBank, 19th Ed.
The Carolina JobBank, 7th Ed.
The Chicago JobBank, 18th Ed.
The Colorado JobBank, 13th Ed.
The Connecticut JobBank, 3rd Ed.
The Dallas-Fort Worth JobBank, 14th Ed.
The Florida JobBank, 15th Ed.
The Houston JobBank, 12th Ed.
The Los Angeles JobBank, 17th Ed.
The New Jersey JobBank, 3rd Ed.
The Metropolitan New York JobBank, 18th Ed.
The Ohio JobBank, 11th Ed.
The Greater Philadelphia JobBank, 14th Ed.
The Phoenix JobBank, 9th Ed.
The San Francisco Bay Area JobBank, 17th Ed.
The Seattle JobBank, 13th Ed.
The Virginia JobBank, 4th Ed.
The Metropolitan Washington DC JobBank, 16th Ed.

The National JobBank, 2005
    (Covers the entire U.S.: $475.00 hc)

Other Career Titles:
The Adams Cover Letter Almanac ($12.95)
The Adams Executive Recruiters Almanac, 2nd Ed. ($17.95)
The Adams Job Interview Almanac ($12.95)
The Adams Jobs Almanac, 8th Ed. ($16.95)
The Adams Resume Almanac ($12.95)

Business Etiquette in Brief ($7.95)
Career Tests ($12.95)
Closing Techniques, 3rd Ed. ($9.95)
Cold Calling Techniques, 5th Ed. ($9.95)
College Grad Job Hunter, 5th Ed. ($14.95)
The Complete Resume & Job Search Book
    for College Students, 2nd Ed. ($12.95)
Cover Letters That Knock 'em Dead, 6th Ed.
    ($12.95)
The Everything Alternative Careers Book
    ($14.95)
The Everything Cover Letter Book ($12.95)
The Everything Get-A-Job Book ($12.95)
The Everything Hot Careers Book
    ($12.95)
The Everything Job Interview Book
    ($14.95)
The Everything Leadership Book
    ($12.95)
The Everything Online Business Book
    ($12.95)
The Everything Online Job Search Book
    ($12.95)
The Everything Resume Book ($14.95)
The Everything Selling Book ($14.95)
Knock 'em Dead, 2005 ($14.95)
Knock 'em Dead Business Presentations
    ($12.95)
Market Yourself and Your Career, 2nd Ed.
    ($12.95)
The New Professional Image ($12.95)
The 150 Most Profitable Home Businesses
    for Women ($9.95)
The Resume Handbook, 4th Ed. ($9.95)
Resumes That Knock 'em Dead, 6th Ed.
    ($12.95)
The Road to CEO ($10.95)
The 250 Job Interview Questions You'll Most
    Likely Be Asked ($9.95)
Your Executive Image ($10.95)

7th Edition

THE

Carolina
JobBank

adams
media

Published by Adams Media, an F+W Publications Company
57 Littlefield Street, Avon, MA 02322 U.S.A.
www.adamsmedia.com

ISBN: 1-59337-220-5
ISSN: 1072-5741
Manufactured in Canada

Because addresses and telephone numbers of smaller companies change rapidly, we recommend you call each company and verify the information before mailing to the employers listed in this book. Mass mailings are not recommended.

While the publisher has made every reasonable effort to obtain and verify accurate information, occasional errors are possible due to the magnitude of the data. Should you discover an error, or if a company is missing, please write the editors at the above address so that we may update future editions.

"This publication is designed to provide accurate and authoritative information with regard to the subject matter covered. It is sold with the understanding that the publisher is not engaged in rendering legal, accounting, or other professional advice. If legal advice or other expert assistance is required, the services of a competent professional person should be sought."
    --From a Declaration of Principles jointly adopted by a Committee of the American Bar Association and a Committee of Publishers and Associations

This book is available on standing order and at quantity discounts for bulk purchases. For information, call 800/872-5627 (in Massachusetts, 508/427-7100) or e-mail: jobbank@adamsmedia.com

TABLE OF CONTENTS

SECTION ONE: INTRODUCTION

How to Use This Book/12
An introduction to the most effective way to use The Carolina JobBank.

SECTION TWO: THE JOB SEARCH

The Basics of Job Winning/16
A review of the elements of a successful job search campaign. Includes advice on developing effective strategies, time planning, and preparing for interviews. Special sections address situations faced by jobseekers who are currently employed, those who have lost a job, and graduates conducting their first job search.

Resumes and Cover Letters/30
Advice on creating strong resumes and cover letters with examples.

SECTION THREE: PRIMARY EMPLOYERS

The Employers/49
The Carolina JobBank is organized according to industry. Many listings include the address and phone number of each major firm listed, along with a description of the company's basic product lines and services, and, in many cases, a contact name and other relevant hiring information.

Accounting and Management Consulting/50
Advertising, Marketing, and Public Relations/53
- Direct Mail Marketers, Market Researchers

Aerospace/55
- Aerospace Products and Services
- Aircraft Equipment and Parts

Apparel, Fashion, and Textiles/58
- Broadwoven Fabric Mills, Knitting Mills, and Yarn and Thread Mills
- Curtains and Draperies
- Footwear
- Nonwoven Fabrics
- Textile Goods and Finishing

Architecture, Construction, and Engineering/71
- Architectural and Engineering Services
- Civil and Mechanical Engineering Firms
- Construction Products, Manufacturers, and Wholesalers
- General Contractors/Specialized Trade Contractor

Arts, Entertainment, Sports, and Recreation/76
- Botanical and Zoological Gardens
- Entertainment Groups
- Motion Picture and Video Tape Production and Distribution
- Museums and Art Galleries
- Physical Fitness Facilities
- Professional Sports Clubs; Sporting and Recreational Camps
- Public Golf Courses and Racing and Track Operations
- Theatrical Producers and Services

Automotive/79
- Automotive Repair Shops
- Automotive Stampings

- *Industrial Vehicles and Moving Equipment*
- *Motor Vehicles and Equipment*
- *Travel Trailers and Campers*

Banking, Savings and Loans, and Other Depository Institutions/82

- *Banks*
- *Bank Holding Companies and Associations*
- *Lending Firms/Financial Services Institutions*

Biotechnology, Pharmaceuticals, and Scientific R&D/89

- *Clinical Labs*
- *Lab Equipment Manufacturers*
- *Pharmaceutical Manufacturers and Distributors*

Business Services and Non-Scientific Research/95

- *Adjustment and Collection Services*
- *Cleaning, Maintenance, and Pest Control Services*
- *Credit Reporting Services*
- *Detective, Guard, and Armored Car Services/Security Systems Services*
- *Miscellaneous Equipment Rental and Leasing*
- *Secretarial and Court Reporting Services*

Charities and Social Services/97

- *Social and Human Service Agencies*
- *Job Training and Vocational Rehabilitation Services*
- *Nonprofit Organizations*

Chemicals, Rubber, and Plastics/101

- *Adhesives, Detergents, Inks, Paints, Soaps, Varnishes*
- *Agricultural Chemicals and Fertilizers*
- *Carbon and Graphite Products*
- *Chemical Engineering Firms*
- *Industrial Gases*

Communications: Telecommunications and Broadcasting/107

- *Cable/Pay Television Services*
- *Communications Equipment*
- *Radio and Television Broadcasting Stations*
- *Telephone, Telegraph, and Other Message Communications*

Computer Hardware, Software, and Services/112

- *Computer Components and Hardware Manufacturers*
- *Consultants and Computer Training Companies*
- *Internet and Online Service Providers*
- *Networking and Systems Services*
- *Repair Services/Rental and Leasing*
- *Resellers, Wholesalers, and Distributors*
- *Software Developers/Programming Services*

Educational Services/126

- *Business/Secretarial/Data Processing Schools*
- *Colleges/Universities/Professional Schools*
- *Community Colleges/Technical Schools/Vocational Schools*
- *Elementary and Secondary Schools*
- *Preschool and Child Daycare Services*

Electronic/Industrial Electrical Equipment and Components/135

- *Electronic Machines and Systems*
- *Semiconductor Manufacturers*

Environmental and Waste Management Services/144

- *Environmental Engineering Firms*
- *Sanitary Services*

Fabricated Metal Products and Primary Metals/146

- *Aluminum and Copper Foundries*
- *Die-Castings*

- *Iron and Steel Foundries/Steel Works, Blast Furnaces, and Rolling Mills*

Financial Services/151
- *Consumer Financing and Credit Agencies*
- *Investment Specialists*
- *Mortgage Bankers and Loan Brokers*
- *Security and Commodity Brokers, Dealers, and Exchanges*

Food and Beverages/Agriculture/153
- *Crop Services and Farm Supplies*
- *Dairy Farms*
- *Food Manufacturers/Processors and Agricultural Producers*
- *Tobacco Products*

Government/158
- *Courts*
- *Executive, Legislative, and General Government*
- *Public Agencies (Firefighters, Military, Police)*
- *United States Postal Service*

Health Care Services, Equipment, and Products/162
- *Dental Labs and Equipment*
- *Home Health Care Agencies*
- *Hospitals and Medical Centers*
- *Medical Equipment Manufacturers and Wholesalers*
- *Offices and Clinics of Health Practitioners*
- *Residential Treatment Centers/Nursing Homes*
- *Veterinary Services*

Hotels and Restaurants/174
Insurance/177
Legal Services/181
Manufacturing: Miscellaneous Consumer/184
- *Art Supplies*
- *Batteries*
- *Cosmetics and Related Products*
- *Household Appliances and Audio/Video Equipment*
- *Jewelry, Silverware, and Plated Ware*
- *Miscellaneous Household Furniture and Fixtures*
- *Musical Instruments*
- *Tools*
- *Toys and Sporting Goods*

Manufacturing: Miscellaneous Industrial/193
- *Ball and Roller Bearings*
- *Commercial Furniture and Fixtures*
- *Fans, Blowers, and Purification Equipment*
- *Industrial Machinery and Equipment*
- *Motors and Generators/Compressors and Engine Parts*
- *Vending Machines*

Mining, Gas, Petroleum, Energy Related/201
- *Anthracite, Coal, and Ore Mining*
- *Mining Machinery and Equipment*
- *Oil and Gas Field Services*
- *Petroleum and Natural Gas*

Paper and Wood Products/203
- *Forest and Wood Products and Services*
- *Lumber and Wood Wholesale*
- *Millwork, Plywood, and Structural Members*
- *Paper and Wood Mills*

Printing and Publishing/211
- *Book, Newspaper, and Periodical Publishers*

- Commercial Photographers
- Commercial Printing Services
- Graphic Designers

Real Estate/218
- Land Subdividers and Developers
- Real Estate Agents, Managers, and Operators
- Real Estate Investment Trusts

Retail/221

Stone, Clay, Glass, and Concrete Products/227
- Cement, Tile, Sand, and Gravel
- Crushed and Broken Stone
- Glass and Glass Products
- Mineral Products

Transportation and Travel/230
- Air, Railroad, and Water Transportation Services
- Courier Services
- Local and Interurban Passenger Transit
- Ship Building and Repair
- Transportation Equipment
- Travel Agencies
- Trucking
- Warehousing and Storage

Utilities: Electric, Gas, and Water/231

Miscellaneous Wholesaling/233
- Exporters and Importers

SECTION FOUR: INDUSTRY ASSOCIATIONS

Associations by Industry/237

SECTION FIVE: INDEX

Index of Primary Employers/299

INTRODUCTION

HOW TO USE THIS BOOK

Right now, you hold in your hands one of the most effective job-hunting tools available anywhere. In *The Carolina JobBank*, you will find valuable information to help you launch or continue a rewarding career. But before you open to the book's employer listings and start calling about current job openings, take a few minutes to learn how best to use the resources presented in *The Carolina JobBank*.

The Carolina JobBank will help you to stand out from other jobseekers. While many people looking for a new job rely solely on newspaper help-wanted ads, this book offers you a much more effective job-search method -- direct contact. The direct contact method has been proven twice as effective as scanning the help-wanted ads. Instead of waiting for employers to come looking for you, you'll be far more effective going to them. While many of your competitors will use trial and error methods in trying to set up interviews, you'll learn not only how to get interviews, but what to expect once you've got them.

In the next few pages, we'll take you through each section of the book so you'll be prepared to get a jump-start on your competition.

Basics of Job Winning

Preparation. Strategy. Time management. These are three of the most important elements of a successful job search. *Basics of Job Winning* helps you address these and all the other elements needed to find the right job.

One of your first priorities should be to define your personal career objectives. What qualities make a job desirable to you? Creativity? High pay? Prestige? Use *Basics of Job Winning* to weigh these questions. Then use the rest of the chapter to design a strategy to find a job that matches your criteria.

In *Basics of Job Winning,* you'll learn which job-hunting techniques work, and which don't. We've reviewed the pros and cons of mass mailings, help-wanted ads, and direct contact. We'll show you how to develop and approach contacts in your field; how to research a prospective employer; and how to use that information to get an interview and the job.

Also included in *Basics of Job Winning*: interview dress code and etiquette, the "do's and don'ts" of interviewing, sample interview questions, and more. We also deal with some of the unique problems faced by those jobseekers who are currently employed, those who have lost a job, and college students conducting their first job search.

Resumes and Cover Letters

The approach you take to writing your resume and cover letter can often mean the difference between getting an interview and never being noticed. In this section, we discuss different formats, as well as what to put on (and what to leave off) your resume. We review the benefits and drawbacks of professional resume writers, and the importance of a follow-up letter. Also included in this section are sample resumes and cover letters which you can use as models.

The Employer Listings

Employers are listed alphabetically by industry. When a company does business under a person's name, like "John Smith & Co.," the company is usually listed by the surname's spelling (in this case "S"). Exceptions occur when a company's name is widely recognized, like "JCPenney" or "Howard Johnson Motor Lodge." In those cases, the company's first name is the key ("J" and "H" respectively).

The Carolina JobBank covers a very wide range of industries. Each company profile is assigned to one of the industry chapters listed below.

Accounting and Management Consulting
Advertising, Marketing, and Public
   Relations
Aerospace
Apparel, Fashion, and Textiles
Architecture, Construction, and Engineering
Arts, Entertainment, Sports, and Recreation
Automotive
Banking/Savings and Loans
Biotechnology, Pharmaceuticals, and
   Scientific R&D
Business Services and Non-Scientific
   Research
Charities and Social Services
Chemicals/Rubber and Plastics
Communications: Telecommunications and
   Broadcasting
Computer Hardware, Software, and
   Services
Educational Services
Electronic/Industrial Electrical Equipment
   and Components

Environmental and Waste Management
   Services
Fabricated/Primary Metals and Products
Financial Services
Food and Beverages/Agriculture
Government
Health Care: Services, Equipment, and
   Products
Hotels and Restaurants
Insurance
Legal Services
Manufacturing: Miscellaneous Consumer
Manufacturing: Miscellaneous Industrial
Mining/Gas/Petroleum/Energy Related
Paper and Wood Products
Printing and Publishing
Real Estate
Retail
Stone, Clay, Glass, and Concrete Products
Transportation/Travel
Utilities: Electric/Gas/Water
Miscellaneous Wholesaling

Many of the company listings offer detailed company profiles. In addition to company names, addresses, and phone numbers, these listings also include contact names or hiring departments, and descriptions of each company's products and/or services. Many of these listings also feature a variety of additional information including:

Positions advertised - A list of open positions the company was advertising at the time our research was conducted. Note: Keep in mind that *The Carolina JobBank* is a directory of major employers in the area, not a directory of openings currently available. Positions listed in this book that were advertised at the time research was conducted may no longer be open. Many of the companies listed will be hiring, others will not. However, since most professional job openings are filled without the placement of help-wanted ads, contacting the employers in this book directly is still a more effective method than browsing the Sunday papers.

Special programs - Does the company offer training programs, internships, or apprenticeships? These programs can be important to first time jobseekers and college students looking for practical work experience. Many employer profiles will include information on these programs.

Parent company - If an employer is a subsidiary of a larger company, the name of that parent company will often be listed here. Use this information to supplement your company research before contacting the employer.

Number of employees - The number of workers a company employs.

Company listings may also include information on other U.S. locations and any stock exchanges the firm may be listed on.

A note on all employer listings that appear in *The Carolina JobBank*: This book is intended as a starting point. It is not intended to replace any effort that you, the jobseeker, should devote to your job hunt. Keep in mind that while a great deal of effort has been put into collecting and verifying the company profiles provided in this book, addresses and contact names change regularly. Inevitably, some contact names listed herein have changed even before you read this. We recommend you contact a company before mailing your resume to ensure nothing has changed.

Industry Associations

This section includes a select list of professional and trade associations organized by industry. Many of these associations can provide employment advice and job-search help, offer magazines that cover the industry, and provide additional information or directories that may supplement the employer listings in this book.

Index of Primary Employers

The Carolina JobBank index is listed alphabetically by company name.

THE JOB SEARCH

THE BASICS OF JOB WINNING: A CONDENSED REVIEW

This chapter is divided into four sections. The first section explains the fundamentals that every jobseeker should know, especially first-time jobseekers. The next three sections deal with special situations faced by specific types of jobseekers: those who are currently employed, those who have lost a job, and college students.

THE BASICS:
Things Everyone Needs to Know

Career Planning

The first step to finding your ideal job is to clearly define your objectives. This is better known as career planning (or life planning if you wish to emphasize the importance of combining the two). Career planning has become a field of study in and of itself.

If you are thinking of choosing or switching careers, we particularly emphasize two things. First, choose a career where you will enjoy most of the day-to-day tasks. This sounds obvious, but most of us have at some point found the idea of a glamour industry or prestigious job title attractive without thinking of the key consideration: Would we enjoy performing the *everyday* tasks the position entails?

The second key consideration is that you are not merely choosing a career, but also a lifestyle. Career counselors indicate that one of the most common problems people encounter in jobseeking is that they fail to consider how well-suited they are for a particular position or career. For example, some people, attracted to management consulting by good salaries, early responsibility, and high-level corporate exposure, do not adapt well to the long hours, heavy travel demands, and constant pressure to produce. Be sure to ask yourself how you might adapt to the day-to-day duties and working environment that a specific position entails. Then ask yourself how you might adapt to the demands of that career or industry as a whole.

Choosing Your Strategy

Assuming that you've established your career objectives, the next step of the job search is to develop a strategy. If you don't take the time to develop a plan, you may find yourself going in circles after several weeks of randomly searching for opportunities that always seem just beyond your reach.

The most common jobseeking techniques are:

- following up on help-wanted advertisements (in the newspaper or online)
- using employment services
- relying on personal contacts
- contacting employers directly (the Direct Contact method)

Each of these approaches can lead to better jobs. However, the Direct Contact method boasts twice the success rate of the others. So unless you have specific reasons to employ other strategies, Direct Contact should form the foundation of your job search.

If you choose to use other methods as well, try to expend at least half your energy on Direct Contact. Millions of other jobseekers have already proven that Direct Contact has been twice as effective in obtaining employment, so why not follow in their footsteps?

Setting Your Schedule

Okay, so now that you've targeted a strategy it's time to work out the details of your job search. The most important detail is setting up a schedule. Of course, since job searches aren't something most people do regularly, it may be hard to estimate how long each step will take. Nonetheless, it is important to have a plan so that you can monitor your progress.

When outlining your job search schedule, have a realistic time frame in mind. If you will be job-searching full-time, your search could take at least two months or more. If you can only devote part-time effort, it will probably take at least four months.

You probably know a few people who seem to spend their whole lives searching for a better job in their spare time. Don't be one of them. If you are presently working and don't feel like devoting a lot of energy to jobseeking right now, then wait. Focus on enjoying your present position, performing your best on the job, and storing up energy for when you are really ready to begin your job search.

> **The first step in beginning your job search is to clearly define your objectives.**

Those of you who are currently unemployed should remember that *job-hunting is tough work, both physically and emotionally*. It is also intellectually demanding work that requires you to be at your best. So don't tire yourself out by working on your job campaign around the clock. At the same time, be sure to discipline yourself. The most logical way to manage your time while looking for a job is to keep your regular working hours.

If you are searching full-time and have decided to choose several different strategies, we recommend that you divide up each week, designating some time for each method. By trying several approaches at once, you can evaluate how promising each seems and alter your schedule accordingly. Keep in mind that the *majority of openings are filled without being advertised*. Remember also that positions advertised on the Internet are just as likely to already be filled as those found in the newspaper!

If you are searching part-time and decide to try several different contact methods, we recommend that you try them sequentially. You simply won't have enough time to put a meaningful amount of effort into more than one method at once. Estimate the length of your job search, and then allocate so many weeks or months for each contact method, beginning with Direct Contact. The purpose of setting this schedule is not to rush you to your goal but to help you periodically evaluate your progress.

The Direct Contact Method

Once you have scheduled your time, you are ready to begin your search in earnest. Beginning with the Direct Contact method, the first step is to develop a checklist for categorizing the types of firms for which you'd like to work. You might categorize firms by product line, size, customer type (such as industrial or consumer), growth prospects, or geographical location. Keep in mind, the shorter the list the easier it will be to locate a company that is right for you.

Next you will want to use this *JobBank* book to assemble your list of potential employers. Choose firms where *you* are most likely to be able to find a job. Try matching your skills with those that a specific job demands. Consider where your skills might be in demand, the degree of competition for employment, and the employment outlook at each company.

Separate your prospect list into three groups. The first 25 percent will be your primary target group, the next 25 percent will be your secondary group, and the remaining names will be your reserve group.

After you form your prospect list, begin working on your resume. Refer to the Resumes and Cover Letters section following this chapter for more information.

Once your resume is complete, begin researching your first batch of prospective employers. You will want to determine whether you would be happy working at the firms you are researching and to get a better idea of what their employment needs might be. You also need to obtain enough information to sound highly informed about the company during phone conversations and in mail correspondence. But don't go all out on your research yet! You probably won't be able to arrange interviews with some of these firms, so save your big research effort until you start to arrange interviews. Nevertheless, you should plan to spend several hours researching each firm.

> **The more you know about a company, the more likely you are to catch an interviewer's eye. (You'll also face fewer surprises once you get the job!)**

Do your research in batches to save time and energy. Start with this book, and find out what you can about each of the firms in your primary target group. For answers to specific questions, contact any pertinent professional associations that may be able to help you learn more about an employer. Read industry publications looking for articles on the firm. (Addresses of associations and names of important publications are listed after each section of employer listings in this book.) Then look up the company on the Internet or try additional resources at your local library. Keep organized, and maintain a folder on each firm.

Information to look for includes: company size; president, CEO, or owner's name; when the company was established; what each division does; and benefits that are important to you. An abundance of company information can now be found electronically, through the World Wide Web or commercial online services. Researching companies online is a convenient means of obtaining information quickly and easily. If you have access to the Internet, you can search from your home at any time of day.

You may search a particular company's Website for current information that may be otherwise unavailable in print. In fact, many companies that maintain a site update their information daily. In addition, you may also search articles written about the company online. Today, most of the nation's largest newspapers, magazines, trade publications, and regional business periodicals have online versions of their publications. To find additional resources, use a search engine like Yahoo! or Alta Vista and type in the keyword "companies" or "employers."

If you discover something that really disturbs you about the firm (they are about to close their only local office), or if you discover that your chances of getting a job there are practically nil (they have just instituted a hiring freeze), then cross them off your prospect list. If possible, supplement your research efforts by contacting individuals who know the firm well. Ideally you should make an informal contact with someone at that particular firm, but often a direct competitor or a major customer will be able to supply you with just as much information. At the very least, try to obtain whatever printed information the company has available -- not just annual reports, but product brochures, company profiles, or catalogs. This information is often available on the Internet.

Getting the Interview

Now it is time to make Direct Contact with the goal of arranging interviews. If you have read any books on job-searching, you may have noticed that most of these books tell you to avoid the human resources office like the plague. It is said that the human resources office never hires people; they screen candidates. Unfortunately, this is often the case. If you can identify the appropriate manager with the authority to hire you, you should try to contact that person directly.

The obvious means of initiating Direct Contact are:

- Mail (postal or electronic)
- Phone calls

Mail contact is a good choice if you have not been in the job market for a while. You can take your time to prepare a letter, say exactly what you want, and of course include your resume. Remember that employers receive many resumes every day. Don't be surprised if you do not get a response to your inquiry, *and don't spend weeks waiting for responses that may never come.* If you do send a letter, follow it up (or precede it) with a phone call. This will increase your impact, and because of the initial research you did, will underscore both your familiarity with and your interest in the firm. Bear in mind that your goal is to make your name a familiar one with prospective employers, so that when a position becomes available, your resume will be one of the first the hiring manager seeks out.

DEVELOPING YOUR CONTACTS: NETWORKING

Some career counselors feel that the best route to a better job is through somebody you already know or through somebody to whom you can be introduced. These counselors recommend that you build your contact base beyond your current acquaintances by asking each one to introduce you, or refer you, to additional people in your field of interest.

The theory goes like this: You might start with 15 personal contacts, each of whom introduces you to three additional people, for a total of 45 additional contacts. Then each of these people introduces you to three additional people, which adds 135 additional contacts. Theoretically, you will soon know every person in the industry.

Of course, developing your personal contacts does not work quite as smoothly as the theory suggests because some people will not be able to introduce you to anyone. The further you stray from your initial contact base, the weaker your references may be. So, if you do try developing your own contacts, try to begin with as many people that you know personally as you can. Dig into your personal phone book and your holiday greeting card list and locate old classmates from school. Be particularly sure to approach people who perform your personal business such as your lawyer, accountant, banker, doctor, stockbroker, and insurance agent. These people develop a very broad contact base due to the nature of their professions.

If you send a fax, always follow with a hard copy of your resume and cover letter in the mail. Often, through no fault of your own, a fax will come through illegibly and employers do not often have time to let candidates know.

Another alternative is to make a "cover call." Your cover call should be just like your cover letter: concise. Your first statement should interest the employer in you. Then try to subtly mention your familiarity with the firm. Don't be overbearing; keep your introduction to three sentences or less. Be pleasant, self-confident, and relaxed. This will greatly increase the chances of the person at the other end of the line developing the conversation. But don't press. If you are asked to follow up with "something in the mail," this signals the conversation's natural end. Don't try to prolong the conversation once it has ended, and don't ask what they want to receive in the mail. Always send your resume and a highly personalized follow-up letter, reminding the addressee of the phone conversation. *Always* include a cover letter if you are asked to send a resume, and treat your resume and cover letter as a total package. Gear your letter toward the specific position you are applying for and prove why you would be a "good match" for the position.

> **Always include a cover letter if you are asked to send a resume.**

Unless you are in telephone sales, making smooth and relaxed cover calls will probably not come easily. Practice them on your own, and then with your friends or relatives.

DON'T BOTHER WITH MASS MAILINGS OR BARRAGES OF PHONE CALLS

Direct Contact does not mean burying every firm within a hundred miles with mail and phone calls. Mass mailings rarely work in the job hunt. This also applies to those letters that are personalized -- but dehumanized -- on an automatic typewriter or computer. Don't waste your time or money on such a project; you will fool no one but yourself.

The worst part of sending out mass mailings, or making unplanned phone calls to companies you have not researched, is that you are likely to be remembered as someone with little genuine interest in the firm, who lacks sincerity -- somebody that nobody wants to hire.

If you obtain an interview as a result of a telephone conversation, be sure to send a thank-you note reiterating the points you made during the conversation. You will appear more professional and increase your impact. However, unless specifically requested, don't mail your resume once an interview has been arranged. Take it with you to the interview instead.

You should never show up to seek a professional position without an appointment. Even if you are somehow lucky enough to obtain an interview, you will appear so unprofessional that you will not be seriously considered.

HELP WANTED ADVERTISEMENTS

Only a small fraction of professional job openings are advertised. Yet the majority of jobseekers -- and quite a few people not in the job market -- spend a lot of time studying the help wanted ads. As a result, the competition for advertised openings is often very severe.

A moderate-sized employer told us about their experience advertising in the help wanted section of a major Sunday newspaper:

It was a disaster. We had over 500 responses from this relatively small ad in just one week. We have only two phone lines in this office and one was totally knocked out. We'll never advertise for professional help again.

If you insist on following up on help wanted ads, then research a firm before you reply to an ad. Preliminary research might help to separate you from all of the other professionals responding to that ad, many of whom will have only a passing interest in the opportunity. It will also give you insight about a particular firm, to help you determine if it is potentially a good match. That said, your chances of obtaining a job through the want ads are still much smaller than they are with the Direct Contact method.

Preparing for the Interview

As each interview is arranged, begin your in-depth research. You should arrive at an interview knowing the company upside-down and inside-out. You need to know the company's products, types of customers, subsidiaries, parent company, principal locations, rank in the industry, sales and profit trends, type of ownership, size, current plans, and much more. By this time you have probably narrowed your job search to one industry. Even if you haven't, you should still be familiar with common industry terms, the trends in the firm's industry, the firm's principal competitors and their relative performance, and the direction in which the industry leaders are headed.

Dig into every resource you can! Surf the Internet. Read the company literature, the trade press, the business press, and if the company is public, call your stockbroker (if you have one) and ask for additional information. If possible, speak to someone at the firm before the interview, or if not, speak to someone at a competing firm. The more time you

> **You should arrive at an interview knowing the company upside-down and inside-out.**

spend, the better. Even if you feel extremely pressed for time, you should set aside several hours for pre-interview research.

If you have been out of the job market for some time, don't be surprised if you find yourself tense during your first few interviews. It will probably happen every time you re-enter the market, not just when you seek your first job after getting out of school.

Tension is natural during an interview, but knowing you have done a thorough research job should put you more at ease. Make a list of questions that you think might be asked in each interview. Think out your answers carefully and practice them with a friend. Tape record your responses to the problem questions. (*See also in this chapter: Informational Interviews.*) If you feel particularly unsure of your interviewing skills, arrange your first interviews at firms you are not as interested in. (But remember it is common courtesy to seem enthusiastic about the possibility of working for any firm at which you interview.) Practice again on your own after these first few interviews. Go over the difficult questions that you were asked.

Take some time to really think about how you will convey your work history. Present "bad experiences" as "learning experiences." Instead of saying "I hated my position as a salesperson because I had to bother people on the phone," say "I realized that cold-calling was not my strong suit. Though I love working with people, I decided my talents would be best used in a more face-to-face atmosphere." Always find some sort of lesson from previous jobs, as they all have one.

Interview Attire

How important is the proper dress for a job interview? Buying a complete wardrobe, donning new shoes, and having your hair styled every morning are not enough to guarantee you a career position as an investment banker. But on the other hand, if you can't find a clean, conservative suit or won't take the time to wash your hair, then you are just wasting your time by interviewing at all.

Personal grooming is as important as finding appropriate clothes for a job interview. Careful grooming indicates both a sense of thoroughness and self-confidence. This is not the time to make a statement -- take out the extra earrings and avoid any garish hair colors not found in nature. Women should not wear excessive makeup, and both men and women should refrain from wearing any perfume or cologne (it only takes a small spritz to leave an allergic interviewer with a fit of sneezing and a bad impression of your meeting). Men should be freshly shaven, even if the interview is late in the day, and men with long hair should have it pulled back and neat.

Men applying for any professional position should wear a suit, preferably in a conservative color such as navy or charcoal gray. It is easy to get away with wearing the same dark suit to consecutive interviews at the same company; just be sure to wear a different shirt and tie for each interview.

Women should also wear a business suit. Professionalism still dictates a suit with a skirt, rather than slacks, as proper interview garb for women. This is usually true even at companies where pants are acceptable attire for female employees. As much as you may disagree with this guideline, the more prudent time to fight this standard is after you land the job.

The final selection of candidates for a job opening won't be determined by dress, of course. However, inappropriate dress can quickly eliminate a first-round candidate. So while you shouldn't spend a fortune on a new wardrobe, you should be sure that your clothes are appropriate. The key is to dress at least as or slightly more formally and conservatively than the position would suggest.

What to Bring

Be complete. Everyone needs a watch, a pen, and a notepad. Finally, a briefcase or a leather-bound folder (containing extra, *unfolded*, copies of your resume) will help complete the look of professionalism.

Sometimes the interviewer will be running behind schedule. Don't be upset, be sympathetic. There is often pressure to interview a lot of candidates and to quickly fill a demanding position. So be sure to come to your interview with good reading material to keep yourself occupied and relaxed.

The Interview

The very beginning of the interview is the most important part because it determines the tone for the rest of it. Those first few moments are especially crucial. Do you smile when you meet? Do you establish enough eye contact, but not too much? Do you walk into the office with a self-assured and confident stride? Do you shake hands firmly? Do you make small talk easily without being garrulous? It is human nature to judge people by that first impression, so make sure it is a good one. But most of all, try to be yourself.

BE PREPARED:
Some Common Interview Questions

Tell me about yourself.

Why did you leave your last job?

What excites you in your current job?

Where would you like to be in five years?

How much overtime are you willing to work?

What would your previous/present employer tell me about you?

Tell me about a difficult situation that you
faced at your previous/present job.

What are your greatest strengths?

What are your weaknesses?

Describe a work situation where you took initiative
and went beyond your normal responsibilities.

Why should we hire you?

Often the interviewer will begin, after the small talk, by telling you about the company, the division, the department, or perhaps, the position. Because of your detailed research, the information about the company should be repetitive for you, and the interviewer would probably like nothing better than to avoid this regurgitation of the company biography. So if you can do so tactfully, indicate to the interviewer that you are very familiar with the firm. If he or she seems intent on providing you with background information, despite your hints, then acquiesce.

But be sure to remain attentive. If you can manage to generate a brief discussion of the company or the industry at this point, without being forceful, great. It will help to further build rapport, underscore your interest, and increase your impact.

> **The interviewer's job is to find a reason to turn you down; your job is to not provide that reason.**
>
> -John L. LaFevre, author,
> *How You Really Get Hired*
>
> Reprinted from the 1989/90 *CPC Annual*, with permission of the National Association of Colleges and Employers (formerly College Placement Council, Inc.), copyright holder.

Soon (if it didn't begin that way) the interviewer will begin the questions, many of which you will have already practiced. This period of the interview usually falls into one of two categories (or somewhere in between): either a structured interview, where the interviewer has a prescribed set of questions to ask; or an unstructured interview, where the interviewer will ask only leading questions to get you to talk about yourself, your experiences, and your goals. Try to sense as quickly as possible in which direction the interviewer wishes to proceed. This will make the interviewer feel more relaxed and in control of the situation.

Remember to keep attuned to the interviewer and make the length of your answers appropriate to the situation. If you are really unsure as to how detailed a response the interviewer is seeking, then ask.

As the interview progresses, the interviewer will probably mention some of the most important responsibilities of the position. If applicable, draw parallels between your experience and the demands of the position as detailed by the interviewer. Describe your past experience in the same manner that you do on your resume: emphasizing results and achievements and not merely describing activities. But don't exaggerate. Be on the level about your abilities.

The first interview is often the toughest, where many candidates are screened out. If you are interviewing for a very competitive position, you will have to make an impression that will last. Focus on a few of your greatest strengths that are relevant to the position. Develop these points carefully, state them again in different words, and then try to summarize them briefly at the end of the interview.

Often the interviewer will pause toward the end and ask if you have any questions. Particularly in a structured interview, this might be the one chance to really show your knowledge of and interest in the firm. Have a list prepared of specific questions that are of real interest to you. Let your questions subtly show your research and your knowledge of the firm's activities. It is wise to have an extensive list of questions, as several of them may be answered during the interview.

Do not turn your opportunity to ask questions into an interrogation. Avoid reading directly from your list of questions, and ask questions that you are fairly certain the interviewer can answer (remember how you feel when you cannot answer a question during an interview).

Even if you are unable to determine the salary range beforehand, do not ask about it during the first interview. You can always ask later. Above all, don't ask about fringe benefits until you have been offered a position. (Then be sure to get all the details.)

Try not to be negative about anything during the interview, particularly any past employer or any previous job. Be cheerful. Everyone likes to work with someone who seems to be happy. Even if you detest your current/former job or manager, do not make disparaging comments. The interviewer may construe this as a sign of a potential attitude problem and not consider you a strong candidate.

Don't let a tough question throw you off base. If you don't know the answer to a question, simply say so -- do not apologize. Just smile. Nobody can answer every question -- particularly some of the questions that are asked in job interviews.

Before your first interview, you may be able to determine how many rounds of interviews there usually are for positions at your level. (Of course it may differ quite a bit even within the different levels of one firm.) Usually you can count on attending at least two or three interviews, although some firms are known to give a minimum of six interviews for all professional positions. While you should be more relaxed as you return for subsequent interviews, the pressure will be on. The more prepared you are, the better.

Depending on what information you are able to obtain, you might want to vary your strategy quite a bit from interview to interview. For instance, if the first interview is a screening interview, then be sure a few of your strengths really stand out. On the other hand, if later interviews are primarily with people who are in a position to veto your hiring, but not to push it forward, then you should primarily focus on building rapport as opposed to reiterating and developing your key strengths.

If it looks as though your skills and background do not match the position the interviewer was hoping to fill, ask him or her if there is another division or subsidiary that perhaps could profit from your talents.

After the Interview

Write a follow-up letter immediately after the interview, while it is still fresh in the interviewer's mind (see the sample follow-up letter format found in the Resumes and Cover Letters chapter). Not only is this a thank-you, but it also gives you the chance to provide the interviewer with any details you may have forgotten (as long as they can be tactfully added in). If you haven't heard back from the interviewer within a week of sending your thank-you letter, call to stress your continued interest in the firm and the position. If you lost any points during the interview for any reason, this letter can help you regain footing. Be polite and make sure to stress your continued interest and competency to fill the position. Just don't forget to proofread it thoroughly. If you are unsure of the spelling of the interviewer's name, call the receptionist and ask.

THE BALANCING ACT:
Looking for a New Job While Currently Employed

For those of you who are still employed, job-searching will be particularly tiring because it must be done in addition to your normal work responsibilities. So don't overwork yourself to the point where you show up to interviews looking exhausted or start to slip behind at your current job. On the other hand, don't be tempted to quit your present job! The long hours are worth it. Searching for a job while you have one puts you in a position of strength.

Making Contact

If you must be at your office during the business day, then you have additional problems to deal with. How can you work interviews into the business day? And if you work in an open office, how can you even call to set up interviews? Obviously, you should keep up the effort and the appearances on your present job. So maximize your use of the lunch hour, early mornings, and late afternoons for calling. If you keep trying, you'll be surprised how often you will be able to reach the executive you are trying to contact during your out-of-office hours. You can catch people as early as 8 a.m. and as late as 6 p.m. on frequent occasions.

Scheduling Interviews

Your inability to interview at any time other than lunch just might work to your advantage. If you can, try to set up as many interviews as possible for your lunch hour. This will go a long way to creating a relaxed atmosphere. But be sure the interviews don't stray too far from the agenda on hand.

Lunchtime interviews are much easier to obtain if you have substantial career experience. People with less experience will often find no alternative to taking time off for interviews. If you have to take time off, you have to take time off. But try to do this as little as possible. Try to take the whole day off in order to avoid being blatantly obvious about your job search, and try to schedule two to three interviews for the same day. (It is very difficult to maintain an optimum level of energy at more than three interviews in one day.) Explain to the interviewer why you might have to juggle your interview schedule; he/she should honor the respect you're showing your current employer by minimizing your days off and will probably appreciate the fact that another prospective employer is interested in you.

> **Try calling as early as 8 a.m. and as late as 6 p.m. You'll be surprised how often you will be able to reach the executive you want during these times of the day.**

References

What do you tell an interviewer who asks for references from your current employer? Just say that while you are happy to have your former employers contacted, you are trying to keep your job search confidential and would rather that your current employer not be contacted until you have been given a firm offer.

IF YOU'RE FIRED OR LAID OFF:
Picking Yourself Up and Dusting Yourself Off

If you've been fired or laid off, you are not the first and will not be the last to go through this traumatic experience. In today's changing economy, thousands of professionals lose their jobs every year. Even if you were terminated with just cause, do not lose heart. Remember, being fired is not a reflection on you as a person. It is usually a reflection of your company's staffing needs and its perception of your recent job performance and attitude. And if you were not performing up to par or enjoying your work, then you will probably be better off at another company anyway.

> **Be prepared for the question "Why were you fired?" during job interviews.**

A thorough job search could take months, so be sure to negotiate a reasonable severance package, if possible, and determine to what benefits, such as health insurance, you are still legally entitled. Also, register for unemployment compensation immediately. Don't be surprised to find other professionals collecting unemployment compensation -- it is for everyone who has lost their job.

Don't start your job search with a flurry of unplanned activity. Start by choosing a strategy and working out a plan. Now is not the time for major changes in your life. If possible, remain in the same career and in the same geographical location, at least until you have been working again for a while. On the other hand, if the only industry for which you are trained is leaving, or is severely depressed in your area, then you should give prompt consideration to moving or switching careers.

Avoid mentioning you were fired when arranging interviews, but be prepared for the question "Why were you fired?" during an interview. If you were laid off as a result of downsizing, briefly explain, being sure to reinforce that your job loss was not due to performance. If you were in fact fired, be honest, but try to detail the reason as favorably as possible and portray what you have learned from your mistakes. If you are confident one of your past managers will give you a good reference, tell the interviewer to contact that person. Do not to speak negatively of your past employer and try not to sound particularly worried about your status of being temporarily unemployed.

Finally, don't spend too much time reflecting on why you were let go or how you might have avoided it. Think positively, look to the future, and be sure to follow a careful plan during your job search.

THE COLLEGE STUDENT:
Conducting Your First Job Search

While you will be able to apply many of the basics covered earlier in this chapter to your job search, there are some situations unique to the college student's job search.

THE GPA QUESTION

You are interviewing for the job of your dreams. Everything is going well: You've established a good rapport, the interviewer seems impressed with your qualifications, and you're almost positive the job is yours. Then you're asked about your GPA, which is pitifully low. Do you tell the truth and watch your dream job fly out the window?

Never lie about your GPA (they may request your transcript, and no company will hire a liar). You can, however, explain if there is a reason you don't feel your grades reflect your abilities, and mention any other impressive statistics. For example, if you have a high GPA in your major, or in the last few semesters (as opposed to your cumulative college career), you can use that fact to your advantage.

Perhaps the biggest problem college students face is lack of experience. Many schools have internship programs designed to give students exposure to the field of their choice, as well as the opportunity to make valuable contacts. Check out your school's career services department to see what internships are available. If your school does not have a formal internship program, or if there are no available internships that appeal to you, try contacting local businesses and offering your services. Often, businesses will be more than willing to have an extra pair of hands (especially if those hands are unpaid!) for a day or two each week. Or try contacting school alumni to see if you can "shadow" them for a few days, and see what their daily duties are like.

Informational Interviews

Although many jobseekers do not do this, it can be extremely helpful to arrange an informational interview with a college alumnus or someone else who works in your desired industry. You interview them about their job, their company, and their industry with questions you have prepared in advance. This can be done over the phone but is usually done in person. This will provide you with a contact in the industry who may give you more valuable information -- or perhaps even a job opportunity -- in the future. Always follow up with a thank you letter that includes your contact information.

The goal is to try to begin building experience and establishing contacts as early as possible in your college career.

What do you do if, for whatever reason, you weren't able to get experience directly related to your desired career? First, look at your previous jobs and see if there's anything you can highlight. Did you supervise or train other employees? Did you reorganize the accounting system, or boost productivity in some way? Accomplishments like these demonstrate leadership, responsibility, and innovation -- qualities that most companies look for in employees. And don't forget volunteer activities and school clubs, which can also showcase these traits.

On-Campus Recruiting

Companies will often send recruiters to interview on-site at various colleges. This gives students a chance to interview with companies that may not have interviewed them otherwise. This is particularly true if a company schedules "open" interviews, in which the only screening process is who is first in line at the sign-ups. Of course, since many more applicants gain interviews in this format, this also means that many more people are rejected. The on-campus interview is generally a screening interview, to see if it is worth the company's time to invite you in for a second interview. So do everything possible to make yourself stand out from the crowd.

The first step, of course, is to check out any and all information your school's career center has on the company. If the information seems out of date, check out the company on the Internet or call the company's headquarters and ask for any printed information.

Many companies will host an informational meeting for interviewees, often the evening before interviews are scheduled to take place. DO NOT MISS THIS MEETING. The recruiter will almost certainly ask if you attended. Make an effort to stay after the meeting and talk with the company's representatives. Not only does this give you an opportunity to find out more information about both the company and the position, it also makes you stand out in the recruiter's mind. If there's a particular company that you had your heart set on, but you weren't able to get an interview with them, attend the information session anyway. You may be able to persuade the recruiter to squeeze you into the schedule. (Or you may discover that the company really isn't the right fit for you after all.)

Try to check out the interview site beforehand. Some colleges may conduct "mock" interviews that take place in one of the standard interview rooms. Or you may be able to convince a career counselor (or even a custodian) to let you sneak a peek during off-hours. Either way, having an idea of the room's setup will help you to mentally prepare.

Arrive at least 15 minutes early to the interview. The recruiter may be ahead of schedule, and might meet you early. But don't be surprised if previous interviews have run over, resulting in your 30-minute slot being reduced to 20 minutes (or less). Don't complain or appear anxious; just use the time you do have as efficiently as possible to showcase the reasons *you* are the ideal candidate. Staying calm and composed in these situations will work to your advantage.

LAST WORDS

A parting word of advice. Again and again during your job search you will face rejection. You will be rejected when you apply for interviews. You will be rejected after interviews. For every job offer you finally receive, you probably will have been rejected many times. Don't let rejections slow you down. Keep reminding yourself that the sooner you go out, start your job search, and get those rejections flowing in, the closer you will be to obtaining the job you want.

RESUMES AND COVER LETTERS

When filling a position, an employer will often have 100-plus applicants, but time to interview only a handful of the most promising ones. As a result, he or she will reject most applicants after only briefly skimming their resumes.

Unless you have phoned and talked to the employer -- which you should do whenever you can -- you will be chosen or rejected for an interview entirely on the basis of your resume and cover letter. *Your cover letter must catch the employer's attention, and your resume must hold it.* (But remember -- a resume is no substitute for a job search campaign. *You* must seek a job. Your resume is only one tool, albeit a critical one.)

RESUME FORMAT:
Mechanics of a First Impression

The Basics

Employers dislike long resumes, so unless you have an unusually strong background with many years of experience and a diversity of outstanding achievements, keep your resume length to one page. If you must squeeze in more information than would otherwise fit, try using a smaller typeface or changing the margins. Watch also for "widows" at the end of paragraphs. You can often free up some space if you can shorten the information enough to get rid of those single words taking up an entire line. Another tactic that works with some word processing programs is to decrease the font size of your paragraph returns and changing the spacing between lines.

Print your resume on standard 8 1/2" x 11" paper. Since recruiters often get resumes in batches of hundreds, a smaller-sized resume may be lost in the pile. Oversized resumes are likely to get crumpled at the edges, and won't fit easily in their files.

First impressions matter, so make sure the recruiter's first impression of your resume is a good one. Never hand-write your resume (or cover letter)! Print your resume on quality paper that has weight and texture, in a conservative color such as white, ivory, or pale gray. Good resume paper is easy to find at many stores that sell stationery or office products. It is even available at some drug stores. Use *matching* paper and envelopes for both your resume and cover letter. One hiring manager at a major magazine throws out all resumes that arrive on paper that differs in color from the envelope!

Do not buy paper with images of clouds and rainbows in the background or anything that looks like casual stationery that you would send to your favorite aunt. Do not spray perfume or cologne on your resume. Do not include your picture with your resume unless you have a specific and appropriate reason to do so.

Another tip: Do a test print of your resume (and cover letter), to make sure the watermark is on the same side as the text so that you can read it. Also make sure it is right-side up. As trivial as this may sound, some recruiters check for this! One recruiter at a law firm in New Hampshire sheepishly admitted this is the first thing he checks. *"I open each envelope and check the watermarks on the resume and cover letter. Those candidates that have it wrong go into a different pile."*

Getting it on Paper

Modern photocomposition typesetting gives you the clearest, sharpest image, a wide variety of type styles, and effects such as italics, bold-facing, and book-like justified margins. It is also too expensive for many jobseekers. The quality of today's laser printers means that a computer-generated resume can look just as impressive as one that has been professionally typeset.

A computer with a word processing or desktop publishing program is the most common way to generate your resume. This allows you the flexibility to make changes almost instantly and to store different drafts on disk. Word processing and desktop publishing programs also offer many different fonts to choose from, each taking up different amounts of space. (It is generally best to stay between 9-point and 12-point font size.) Many other options are also available, such as bold-facing or italicizing for emphasis and the ability to change and manipulate spacing. It is generally recommended to leave the right-hand margin unjustified as this keeps the spacing between the text even and therefore easier to read. It is not wrong to justify both margins of text, but if possible try it both ways before you decide.

For a resume on paper, the end result will be largely determined by the quality of the printer you use. Laser printers will generally provide the best quality. Do not use a dot matrix printer.

Many companies now use scanning equipment to screen the resumes they receive, and certain paper, fonts, and other features are more compatible with this technology. White paper is preferable, as well as a standard font such as Courier or Helvetica. You should use at least a 10-point font, and avoid bolding, italics, underlining, borders, boxes, or graphics.

Household typewriters and office typewriters with nylon or other cloth ribbons are *not* good enough for typing your resume. If you don't have access to a quality word processing program, hire a professional with the resources to prepare your resume for you. Keep in mind that businesses such as Kinko's (open 24 hours) provide access to computers with quality printers.

Don't make your copies on an office photocopier. Only the human resources office may see the resume you mail. Everyone else may see only a copy of it, and copies of copies quickly become unreadable. Furthermore, sending photocopies of your resume or cover letter is completely unprofessional. Either print out each copy individually, or take your resume to a professional copy shop, which will generally offer professionally-maintained, extra-high-quality photocopiers and charge fairly reasonable prices. You want your resume to represent you with the look of polished quality.

Proof with Care

Whether you typed it or paid to have it produced professionally, mistakes on resumes are not only embarrassing, but will usually remove you from consideration (particularly if something obvious such as your name is misspelled). No matter how much you paid someone else to type, write, or typeset your resume, *you* lose if there is a mistake. So proofread it as carefully as possible. Get a friend to help you. Read your draft aloud as your friend checks the proof copy. Then have your friend read aloud while you check. Next, read it letter by letter to check spelling and punctuation.

If you are having it typed or typeset by a resume service or a printer, and you don't have time to proof it, pay for it and take it home. Proof it there and bring it back later to get it corrected and printed.

If you wrote your resume with a word processing program, use the built-in spell checker to double-check for spelling errors. Keep in mind that a spell checker will not find errors such as "to" for "two" or "wok" for "work." Many spell check programs do not recognize missing or misused punctuation, nor are they set to check the spelling of capitalized words. It's important that you still proofread your resume to check for grammatical mistakes and other problems, even <u>after</u> it has been spellchecked. If you find mistakes, do not make edits in pen or pencil or use white-out to fix them on the final copy!

Electronic Resumes

As companies rely increasingly on emerging technologies to find qualified candidates for job openings, you may opt to create an electronic resume in order to remain competitive in today's job market. Why is this important? Companies today sometimes request that resumes be submitted by e-mail, and many hiring managers regularly check online resume databases for candidates to fill unadvertised job openings. Other companies enlist the services of electronic employment database services, which charge jobseekers a nominal fee to have their resumes posted to the database to be viewed by potential employers. Still other companies use their own automated applicant tracking systems, in which case your resume is fed through a scanner that sends the image to a computer that "reads" your resume, looking for keywords, and files it accordingly in its database.

Whether you're posting your resume online, e-mailing it directly to an employer, sending it to an electronic employment database, or sending it to a company you suspect uses an automated applicant tracking system, you must create some form of electronic resume to take advantage of the technology. Don't panic! An electronic resume is simply a modified version of your conventional resume. An electronic resume is one that is sparsely formatted, but filled with keywords and important facts.

In order to post your resume to the Internet -- either to an online resume database or through direct e-mail to an employer -- you will need to change the way your resume is formatted. Instead of a Word, WordPerfect, or other word processing document, save your resume as a plain text, DOS, or ASCII file. These three terms are basically interchangeable, and describe text at its simplest, most basic level, without the formatting such as boldface or italics that most jobseekers use to make their resumes look more interesting. If you use e-mail, you'll notice that all of your messages are written and received in this format. First, you should remove all formatting from your resume including boldface, italics, underlining, bullets, differing font sizes, and graphics. Then, convert and save your resume as a plain text file. Most word processing programs have a "save as" feature that allows you to save files in different formats. Here, you should choose "text only" or "plain text."

Another option is to create a resume in HTML (hypertext markup language), the text formatting language used to publish information on the World Wide Web. However, the real usefulness of HTML resumes is still being explored. Most of the major online databases do not accept HTML resumes, and the vast majority of companies only accept plain text resumes through their e-mail.

Finally, if you simply wish to send your resume to an electronic employment database or a company that uses an automated applicant tracking system, there is no need to convert your resume to a plain text file. The only change you need to make is to organize the information in your resume by keywords. Employers are likely to do keyword searches for information, such as degree held or knowledge of particular types of software. Therefore, using the right keywords or key phrases in your resume is critical to its ultimate success. Keywords are usually nouns or short phrases that the computer searches for which refer to experience, training, skills, and abilities. For example, let's say an employer searches an employment database for a sales representative with the following criteria:

> BS/BA
> exceeded quota
> cold calls
> high energy
> willing to travel

Even if you have the right qualifications, neglecting to use these keywords would result in the computer passing over your resume. Although there is no way to know for sure which keywords employers are most likely to search for, you can make educated guesses by checking the help-wanted ads or online job postings for your type of job. You should also arrange keywords in a keyword summary, a paragraph listing your qualifications that immediately follows your name and address (see sample letter in this chapter). In addition, choose a nondecorative font with clear, distinct characters, such as Helvetica or Times. It is more difficult for a scanner to accurately pick up the more unusual fonts. Boldface and all capital letters are best used only for major section headings, such as "Experience" and "Education." It is also best to avoid using italics or underlining, since this can cause the letters to bleed into one another.

Types of Resumes

The most common resume formats are the functional resume, the chronological resume, and the combination resume. (Examples can be found at the end of this chapter.) A functional resume focuses on skills and de-emphasizes job titles, employers, etc. A functional resume is best if you have been out of the work force for a long time or are changing careers. It is also good if you want to highlight specific skills and strengths, especially if all of your work experience has been at one company. This format can also be a good choice if you are just out of school or have no experience in your desired field.

Choose a chronological format if you are currently working or were working recently, and if your most recent experiences relate to your desired field. Use reverse chronological order and include dates. To a recruiter your last job and your latest schooling are the most important, so put the last first and list the rest going back in time.

A combination resume is perhaps the most common. This resume simply combines elements of the functional and chronological resume formats. This is used by many jobseekers with a solid track record who find elements of both types useful.

Organization

Your name, phone number, e-mail address (if you have one), and a complete mailing address should be at the top of your resume. Try to make your name stand out by using a slightly larger font size or all capital letters. Be sure to spell out everything. Never abbreviate St. for Street or Rd. for Road. If you are a college student, you should also put your home address and phone number at the top. Change your message on your answering machine if necessary – RUSH blaring in the background or your sorority sisters screaming may not come across well to all recruiters. If you think you may be moving within six months then include a second address and phone number of a trusted friend or relative who can reach you no matter where you are.

> *Remember that employers will keep your resume on file and*
> *may contact you months later if a position opens that fits your qualifications.*
> *All too often, candidates are unreachable because they have moved and had not*
> *previously provided enough contact options on their resume.*

Next, list your experience, then your education. If you are a recent graduate, list your education first, unless your experience is more important than your education. (For example, if you have just graduated from a teaching school, have some business experience, and are applying for a job in business, you would list your business experience first.)

Keep everything easy to find. Put the dates of your employment and education on the left of the page. Put the names of the companies you worked for and the schools you attended a few spaces to the right of the dates. Put the city and state, or the city and country, where you studied or worked to the right of the page.

The important thing is simply to break up the text in some logical way that makes your resume visually attractive and easy to scan, so experiment to see which layout works best for your resume. However you set it up, *stay consistent*. Inconsistencies in fonts, spacing, or tenses will make your resume look sloppy. Also, be sure to use tabs to keep your information vertically lined up, rather than the less precise space bar.

RESUME CONTENT:
Say it with Style
Sell Yourself

You are selling your skills and accomplishments in your resume, so it is important to inventory yourself and know yourself. If you have achieved something, say so. Put it in the best possible light, but avoid subjective statements, such as "I am a hard worker" or "I get along well with my coworkers." Just stick to the facts.

While you shouldn't hold back or be modest, don't exaggerate your achievements to the point of misrepresentation. Be honest. Many companies will immediately drop an applicant from consideration (or fire a current employee) upon discovering inaccurate or untrue information on a resume or other application material.

Write down the important (and pertinent) things you have done, but do it in as few words as possible. Your resume will be scanned, not read, and short, concise phrases are much more effective than long-winded sentences. Avoid the use of "I" when emphasizing your accomplishments. Instead, use brief phrases beginning with action verbs.

While some technical terms will be unavoidable, you should try to avoid excessive "technicalese." Keep in mind that the first person to see your resume may be a human resources person who won't necessarily know all the jargon -- and how can they be impressed by something they don't understand?

Keep it Brief

Also, try to hold your paragraphs to six lines or less. If you have more than six lines of information about one job or school, put it in two or more paragraphs.

A short resume will be examined more carefully. Remember: Your resume usually has between eight and 45 seconds to catch an employer's eye. So make every second count.

Job Objective

A functional resume may require a job objective to give it focus. One or two sentences describing the job you are seeking can clarify in what capacity your skills will be best put to use. Be sure that your stated objective is in line with the position you're applying for.

Examples:

An entry-level editorial assistant position in the publishing industry.
A senior management position with a telecommunications firm.

Don't include a job objective on a chronological resume unless your previous work experiences are completely unrelated to the position for which you're applying. The presence of an overly specific job objective might eliminate you from consideration for other positions that a recruiter feels are a better match for your qualifications. But even if you don't put an objective on paper, having a career goal in mind as you write can help give your resume a solid sense of direction.

USE ACTION VERBS

How you write your resume is just as important as *what* you write. In describing previous work experiences, the strongest resumes use short phrases beginning with action verbs. Below are a few you may want to use. (This list is not all-inclusive.)

achieved	developed	integrated	purchased
administered	devised	interpreted	reduced
advised	directed	interviewed	regulated
arranged	distributed	launched	represented
assisted	established	managed	resolved
attained	evaluated	marketed	restored
budgeted	examined	mediated	restructured
built	executed	monitored	revised
calculated	expanded	negotiated	scheduled
collaborated	expedited	obtained	selected
collected	facilitated	operated	served
compiled	formulated	ordered	sold
completed	founded	organized	solved
computed	generated	participated	streamlined
conducted	headed	performed	studied
consolidated	identified	planned	supervised
constructed	implemented	prepared	supplied
consulted	improved	presented	supported
controlled	increased	processed	tested
coordinated	initiated	produced	trained
created	installed	proposed	updated
determined	instructed	published	wrote

Some jobseekers may choose to include both "Relevant Experience" and "Additional Experience" sections. This can be useful, as it allows the jobseeker to place more emphasis on certain experiences and to de-emphasize others.

Emphasize continued experience in a particular job area or continued interest in a particular industry. De-emphasize irrelevant positions. It is okay to include one opening line providing a general description of each company you've worked at. Delete positions that you held for less than four months (unless you are a very recent college grad or still in school). Stress your <u>results</u> and your achievements, elaborating on how you contributed in your previous jobs. Did you increase sales, reduce costs, improve a product, implement a new program? Were you promoted? Use specific numbers (i.e., quantities, percentages, dollar amounts) whenever possible.

Education

Keep it brief if you have more than two years of career experience. Elaborate more if you have less experience. If you are a recent college graduate, you may choose to include any high school activities that are directly relevant to your career. If you've been out of school for a while you don't need to list your education prior to college.

Mention degrees received and any honors or special awards. Note individual courses or projects you participated in that might be relevant for employers. For example, if you are an English major applying for a position as a business writer, be sure to mention any business or economics courses. Previous experience such as Editor-in-Chief of the school newspaper would be relevant as well.

If you are uploading your resume to an online job hunting site such as CareerCity.com, action verbs are still important, but the key words or key nouns that a computer would search for become more important. For example, if you're seeking an accounting position, key nouns that a computer would search for such as "Lotus 1-2-3" or "CPA" or "payroll" become very important.

Highlight Impressive Skills

Be sure to mention any computer skills you may have. You may wish to include a section entitled "Additional Skills" or "Computer Skills," in which you list any software programs you know. An additional skills section is also an ideal place to mention fluency in a foreign language.

Personal Data

This section is optional, but if you choose to include it, keep it brief. A one-word mention of hobbies such as fishing, chess, baseball, cooking, etc., can give the person who will interview you a good way to open up the conversation.

Team sports experience is looked at favorably. It doesn't hurt to include activities that are somewhat unusual (fencing, Akido, '70s music) or that somehow relate to the position or the company to which you're applying. For instance, it would be worth noting if you are a member of a professional organization in your industry of interest. Never include information about your age, alias, date of birth, health, physical characteristics, marital status, religious affiliation, or political/moral beliefs.

References

The most that is needed is the sentence "References available upon request" at the bottom of your resume. If you choose to leave it out, that's fine. This line is not really necessary. It is understood that references will most likely be asked for and provided by you later on in the interviewing process. Do not actually send references with your resume and cover letter unless specifically requested.

HIRING A RESUME WRITER:
Is it the Right Choice for You?

If you write reasonably well, it is to your advantage to write your own resume. Writing your resume forces you to review your experiences and figure out how to explain your accomplishments in clear, brief phrases. This will help you when you explain your work to interviewers. It is also easier to tailor your resume to each position you're applying for when you have put it together yourself.

If you write your resume, everything will be in your own words; it will sound like you. It will say what you want it to say. If you are a good writer, know yourself well, and have a good idea of which parts of your background employers are looking for, you should be able to write your own resume better than someone else. If you decide to write your resume yourself, have as many people as possible review and proofread it. Welcome objective opinions and other perspectives.

When to Get Help

If you have difficulty writing in "resume style" (which is quite unlike normal written language), if you are unsure which parts of your background to emphasize, or if you think your resume would make your case better if it did not follow one of the standard forms outlined either here or in a book on resumes, then you should consider having it professionally written.

Even some professional resume writers we know have had their resumes written with the help of fellow professionals. They sought the help of someone who could be objective about their background, as well as provide an experienced sounding board to help focus their thoughts.

If You Hire a Pro

The best way to choose a writer is by reputation: the recommendation of a friend, a personnel director, your school placement officer, or someone else knowledgeable in the field.

Important questions:
- "How long have you been writing resumes?"
- "If I'm not satisfied with what you write, will you go over it with me and change it?"
- "Do you charge by the hour or a flat rate?"

There is no sure relation between price and quality, except that you are unlikely to get a good writer for less than $50 for an uncomplicated resume and you shouldn't have to pay more than $300 unless your experience is very extensive or complicated. There will be additional charges for printing. Assume nothing no matter how much you pay. It is your career at stake if there are mistakes on your resume!

Few resume services will give you a firm price over the phone, simply because some resumes are too complicated and take too long to do for a predetermined price. Some services will quote you a price that applies to almost all of their customers. Once you decide to use a specific writer, you should insist on a firm price quote *before* engaging their services. Also, find out how expensive minor changes will be.

COVER LETTERS:
Quick, Clear, and Concise

Always mail a cover letter with your resume. In a cover letter you can show an interest in the company that you can't show in a resume. You can also point out one or two of your skills or accomplishments the company can put to good use.

Make it Personal

The more personal you can get, the better, so long as you keep it professional. If someone known to the person you are writing has recommended that you contact the company, get permission to include his/her name in the letter. If you can get the name of a person to send the letter to, address it directly to that person (after first calling the company to verify the spelling of the person's name, correct title, and mailing address). Be sure to put the person's name and title on both the letter and the envelope. This will ensure that your letter will get through to the proper person, even if a new person now occupies this position. It will not always be possible to get the name of a person. Always strive to get at least a title.

Be sure to mention something about why you have an interest in the company -- *so many candidates apply for jobs with no apparent knowledge of what the company does!* This conveys the message that they just want any job.

Type cover letters in full. Don't try the cheap and easy ways, like using a computer mail merge program or photocopying the body of your letter and typing in the inside address and salutation. You will give the impression that you are mailing to a host of companies and have no particular interest in any one.

Print your cover letter on the same color and same high-quality paper as your resume.

Cover letter basic format

<u>Paragraph 1:</u> State what the position is that you are seeking. It is not always necessary to state how you found out about the position -- often you will apply without knowing that a position is open.

<u>Paragraph 2:</u> Include what you know about the company and why you are interested in working there. Mention any prior contact with the company or someone known to the hiring person if relevant. Briefly state your qualifications and what you can offer. (Do not talk about what you cannot do).

<u>Paragraph 3:</u> Close with your phone number and where/when you can be reached. Make a request for an interview. State when you will follow up by phone (or mail or e-mail if the ad requests no phone calls). Do not wait long -- generally five working days. If you say you're going to follow up, then actually do it! This phone call can get your resume noticed when it might otherwise sit in a stack of 225 other resumes.

Cover letter do's and don'ts

- *Do* keep your cover letter brief and to the point.
- *Do* be sure it is error-free.
- *Do* accentuate what you can offer the company, not what you hope to gain.

- *Do* be sure your phone number and address is on your cover letter just in case it gets separated from your resume (this happens!).
- *Do* check the watermark by holding the paper up to a light -- be sure it is facing forward so it is readable -- on the same side as the text, and right-side up.
- *Do* sign your cover letter (or type your name if you are sending it electronically). Blue or black ink are both fine. Do not use red ink.
- *Don't* just repeat information verbatim from your resume.
- *Don't* overuse the personal pronoun "I."
- *Don't* send a generic cover letter -- show your personal knowledge of and interest in that particular company.

THANK YOU LETTERS:
Another Way to Stand Out

As mentioned earlier, *always* send a thank you letter after an interview (see the sample later in this section). So few candidates do this and it is yet another way for you to stand out. Be sure to mention something specific from the interview and restate your interest in the company and the position.

It is generally acceptable to handwrite your thank you letter on a generic thank you card (but *never* a postcard). Make sure handwritten notes are neat and legible. However, if you are in doubt, typing your letter is always the safe bet. If you met with several people it is fine to send them each an individual thank you letter. Call the company if you need to check on the correct spelling of their names.

Remember to:
- Keep it short.
- Proofread it carefully.
- Send it *promptly*.

FUNCTIONAL RESUME

C.J. RAVENCLAW
129 Pennsylvania Avenue
Washington DC 20500
202/555-6652
e-mail: ravenclaw@dcpress.net

Objective
A position as a graphic designer commensurate with my acquired skills and expertise.

Summary
Extensive experience in plate making, separations, color matching, background definition, printing, mechanicals, color corrections, and personnel supervision. A highly motivated manager and effective communicator. Proven ability to:

- **Create Commercial Graphics**
- **Produce Embossed Drawings**
- **Color Separate**
- **Control Quality**
- **Resolve Printing Problems**
- **Analyze Customer Satisfaction**

Qualifications
Printing:
Knowledgeable in black and white as well as color printing. Excellent judgment in determining acceptability of color reproduction through comparison with original. Proficient at producing four- or five-color corrections on all media, as well as restyling previously reproduced four-color artwork.

Customer Relations:
Routinely work closely with customers to ensure specifications are met. Capable of striking a balance between technical printing capabilities and need for customer satisfaction through entire production process.

Specialties:
Practiced at creating silk screen overlays for a multitude of processes including velo bind, GBC bind, and perfect bind. Creative design and timely preparation of posters, flyers, and personalized stationery.

Personnel Supervision:
Skillful at fostering atmosphere that encourages highly talented artists to balance high-level creativity with maximum production. Consistently beat production deadlines. Instruct new employees, apprentices, and students in both artistry and technical operations.

Experience
Graphic Arts Professor, Ohio State University, Columbus OH (1997-2001).
Manager, Design Graphics, Washington DC (2002-present).

Education
Massachusetts Conservatory of Art, Ph.D. 1995
University of Massachusetts, B.A. 1993

CHRONOLOGICAL RESUME

HARRY SEABORN
557 Shoreline Drive
Seattle, WA 98404
(206) 555-6584
e-mail: hseaborn@centco.com

EXPERIENCE

THE CENTER COMPANY   Seattle, WA
Systems Programmer   2001-present
  • Develop and maintain customer accounting and order tracking
  database using a Visual Basic front end and SQL server.
  • Plan and implement migration of company wide transition from
  mainframe-based dumb terminals to a true client server environment
  using Windows NT Workstation and Server.
  • Oversee general local and wide area network administration
  including the development of a variety of intranet modules to
  improve internal company communication and planning across
  divisions.

INFO TECH, INC.   Seattle, WA
Technical Manager   1995-2001
  • Designed and managed the implementation of a network providing
  the legal community with a direct line to Supreme Court cases
  across the Internet using SQL Server and a variety of Internet tools.
  • Developed a system to make the entire library catalog available on
  line using PERL scripts and SQL.
  • Used Visual Basic and Microsoft Access to create a registration
  system for university registrar.

EDUCATION

SALEM STATE UNIVERSITY   Salem, OR
          M.S. in Computer Science.   1998
          B.S. in Computer Science.   1996

COMPUTER SKILLS

  • Programming Languages: Visual Basic, Java, C++, SQL, PERL
  • Software: SQL Server, Internet Information Server, Oracle
  • Operating Systems: Windows NT, UNIX, Linux

FUNCTIONAL RESUME

Donna Hermione Moss
703 Wizard's Way
Chicago, IL 60601
(312) 555-8841
e-mail: donna@cowfire.com

OBJECTIVE:
To contribute over five years of experience in promotion, communications, and administration to an entry-level position in advertising.

SUMMARY OF QUALIFICATIONS:
- Performed advertising duties for small business.
- Experience in business writing and communications skills.
- General knowledge of office management.
- Demonstrated ability to work well with others, in both supervisory and support staff roles.
- Type 75 words per minute.

SELECTED ACHIEVEMENTS AND RESULTS:
Promotion:
Composing, editing, and proofreading correspondence and public relations materials for own catering service. Large-scale mailings.

Communication:
Instruction; curriculum and lesson planning; student evaluation; parent-teacher conferences; development of educational materials. Training and supervising clerks.

Computer Skills:
Proficient in MS Word, Lotus 1-2-3, Excel, and Filemaker Pro.

Administration:
Record-keeping and file maintenance. Data processing and computer operations, accounts receivable, accounts payable, inventory control, and customer relations. Scheduling, office management, and telephone reception.

PROFESSIONAL HISTORY:
Teacher; Self-Employed (owner of catering service); Floor Manager; Administrative Assistant; Accounting Clerk.

EDUCATION:
Beloit College, Beloit, WI, BA in Education, 1996

CHRONOLOGICAL RESUME

PERCY ZIEGLER
16 Josiah Court
Marlborough CT 06447
203/555-9641 (h)
203/555-8176, x14 (w)

EDUCATION

Keene State College, Keene NH
Bachelor of Arts in Elementary Education, 2002
• Graduated *magna cum laude*
• English minor
• Kappa Delta Pi member, inducted 2000

EXPERIENCE
September 2002-
Present

Elmer T. Thienes Elementary School, Marlborough CT
Part-time Kindergarten Teacher
• Instruct kindergartners in reading, spelling, language arts, and
  music.
• Participate in the selection of textbooks and learning aids.
• Organize and supervise class field trips and coordinate in-class
  presentations.

Summers
1999-2001

Keene YMCA, Youth Division, Keene NH
Child-care Counselor
• Oversaw summer program for low-income youth.
• Budgeted and coordinated special events and field trips,
  working with Program Director to initiate variations in the
  program.
• Served as Youth Advocate in cooperation with social worker to
  address the social needs and problems of participants.

Spring 2001

Wheelock Elementary School, Keene NH
Student Teacher
• Taught third-grade class in all elementary subjects.
• Designed and implemented a two-week unit on Native
  Americans.
• Assisted in revision of third-grade curriculum.

Fall 2000

Child Development Center, Keene NH
Daycare Worker
• Supervised preschool children on the playground and during art
  activities.
• Created a "Wishbone Corner," where children could quietly
  look at books or take a voluntary "time-out."

ADDITIONAL INTERESTS

Martial arts, Pokemon, politics, reading, skiing, writing.

ELECTRONIC RESUME

GRIFFIN DORE
69 Dursley Drive
Cambridge, MA 02138
(617) 555-5555

KEYWORD SUMMARY

Senior financial manager with over ten years experience in Accounting and Systems Management, Budgeting, Forecasting, Cost Containment, Financial Reporting, and International Accounting. MBA in Management. Proficient in Lotus, Excel, Solomon, and Windows.

EXPERIENCE

COLWELL CORPORATION, Wellesley, MA
Director of Accounting and Budgets, 1995 to present
   Direct staff of twenty in General Ledger, Accounts Payable, Accounts Receivable, and International Accounting.
   Facilitate month-end closing process with parent company and auditors.
   Implemented team-oriented cross-training program within accounting group, resulting in timely month-end closings and increased productivity of key accounting staff.
   Developed and implemented a strategy for Sales and Use Tax Compliance in all fifty states.
   Prepare monthly financial statements and analyses.

FRANKLIN AND DELANEY COMPANY, Melrose, MA
Senior Accountant, 1992-1995
   Managed Accounts Payable, General Ledger, transaction processing, and financial reporting. Supervised staff of five.

Staff Accountant, 1990-1992
   Managed Accounts Payable, including vouchering, cash disbursements, and bank reconciliation.
   Wrote and issued policies.
   Maintained supporting schedules used during year-end audits.
   Trained new employees.

EDUCATION

MBA in Management, Northeastern University, Boston, MA, 1994
BS in Accounting, Boston College, Boston, MA, 1990

ASSOCIATIONS

National Association of Accountants

GENERAL MODEL
FOR A COVER LETTER

Your mailing address
Date

Contact's name
Contact's title
Company
Company's mailing address

Dear Mr./Ms. _____ :

Immediately explain why your background makes you the best candidate for the position that you are applying for. Describe what prompted you to write (want ad, article you read about the company, networking contact, etc.). Keep the first paragraph short and hard-hitting.

Detail what you could contribute to this company. Show how your qualifications will benefit this firm. Describe your interest in the corporation. Subtly emphasizing your knowledge about this firm and your familiarity with the industry will set you apart from other candidates. Remember to keep this letter short; few recruiters will read a cover letter longer than half a page.

If possible, your closing paragraph should request specific action on the part of the reader. Include your phone number and the hours when you can be reached. Mention that if you do not hear from the reader by a specific date, you will follow up with a phone call. Lastly, thank the reader for their time, consideration, etc.

Sincerely,

(signature)

Your full name (typed)

Enclosure (use this if there are other materials, such as your resume,
              that are included in the same envelope)

SAMPLE COVER LETTER

16 Josiah Court
Marlborough CT 06447
January 16, 2005

Ms. Leona Malfoy
Assistant Principal
Laningham Elementary School
43 Mayflower Drive
Keene NH 03431

Dear Ms. Malfoy:

Toby Potter recently informed me of a possible opening for a third grade teacher at Laningham Elementary School. With my experience instructing third-graders, both in schools and in summer programs, I feel I would be an ideal candidate for the position. Please accept this letter and the enclosed resume as my application.

Laningham's educational philosophy that every child can learn and succeed interests me, since it mirrors my own. My current position at Elmer T. Thienes Elementary has reinforced this philosophy, heightening my awareness of the different styles and paces of learning and increasing my sensitivity toward special needs children. Furthermore, as a direct result of my student teaching experience at Wheelock Elementary School, I am comfortable, confident, and knowledgeable working with third-graders.

I look forward to discussing the position and my qualifications for it in more detail. I can be reached at 203/555-9641 evenings or 203/555-8176, x14 weekdays. If I do not hear from you before Tuesday of next week, I will call to see if we can schedule a time to meet. Thank you for your time and consideration.

Sincerely,

Percy Ziegler

Percy Ziegler

Enclosure

GENERAL MODEL FOR A
THANK YOU/FOLLOW-UP LETTER

Your mailing address
Date

Contact's name
Contact's title
Company
Company's mailing address

Dear Mr./Ms._____:

Remind the interviewer of the reason (i.e., a specific opening, an informational interview, etc.) you were interviewed, as well as the date. Thank him/her for the interview, and try to personalize your thanks by mentioning some specific aspect of the interview.

Confirm your interest in the organization (and in the opening, if you were interviewing for a particular position). Use specifics to re-emphasize that you have researched the firm in detail and have considered how you would fit into the company and the position. This is a good time to say anything you wish you had said in the initial meeting. Be sure to keep this letter brief; a half page is plenty.

If appropriate, close with a suggestion for further action, such as a desire to have an additional interview, if possible. Mention your phone number and the hours you can be reached. Alternatively, you may prefer to mention that you will follow up with a phone call in several days. Once again, thank the person for meeting with you, and state that you would be happy to provide any additional information about your qualifications.

Sincerely,

(signature)

Your full name (typed)

PRIMARY EMPLOYERS

ACCOUNTING & MANAGEMENT CONSULTING

You can expect to find the following types of companies in this section:
Consulting and Research Firms • Industrial Accounting Firms • Management Services • Public Accounting Firms • Tax Preparation Companies

North Carolina

DELOITTE & TOUCHE
150 Fayetteville Street Mall, Suite 1800, Raleigh NC 27601. 919/546-8000. **Fax:** 919/833-3276. **Contact:** Office Administrator. **E-mail address:** dtcareers@deloitte.com. **World Wide Web address:** http://www.us.deloitte.com. **Description:** An international firm of certified public accountants providing professional accounting, auditing, tax, and management consulting services to widely diversified clients. The company has a specialized program consisting of national industry groups and functional groups that cross industry lines. Groups are involved in various disciplines including accounting, auditing, taxation management advisory services, small and growing businesses, mergers and acquisitions, and computer applications. **NOTE:** Please visit website to search for jobs and apply online. **Corporate headquarters location:** New York NY. **Other area locations:** Charlotte NC; Hickory NC; Research Triangle Park NC. **Other U.S. locations:** Nationwide. **International locations:** Worldwide.

ERNST & YOUNG LLP
101 Independence Center, Suite 1100, 101 North Tryon Street, Charlotte NC 28246. 704/372-6300. **Contact:** Human Resources. **World Wide Web address:** http://www.ey.com. **Description:** A certified public accounting firm that also provides management consulting services. Services include data processing, financial modeling, financial feasibility studies, production planning and inventory management, management sciences, health care planning, human resources, cost accounting, and budgeting systems. **NOTE:** Please visit website to search for jobs and apply online. **Positions advertised include:** Technology and Security Risk Services; Assurance Senior; Risk Management Services Manager; Business Risk Services Senior Auditor – Internal Audit Services. **Corporate headquarters location:** New York NY. **Other area locations:** Raleigh NC; Greensboro NC. **Other U.S. locations:** Nationwide.

KPMG
301 North Elm Street, Suite 700, Greensboro NC 27401. 336/275-3394. **Contact:** Manager. **World Wide Web address:** http://www.us.kpmg.com. **Description:** KPMG delivers a wide range of value-added assurance, tax, and consulting services. **NOTE:** Please visit http://kpmgcareers.com/index.asp to search for jobs. **Corporate headquarters location:** Washington DC. **Parent company:** KPMG

International is a leader among professional services firms engaged in capturing, managing, assessing, and delivering information to create knowledge that will help its clients maximize shareholder value. **Other U.S. locations:** Nationwide. **International locations:** Worldwide. **Number of employees at this location:** 50.

McGLADREY & PULLEN, LLP
P.O. Box 2470, Greensboro NC 27402-2470. 336/273-4461. **Physical address:** 230 North Elm Street, Suite 1100, Greensboro NC 27401. **Fax:** 336/274-2519. **Contact:** Jennifer Parish, Personnel. **World Wide Web address:** http://www.mcgladrey.com. **Description:** A certified public accounting firm providing audit, tax, management, data processing, and cost systems services. **Corporate headquarters location:** Bloomington MN. **Other area locations:** Statewide. **Other U.S. locations:** Nationwide.

PRICEWATERHOUSECOOPERS
214 North Tryon Street, Suite 3600, Charlotte NC 28202. 704/344-7500. **Fax:** 704/344-4100. **Contact:** Personnel. **World Wide Web address:** http://www.pricewaterhousecoopers.com. **Description:** One of the largest certified public accounting firms in the world. PricewaterhouseCoopers provides public accounting, business advisory, management consulting, and taxation services. **NOTE:** Please visit website to search for jobs and apply online. **Positions advertised include:** HCP Manager; ITS Senior Associate; ISG Manager; SALT Senior Associate; Income Franchise Manager; Assurance Senior Associate; Financial Services IAS Senior Associate; Executive Assistant – Tax Services; Manager – FORCe; SPA Senior Associate; Credit Risk Management Senior Associate. **Corporate headquarters location:** New York NY. **Other U.S. locations:** Nationwide. **International locations:** Worldwide. **Number of employees worldwide:** 120,000.

South Carolina

ELLIOT DAVIS & COMPANY LLP
P.O. Box 6286, Greenville SC 29606. 864/242-3370. **Physical address:** 200 East Broad Street, Greenville SC 29601. **Fax:** 864/232-7161. **Contact:** Nancy Browder, Office Manager. **E-mail address:** hr@elliottdavis.com. **World Wide Web address:** http://www.elliottdavis.com. **Description:** The company ranks in the top 40 corporate accounting firms in the U.S. offering comprehensive tax, audit, and consulting services and is affiliated with the international firm Moore Stephens Elliot Davis, LLC. Founded in 1925. **NOTE:** Apply online. **Positions advertised include:** Senior Tax Accountant; Senior Auditor. **Corporate headquarters location:** This location. **Other locations:** Statewide.

ERNST & YOUNG LLP
P.O. Box 10647, Greenville SC 29603. 864/242-5740. **Contact:** Phil Snipes, Partner. **World Wide Web address:** http://www.ey.com.

Description: A certified public accounting firm that also provides management consulting services. Services include data processing, financial modeling, financial feasibility studies, production planning and inventory management, management sciences, health care planning, human resources, cost accounting, and budgeting systems. **NOTE:** The company requests resumes to be submitted online. **Positions advertised include:** Technology Support Specialist. **Corporate headquarters location:** New York NY. **Other locations:** Worldwide. **Chairman/CEO:** James (Jim) S. Turley. **Annual sales/revenues:** $10.1 billion. **Number of employees:** 110,000.

KPMG
55 Beattie Place, Suite 900, Greenville SC 29601. 864/250-2600. **Contact:** Human Resources. **World Wide Web address:** http://www.kpmg.com. **Description:** Delivers a wide range of value-added auditing, accounting, taxation, and consulting services. **Other area locations:** Greensboro SC. **Other locations:** Worldwide. **Parent company:** KPMG International (Amstelveen, Netherlands). **Number of employees at this location:** 75.

PRESIDION SOLUTIONS, INC.
One Harbison Way, Suite 114, Columbia SC 29212. 803/781-7810. **Toll-free phone:** 800/948-8524. **Contact:** Human Resources Manager. **World Wide Web address:** http://www.presidionsolutions.com. **Description:** Performs general accounting functions, as well as human resources, payroll, and workers' compensation for other companies. **Corporate headquarters location:** Troy MI. **Other locations:** Ten sales offices throughout the state of Florida. **Parent company:** Presidion Corporation (Troy MI). **President/CEO:** Craig Vanderburg.

ADVERTISING, MARKETING, AND PUBLIC RELATIONS

You can expect to find the following types of companies in this section:
Advertising Agencies • Direct Mail Marketers • Market Research Firms • Public Relations Firms

North Carolina

ADSTREET INC.
1638 South Saunders Street, Raleigh NC 27603. 919/828-2990. **Contact:** Rich Styles, President. **World Wide Web address:** http://www.adstreet.com. **Description:** A full-service advertising and public relations agency. The company offers creative advertising work, sports marketing, and media buying services. **Corporate headquarters location:** This location. **Other U.S. locations:** Orlando FL. **CEO:** Rich Styles.

COX TARGET MEDIA (CTM)
6030 US Highway 301 North, Elm City NC 27822-9144. 252/236-4301. **Contact:** Human Resources Manager. **E-mail address:** elmcity_humanresources3@coxtarget.com. **World Wide Web address:** http://www.coxtarget.com. **Description:** A direct marketing company. **NOTE:** Please visit website to view job listings and apply online. **Positions advertised include:** Inserting Supervisor. **Corporate headquarters location:** Largo FL. **Other U.S. locations:** Los Angeles CA; Tampa FL; St. Petersburg FL; Boston MA; Minneapolis MN; Houston TX. **Parent company:** CTM is a subsidiary of Cox Newspapers, which is owned by Cox Enterprises.

FFWD
325 Arlington Avenue, Suite 1000, Charlotte NC 28203. 704/344-7900. **Contact:** Human Resources. **E-mail address:** hr@ffwdgroup.com. **World Wide Web address:** http://www.ffwdgroup.com. **Description:** A marketing agency providing direct marketing, advertising, branding, online marketing, customer loyalty, and database marketing services. **Other U.S. locations:** New York NY; Denver CO; Chicago IL; Minneapolis MN; Dallas TX.

McKINNEY & SILVER
333 Corporate Plaza, Raleigh NC 27601. 919/828-0691. **Fax:** 919/821-5122. **Contact:** Lea Daughtridge, Human Resources. **E-mail address:** adaughtr@mckinney-silver.com. **World Wide Web address:** http://www.mckinney-silver.com. **Description:** An advertising agency offering broadcast, media, and print production services. **NOTE:** Contact Human Resources directly at 919/821-6417. **CEO:** Brad Brinegar.

NATIONWIDE ADVERTISING SERVICE INC.

2920 Highwoods Boulevard, Suite 110, Raleigh NC 27604-1053. 919/872-6800. **Fax:** 919/872-3926. **Contact:** Regional Manager. **E-mail address:** nas.ra@hrads.com. **World Wide Web address:** http://www.hrads.com. **Description:** With offices in 36 major U.S. and Canadian cities, Nationwide Advertising Service is one of the largest and oldest, independent, full-service advertising agencies exclusively specializing in human resource communications, promotions, and advertising. The company offers consultations, campaign planning, ad placement, research, and creative production. **NOTE:** Please visit website to search for jobs. **Corporate headquarters location:** Cleveland OH. **Other area locations:** Charlotte NC. **Other U.S. locations:** Nationwide. **International locations:** Toronto, Canada. **Parent company:** McCann-Erickson WorldGroup.

SADDLE CREEK COPAK CORPORATION

3555 Shamrock Road, Harrisburg NC 28075. 704/454-6300. **Fax:** 704/454-6301. **Contact:** Maria Russell, Human Resources. **E-mail address:** mariar@saddlecrk.com. **World Wide Web address:** http://www.saddlecrk.com. **Description:** A direct mail advertising agency with a broad range of clients. Founded 1966. **NOTE:** Please visit http://www.monster.com to search for jobs and apply online. **Positions advertised include:** Mid-Senior Manager; Warehouse Manager; Forklift Driver; Tractor/Trailer Driver; Customer Service Coordinator. **Corporate headquarters location:** Lakeland FL. **Other U.S. locations:** Southern and Southeastern U.S. **CEO:** David Lyons.

South Carolina

ANCHOR SIGN

P.O. Box 6009, 2200 Discher Avenue, Charleston SC 28405. 843/747-5901. **Toll-free phone:** 800/213-3331. **Fax:** 843/747-5807. **Contact:** Darrell Edwards, Human Resources. **E-mail address:** dedwards@anchorsign.com. **World Wide Web address:** http://www.anchorsign.com. **Description:** A sign making company specializing in business-to-business solutions. **Positions advertised include:** Accounts Payable Clerk.

McLEOD & ASSOCIATES INCORPORATED

P.O. Box 3518, West Columbia SC 29171. 803/739-6900. **Toll-free number:** 800/951-3977. **Fax:** 803/739-6901. **Contact:** Office Manager. **E-mail address:** marketing@realestate-guides.com. **World Wide Web address:** http:// www.realestate-guides.com. **Description:** A publishing and public relations firm serving over 400 cities offering several publications for the real estate industry and providing advertising through three publications for realtors which welcome new residents to the area. **Corporate headquarters location:** This location. **Other locations:** Camden SC; Cayce SC.

AEROSPACE

You can expect to find the following types of companies in this section:
Aerospace Products and Services • Aircraft Equipment and Parts

North Carolina

B/E AEROSPACE, INC.
1455 Fairchild Road, Winston-Salem NC 27105. 336/767-2000. **Fax:** 336/744-1009. **Contact:** Human Resources. **World Wide Web address:** http://www.beaerospace.com. **Description:** B/E Aerospace, Inc. designs, manufactures, sells, and supports a wide range of commercial aircraft cabin interior product lines including seating products, passenger entertainment and service systems, and galley structures and inserts. The company supplies major airlines and airframe manufacturers. **NOTE:** Please visit website to search for jobs and apply online. **Positions advertised include:** Quality Engineer; Security Administrator; System Administrator. **Corporate headquarters location:** Wellington FL. **Other U.S. locations:** Nationwide. **International locations:** England; Singapore; Wales. **Operations at this facility include:** This location manufactures airplane seats. **Listed on:** NASDAQ. **Stock exchange symbol:** BEAV. **President/CEO:** Robert J. Khoury. **Annual sales/revenues:** More than $100 million. **Number of employees at this nationwide:** 3,300.

CURTISS-WRIGHT CORPORATION
201 Old Boiling Springs Road, Shelby NC 28152. 704/481-1150. **Fax:** 704/481-2267. **Contact:** Michelle Stalder, Senior Human Resources Manager. **World Wide Web address:** http://www.curtisswright.com. **Description:** Manufactures flight control systems. **NOTE:** Please visit website to search for jobs. **Corporate headquarters location:** Roseland NJ. **Other area locations:** Gastonia NC. **Other U.S. locations:** Nationwide. **International locations:** Denmark; Switzerland. **Parent company:** Curtiss-Wright Corporation. **Listed on:** New York Stock Exchange. **Stock exchange symbol:** CW. **Annual sales/revenues:** $51 - $100 million. **Number of employees at this location:** 250. **Number of employees worldwide:** 4,655.

GOODRICH CORPORATION
4 Coliseum Centre, 2730 West Tyvola Road, Charlotte NC 28217-4578. 704/423-7000. **Fax:** 704/423-7002. **Contact:** Human Resources. **World Wide Web address:** http://www.goodrich.com. **Description:** Provides components and systems for general aviation, regional, business, commercial, and military aircraft and space vehicles. The company also manufactures performance polymer systems and additives. **NOTE:** Please visit website to search for jobs and apply online. **Positions advertised include:** Executive Administrative Assistant; Manager – Global Sourcing; Legal Administrative Assistant; Supply Chain Leadership Program Worker; Financial Analyst; Senior Internal Auditor;

Material Handler; Warehouse Lead. **Corporate headquarters location:** This location. **Other U.S. locations:** Nationwide. **International locations:** Worldwide. **Listed on:** New York Stock Exchange. **Stock exchange symbol:** GR. **Annual sales/revenues:** More than $100 million. **Number of employees worldwide:** 20,000.

HONEYWELL

3475 North Wesleyan Boulevard North, Rocky Mount NC 27804. 252/977-2100. **Contact:** Human Resources. **World Wide Web address:** http://www.honeywell.com. **Description:** Honeywell is engaged in the research, development, manufacture, and sale of advanced technology products and services in the fields of chemicals, electronics, automation, and controls. The company's major businesses are home and building automation and control, performance polymers and chemicals, industrial automation and control, space and aviation systems, and defense and marine systems. **NOTE:** Please visit website to search for jobs and apply online. Resumes will not be accepted by mail. **Positions advertised include:** Engineer. **Special programs:** Internships. **Corporate headquarters location:** Morristown NJ. **Other area locations:** Statewide. **Other U.S. locations:** Nationwide. **International locations:** Worldwide. **Operations at this facility include:** This location manufactures aircraft parts and equipment. **Listed on:** New York Stock Exchange. **Stock exchange symbol:** HON. **Number of employees worldwide:** 100,000.

KIDDE AEROSPACE, INC.

4200 Airport Drive NW, Wilson NC 27896-8630. 252/237-7004. **Fax:** 252/246-7184. **Contact:** Human Resources. **E-mail address:** hr@kiddeaerospace.com. **World Wide Web address:** http://www.walterkidde.com. **Description:** Develops and manufactures fire detection and suppression equipment for use in aerospace and marine applications. Products are sold to aircraft manufacturers and to airlines as replacement/repair parts, and are used in defense applications. **Positions advertised include:** Lead Engineer; Senior Project Engineer; Systems Program Manager; Systems Integration Engineer. **Corporate headquarters location:** Colnbrook, England. **International locations:** Russia; Singapore; United Arab Emirates. **Parent company:** Kidde plc. **Number of employees at this location:** 240.

South Carolina

LOCKHEED MARTIN AIRCRAFT AND LOGISTICS CENTER

107 Frederick Street, 105 Edinburgh Court, Greenville SC 29607. 864/422-6262. **Fax:** 864/422-6397. **Contact:** Human Resources Department. **World Wide Web address:** http://lmalc.external.lmco.com. **Description:** Manufactures aircraft parts and equipment at over 90 facilities worldwide supporting defense departments of the U.S. government, other federal agencies, other Lockheed Martin companies, international and national customers. **Positions advertised include:** Aircraft Mechanic; Aeronautical Engineer; Aircraft Maintenance;

Electronics Technician; Business Operations Manager; Production Control Clerk; Program Manager; Proposal Analyst; Sales Representative. **Parent company:** Lockheed Martin Corporation (Bethesda MD), a diversified defense contractor has businesses in engineering contracting, civil space programs, government services, commercial electronics, aeronautical systems, avionics, aerodynamics, and materials. Subsidiaries of Lockheed Martin include a missiles and space systems group, an aeronautical systems group, a technology services group, an electronic systems group, and Lockheed Financial Corporation.

PARKER HANNIFIN CORPORATION
3025 West Croft Circle, P.O. Box 15009, Spartanburg SC 29302-0201. 864/573-7332. **Fax:** 864/515-6086. **Contact:** Human Resources. **E-mail address:** tsdjobs@parker.com. **World Wide Web address:** http://www.parker.com. **Description:** Designs and manufactures flight, missile, and engine controls for both commercial and military programs. The company's product lines consist of electronics, hydraulics, and electrohydraulic components. **Positions advertised include:** Administrative Sales Manager; Inside Sales Representative; Accounting Manager; Network Applications Manager. **Corporate headquarters location:** Cleveland OH. **Operations at this facility include:** TechSeal Division manufacturing. **Annual sales/revenues:** $6 billion. **Number of employees worldwide:** 48,000.

APPAREL, FASHION, AND TEXTILES

You can expect to find the following types of companies in this section:
Broadwoven Fabric Mills • Knitting Mills • Yarn and Thread Mills • Curtains and Draperies • Footwear • Nonwoven Fabrics • Textile Goods and Finishing

North Carolina

ACME-MCCRARY CORPORATION
P.O. Box 1287, Asheboro NC 27204. 336/625-2161. **Physical address:** 159 North Street, Asheboro NC 27203. **Fax:** 336/629-2263. **Contact:** Human Resources Manager. **E-mail address:** acmehose@acme-mccrary.com. **World Wide Web address:** http://www.acme-mccrary.com. **Description:** Manufactures women's sheer hosiery. **Corporate headquarters location:** This location.

ALBA-WALDENSIAN, INC.
P.O. Box 100, Valdese NC 28690. 828/879-6500. **Physical address:** 201 St. Germain Avenue SW, Valdese NC 28690. **Toll-free phone:** 800/554-2522. **Contact:** Human Resources Manager. **E-mail address:** info@alba1.com. **World Wide Web address:** http://www.alba1.com. **Description:** A national, multifacility apparel-manufacturing company offering a variety of knit products. The company primarily produces women's knit hosiery and stretch panties. Alba-Waldensian also produces knit health care products, which are used in hospitals and nursing homes, and are distributed throughout the United States, Canada, England, Europe, and the Middle East. Founded in 1901. **Corporate headquarters location:** This location. **International locations:** Israel. **Parent company:** Tefron Limited Group. **President/CEO:** Lee N. Mortenson.

AMERICAN & EFIRD, INC.
22 American Street, P.O. Box 507, Mount Holly NC 28120. 704/827-4311. **Toll-free phone:** 704/82-4311. **Contact:** Human Resources. **E-mail address:** ae.careers@amefird.com. **World Wide Web address:** http://www.amefird.com. **Description:** Manufactures and distributes sewing thread internationally for industrial and consumer markets. American & Efird, Inc. has 12 manufacturing facilities in North Carolina. **NOTE:** All hiring for American & Efird, Inc. is done at this location. **Corporate headquarters location:** This location. **Other U.S. locations:** Nationwide. **International locations:** Worldwide. **Parent company:** Ruddick Corporation is a diversified holding company operating through its wholly-owned subsidiaries American & Efird, Inc.; Harris Teeter, Inc. (Charlotte NC) operates a regional supermarket chain and handles its own hiring; and Ruddick Investment Company.

BURKE MILLS, INC.
P.O. Box 190, Valdese NC 28690. 828/874-6341. **Physical address:** 191 Sterling Street, Valdese NC. **Fax:** 828/879-7188. **Contact:** Human Resources. **World Wide Web address:** http://www.burkemills.com. **Description:** Engaged in twisting, texturing, winding, dyeing, processing, and selling filament, novelty, and spun yarns and also in the dyeing and processing of these yarns for others on a commission basis. The company's products have upholstery, apparel, and industrial uses for the knitting and weaving industry. **Corporate headquarters location:** This location. **Listed on:** Over-the-Counter. **Stock exchange symbol:** BMLS. **CEO:** Humayan N. Shaikh. **Number of employees nationwide:** 167.

BURLINGTON INDUSTRIES
3330 West Friendly Avenue, Greensboro NC 27410-4800. 336/379-2000. **Fax:** 336/332-0815. **Contact:** Mark Collins, Human Resources. **World Wide Web address:** http://www.burlington.com. **Description:** A major producer of textiles including apparel and interior furnishings. Apparel products, which are designed, manufactured, and sold by five divisions within the company include yarns, wools, woven synthetics, clothes, denims, industrial uniforms, and sportswear. The interior furnishings division includes Burlington House, which manufactures drapes, upholstery, and bedroom ensembles; the carpet division, which uses the Lees brand name; and the Burlington House Area Rugs unit. **Special programs:** Internships. **Corporate headquarters location:** This location. **Parent company:** W.L. Ross & Co.

CLAYTON MARCUS
P.O. Box 100, Hickory NC 28603. 828/495-2200. **Physical address:** 166 Teague Town Road, Hickory NC 28601. **Fax:** 828/495-1378. **Contact:** Human Resources. **E-mail address:** info@claytonmarcus.com. **World Wide Web address:** http://www.claytonmarcus.com. **Description:** A furniture upholsterer. **NOTE:** Entry-level positions and second and third shifts are offered. **Special programs:** Internships; Summer Jobs. **Office hours:** Monday – Friday, 8:00 a.m. – 4:30 p.m. **Corporate headquarters location:** Greensboro NC. **Parent company:** La-Z-Boy Inc. **Operations at this facility include:** Divisional Headquarters. **President:** Michael Delgatti.

COATS NORTH AMERICA
Two LakePointe Plaza, 4135 South Stream Boulevard, Charlotte NC 28217. 704/329-5800. **Toll-free phone:** 800/631-0965. **Fax:** 704/329-5829. **Contact:** Human Resources Department. **World Wide Web address:** http://www.coatscna.com. **Description:** A manufacturer and supplier of sewing thread and associated products for the industrial and consumer markets. The company is also engaged in manufacturing cotton and synthetic thread and yarn; metal and coil slide fasteners, tapes, trimmings, and small diecastings; wood turnings and novelties; and special machinery spools, nylon travelers, and other plastic injection moldings. **Corporate headquarters location:** This location. **Other area locations:** Gastonia NC; Marble NC; Marlon NC; Old Fort NC; Rosman NC; Stanley NC. **Other U.S. locations:** Nationwide. **Subsidiaries**

include: Barbour Threads; Coats Bell; Coats Timon; Coats Caribbean and Central America. **Parent company:** Coats Viyella Group (London England). **Operations at this facility include:** Administration; Sales; Service. **CEO:** Max Perks. **Number of employees at this location:** 215. **Number of employees nationwide:** 4,225.

COLLINS & AIKMAN HOLDINGS CORPORATION
P.O. Box 580 Albemarle NC 28001. 704/983-5166. **Contact:** Human Resources Department. **E-mail address:** resume@colaik.com. **World Wide Web address:** http://www.collinsaikman.com. **Description:** Collins & Aikman Holdings Corporation and its subsidiaries manufacture home furnishings and hosiery products, as well as textile products for major automobile manufacturers. The home furnishings division produces and sells decorative upholstery fabrics through 15 manufacturing facilities and 11 showrooms across the nation. Consumer leg wear includes the brand name No-Nonsense. **NOTE:** Please send resumes to corporate office location at 250 Stephenson Highway, Troy MI 48083; fax is 248/824-1613. No phone calls regarding employment. **Special programs:** Internships. **Corporate headquarters location:** Troy MI. **Listed on:** New York Stock Exchange. **Stock exchange symbol:** CKC. **President:** Millard L. King, Jr. **Number of employees nationwide:** 23,000.

CONE MILLS CORPORATION
P.O. Box 26540, Greensboro NC 27415-6540. 336/379-6220. **Physical address:** 804 Green Valley Road, Suite 300, Greensboro NC 27408. **Fax:** 336/379-6287. **Contact:** Director of Human Resources. **World Wide Web address:** http://www.cone.com. **Description:** Cone Mills is a major manufacturer of denim and home furnishing fabrics. The denim division produces about 400 styles and is one of the largest suppliers for Levi Strauss & Company. The division also manufactures specialty fabrics including plaids, chamois flannel, and uniform and sportswear fabrics. Founded 1891. **Corporate headquarters location:** This location. **Other area locations:** Statewide. **Other U.S. locations:** San Francisco CA; Los Angeles CA; New York NY; Dallas TX. **International locations:** Brussels, Belgium; Mexico. **Subsidiaries include:** Carlisle Finishing Company, one of the largest U.S. commission printers of home furnishing fabrics; John Wolf Decorative Fabrics, a maker of fabrics for upholstery, drapes, and bedroom products; Olympic Products Company, which manufactures foams for beds, carpets, and furniture used in the medical and consumer markets. **Listed on:** Pink Sheets. **Stock exchange symbol:** CJML. **President/CEO:** John L. Bakane. **Number of employees worldwide:** 3,000.

CROSS CREEK APPAREL INC.
P.O. Drawer 1107, Mount Airy NC 27030. 336/783-3800. **Physical address:** 510 Riverside Drive, Mount Airy NC. **Fax:** 336/783-3795. **Contact:** Human Resources. **E-mail address:** jobs@crosscreek.com. **World Wide Web address:** http://www.crosscreek.com. **Description:** Produces men's apparel including knit shirts, turtlenecks, sweaters, shorts, and pants. Cross Creek Apparel also produces placket shirts for

women and children. Founded in 1935. **Corporate headquarters location:** Atlanta GA. **Parent company:** Russell Corporation manufactures athletic wear and leisurewear for men, women, and children.

GALEY & LORD, INC.
P.O. Box 35528, Greensboro NC 27425-0528. 336/665-3037. **Physical address:** 7736 McCloud Road, One Triad Center, Suite 300, Greensboro NC 27409. **Fax:** 336/665-3130. **Contact:** Personnel Manager. **Description:** Galey & Lord is a leading manufacturer and marketer of fabric sold to clothing manufacturers. The company is a major producer of wrinkle-free cotton fabrics for uniforms and printed fabrics for the home. **Corporate headquarters location:** New York NY. **Other U.S. locations:** CA; GA; SC; TX. **International locations:** Mexico. **Subsidiaries include:** Galey & Lord Industries, Inc; Klopman International; Swift Denim Group. **Operations at this facility include:** This location is a manufacturing plant. **Listed on:** Over-the-Counter. **Stock exchange symbol:** GYLDQ. **Chairman/CEO:** John J. Heldrich. **Number of employees nationwide:** 4,790.

GRANITE KNITWEAR, INC.
P.O. Box 498, Granite Quarry NC 28072-0498. 704/279-5526. **Toll-free phone:** 800/476-9944. **Fax:** 704/279-8205. **Contact:** Georgette White, Human Resources. **World Wide Web address:** http://www.calcru.com. **Description:** A sportswear and fleece wear apparel manufacturer. **Corporate headquarters location:** This location. **Parent company:** Cal Cru Company Inc. **Number of employees at this location:** 170.

GUILFORD MILLS, INC.
6001 West Market Street, Greensboro NC 27409. 336/316-4000. **Contact:** Richard Novak, Human Resources. **World Wide Web address:** http://www.guilfordmills.com. **Description:** A manufacturer, processor, and marketer of warp knit fabrics for the apparel, automotive, home furnishing, swimwear, dress, and sportswear industries. **Corporate headquarters location:** This location. **Other area locations:** Kenansville NC. **Other U.S. locations:** Madison Heights MI. **International locations:** Germany; United Kingdom. **President/CEO:** John A. Emrich. **Number of employees worldwide:** 3,600.

HANES INDUSTRIES
P.O. Box 457, Conover NC 28613-0457. 828/464-4673. **Physical address:** 500 North McLin Creek Road, Conover NC. **Toll-free phone:** 800/438-9124. **Fax:** 828/464-0459. **Contact:** Human Resources. **World Wide Web address:** http://www.hanesindustries.com. **Description:** Converts fabric and related materials for the bedding and drapery industry. **Office hours:** Monday – Friday, 8:00 a.m. – 5:00 p.m. **Corporate headquarters location:** This location. **Other U.S. locations:** Phoenix AZ; Cerritos CA; Indianapolis IN; Pontotoc MS; Carlstadt NJ; Cincinnati OH; Cleveland TN; Dallas TX; Auburn WA. **International locations:** Canada; England; Mexico. **Parent company:** Hanes Companies is a subsidiary of Leggett & Platt Inc.

HOLT HOSIERY

P.O. Box 1757, Burlington NC 27216. 336/227-1431. **Physical address:** 733 Koury Drive, Burlington NC. **Fax:** 336/227-8614. **Contact:** Tammy Dalrymple, Personnel. **Description:** A manufacturer and wholesaler of women's sheer hosiery. **Corporate headquarters location:** This location. **Operations at this facility include:** Manufacturing; Sales. **Number of employees at this location:** 200.

HOLT SUBLIMATION

P.O. Box 2017, Burlington NC 27216-2017. 336/222-3600. **Physical address:** 2208 Air Park Drive, Burlington NC 27216. **Fax:** 336/229-7580. **Contact:** Human Resources. **World Wide Web address:** http://www.holtsublimation.com. **Description:** An apparel design company whose disperse dye printing process allows the color and detail of artwork to be transferred to material. Engineered designs using the company's techniques are placed on active wear, swimwear, athletic wear, sleepwear, scarves, rugs, mats, domestics, narrow-web elastic, lace trim, labels, ribbons, shoelaces, and other products. **Special programs:** Internships. **Corporate headquarters location:** This location. **Operations at this facility include:** Administration; Manufacturing; Research and Development; Sales; Service. **Listed on:** Privately held. **President/CEO:** Frank Holt III. **Number of employees at this location:** 220.

HONEYWELL

P.O. Box 166, Moncure NC 27559. 919/542-2200. **Physical address:** 338 Pea Ridge Road Moncure NC 27562. **Contact:** Manager of Personnel. **World Wide Web address:** http://www.honeywell.com. **Description:** Honeywell is engaged in the research, development, manufacture, and sale of advanced technology products and services in the fields of chemicals, electronics, automation, and controls. The company's major businesses are home and building automation and control, performance polymers and chemicals, industrial automation and control, space and aviation systems, and defense and marine systems. **NOTE:** Please visit website to search for jobs and apply online. **Positions advertised include:** Process Development and Technical Group Manager. **Special programs:** Internships. **Corporate headquarters location:** Morristown NJ. **Other area locations:** Statewide. **Other U.S. locations:** Nationwide. **International locations:** Worldwide. **Operations at this facility include:** This location manufactures polyester filament yarns for cord, seatbelts, and other industrial applications, and also produces polyester resins. **Listed on:** New York Stock Exchange. **Stock exchange symbol:** HON. **Number of employees worldwide:** 100,000.

KAYSER-ROTH CORPORATION

102 Corporate Center Boulevard, Greensboro NC 27408. 336/852-2030. **Contact:** Sara Newby, Human Resources. **World Wide Web address:** http://www.nononsense.com. **Description:** Distributes sheer hosiery to food and drug stores, mass merchandisers, and discount stores. Brands

include No Nonsense, Renew!, Great Shapes, Almost Bare, Sheer Endurance, and Business Casuals. **Other U.S. locations:** Nationwide.

KIMBERLY-CLARK CORPORATION
32 Smyth Avenue, Hendersonville NC 28792-8503. 828/692-9611. **Contact:** Human Resources Director. **World Wide Web address:** http://www.kimberly-clark.com. **Description:** Kimberly-Clark Corporation manufactures and markets products for personal, business, and industrial uses throughout the world. Most of the company's products are made from natural and synthetic fibers using advanced technologies in absorbency, fibers, and nonwovens. The name brands of Kimberly-Clark Corporation include Kleenex facial and bathroom tissue, Huggies diapers and baby wipes, Pull-Ups training pants, Kotex and New Freedom feminine care products, Depend and Poise incontinence care products, Hi-Dri household towels, Kimguard sterile wrap, Kimwipes industrial wipes, and Classic business and correspondence papers. **NOTE:** Please visit website to search for job by category and apply online. Resumes are not accepted at this location. Please apply through Blue Ridge Community College. **Corporate headquarters location:** Dallas TX. **Other U.S. locations:** Nationwide. **International locations:** Worldwide. **Operations advertised include:** This location is a nonwoven fabric mill. **Listed on:** New York Stock Exchange. **Stock exchange symbol:** KMB. **CEO:** Thomas J. Falk. **Number of employees worldwide:** 62,000.

KOSA
P.O. Box 37388, Charlotte NC 28237. 704/586-7300. **Physical address:** 4501 Charlotte Park Drive, Charlotte NC. **Fax:** 704/586-7500. **Contact:** Human Resources. **World Wide Web address:** http://www.kosa.com. **Description:** One of the world's largest producers of polyester fibers, resins, and polymer products. KoSa is a joint venture between Koch Industries Inc. (Witchita KS) and IMASAB S.A. de C.V. (Mexico). **Corporate headquarters location:** Houston TX. **Other area locations:** Wilmington NC; Salisbury NC; Shelby NC. **Other U.S. locations:** Spartanburg SC; Winnsboro SC. **International locations:** Canada; Germany; Mexico; Netherlands. **Parent company:** Koch International Equity Investments BV. **Operations at this facility include:** Regional Headquarters. **Number of employees worldwide:** 6,500.

LEE INDUSTRIES
402 West 25th Street, Newton NC 28658. 828/464-8318. **Fax:** 828/465-0614. **Contact:** Angie Doane Human Resources. **World Wide Web address:** http://www.leeindustries.com. **Description:** An upholstery manufacturer. **Corporate headquarters location:** This location.

NATIONAL SPINNING COMPANY INC.
1632 Wards Bridge Road, Warsaw NC 28398. 910/293-7101. **Toll-free phone:** 800/868-7104. **Contact:** Human Resources. **World Wide Web address:** http://www.natspin.com. **Description:** Engaged in the manufacture, marketing, and distribution of yarn products for knitwear manufacturers. National Spinning Company also produces hand-knitting yarn and rug kits for distribution to retail chains throughout the United

States. Founded 1921. **Corporate headquarters location:** New York NY. **Other area locations:** Beulaville NC; Glen Raven NC; Kinston NC; Washington NC; Whiteville NC. **Other U.S. locations:** LaFayette GA. **International locations:** Canada. **Operations at this facility include:** This location is a yarn plant. **President/CEO:** Jim Chesnutt.

REGAL MANUFACTURING COMPANY
212 12th Avenue NE, P.O. Box 2363, Hickory NC 28603-2363. 828/328-5381. **Fax:** 828/328-4936. **Contact:** Personnel Manager. **E-mail address:** info@regalmfgcoinc.com. **World Wide Web address:** http://www.regalmfgcoinc.com. **Description:** Develops, manufactures, and markets elastic yarn for the garment industry. Founded 1956. **Corporate headquarters location:** This location. **Subsidiaries include:** Filix-Lastex S.A.; Rubyco Inc.; Fibrexa Ltda.; Elastic Corporation of America; Elastex Inc. **Parent company:** Worldtex, Inc. **Operations at this facility include:** Administration; Manufacturing; Research and Development; Sales; Service.

ROCKY MOUNT CORD COMPANY
P.O. Drawer 4304, Rocky Mount NC 27803-0304. 252/977-9130. **Fax:** 252/977-9123. **Contact:** Human Resources Director. **World Wide Web address:** http://www.rmcord.com. **Description:** Manufactures braided cord and twisted rope. **Corporate headquarters location:** This location.

ROYAL HOME FASHIONS INC.
P.O. Box 930, Durham NC 27702. 919/683-8011. **Physical address:** 2102 Fay Street, Durham NC 27704. **Fax:** 252/431-0470. **Contact:** Human Resources. **E-mail address:** jobapps@croscill.com. **World Wide Web address:** http://www.croscill.com. **Description:** Manufactures home furnishings such as window treatments, comforters, sheets, and pillows. **NOTE:** Please visit website to view job listings and apply online. Hiring for Royal Home Fashions and Croscill Home Fashions is done through the same online application, e-mail, and fax contacts. **Corporate headquarters location:** This location. **Other area locations:** Henderson NC. **Parent company:** Croscill Home Fashions. **Operations at this facility include:** Administration; Manufacturing. **Listed on:** Privately held. **Number of employees nationwide:** 1,500.

SARA LEE HOSIERY
5660 University Parkway, Winston-Salem NC 27105. 336/519-8400. **Toll-free phone:** 800/206-9196. **Fax:** 336/519-3941. **Contact:** Personnel. **World Wide Web address:** http://www.saraleehosiery.com. **Description:** Manufactures and markets a nationally distributed line of women's hosiery products. **Corporate headquarters location:** This location. **Parent company:** Sara Lee Corporation. **Listed on:** New York Stock Exchange. **Stock exchange symbol:** SLE.

SARA LEE INTIMATE APPAREL
P.O. Box 5100, Winston-Salem NC 27113-5100. 336/519-6053. **Physical address:** 3330 Healy Drive, Winston-Salem NC 27103. **Contact:** Employee Relations. **World Wide Web address:**

http://www.balinet.com. **Description:** Manufactures women's intimate apparel. Brands include BALI, Wonderbra, Playtex, and Just My Size. **NOTE:** Please visit corporate website http://www.saralee.com to search for jobs and apply online. **Positions advertised include:** Manager – Financial Controls Compliance. **Corporate headquarters location:** This location. **Parent company:** Sara Lee Corporation.

SHADOWLINE INC.
550 Lenoir Road, Morganton NC 28655. 828/437-3821. **Fax:** 828/437-8900. **Contact:** Personnel Manager. **World Wide Web address:** http://www.shadowline-lingerie.com. **Description:** A manufacturer of lingerie. **Special programs:** Internships. **Corporate headquarters location:** This location. **Other area locations:** Boone NC; Fallston NC; Mars Hill NC. **Other U.S. locations:** SC; TN; MO; AL; FL; OH; TX. **Operations at this facility include:** Administration; Manufacturing; Research and Development; Sales; Service. **Listed on:** Privately held.

M.J. SOFFE COMPANY, INC.
P.O. Box 2507, One Soffe Drive, Fayetteville NC 28312. 910/483-2500. **Fax:** 910/486-9030. **Contact:** Human Resources Director. **World Wide Web address:** http://www.mjsoffe.com. **Description:** A manufacturer of sportswear. **Corporate headquarters location:** This location. **Other area locations:** Maxton NC; Rowland NC; Bladenboro NC. **Other U.S. locations:** Lansing MI; Jacksonville FL; Springfield MA. **Listed on:** Privately held.

THOMASVILLE FURNITURE
401 East Main Street, P.O. Box 339, Thomasville NC 27361-0339. 336/472-4000. **Fax:** 336/472-4085. **Contact:** Personnel. **World Wide Web address:** http://www.thomasville.com. **Description:** Manufactures furniture upholstery for the nationwide Thomasville furniture chain and related stores. **Corporate headquarters location:** This location. **Other area locations:** Statewide. **President/CEO:** Thomas G. Tilley.

UNIFI, INC.
P.O. Box 19109, Greensboro NC 27419-9109. 336/294-4410. **Physical address:** 7201 West Friendly Avenue, Greensboro NC 27410. **Fax:** 336/316-5422. **Contact:** Human Resources Director. **E-mail address:** careers@unifi-inc.com. **World Wide Web address:** http://www.unifi-inc.com. **Description:** Unifi, Inc. and its subsidiaries are engaged in the processing of yarns by texturing synthetic filament polyester and nylon fibers and spinning cotton and cotton-blend fibers. The company supplies knitters and weavers for apparel, women's and men's hosiery, high-performance stretch active wear, medical products including tape and bandages that contain the company's textured nylon and covered lycra and rubber products, industrial hosiery, home furnishing, automotive upholstery, and other end use markets. **Office hours:** Monday – Friday, 8:00 a.m. – 5:00 p.m. **Corporate headquarters location:** This location. **Other area locations:** Altamahaw NC; Reidsville NC; Mayodan NC; Yadkinville NC. **International locations:** Ireland; Colombia; Brazil; China; United Kingdom; Germany; Italy. **Subsidiaries**

include: Unifi Spun Yarns, Inc.; Vintage Yarns, Inc. **Listed on:** New York Stock Exchange. **Stock exchange symbol:** UFI. **Number of employees nationwide:** 4,500.

UNIFI, INC.
2920 Vance Street, P.O. Box 1437, Reidsville NC 27323. 336/342-3361. **Fax:** 336/348-6535. **Contact:** Employment Manager. **E-mail address:** careers@unifi-inc.com. **World Wide Web address:** http://www.unifi-inc.com. **Description:** The company and its subsidiaries are engaged in the processing of yarns by texturing synthetic filament polyester and nylon fiber and spinning cotton and cotton-blend fibers. The company supplies knitters and weavers for apparel, women's and men's hosiery, high-performance stretch active wear, medical products including tape and bandages that contain the company's textured nylon and covered lycra and rubber products, industrial hosiery, home furnishing, automotive upholstery, and other end use markets. **Corporate headquarters location:** Greensboro NC. **Other area locations:** Altamahaw NC; Mayodan NC; Yadkinville NC. **International locations:** Ireland; Colombia; Brazil; China; United Kingdom; Germany; Italy. **Subsidiaries include:** Unifi Spun Yarns, Inc.; Vintage Yarns, Inc. **Operations at this facility include:** This location processes and dyes yarn. **Listed on:** New York Stock Exchange. **Stock exchange symbol:** UFI. **Number of employees nationwide:** 4,500.

UNIFI, INC.
802 South Ayersville Road, Mayodan NC 27027. 336/427-1500. **Fax:** 336/427-1529. **Contact:** Employment Manager. **E-mail address:** careers@unifi-inc.com. **World Wide Web address:** http://www.unifi-inc.com. **Description:** The company and its subsidiaries are engaged in the processing of yarns by texturing synthetic filament polyester and nylon fiber and spinning cotton and cotton-blend fibers. The company supplies knitters and weavers for apparel, women's and men's hosiery, high-performance stretch active wear, medical products including tape and bandages that contain the company's textured nylon and covered lycra and rubber products, industrial hosiery, home furnishing, automotive upholstery, and other end use markets. **Corporate headquarters location:** Greensboro NC. **Other area locations:** Altamahaw NC; Yadkinville NC; Reidsville NC; Greensboro NC. **International locations:** Ireland; Colombia; Brazil; China; United Kingdom; Germany; Italy. **Subsidiaries include:** Unifi Spun Yarns, Inc.; Vintage Yarns, Inc. **Operations at this facility include:** This location produces ultra-fine to mid-denier textured nylon with various filament counts including microfibers. A portion of these products are package-dyed. **Listed on:** New York Stock Exchange. **Stock exchange symbol:** UFI. **Number of employees nationwide:** 4,500.

VF CORPORATION
P.O. Box 21488, Greensboro NC 27420-1488. 336/424-6000. **Physical address:** 105 Corporate Center Boulevard, Greensboro NC 27408. **Fax:** 336/424-7631. **Contact:** Vice President of Human Resources. **World Wide Web address:** http://www.vfc.com. **Description:** A manufacturer

of jeans wear, decorative knitwear, intimate apparel, playwear, and specialty apparel sold worldwide. VF Corporation markets its products under the brand names Vanity Fair, Barbizon, JanSport, Rustler, Girbaud, Lee, and Wrangler. Founded 1899. **NOTE:** Please visit website to search for jobs and apply online. **Positions advertised include:** AS400 Software Systems Analyst; Senior Accountant; SAP F1 Systems Analyst; Senior Business Development Analyst; Senior Strategic Planning Analyst; UNIX Systems Analyst; SAP Product Costing Team Member. **Corporate headquarters location:** This location. **Other U.S. locations:** Shawnee Mission KS; Alpharetta GA; New York NY; Appleton WI; San Leandro CA; Nashville TN; Wyoming PA; Tampa FL. **International locations:** Mexico; Argentina; Spain; Belgium; Italy; China. **Subsidiaries include:** Eastpak; Jansport; Lee Sport; Red Kap Industries; Wrangler. **Listed on:** New York Stock Exchange. **Stock exchange symbol:** VFC. **Number of employees worldwide:** 52,300.

WAVERLY MILLS INCORPORATED
23 Third Street, Laurinburg NC 28352. 910/276-1441. **Fax:** 910/276-5826. **Contact:** Personnel Director. **World Wide Web address:** http://www.waverlymills.com. **Description:** Manufactures synthetic spun yarn. **Parent company:** R.J. Kunik & Co. **President:** Robert Kunik.

South Carolina

AMERICAN FIBER & FINISHING
P.O. Box 379, Newberry SC 29108. 803/276-2843. **Physical address:** 2802 Fair Avenue, Newbury SC 29108. **Toll-free number:** 800/949-8203. **Fax:** 803/276-2324. **Contact:** Human Resources Manager. **E-mail address:** sales@affinc.com. **World Wide Web address:** http://www.affinc.com. **Description:** Manufactures cloth from cotton. The company wholesales this material to other companies that make finished apparel and textile products. Founded in 1986. **Corporate headquarters location:** Albemarle NC. **Operations at this facility include:** Greiger Cloth production.

BASF CORPORATION
P.O. Drawer 13025, Anderson SC 29624. 864/260-7000. **Physical address:** 411 Masters Boulevard, Anderson SC 29626. **Fax:** 864/260-7641. **Contact:** Human Resources. **World Wide Web address:** http://www.basf.com. **Description:** The company, the North American arm of the German chemical company BASF, manufactures and markets industrial chemicals, yarns, and man-made fibers through seven groups: Fine Chemicals/Pharmaceuticals; Agricultural Chemicals; Biotechnology; Automotive and Coil Coatings; Chemicals; Plastics; and Fibers, and is the parent company's NAFTA region representative. Founded in 1968. **Corporate headquarters location:** Mount Olive NJ. **Other area locations:** Clemson SC; Whitestone SC. **Other U.S. locations:** Nationwide. **International locations:** Canada; Mexico. **Parent company:** BASF AG (Ludwigshafen, Germany). **Operations at this facility include:** Anderson Plant Production; Fiber Products Division

Manufacturing. **Chairman:** Peter Oakley. **Number of employees at this location:** 1,200. **Number of employees in North America:** 14,600.

BP FABRICS AND FIBERS
320 Shiloh Road, Seneca SC 29678. 864/882-5660. **Fax:** 864/882-4981. **Contact:** Human Resources. **World Wide Web address:** http://www.fabricsandfibers.com. **E-mail address:** fabrics.info@usa.com. **Description:** BP Fabrics and Fibers Company is part of BP's conversion and specialty chemicals division, converting polypropylene into woven carpet-backing and fabrics and yarns for home, automotive, industrial, and medical applications. The company's products include non-woven fabrics, multifilament yarns, and fibers. Since 1965. **Positions advertised include:** Transport Driver; Chemical Engineer. **Corporate headquarters location:** Austell GA. **Other U.S. locations:** AL CA; GA. **International locations:** Australia; Brazil; China; Mexico. **Operations at this facility include:** The Seneca Mills manufactures furniture, bedding, and automotive non-woven fabrics and civil engineering non-woven fabrics. **Number of employees worldwide:** 3,500.

DELTA WOODSIDE INDUSTRIES, INC.
100 Augusta Street, P.O. Box 6126, Greenville SC 29606. 864/255-4100. **Fax:** 864/255-4165. **Contact:** Jerry Tucker, Personnel. **World Wide Web address:** http://www.deltawoodside.com. **Description:** Manufactures and sells textiles and finished apparel fabrics operating six manufacturing plants in North and South Carolina. **Corporate headquarters:** This location. **Other area locations:** Edgefield SC; Wallace SC. **Subsidiaries include:** Delta Mills, Inc. **Listed on:** New York Stock Exchange. **Stock exchange symbol:** DLW. **Director/President/CEO:** William F. Garrett. **Annual sales/revenues:** $175 million. **Number of employees:** 1,750.

GREENWOOD MILLS, INC.
P.O. Box 1017, Greenwood SC 29648-1017. 864/229-2571. **Physical address:** 300 Morgan Avenue, Greenwood SC 29646. **Fax:** 864/229-1111. **Contact:** Warren Moore, Vice President of Human Resources. **Description:** A family-owned textile manufacturer specializing in finished fabrics for clothing, bed linens, garments, jeans and denim products as well as operating golf courses, resorts, and real estate developments. Founded in 1888. **Other locations:** Orangeburg SC; Mexico. **Affiliates include:** SingleSource Apparel. **Listed on:** Privately held. **Chairman:** William Self. **Annual sales/revenues:** $400 million. **Number of employees:** 4,000.

HAMPSHIRE DESIGNERS, INC.
215 Commerce Boulevard, Anderson SC 29625. 864/225-6232. **Fax:** 864/225-4421. **Contact:** Martha Camberrell, Human Resources. **E-mail address:** hr@ hamp.com. **World Wide Web address:** http://www.hamp.com. **Description:** One of the largest manufacturers of full-fashion sweaters in the United States. The company designs, manufactures, and markets sweaters under the brand name Designers Originals. **Positions advertised include:** Customer Service

Representative; Designer; Financial Specialist; Accountant; Information Technology Associate; Merchandiser; Production Manager; Sales Representative; Sourcing Specialist. **Corporate headquarters location:** This location. **Other locations:** Hauppauge NY; New York NY. **Affiliates include:** Hampshire Investments, Limited; Item-Eyes, Inc. **Parent company:** Hampshire Group, Limited (also at this location). **Listed on**: Nasdaq. **Stock exchange symbol:** HAMP.

HONEYWELL

4401 St. Andrews Road, Columbia SC 29210. 803/772-2700. **Contact:** Personnel Manager. **World Wide Web address:** http://www.honeywell.com. **Description:** Honeywell is engaged in the research, development, manufacture, and sale of advanced technology products and services in the fields of chemicals, electronics, automation, and controls. The company's major businesses are home and building automation and control, performance polymers and chemicals, industrial automation and control, space and aviation systems, and defense and marine systems. **Operations at this facility include:** Production of nylon textile yarns and related products. **Listed on:** New York Stock Exchange. **Stock exchange symbol:** HON.

JPS INDUSTRIES

555 North Pleasantburg Drive, Suite 202, Greenville SC 29607. 864/239-3900. **Fax:** 864/271-9939. **Contact:** Monnie L. Broome, Human Resources Manager. **Description:** A holding company with companies that are engaged in the following areas of business: manufacturing industrial roofing; automotive products; home furnishings; and residential and commercial carpets. Founded in 1964. **Corporate headquarters location:** This location. **Other locations:** Nationwide. **Subsidiaries include:** JPS Elastomerics; JPS Glass; AstroQuartz. **Listed on:** NASDAQ. **Stock exchange symbol:** JPST. **Chairman/President/CEO:** Michael L. Fulbright. **Annual sales/revenues:** $127 million. **Number of employees:** 620.

KOSA

1551 Sha Lane, Spartanburg SC 29304. 864/579-5750. **Fax:** 864/579-5678. **Contact:** Human Resources. **World Wide Web address:** http://www.kosa.com. **Description:** One of the world's largest producers of polyester fibers, resins, and polymer products. KoSa is a joint venture between Koch Industries Inc. (Wichita KS) and IMASAB S.A. de C.V. (Mexico). **Corporate headquarters location:** Houston TX. **Other U.S. locations:** NC. **International locations:** Canada; Germany; Mexico; Netherlands. **Site Manager:** Bill Every. **Number of employees:** 6,500.

TIETEX INTERNATIONAL

P.O. Box 6218, Spartanburg SC 29304. 864/574-0500. **Physical address:** 3010 North Blackstock Road, Spartanburg SC 29301. **Toll-free phone:** 800/843-8390. **Fax:** 864/574-9476. **Contact:** Mr. Jackie Johnson, Director of Human Resources. **E-mail address:** info@tietex.com. **World Wide Web address:** http://www.tietex.com. **Description:** One of the world's largest manufacturers of stitch-bonded fabrics. Other services provided by the company include warp knitting and textile finishing. Finishing processes include flexographic printing, dyeing, acrylic foam coating, heat transfer printing, napping, hot melt adhesive laminating, and embossing. Tietex products include mattress ticking (printed tickings, box spring filler cloth, and commercial tickings with flame retardants); vertical blinds (custom and ready-made vertical and pleated shade fabrics); bedding (prints and solids for comforters, bedspreads, pillow shams, and dust ruffles); upholstery (prints, faux leathers, and suedes); outdoor furniture (cushion and umbrella prints); drapery and curtains (prints and solids that can be napped, latex foam-backed, or flame-retarded); industrial fabrics; vacuum cleaner bags (foam-backed filter media for outside of the bags on residential and commercial uprights and stick brooms); roofing (reinforcement for cold process roofing and modified bitumen membranes); shoes (shoe lining and innersole fabrics); medical (fabrics for orthopedic soft goods, arm slings, and restraint vests); sleeping bags (shells and linings for sleeping bags); and home furnishings (Tietex's largest area of business). Founded in 1972. **Corporate headquarters location:** This location. **Other locations:** Chonburi, Thailand. **Listed on:** Privately held.

ARCHITECTURE, CONSTRUCTION, AND ENGINEERING

You can expect to find the following types of companies
in this section:
Architectural and Engineering Services • Civil and Mechanical
Engineering Firms • Construction Products, Manufacturers, and
Wholesalers • General Contractors/Specialized Trade Contractors

North Carolina

APAC
P.O. Box 6939, Asheville NC 28816. 828/665-1180. **Physical address:**
1188 Smokey Park Highway, Candler NC 28715. **Fax:** 828/665-9345.
Contact: Human Resources. **World Wide Web address:**
http://www.apac.com. **Description:** APAC is a leading transportation
construction company, providing service and materials to customers
across the country. **NOTE:** Please visit website to search for jobs and
apply online. **Positions advertised include:** Marketing Representative.
Corporate headquarters location: Alpharetta GA. **Other area
locations:** Statewide. **Other U.S. locations:** Nationwide. **Operations at
this facility include:** This location is engaged in the production of
asphalt and asphalt paving services. **President:** Garry M. Higdem.

FM GLOBAL
14120 Ballantyne Corporate Place, Suite 460, Charlotte NC 28217.
704/752-3080. **Contact:** Human Resources. **E-mail address:**
jobs@fmglobal.com. **World Wide Web address:**
http://www.fmglobal.com. **Description:** A loss control service
organization. FM Global's primary objective is to help owner company
policyholders to protect their properties and occupancies from damage
from fire, wind, flood, and explosion; from boiler, pressure vessel, and
machinery accidents; and from many other insured hazards. To
accomplish this objective, a wide range of engineering, research, and
consulting services are provided, primarily in the field of loss control.
NOTE: Please visit website to search for jobs and apply online. **Special
programs:** Internships; Co-ops. **Corporate headquarters location:**
Johnston RI. **Other U.S. locations:** Nationwide. **International
locations:** Worldwide.

HLM DESIGN
121 West Trade Street, Suite 2950, Charlotte NC 28202. 704/358-0779.
Fax: 704/358-0229. **Contact:** Professional Recruitment. **World Wide
Web address:** http://www.hlmdesign.com. **Description:** An architectural,
engineering, and planning firm for commercial facilities. **NOTE:** Entry-
level positions are offered. **Special programs:** Internships. **Corporate
headquarters location:** This location. **Other U.S. locations:** San
Francisco CA; Denver CO; Orlando FL; Atlanta GA; Chicago IL; Iowa
City IA; Bethesda MD; Philadelphia PA; Dallas TX. **International
locations:** United Kingdom. **Number of employees at this location:**
120. **Number of employees nationwide:** 434.

OAKWOOD HOMES

P.O. Box 27081, Greensboro NC 27425-7081. 336/664-2400. **Toll-free phone:** 800/556-2080. **Fax:** 336/664-3041. **Contact:** Melissa Lee, Human Resources. **World Wide Web address:** http://www.oakwoodhomes.com. **Description:** Manufactures and sells prefabricated housing under the Oakwood and Freedom brand names. Oakwood Homes also finances a portion of its installment contracts through its finance unit. **NOTE:** Please visit website to search for jobs and apply online. **Positions advertised include:** Collections Representative. **Special programs:** Internships. **Corporate headquarters location:** This location. **Other U.S. locations:** Nationwide. **Operations at this facility include:** Administration. **Listed on:** New York Stock Exchange. **Stock exchange symbol:** OH.

SPX CORPORATION

13515 Ballantyne Corporate Place, Charlotte NC 28277. 704/752-4400. **Fax:** 704/752-7511. **Contact:** Human Resources. **World Wide Web address:** http://www.spx.com. **Description:** The company operates in three segments: industrial products, building products, and engineering. The industrial products segment produces sanitary pumps for the food and industrial processing industries; submersible water and petroleum pumps; petroleum leak detection equipment; compacting equipment for soil, asphalt, and refuse applications; cooling towers for power generation, industrial, and heating and cooling applications; cast-iron boilers and electrical resistance heaters for industrial and residential customers; industrial machinery and process equipment; and aerospace components. The building products segment manufactures complementary products that encompass architectural metal roofing; side-hinged and rolling steel doors; residential garage doors; pre-engineered metal buildings; loading dock systems and related equipment; and wall, roof, floor, and window systems. It also provides general and specialized contractor services. The engineering segment is comprised of the Litwin companies, which provide worldwide engineering and construction services for the refining and petrochemical, polymers, specialty chemicals, and environmental control markets. Litwin also provides advanced process control and instrumentation capabilities. **NOTE:** Please visit http://www.monster.com to search for jobs and apply online. **Corporate headquarters location:** This location. **International locations:** Worldwide. **Operations at this facility include:** This location houses the executive offices. **Listed on:** New York Stock Exchange. **Stock exchange symbol:** SPW. **Number of employees worldwide:** 22,000.

SOUTHERN INDUSTRIAL CONSTRUCTORS, INC.

6101 Triangle Drive, Raleigh NC 27617-4717. 919/782-4600. **Recorded jobline:** 888/874-2778x4202. **Fax:** 919/782-2935. **Contact:** Human Resources Department. **World Wide Web address:** http://www.southernindustrial.com. **Description:** An industrial construction firm specializing in the installation of manufacturing processes and equipment. The company operates in 33 states. **Office hours:** Monday – Friday, 8:00 a.m. – 5:00 p.m. **Corporate**

headquarters location: This location. **Other area locations:** Wilmington NC; Raleigh NC. **Other U.S. locations:** Columbia SC. **Listed on:** Privately held. **President:** John G. Wilson.

UNDERWRITERS LABORATORIES

12 Laboratory Drive, P.O. Box 13995, Research Triangle Park NC 27709. 919/549-1400. **Fax:** 919/547-6000. **Contact:** Human Resources Director. **E-mail address:** rtpjobs@us.ul.com. **World Wide Web address:** http://www.ul.com. **Description:** An independent, nonprofit corporation established to help reduce or prevent bodily injury, loss of life, and property damage. The organization is engaged in the scientific investigation of various materials, devices, equipment, and construction methods and systems, and in the publication of standards, classifications, specifications, and other information. The company's engineering functions are divided among six departments including electrical; burglary protection and signaling; casualty and chemical hazards; fire protection; heating, air conditioning, and refrigeration; and marine. Underwriters Laboratories also provides a factory inspection service through offices located throughout the United States and in 54 other countries. **NOTE:** Please visit website to view job listings. **Office hours:** Monday - Friday, 7:30 a.m. - 4:30 p.m. **Other U.S. locations:** Nationwide. **International locations:** Worldwide. **Number of employees at this location:** 400. **Number of employees worldwide:** 4,000.

WESTMINSTER HOMES

2706 North Church Street, Greensboro NC 27405. 336/375-6200. **Fax:** 336/375-6355. **Contact:** Human Resources. **World Wide Web address:** http://www.greensboro.com/westminster. **Description:** A real estate and construction company. Westminster Homes specializes in single-family home development and sales in North Carolina. **Corporate headquarters location:** This location. **Other U.S. locations:** Cary NC. **Parent company:** Washington Homes, Inc. **Operations at this facility include:** Administration; Sales; Service. **Number of employees at this location:** 60. **Number of employees nationwide:** 100.

South Carolina

ADC ENGINEERING

1226 Yeamans Hall Road, Hanahan SC 29406. 843/506-1044. **Fax:** 843/566-0162. **Contact:** Rich Cook, Human Resources. **E-mail address:** email@ adcengineering.com. **World Wide Web address:** http://www.adcengineering.com. **Description:** Full service structural engineering roofing, water proofing, consulting and landscaping company. **Positions advertised include:** Auto Cad Technician.

DAVIS ELECTRICAL CONSTRUCTORS, INC.

429 North Main Street, P.O. Box 1907, Greenville SC 29602. 864/250-2500. **Fax:** 864/250-2567. **Contact:** Bill Dyar, Human Resources. **World Wide Web address:** http://www.daviselectrical.com. **Description:** An electrical and instrumentation contractor for power plants, textile

manufacturers, and chemical producers. Founded in 1965. **NOTE:** Human Resources phone: 864/250-2471. **Positions advertised include:** Electrical Engineer; Project Coordinator. **Corporate headquarters location:** This location. **Other U.S. locations:** Baton Rouge LA; Debary FL; Shelby NC; Gulfport MS.

FLUOR CORPORATION
100 Fluor Daniel Drive, Greenville SC 29607-2762. 864/281-4400. **Fax:** 864/281-6913. **Contact:** Human Resources. **E-mail address:** careers@fluor.com. **World Wide Web address:** http://www.fluor.com. **Description:** Operates within the fields of engineering, global services, coal production, and procurement and construction through four operation groups. Fluor Daniel provides engineering, procurement, and construction services. Fluor Global Services provides a wide range of products and related services including consulting services; equipment rental sales and service; operations; and maintenance services. Fluor Signature Services provides business support services to Fluor Corporation. A.T. Massey Coal Group produces coal for the steel industry. **NOTE:** Human Resources phone: 864/281-8600. **Positions advertised include:** Safety Technician; Senior Maintenance Engineering Manager; Senior Estimator; Senior Auditor; Audit Manager; Business Project Analyst; Sales Director; Principal Estimator; Project Manager; Senior Mechanical Estimator; Operations Director. **Corporate headquarters location:** Aliso Viejo CA. **Other U.S. locations:** Nationwide. **International locations:** Worldwide. **Subsidiaries include:** Duke/Fluor Daniel; ICA Fluor Daniel; Del-Jen, Inc.; Plant Performance Services, LLC; Fluor and Aspentech Integrated Process Solutions; ICI & ETB/Fluor Daniel Chlor-Alkali Technology. **Operations at this facility include:** Fluor Enterprises, Inc.; Fluor Constructors International, Inc. (250 Executive Center Drive, Greenville SC 29615). **Listed on:** New York Stock Exchange. **Stock exchange symbol:** FLR. **Chairman/CEO:** Alan L. Boeckmann. **Annual sales/revenues:** $10 billion. **Number of employees worldwide:** 51,300.

JACOBS APPLIED TECHNOLOGY
2040 Bushy Park Road, Goose Creek SC 29445. 843/824-1100. **Fax:** 843/824-1103. **Contact:** Human Resources Manager. **World Wide Web address:** http://www.jacobs.com. **Description:** Designs, fabricates, and constructs propane-air gas plants and process plants for the chemical, petrochemical, fine chemical, specialty chemical, food and beverage, pharmaceutical, and consumer industries. Founded in 1947. **Positions advertised include:** Project Manager. **Parent company:** Jacobs Engineering Group, Inc. (Pasadena CA) provides engineering, procurement, construction, and maintenance services to the chemicals and polymers, federal programs, pulp and paper, semiconductor, petroleum refining, facilities and transportation, food and consumer products, pharmaceutical and biotechnology, and basic resources industries. Through Jacobs College and other site-specific programs, the company trains more than 5,000 employees per year. **Operations at this facility include:** Administration; Manufacturing; Sales.

JACOBS SIRRINE ENGINEERS, INC.

1041 East Butler Road, P.O. Box 5456, Greenville SC 29607. 864/676-6000. **Fax:** 864/676-5096. **Contact:** Mary Johnson, Human Resources Representative. **World Wide Web address:** http://www.jacobs.com. **Description:** Provides architectural, engineering, and construction management consulting services. **Positions advertised include:** Civil Inspector; Customer Service Representative; Sales Manager; Civil Engineer; Electrical Engineer; Mechanical Engineer.

LOCKWOOD GREENE ENGINEERS, INC.

P.O. Box 491, Spartanburg SC 29304. 864/578-2000. **Toll-free phone:** 888/(LOCKWOOD) 5625-9663. **Fax:** 864/599-6400. **E-mail address:** careers@lg.com. **Contact:** Trudy Wofford, Personnel Manager. **World Wide Web address:** http://www.lg.com. **Description:** A consulting firm providing engineering and architectural design for industrial and commercial clients. Specifically, the company is involved in the planning and project management of industrial plants and production facilities. **Positions advertised include:** Electrical Design Engineer; Marketing Coordinator; Project Manager; Architectural Engineer; Chemical Engineer; Civil Engineer; Computer Programmer; Draftsperson; Electrical Engineer; Industrial Engineer; Mechanical Engineer; Systems Analyst. **Corporate headquarters location:** This location. **Parent company:** J.A. Jones, Inc. (Charlotte NC). **Operations at this facility include:** Computer-aided design, process, and environmental engineering, control systems engineering, computer systems integration and testing, and construction. **Annual sales/revenues:** $1 billion. **Number of employees:** 3,000.

SUITT CONSTRUCTION COMPANY INC.

P.O. Box 8858, Greenville SC 29604. 864/250-5000. **Physical address:** 201 East McBee Avenue, Suite 300, Greenville SC 29601. **Fax:** 864/250-5230. **Contact:** Human Resources. **E-mail address:** careers@suitt.com. **World Wide Web address:** http://www.suitt.com. **Description:** A diversified, single-source provider of construction and design-build services engaged in new construction, renovation and expansion. Founded in 1968. **Positions advertised include:** Project Engineer; Project Manager. **Corporate headquarters location:** This location. **Other U.S. locations:** Atlanta GA; Orlando FL; Providence RI; Raleigh NC; Richmond VA. **International locations:** Mexico. **Parent company:** BE&K Inc. (Birmingham AL). **Number of employees:** 1,500.

TRICO ENGINEERING

4425 Belle Oaks Drive, North Charleston SC 29405. 843/740-7700. **Contact:** Human Resources. **E-mail address:** jobs@tricoengineering.com. **World Wide Web address:** http://www.tricoengineering.com. **Description:** An engineering company that does surveying projects. **Positions advertised include:** Survey Instrument Person. **Corporate headquarters location:** This location.

ARTS, ENTERTAINMENT, SPORTS, AND RECREATION

You can expect to find the following types of companies in this section:
Botanical and Zoological Gardens • Entertainment Groups • Motion Picture and Video Tape Production and Distribution • Museums and Art Galleries • Physical Fitness Facilities • Professional Sports Clubs; Sporting and Recreational Camps • Public Golf Courses and Racing and Track Operations • Theatrical Producers and Services

North Carolina

THE BILTMORE COMPANY/BILTMORE HOUSE
One Approach Road, Asheville NC 28803. 828/255-1333. **Toll-free phone:** 800/624-1575. **Fax:** 828/225-6744. **Contact:** Human Resources Manager. **E-mail address:** humanresouces@biltmore.com. **World Wide Web address:** http://www.biltmore.com. **Description:** The Biltmore Company is an organization dedicated to the preservation of the largest privately-owned historic house in America (Biltmore House) and its 50,000-object collection. Founded in 1986. **NOTE:** Please visit website to download application form. **Positions advertised include:** Systems Support Trainee; Parking Host; Retail Stockroom Supervisor; Sales Manager; Administrative Assistant; Education Program Coordinator; Floral Display Staff; Engineering Services Staff; Housekeeping Staff; Winery Production Staff; Call Direction Host; Food and Beverage Director; Front Desk Supervisor; Operations Specialist; Engineer; Facility Services Crew Leader; Reservation Sales Agent; Concierge; Reception and Ticket Center Host; E-commerce Customer Service and Sales Representative. **Special programs:** Internships. **Office hours:** Monday – Friday, 9:00 a.m. – 4:00 p.m. **Number of employees at this location:** 1,500.

CHARLOTTE SYMPHONY ORCHESTRA
201 South College Street, Suite 110, College Street Level, Charlotte NC 28244. 704/972-2003. **Fax:** 704/972-2011. **Contact:** Frederick Boyd, Orchestra Personnel Manager. **E-mail address:** fredb@charlottesymphony.org. **World Wide Web address:** http://www.charlottesymphony.org. **Description:** Offices of the local symphony orchestra. The symphony plays 115 performances every season, to an accumulated audience of over 250,000. Founded in 1932. **Operations at this facility include:** Administration; Sales; Service. **President:** Richard L. Early.

SPEEDWAY MOTORSPORTS, INC.
P.O. Box 600, Concord NC 28026. 704/455-3239. **Physical address:** 5555 Concord Parkway South, Concord NC 28027. **Fax:** 704/532-3312. **Contact:** Personnel. **World Wide Web address:** http://www.speedwaymotorsports.com. **Description:** Promotes, markets, and sponsors motor sports activities including eight racing events annually sanctioned by NASCAR, five of which are associated with the

Winston Cup professional stock car racing circuit and three of which are associated with the Busch Grand National circuit. The company also operates, sanctions, and promotes its Legends Cars, 5/8-scale modified cars, modeled after those driven by legendary early NASCAR racers, for use on its Legends Car Racing Circuit, which is an entry-level stock car racing series. Other Speedway Motorsports operations include two ARCA annual stock car races. **NOTE:** Please send resumes to P.O. Box 18747, Charlotte NC 28218. **Special programs:** Internships. **Office hours:** Monday - Friday, 9:00 a.m. - 5:00 p.m. **Corporate headquarters location:** This location. **Subsidiaries include:** Atlanta Motor Speedway; Bristol Motor Speedway; Infineon Raceway; Las Vegas Motor Speedway; Lowe's Motor Speedway; PRN Radio; Texas Motor Speedway. **Listed on:** New York Stock Exchange. **Stock exchange symbol:** TRK. **CEO:** O. Bruton Smith. **Number of employees at this location:** 255.

South Carolina

ALABAMA THEATRE
4750 Highway 17 South, North Myrtle Beach SC 29582. 843/272-5758. **Fax:** 843/272-1111. **Contact:** Talent Department. **E-mail address:** bradshaw@alabama-theatre. com. (for audition information). **World Wide Web address:** http:// www.alabama-theatre.com. **Description:** A performing arts showcase featuring dance, comedy and country music performances. **Positions advertised include:** Singer; Dancer; Musician.

CHARLESTON MUSEUM
360 Meeting Street, Charleston SC 29403. 843/722-2996. **Contact:** Human Resources. **E-mail address:** info@charlestownmuseum.org. **World Wide Web address:** http://www.charlestonmuseum.org. **Description:** One of the oldest municipal museums, the Charleston Museum features collections of arts, crafts, textiles, and furniture with an emphasis on the history of South Carolina.

RIVERBANKS ZOO & GARDEN
P.O. Box 1060, Columbia SC 29202-1060. 803/779-8717. **Fax:** 803/253-6381. **Contact:** Human Resources Director. **E-mail address:** jobs@riverbanks.org. **World Wide Web address:** http://www.riverbanks.org. **Description:** A zoo featuring over 2,000 animals and a 70-acre botanical garden. **NOTE:** For positions with the zoo's food service, catering and merchandiser, Aramark Sports and Entertainment Services, phone: 803/779-8717 ext1303. **Positions advertised include:** Horticulturist; Mammal Keeper; Herpetological Keeper; Night Watch Person; Pony Ride Attendant; Development Director; Hospital Keeper; Guest Services Representative; Curator; Lorikeet Aviary Attendant.

SOUTH CAROLINA STATE MUSEUM
P.O. Box 100107, Columbia SC 29202-3107. 803/898-4921. **Physical address:** 301 Gervais Street, Columbia SC 29201. **E-mail address:** PublicRelations@ museum.state.sc.us. **Contact:** Charles Lee, Director

of Human Resources. **World Wide Web address:** http://www.museum.state.sc.us. **Description:** A museum featuring art, history, natural history, and science and technology. **Corporate headquarters location:** This location.

WOODLANDS RESORT & INN
125 Parsons Road, Summerville SC 29483. 843/875-2600. **Toll-free phone:** 800/774-9999. **Fax:** 843/875-2603. **Contact:** Human Resources. **E-mail address:** dlester@woodlands.com. **World Wide Web address:** http://www. woodlandinn.com. **Description:** One of Charleston's most luxurious hotels AAA Five Diamond. **Positions advertised include:** Pastry Chef; Maintenance Help; Dishwasher; Server.

AUTOMOTIVE

**You can expect to find the following types of companies
in this section:**
Automotive Repair Shops • Automotive Stampings • Industrial Vehicles
and Moving Equipment • Motor Vehicles and Equipment • Travel Trailers
and Campers

North Carolina

GOERLICH'S EXHAUST SYSTEMS
300 Dixie Trail, Goldsboro NC 27530. 919/580-2000. **Fax:** 919/580-1925. **Contact:** David Mozingo, Personnel Director. **E-mail address:** dmozingo@goerlichs.com. **World Wide Web address:** http://www.goerlichs.com. **Description:** Manufactures motor vehicle parts and accessories. **Positions advertised include:** Marketing Data Analyst; Product Line Coordinator; Master Scheduler/Purchasing Manager; Tubemill Manager; Senior Pricing Analyst; Engineering Technician; Machinist; Coach; Electrician; Production Scheduler. **Corporate headquarters location:** This location. **Other U.S. locations:** CT; DE; DC; MD; MA; NH; RI; VT. **President:** Vange Proimos.

HACKNEY & SONS INC.
P.O. Box 880, Washington NC 27889. 252/946-6521. **Physical address:** 911 West Fifth Street, Washington NC 27889. **Toll-free phone:** 800/763-0700. **Fax:** 252/975-8344. **Contact:** Pam Pippin, Human Resources Director. **World Wide Web address:** http://www.hackneyandsons.com. **Description:** Manufactures trucks and trailers for the beverage industry. Hackney & Sons also manufactures emergency service vehicles. Founded 1946. **Corporate headquarters location:** This location. **Other U.S. locations:** KS. **International locations:** Worldwide. **Listed on:** Privately held. **Number of employees at this location:** 250. **Number of employees nationwide:** 500.

STANADYNE AUTOMOTIVE CORPORATION
230 Clarks Neck Road, P.O. Box 1105, Washington NC 27889. 252/975-2553. **Contact:** Human Resources Manager. **E-mail address:** hr@stanadyne.com. **World Wide Web address:** http://www.stanadyne.com. **Description:** Manufactures fuel injection systems for diesel engines. **Corporate headquarters location:** Windsor CT. **NOTE:** Please visit website to view job listings and apply online. **Other area locations:** Jacksonville NC. **Other U.S. locations:** Tallahassee FL. **International locations:** Brazil; Italy; France; India. **Operations at this facility include:** Manufacturing. **Number of employees at this location:** 350.

THOMAS BUILT BUSES, INC.
1408 Courtesy Road, High Point NC 27260. . 336/889-4871. **Fax:** 336/881-6509. **Contact:** Personnel Director. **World Wide Web address:** http://www.thomasbus.com. **Description:** Manufactures motor vehicles

and passenger car bodies. **NOTE:** Please contact the local NC Employment Security Commission office about employment opportunities. Mail to 919 Phillips Avenue, High Point NC 27262. **Corporate headquarters location:** This location. **Other area locations:** Jamestown NC. **International locations:** Canada. **Parent company:** Freightliner, LLC. **President/CEO:** John O'Leary. **Number of employees nationwide:** 1,600.

South Carolina

BMW MANUFACTURING CORPORATION
P.O. Box 11000, Spartanburg SC 29304. 864/968-6000. **Contact:** Human Resources. **World Wide Web address:** http://www.bmwusa.com. **Description:** As the only production facility in the U.S., BMW Manufacturing is responsible for production of all BMW roadsters, coupes, and X5 Sports Activity Vehicles. The company also operates a Visitor's Center with the BMW Zentrum Museum of BMW's engineering and manufacturing. Since 1993. **NOTE:** Resumes, along with salary history and a job reference code, may be sent to the parent company's address: BMW of North America, LLC, P.O. Box 964, Hewitt NJ 07461. E-mail address (with the word 'resume' in the subject field): bmwna@hreasy.com. **Positions advertised include:** Inventory Accuracy Analyst; Operations Manager; Mechanical Engineer; Field Service Manager. **Other area locations:** Greer SC. **U.S. locations:** Houston TX. **Parent company:** BMW of North America, LLC (Woodcliff Lake NJ); Bayerische Motoren Werke AG (Munich, Germany). **Operations at this facility include:** Spartanburg Factory (X5 and Z3 model production; Zentrum Museum. **Number of employees at this location:** 4,300.

COLLINS & AIKMAN CORPORATION
199 Blackhawk Road, Greenville SC 29611. 864/295-5000. **Contact:** Director of Human Resources. **World Wide Web address:** http://www.colaik.com. **Description:** Manufactures automotive products including carpet and trunk liners for automobiles. **NOTE:** Resumes should be sent to the company headquarters address: Human Resources, 250 Stephenson Highway, Troy MI 48083. Fax: 248/824-1613. **Special programs:** Internships. **Corporate headquarters location:** Troy MI. **Other locations:** Nationwide. **International locations:** Worldwide. **Operations at this facility include:** Manufacturing. **Listed on:** New York Stock Exchange. **Stock exchange symbol:** CKC. **Annual sales/revenues:** $3.9 billion. **Number of employees worldwide:** 26,000.

MACK TRUCKS INC.
One Bulldog Boulevard, Winnsboro SC 29180. 803/635-8000. **Contact:** Dave Frueauf, Director of Personnel. **E-mail address:** job_opportunities@macktrucks.com. **World Wide Web address:** http://www.macktrucks.com. **Description:** Manufactures and sells heavy-duty trucks, truck tractors, and truck replacement parts; and provides repair and maintenance service for these products. **NOTE:** Resumes should be

sent to the company's headquarters address: P.O. Box M, Allentown PA 18105, or fax to: 610/709-3699. **Positions advertised include:** Truck Technician; Sales Administrator; Leasing Agent; Recovery Specialist; Production Advisor. **Other area locations:** Greenville SC. **Parent company:** Volvo Group (Gothenburg, Sweden).

THE TIMKEN COMPANY
P.O. Box 565, Honea Path SC 29654. 864/369-7395. **Contact:** Human Resources Manager. **E-mail address:** careers@timken.com. **World Wide Web address:** http://www.torrington.com. **Description:** Formerly the Torrington Company, Timken develops, manufactures, and markets antifriction bearings and produces universal joints and precision metal components and assemblies for the automotive industry with operations in 24 countries. **NOTE:** Due to the February 2003 acquisition of Torrington, resumes should be sent to the parent company headquarters address: 1835 Dueber Avenue SW, P.O. Box 6932, Canton OH 44706-0932. Fax: 330/471-4551. **Positions advertised include:** Draftsperson; Electrical Engineer; Mechanical Engineer. **Corporate headquarters location:** Canton OH. **Operations at this facility include:** Manufacturing. **Listed on:** New York Stock Exchange. **Stock exchange symbol:** TKR. **Annual sales/revenues:** $2.4 billion. **Number of employees:** 18,200.

UNITED DEFENSE
15 Windham Boulevard, Aiken SC 29805. 803/643-2500. **Contact:** Human Resources. **World Wide Web address:** http://www.uniteddefense.com. **Description:** Fabricates, machines, and welds aluminum, steel, and titanium component parts for medium and heavy armored combat vehicles. **Positions advertised include:** Project Engineer; Systems Engineer; Internal Auditor; Program Manager; Electrical Engineer. **Operations at this facility includes:** Ground System Division. **Corporate headquarters location:** Arlington VA. **Other U.S. locations:** Nationwide. **International locations:** Japan; Turkey; Korea.

BANKING, SAVINGS & LOANS, AND OTHER DEPOSITORY INSTITUTIONS

You can expect to find the following types of companies in this section:
Banks • Bank Holding Companies and Associations • Lending Firms/Financial Services Institutions

North Carolina

BB&T CORPORATION
200 West Second Street, Winston-Salem NC 27101. 336/733-2000. **Fax:** 336/733-2009. **Contact:** Human Resources. **World Wide Web address:** http://www.bbandt.com. **Description:** BB&T Corporation is a multibank holding company. Founded in 1872. **NOTE:** Please visit website to search for jobs and apply online. Entry-level positions and part-time jobs are offered. **Positions advertised include:** Accounting Policy Manager; Compensation and Benefits Plan Administration Merger Analyst; Credit Risk Quantitative Analyst; Financial Audit Coordinator; Internal Auditor; Securities Compliance Manager; Senior Interior Designer. **Company slogan:** Respect the individual. Value the relationship. **Special programs:** Internships; Training; Summer Jobs. **Office hours:** Monday - Friday, 8:30 a.m. - 5:00 p.m. **Corporate headquarters location:** This location. **Other U.S. locations:** Eastern and Southeastern U.S. **Subsidiaries include:** BB&T of North Carolina, which offers full-service commercial and retail banking and additional financial services such as investments, leasing, factoring, and trust. **Listed on:** New York Stock Exchange. **Stock exchange symbol:** BBT. **CEO:** John Allison. **President:** Kelly King. **Purchasing Manager:** Steve Paige. **Annual sales/revenues:** More than $100 million. **Number of employees at this location:** 750. **Number of employees nationwide:** 26,300.

BB&T
500 North Chestnut Street, Lumberton NC 28359. 910/272-2131. **Fax:** 910/272-2103. **Contact:** Human Resources. **World Wide Web address:** http://www.bbandt.com. **Description:** A bank engaged in commercial banking, mortgages, discount brokerage, mutual funds, leasing, insurance, retail banking, trust services, annuities, international banking, cash management, and sales finance. **NOTE:** Please visit website to search for jobs and apply online. **Corporate headquarters location:** Winston-Salem NC. **Other U.S. locations:** Eastern and Southeastern U.S. **Parent company:** BB&T-Southern National Corporation was formed by the 1994 merger of Branch Bank & Trust Financial Corporation and Southern National Corporation. Its subsidiaries form a network of hundreds of branches in cities and communities across the Carolinas and Virginia. Other subsidiaries of BB&T-Southern National Corporation include: BB&T-Southern National Bank of South Carolina; BB&T-Southern National Savings Bank, Inc.; Branch Banking & Trust (BB&T-NC); Commerce Bank of Virginia Beach; Community Bank of

South Carolina; and Lexington State Bank. **Stock exchange symbol:** BBT. **CEO:** John Allison. **Number of employees nationwide:**26,300.

BANK OF AMERICA
100 North Tryon Street, Charlotte NC 28255. 704/386-1845. **Toll-free phone:** 800/432-1000. **Fax:** 704/386-6699. **Contact:** Personnel. **World Wide Web address:** http://www.bankofamerica.com. **Description:** A full-service banking and financial institution. Bank of America operates through four business segments: Global Corporate and Investment Banking, Principal Investing and Asset Management, Commercial Banking, and Consumer Banking. **Corporate headquarters location:** This location. **Other U.S. locations:** Nationwide. **Listed on:** New York Stock Exchange. **Stock exchange symbol:** BAC. **CEO:** Kenneth D. Lewis. **Number of employees worldwide:** 133,549.

CCB FINANCIAL CORPORATION
111 Corcoran Street, Durham NC 27701. 919/683-7621. **Toll-free phone:** 800/422-2226. **Fax:** 919/683-7662. **Contact:** Human Resources. **E-mail address:** human_resources@ccbf.com. **World Wide Web address:** http://www.ccbonline.com. **Description:** CCB Financial is a bank holding company offering a complete line of traditional banking services, as well as a full array of financial products such as investments, insurance, and trust services. This location also hires seasonally. Founded in 1903. **NOTE:** Entry-level positions and part-time jobs are offered. Please visit website to search for jobs and apply online. **Positions advertised include:** Loan Servicing Representative; Summer Teller. **Special programs:** Summer Jobs. **Corporate headquarters location:** Memphis TN. **Parent company:** National Commerce Financial Corporation. **Other U.S. locations:** Southeast U.S. **Listed on:** New York Stock Exchange. **Stock exchange symbol:** NCF. **CEO:** Bill Reed. **Number of employees nationwide:** 3,000.

CAROLINA FARM CREDIT
P.O. Box 1827, Statesville NC 28687. 704/873-0276. **Physical address:** 1704 Wilkesboro Highway, Statesville NC 28625. **Toll-free phone:** 800/521-9952. **Fax:** 704/873-6900. **Contact:** Human Resources. **E-mail address:** jobs@carolinafarmcredit.com. **World Wide Web address:** http://www.carolinafarmcredit.com. **Description:** Farm Credit Services provides financial services through 39 branch offices across the United States. FCS offers long-, intermediate-, and short-term financing to agricultural producers, farm-related businesses, fishermen, part-time farmers, and rural homeowners. **NOTE:** Please visit http://www.agfirst.com and click the 'Employment Opportunities' button to search for jobs. **Positions advertised include:** Appraiser; Credit Analyst. **Corporate headquarters location:** This location. **Other area locations:** Statewide.

COOPERATIVE BANKSHARES, INC.
P.O. Box 600, Wilmington NC 28402. 910/343-0181. **Physical address:** 201 Market Street, Wilmington NC 28405. **Toll-free phone:** 800/672-0443. **Contact:** Human Resources. **E-mail address:** info@coop-

bank.com. **World Wide Web address:** http://www.coop-bank.com. **Description:** A savings bank holding company. **Corporate headquarters location:** This location. **Other area locations:** Statewide. **Subsidiaries include:** Cooperative Bank For Savings, Inc., SSB is engaged in general banking activities. **Listed on:** NASDAQ. **Stock exchange symbol:** COOP.

EQUIFIRST
500 Forest Point Circle, Charlotte NC 28273. 704/679-4400. **Contact:** Recruiter. **E-mail address:** recruiter@equifirst.com. **World Wide Web address:** http://www.equifirst.com. **Description:** Provides products and assistance to mortgage lenders. **NOTE:** Please visit website to view job listings. Human Resources phone is 704/679-4611. **Positions advertised include:** Account Executive; Underwriter; Loan Processor. **Corporate headquarters location:** This location.

FIRST BANCORP
FIRST BANK
P.O. Box 508, Troy NC 27371. 910/576-6171. **Physical address:** 341 North Main Street, Troy NC 27371-0508. **Toll-free phone:** 866/256-2273. **Fax:** 910/572-2884. **Contact:** Patricia McCormick, Human Resources Director. **E-mail address:** pmmcormick@firstbankcorp.com. **World Wide Web address:** http://www.firstbancorp.com. **Description:** First Bancorp is a bank holding company that owns and operates First Bank (also at this location). Founded in 1983. **Corporate headquarters location:** This location. **Other area locations:** Statewide. **Other U.S. locations:** VA; SC. **Listed on:** NASDAQ. **Stock exchange symbol:** FBNC. **President/CEO:** James H. Garner. **Number of employees nationwide:** 500.

FIRST CHARTER CORPORATION
FIRST CHARTER NATIONAL BANK
P.O. Box 37937, Charlotte NC 28237. 704/365-2880. **Fax:** 704/688-4475. **Contact:** Human Resources. **E-mail address:** careers@firstcharter.com. **World Wide Web address:** http://www.firstcharter.com. **Description:** First Charter Corporation is a holding company that operates 50 banks throughout the greater Charlotte metropolitan area. Assets total $2.7 million. **NOTE:** Applications are active for 90 days. Please visit website to view job listings. **Positions advertised include:** CAM Client Advisor; Commercial Credit Analyst; Commercial Sales Assistant; Conversion Technician; Financial Center Manager; Mail Services Clerk; PAM Client Advisor; Personal Banker; Check Processor; Data Capture Operator; Data Entry Check Processor. **Corporate headquarters location:** This location. **Other area locations:** Statewide. **Subsidiaries include:** First Charter National Bank provides businesses and individuals with a broad range of financial services including banking, financial planning, funds management, investments, insurance mortgages, and employee benefits programs. **Listed on:** NASDAQ. **Stock exchange symbol:** FCTR. **President/CEO:** Lawrence M. Kimbrough.

FIRST CITIZENS BANK & TRUST
3128 Smoketree Court, Raleigh NC 27602. 919/755-7000. **Recorded jobline:** 919/755-2070. **Contact:** Human Resources. **World Wide Web address:** http://www.firstcitizens.com. **Description:** A bank founded in 1898. **NOTE:** Please visit website to search for jobs and apply online. Entry-level positions and second and third shifts are offered. **Positions advertised include:** Financial Consultant; Administrative Assistant; Audit Specialist; Banker Assistant; Benefits Planning Analyst; Commercial Credit Analyst; Float Teller; Image Specialist; Investment Counselor; Market Executive; Mortgage Banker; Regional Leasing Officer; Senior Teller. **Special programs:** Training; Summer Jobs. **Office hours:** Monday - Friday, 9:00 a.m. - 5:00 p.m. **Corporate headquarters location:** This location. **Other U.S. locations:** VA; WV. **Annual sales/revenues:** $5 - $10 million. **Number of employees nationwide:** 5,000.

RBC CENTURA
1417 Centura Highway, P.O. Box 1220, Rocky Mount NC 27802. 252/454-4400. **Fax:** 252/454-4806. **Toll-free phone:** 800/CENTURA. **Contact:** Human Resources. **World Wide Web address:** http://www.rbccentura.com. **Description:** A bank holding company that provides a full range of banking, investment, and insurance services for individuals and businesses. **NOTE:** Please visit website to search for jobs and apply online. **Positions advertised include:** Mortgage Cashiering Associate; Centura Support Specialist. **Corporate headquarters location:** This location. **Parent company:** RBC Financial Group. **Listed on:** New York Stock Exchange. **Stock exchange symbol:** RY. **CEO:** H. Kel Landis. **Number of employees nationwide:** 1,870.

U.S. FEDERAL RESERVE BANK OF RICHMOND
P.O. Box 30248, Charlotte NC 28230. 704/358-2100. **Physical address:** 530 East Trade Street, Charlotte NC 28202. **Contact:** Personnel Manager. **World Wide Web address:** http://www.rich.frb.org. **Description:** One of 12 regional Federal Reserve banks that, along with the Federal Reserve Board of Governors in Washington DC, and the Federal Open Market Committee (FOMC), comprise the Federal Reserve System, the nation's central bank. As the nation's central bank, the Federal Reserve is charged with three major responsibilities: monetary policy, banking supervision and regulation, and processing payments. **NOTE:** Please visit website to search for jobs and apply online. **Positions advertised include:** Supervisor; Senior Supervisor; Senior Examiner; LCBO Risk Modeling Specialist; Central Point of Contact – LCBOs. **Corporate headquarters location:** Richmond VA.

WACHOVIA CORPORATION
301 South College Street, Suite 4000, One Wachovia Center, Charlotte NC 28288-0013. 704/374-6161. **Recorded jobline:** 800/FUN-HIRE (for customer service positions). **Contact:** Human Resources Director. **World Wide Web address:** http://www.wachovia.com. **Description:** A securities brokerage firm. **NOTE:** Please visit website to search for jobs

and apply online. **Positions advertised include:** Manager – Financial Analysis and Production; Senior Credit Default Swap Trader; CIB Risk Officer; Quality Assurance Analyst; Senior Trader; Finance Senior Consultant; Junior High Yield Trader; Systems Analyst; Loan Market Research Analyst; Client Manager. **Corporate headquarters location:** This location. **Other area locations:** Statewide. **Other U.S. locations:** Nationwide. **International locations:** Worldwide. **Listed on:** New York Stock Exchange. **Stock exchange symbol:** WB. **CEO:** G. Kennedy Thompson. **Number of employees worldwide:** 87,000.

WACHOVIA CORPORATION
100 North Main Street, Winston-Salem NC 27101. 336/732-5391. **Recorded jobline:** 888/WCE-MPLO. **Contact:** Employment Manager. **World Wide Web address:** http://www.wachovia.com. **Description:** A holding company whose member companies provide a variety of banking and financial services. **NOTE:** Entry-level positions, part-time jobs, and second and third shifts are offered. Please visit website to search for jobs and apply online. **Company slogan:** We are more than a bank. **Positions advertised include:** Finance Manager; Teller; Administrative Assistant; Credit Products Manager; Issues Management and Research Manager; Learning Strategist. **Special programs:** Internships; Training; Co-ops; Summer Jobs. **Corporate headquarters location:** Charlotte NC. **Other U.S. locations:** Nationwide. **International locations:** Worldwide. **Operations at this facility include:** This office is a financial center. **Listed on:** New York Stock Exchange. **Stock exchange symbol:** WB. **CEO:** G. Kennedy Thompson. **Number of employees nationwide:** 87,000.

South Carolina

AGFIRST FARM CREDIT BANK
P.O. Box 1499, Columbia SC 29202. 803/799-5000. **Physical address:** 1401 Hampton Street, Columbia SC 29201. **Fax:** 803/771-0752. **Contact:** Recruiter. **E-mail address:** cmccroskey@agfirst.com. **World Wide Web address:** http:// www.agfirst.com. **Description:** A cooperative set up by Congress in 1916 which acts as an agricultural lender to 80,000 farmers, ranchers, rural homeowners, and agribusinesses in 15 United States and Puerto Rico as well as offering crop, life, and timber insurance; equipment leasing; tax services; and record keeping. The company provides more than $10 billion in loans and originates real estate, operating, and home mortgages. Instead of accepting deposits, it funds activities by selling bonds and notes on capital markets. **NOTE:** Entry-level positions are offered. **Positions advertised include:** Lead Network Analyst; Customer Support Analyst; Special Events Assistant; Loan Officer; Accountant; Administrative Assistant; Systems Analyst. **Corporate headquarters location:** This location. **Other locations:** Nationwide. **Chairman:** F.A. (Andy) Lowrey. **Annual sales/revenues:** $754 million.

FIRST CITIZENS BANCORPORATION OF SOUTH CAROLINA, INC.
dba FIRST CITIZENS BANK

Drawer I, P.O. Box 29, Columbia SC 29202. 803/771-8700. **Physical address:** 1230 Main Street, Columbia SC 29201. **Fax:** 803/733-3480. **Recorded jobline:** 866/733-3482. **Contact:** Annette Rollins, Human Resources Department. **E-mail address:** jobs@fcbsc.com. **World Wide Web address:** http://www.fcbsc.com. **Description:** A bank holding company with statewide subsidiaries engaged in commercial banking, credit card services, and mortgage banking. Founded in 1913. **NOTE:** Human Resources address: 1213 Lady Street, Columbia SC 29201. Human Resources phone: 803/733-3482. **Positions advertised include:** Personal Banker; Teller. **Office Hours:** Monday – Friday, 9:00 a.m. – 4:00 p.m. **Corporate headquarters location:** This location. **Other locations:** Statewide. **Subsidiaries/Affiliates include:** First Citizens Bank & Trust Company of South Carolina; The Exchange Bank of South Carolina; First Citizens BancShares. **Listed on:** Over The Counter. **Stock exchange symbol:** FBCN. **Chairman/CEO:** Jim B. Apple. **Annual sales/revenues:** $282.7 million. **Number of employees:** 1,550.

FIRST FINANCIAL HOLDINGS, INC.

P.O. Box 118068, Charleston SC 29423-8068. 843/529-5933. **Physical address:** 34 Broad Street, Charleston SC 29401. **Fax:** 843/529-5929. **Contact:** Jerry P. Gazes, Human Resources. **World Wide Web address:** http://www. firstfinancialholdings.com. **Description:** A multiple thrift holding company serving retail banking markets. **Corporate headquarters location:** This location. **Subsidiaries include:** First Federal Savings and Loan Association of Charleston; First Southeast Fiduciary & Trust Services, Inc.; First Southeast Insurance Services, Inc.; First Southeast Investor Services, Inc. **Listed on:** NASDAQ. **Stock exchange symbol:** FFCH. **Chairman:** A.L. Hutchinson Jr. **Annual sales/revenues:** $185 million. **Number of employees:** 763.

FIRST NATIONAL CORPORATION
dba SOUTH CAROLINA BANK & TRUST, N.A.

P.O. Box 1287, Orangeburg SC 29116-1287. 803/531-0511. **Physical address:** 950 John C. Calhoun Drive South East, Orangeburg SC 29115. **Fax:** 803/531-8757. **Recorded jobline:** 866/722-8562. **Contact:** Human Resources. **E-mail address:** jobs@scbandt.com. **World Wide Web address:** http://www.bankfcnb.com. **Description:** A bank holding company whose subsidiaries perform commercial banking operations and provide other financial services. **Positions advertised include:** Client Server Engineer I; Account Service Representative; Financial Sales Representative; Teller. **Corporate headquarters location:** This location. **Other locations:** Statewide. **Subsidiaries include:** South Carolina Bank & Trust, N.A.; South Carolina Bank & Trust of Piedmont; South Carolina Bank & Trust of Pee Dee; CreditSouth Financial Services. **Listed on:** American Stock Exchange. **Stock exchange symbol:** FNC. **Chairman:** Robert R. Horger. **Annual sales/revenues:** $88.2 million. **Number of employees:** 442.

SOUTH COAST COMMUNITY BANK

P.O. Box 1561, Mount Pleasant SC 29465. 843/884-0504. **Fax:** 843/216-3071. **Physical address:** 530 Johnnie Dodds Boulevard, Mount Pleasant SC 29464. **Contact:** Human Resources. **E-mail address:** lcalhoun@southcoastbank.com. **World Wide Web address:** http://www.southcoastbank.com. **Description:** A state chartered commercial bank. **Positions advertised include:** Branch Manager.

SOUTH TRUST

145 King Suite 302, Charleston SC 29401. 843/7200-2026. **Contact:** Human Resources. **E-mail address:** careers@southtrust.com. **World Wide Web address:** http://www.southtrust.com. **Description:** A full service bank offering financial and banking services for personal and business accounts. **Positions advertised include:** Teller; Teller Supervisor. **Corporate headquarters:** Birmingham, Alabama. **Listed on:** NASDAQ. **Stock exchange symbol:** SOTR. **Annual Sales / Revenue:** 51.9 billion.

WACHOVIA CORPORATION
FIRST UNION/WACHOVIA

P.O. Box 1329, Greenville SC 29602. 864/467-2500. **Physical address:** 15 South Main Street, Greenville SC 29601. **Contact:** Paul G. George, Human Resources. **World Wide Web address:** http://www.firstunion.com. **Description:** Formerly First Union National Bank of South Carolina, Wachovia is a full-service commercial bank providing corporate and consumer services with 2,700 locations in East Coast states and some 65 branches in South Carolina. Founded in 1879. **Positions advertised include:** Profit Family Analyst; Teller; Small Business Banker; Conservative Lending Specialist; Teller Management; Community Bank Market. **NOTE:** Contact Corporate Human Resources at: 800386HIRE (800/386-4473). **Corporate headquarters location:** Charlotte NC. **Subsidiaries include:** OFFITBANK; Wachovia Securities, Inc. **Listed on:** New York Stock Exchange. **Stock exchange symbol:** WB. **Chairman/President/CEO:** G. Kennedy (Ken) Thompson. **Number of employees nationwide:** 84,000.

BIOTECHNOLOGY, PHARMACEUTICALS, AND SCIENTIFIC R&D

You can expect to find the following types of companies in this section:
Clinical Labs • Lab Equipment Manufacturers • Pharmaceutical Manufacturers and Distributors

North Carolina

BAYER CROP SCIENCE
2 T.W. Alexander Drive, P.O. Box 12, Research Triangle Park NC 27709. 919/549-2000. **Toll-free phone:** 800/842-8020. **Contact:** Human Resources. **World Wide Web address:** http://www.bayercropscienceus.com. **Description:** Involved in the research and development of pesticides and herbicides. **NOTE:** Please visit http://www.bayerjobs.com to search for jobs. **Corporate headquarters location:** This location. **Other U.S. locations:** Kansas City MO. **International locations:** Worldwide. **Parent company:** Bayer AG. **Listed on:** New York Stock Exchange. **Stock exchange symbol:** BAY. **Number of employees at this location:** 500.

EMBREX INC.
P.O. Box 13989, Research Triangle Park NC 27709-3989. 919/941-5185. **Physical address:** 1040 Swabia Court, Durham NC 27703. **Fax:** 919/314-2550. **Contact:** Personnel. **E-mail address:** employment@embrex.com. **World Wide Web address:** http://www.embrex.com. **Description:** Develops and manufactures an automated, egg-injection system, eliminating the need for manual vaccination of newly hatched broiler chicks. Its patented INOVOJECT system inoculates up to 50,000 eggs per hour. The company's research also includes viral neutralizing factors, immunomodulators, gene vaccines, and performance enhancement products that alter bird physiology for early delivery. **NOTE:** Please visit website to search for jobs and apply online. **Positions advertised include:** Facilities Technician; Inventory and Manufacturing Accountant; Research Associate; Supervisor – Shipping and Receiving; Production Manager; Lead Process Operator. **Corporate headquarters location:** This location. **International locations:** Argentina; Brazil; China; Korea; Malaysia. **Subsidiaries include:** Embrex Europe Ltd. **Listed on:** NASDAQ. **Stock exchange symbol:** EMBX. **President/CEO:** Randall L. Marcuson. **Number of employees nationwide:** 240.

GLAXOSMITHKLINE
5 Moore Drive, Durham NC 27709-3398. 919/483-2100. **Toll-free phone:** 888/825-5249. **Contact:** Director or Human Resources Operations. **World Wide Web address:** http://www.gsk.com. **Description:** A pharmaceutical preparations company whose products include AZT, an AIDS treatment drug; Zantac; and Malarone, a medication for malaria. **NOTE:** Please visit website to search for jobs

and apply online. **Positions advertised include:** Administrative Assistant; Advisor/Manager Respiratory Commercial Analysis; Assistant Scientist; Assistant Clinical Supplies Project Leader; Associate Program Manager; Chemical Engineer; Clinical Pharmacokineticist; Clinical Pharmacology Disease Area Manager; Director of Business Integration; Health Enhancement Manager; Epidemiologist; Manager – Various Departments; Pharmaceutical Sales Representative. **Special programs:** Internships. **Corporate headquarters location:** London, England. **Other area locations:** Zebulon NC. **Other U.S. locations:** PA; NJ; DE; MA; MI; SC. **International locations:** Worldwide. **Operations at this facility include:** Administration; Research and Development. **Listed on:** New York Stock Exchange. **Stock exchange symbol:** GSK. **Number of employees worldwide:** 100,000.

INVERESK RESEARCH
11000 Weston Parkway, Cary NC 27513. 919/460-9005. **Fax:** 919/462-2200. 46. **Contact:** Human Resources. **E-mail address:** hr.usa@inveresk.com. **World Wide Web address:** http://www.inveresk.com. **Description:** Provides research services to pharmaceutical companies for studies that include FDA drug approval. **NOTE:** Please visit website to search for jobs and apply online. You can either apply through the website, or e-mail your resume. **Positions advertised include:** Manager – Clinical Monitoring; Project Team Assistant; Telecommunications/Facility Specialist; Financial Analyst; Associate Director Systems; Medical Director; Senior Clinical Research Associate; Clinical Research Associate; Executive Assistant; Associate Director; Clinical Project Manager; Senior Biostatistician; Director – Proposal Development. **Corporate headquarters location:** This location. **Other area locations:** Wilmington NC. **International locations:** Belgium; Canada; Czech Republic; France; Germany; Israel; Italy; Japan; Poland; Spain.

KING PHARMACEUTICALS, INC.
7001 Weston Parkway, Suite 300, Cary NC 27513. 919/653-7001. **Contact:** Human Resources. **World Wide Web address:** http://www.kingpharm.com. **Description:** A pharmaceutical development firm specializing in cardiovascular drugs. Founded 1994. **Corporate headquarters location:** Bristol TN. **Other area locations:** Statewide. **Other U.S. locations:** Nationwide. **Listed on:** New York Stock Exchange. **Stock exchange symbol:** KG.

LABORATORY CORPORATION OF AMERICA (LABCORP)
309 East Davis Street, P.O. Box 2230, Burlington NC 27216. 336/229-1127. **Contact:** Human Resources. **World Wide Web address:** http://www.labcorp.com. **Description:** One of the nation's leading clinical laboratory companies, providing services primarily to physicians, hospitals, clinics, nursing homes, and other clinical labs nationwide. LabCorp performs tests on blood, urine, and other body fluids and tissue, aiding the diagnosis of disease. **NOTE:** Please visit website to search for jobs and apply online. **Positions advertised include:** Sr. Cytogenetics Technologist; Laboratory Director; national Managed Care Executive

Director; Sr. Programmer/Analyst; Lead Project Analyst/Engineer. **Special programs:** Internships. **Corporate headquarters location:** This location. **Other U.S. locations:** Nationwide. **Operations at this facility include:** Administration; Regional Headquarters; Research and Development; Sales; Service. **Listed on:** New York Stock Exchange. **Stock exchange symbol:** LH. **Number of employees nationwide:** 23,000.

LABORATORY CORPORATION OF AMERICA (LABCORP)
1904 Alexander Drive, Research Triangle Park NC 27709. 919/572-6900. **Toll-free phone:** 800/800-4522. **Contact:** Human Resources. **World Wide Web address:** http://www.labcorp.com. **Description:** LabCorp is one of the nation's leading clinical laboratory companies, providing services primarily to physicians, hospitals, clinics, nursing homes, and other clinical labs nationwide. LabCorp performs tests on blood, urine, and other body fluids and tissue, aiding the diagnosis of disease. **NOTE:** Please visit website to search for jobs and apply online. **Corporate headquarters location:** Burlington NC. **Operations at this facility include:** This location is part of the Occupational Testing Division, and provides forensic drug testing services to various clients. **Listed on:** New York Stock Exchange. **Stock exchange symbol:** LH. **Number of employees nationwide:** 23,000.

MERCK MANUFACTURING
4633 Merck Road, Wilson NC 27893. 252/243-2011. **Contact:** Human Resources. **World Wide Web address:** http://www.merck.com. **Description:** Manufactures pharmaceuticals for Merck & Company, Inc. **Corporate headquarters location:** Whitehouse Station NJ. **Other U.S. locations:** Nationwide. **International locations:** Worldwide. **Parent company:** Merck & Company, Inc. is a worldwide organization engaged primarily in the business of discovering, developing, producing, and marketing products for the maintenance of health and the environment. Products include human and animal pharmaceuticals and chemicals sold to the health care, oil exploration, food processing, textile, paper, and other industries. Merck & Company, Inc. also runs an ethical drug mail-order marketing business. **Listed on:** New York Stock Exchange. **Stock exchange symbol:** MRK.

NATIONAL INSTITUTE OF ENVIRONMENTAL HEALTH SCIENCES
111 Alexander Drive, P.O. Box 12233, Research Triangle Park NC 27709. 919/541-0218. **Recorded jobline:** 919/541-4331. **Contact:** Human Resources. **World Wide Web address:** http://www.niehs.nih.gov. **Description:** A component of the Department of Health and Human Services, the National Institute of Environmental Health Services specializes in biomedical research programs, communication strategies, and prevention and intervention efforts. The focus of the Institute is to reduce human illness and dysfunction caused by the environment. **NOTE:** Please visit http://www.niehs.nih.gov/vacancy/niehsvac.htm or http://www.jobs.nih.gov to search for jobs. **Positions advertised include:** Health Science Administrator; Administrative Assistant;

External Program Specialist; Secretary – Office Automation; Student Assistant; Program Specialist. **Special programs:** Fellowships in environmental medicine for medical students; Internships. **Corporate headquarters location:** This location. **Other U.S. locations:** Bethesda MD.

QUINTILES INC.
P.O. Box 13979, Research Triangle Park NC 27709-3979. 919/998-2000. **Physical address:** 4709 Creekstone Drive Durham NC 27703. **Fax:** 919/998-2094. **Contact:** Human Resources. **E-mail address:** hr.info@quintiles.com. **World Wide Web address:** http://www.quintiles.com. **Description:** A contract pharmaceutical research company. Provides professional services for pharmaceutical and biotechnology companies, as well as healthcare providers. Founded 1982. **NOTE:** Please visit website to search for jobs and apply online. **Positions advertised include:** Administrative Assistant; Alliance Management Director; Analyst; Associate Clinical Scientist; Associate Director – Various Departments; Employee Premium Services; Global Account Executive; IT Security Architect; Pricing Analyst; Project Manager; Project Specialist; Scientific Specialist; Senior Administrative Assistant; Senior Contracts Manager; Vice President – Market Development. **Corporate headquarters location:** This location. **Other area locations:** Morrisville NC. **Other U.S. locations:** Nationwide. **International locations:** Worldwide. **Parent company:** Pharma Services Acquisition Corp.

RESEARCH TRIANGLE INSTITUTE (RTI)
3040 Cornwallis Road, P.O. Box 12194, Research Triangle Park NC 27709-2194. 919/541-6000. **Fax:** 919/541-5985. **Contact:** Supervisor of Employment Services. **E-mail address:** jobs@rti.org. **World Wide Web address:** http://www.rti.org. **Description:** A nonprofit, independent research organization involved in many scientific fields, under contract to business; industry; federal, state, and local governments; industrial associations; and public service agencies. The institute was created as an independent entity by the joint action of North Carolina State University, Duke University, and the University of North Carolina at Chapel Hill; however, close ties are maintained with the universities' scientists, both through the active research community of the Research Triangle Park region and through collaborative research for government and industry clients. RTI responds to national priorities in health, the environment, advanced technology, and social policy with contract research for the U.S. government including applications in statistics, social sciences, chemistry, life sciences, environmental sciences, engineering, and electronics. Founded in 1958. **NOTE:** Entry-level positions are offered. Please visit website to search for jobs and apply online. **Positions advertised include:** Accountant; Accounting Manager; Acquisitions Specialist; Administrative Assistant; Analyst; Biological Lab Assistant; Biologist; Business Development Director; Call Center Services Supervisor; Chemist; Contract Billing Specialist; Economist; Engineer; Environmental Engineer; Maintenance Supervisor; Postdoctoral Chemist; Senior Research Scientist Toxicologist.

Corporate headquarters location: This location. **Other area locations:** Durham NC; Raleigh NC; Greenville NC. **Other U.S. locations:** Washington DC; Cocoa Beach FL; Hampton VA; Rockville MD; Atlanta GA; Chicago IL; Waltham MA; Anniston AL. **International locations:** United Arab Emirates; Indonesia; England; South Africa; El Salvador. **Subsidiaries include:** RTI Polska LLC. **Listed on:** Privately held. **Annual sales/revenues:** More than $100 million. **Number of employees at this location:** 1,400.

SYNGENTA BIOTECHNOLOGY, INC.
3054 Cornwallis Road, Research Triangle Park NC 27709-2257. 919/541-8500. **Contact:** Human Resources. **World Wide Web address:** http://www.syngentabiotech.com. **Description:** Researches and develops products to improve crop protection and to increase crop production. **NOTE:** Please visit website to view job listings and apply online. **Corporate headquarters location:** Basel Switzerland. **Other area locations:** Greensboro NC. **Other U.S. locations:** Longmont CO; Wilmington DE; Boise ID; Des Moines IA; Downers Grove IL; Golden Valley MN; Cordova TN. **International locations:** Worldwide. **Parent company:** Syngenta. **Listed on:** New York Stock Exchange. **Stock exchange symbol:** SYT. **CEO:** Michael Pragnell. **Number of employees worldwide:** 19,000.

TYCO HEALTHCARE/MALLINCKRODT
8800 Durant Road, Raleigh NC 27616. 919/878-2930. **Contact:** Human Resources. **World Wide Web address:** http://www.mallinckrodt.com. **Description:** Tyco Healthcare/Mallinckrodt, Inc. provides specialty chemicals and human and animal health products worldwide through Tyco Healthcare/Mallinckrodt and two other technology-based businesses: Mallinckrodt Chemical, Inc. and Mallinckrodt Veterinary, Inc. Mallinckrodt Chemical is a producer of pharmaceutical and specialty industrial chemicals. It is also a joint venture partner in a worldwide flavors business. The company is one of the world's largest producers of acetaminophen and a major producer of medicinal narcotics and laboratory chemicals. Mallinckrodt Veterinary is one of the world's leading animal health and nutrition companies, with approximately 1,000 products sold in more than 100 countries. Products include pharmaceuticals, livestock and pet vaccines, pesticides, surgical supplies, anesthetics, and mineral feed ingredients. **NOTE:** Please visit website to search for jobs and apply online. **Corporate headquarters location:** Hazelwood MO. **Other U.S. locations:** Nationwide. **International locations:** Worldwide. **Operations at this facility include:** This location manufactures dyes used in CT scans. Tyco Healthcare/Mallinckrodt is a provider of technologically-advanced, cost-effective products and services to five medical specialties: anesthesiology, cardiology, critical care, nuclear medicine, and radiology. **President:** Michael J. Collins.

South Carolina

GLAXOSMITHKLINE PLC
65 Windham Boulevard, Aiken SC 29805. 803/649-3471. **Contact:** Human Resources Manager. **World Wide Web address:** http://www.gsk.com. **Description:** GlaxoSmithKline Corporation is a health care company engaged in the research, development, manufacture, and marketing of ethical pharmaceuticals, animal health products, ethical and proprietary medicines, and eye care products. **Positions advertised include:** Sales Representative. **Corporate headquarters location:** London, England. **Operations at this facility include:** Production of Aquafresh toothpaste and Vivarin sleep inhibitors. **Listed on:** New York Stock Exchange. **Stock exchange symbol:** GSK. **Chairman:** Sir Christopher A. Hogg. **Annual sales/revenues:** $32 billion. **Number of employees worldwide:** 100,000.

LABORATORY CORPORATION OF AMERICA (LABCORP)
25 Woods Lake Road, Suite 602, Greenville SC 29607. 864/232-0636. **Contact:** Human Resources. **World Wide Web address:** http://www.labcorp.com. **Description:** One of the nation's leading clinical laboratory companies, providing services primarily to physicians, hospitals, clinics, nursing homes, and other clinical labs nationwide. LabCorp performs tests of blood, urine, and other body fluids and tissue, as well as aiding the diagnosis of disease. Founded in 1971. **Positions advertised include:** Technical Specialist; Service Representative. **NOTE:** Resumes should be sent to the company's headquarters address: LabCorp, Human Resources, 309 East Davis Street, Burlington NC 27215. **Corporate headquarters location:** Burlington NC. **Listed on:** New York Stock Exchange. **Stock exchange symbol:** LH. **Annual sales/revenues:** $2.5 billion. **Number of employees:** 20,000.

PERRIGO COMPANY
P.O. Box 1968, Greenville SC 29602. 864/288-5521. **Physical address:** 4615 Dairy Drive, Greenville SC 29607. **Contact:** Ms. Jimmie Fannell, Personnel Manager. **World Wide Web address:** http://www.perrigo.com. **Description:** Manufactures and sells generic pharmaceuticals, vitamins, and personal care products for the store brand market, nationally and internationally. **Positions advertised include:** Research & Development Formulator. **Corporate headquarters location:** Allegan MI. **Other locations:** CA; MI; NJ. **International locations:** England; Mexico. **Operations at this facility include:** Vitamin manufacturing; Warehouse and Distribution Center also in Greenville SC. **Listed on:** NASDAQ. **Stock exchange symbol:** PRGO. **Annual sales/revenues:** $826. **Number of employees nationwide:** 4,250.

BUSINESS SERVICES & NON-SCIENTIFIC RESEARCH

You can expect to find the following types of companies in this section:
Adjustment and Collection Services • Cleaning, Maintenance, and Pest Control Services • Credit Reporting Services • Detective, Guard, and Armored Car Services • Security Systems Services • Miscellaneous Equipment Rental and Leasing • Secretarial and Court Reporting Services

North Carolina

JEFFERSON-PILOT FINANCIAL

P.O. Box 21008, Greensboro NC 27420. 336/691-3000. **Physical address:** 100 North Greene Street, Greensboro NC 27401. **Contact:** Human Resources. **E-mail address:** gsojobs@jpfinancial.com. **World Wide Web address:** http://www.jpfinancial.com. **Description:** A holding company whose principal insurance subsidiaries are Jefferson-Pilot Life Insurance Company, Jefferson-Pilot Fire and Casualty Company, and Jefferson-Pilot Title Insurance Company. The company also operates radio and television stations and produces televised sports programs. **Positions advertised include:** Manager – Internal Auditing; Supply Clerk; Quality Assurance Analyst; Audio-Visual Specialist; Customer Service Team Leader; Production Supervisor; Manager – Financial Reporting; Senior Accountant; Quality Assurance Analyst; JPSC Marketing Assistant; Business Analyst; Communications Specialist; Insurance Agent; Actuarial Clerk; Manager – Annuity Product Compliance; Marketing Specialist; File Clerk. **Corporate headquarters location:** This location. **Other U.S. locations:** Concord NH; Omaha NE. **Listed on:** New York Stock Exchange. **Stock exchange symbol:** JP.

RENTAL SERVICE CORPORATION

3022 Griffith Street, Charlotte NC 28203. 704/522-8338. **Fax:** 704/522-6449. **Contact:** Ronnie Rockett, General Manager. **E-mail address:** s472mgr@rentalservice.com. **World Wide Web address:** http://www.rentalservice.com. **Description:** Engaged in equipment rental and sale to the industrial and construction markets. **Office hours:** Monday – Friday, 7;00 a.m. – 5:00 p.m. **NOTE:** Please visit website to search for jobs. **Corporate headquarters location:** Scottsdale AZ. **Other area locations:** Statewide. **Other U.S. locations:** Nationwide. **International locations:** Canada; Mexico. **Parent company:** Atlas Copco Group. **Operations at this facility include:** Sales; Service. **Listed on:** Privately held. **CEO:** Freek Nijdam.

SECURITAS

5108 North Interstate 85 Service Road, Charlotte NC 28206. 704/597-0626. **Toll-free phone:** 800/232-7465. **Recorded jobline:** 888/591-4473. **Contact:** Vicki Giacomin, Human Resources. **World Wide Web address:** http://www.securitasinc.com. **Description:** Offers a wide range of protective services and contract security guard programs to businesses and government. Burns International Security Services also provides electronic security systems and security planning consultation. **Office hours:** Monday - Friday, 8:00 a.m. - 5:00 p.m. **Corporate headquarters location:** Chicago IL. **Other U.S. locations:** Nationwide.

TEXTILEASE
4700 Dwight Evans Road, Charlotte NC 28217. 704/523-9593. **Toll-free phone:** 800/888-4425. **Fax:** 704/525-9443. **Contact:** Human Resources. **World Wide Web address:** http://www.unifirst.com. **Description:** Provides laundry rental and cleaning services for hotels and restaurants. **Corporate headquarters:** Wilmington MA. **Other area locations:** Durham NC; Goldsboro NC; Kernersville NC; Rocky Mount NC; Wilmington NC. **Other U.S. locations:** Nationwide. **International locations:** Canada. **Parent company:** UniFirst Corporation. **Listed on:** New York Stock Exchange. **Stock exchange symbol:** UNF.

South Carolina

DEFENDER SERVICES
P.O. Box 1775, Columbia SC 29202-1775. 803/776-4220. **Physical address:** 9031 Garner's Ferry Road, Columbia SC 29209. **Fax:** 803/776-1580. **Contact:** Personnel Department. **E-mail address:** johns@defenderservices.com or humanresources@defenderservices.com. **World Wide Web address:** http://www.defenderservices.com. **Description:** Defender Services offers cleaning, painting, floor sanding, maintenance, yard work, grounds work, housekeeping, trash removal, and security. **Corporate headquarters location:** This location. **Other area locations:** Anderson SC; Charleston SC; Greenwood SC; Lancaster SC. **Other U.S. locations:** Nationwide. **Number of employees nationwide:** 7,000.

DIVERSCO INC.
105 Diversco Drive, P.O. Box 5527, Spartanburg SC 29304. 864/579-3420. **Toll-free phone:** 800/277-3420. **Fax:** 864/579-9578. **Contact:** Raina Tuten, Human Resources Manager. **World Wide Web address:** http://www.diversco.com. **Description:** Provides outsourcing services including janitorial and building maintenance, security, temporary staffing, food processing equipment, sanitation, and contract services to industrial clients. **Corporate headquarters location:** This location. **Other locations:** Nationwide. **Parent company:** Diversco Holdings, Inc. (also at this location). **Subsidiaries include:** Personnel Management, Inc.; Spartan Security.

GENERAL PHYSICS CORPORATION
2391 Centennial Avenue, Suite 100, Aiken SC 29803. 803/649-0515. **Fax:** 803/649-3017. **Contact:** Human Resources. **World Wide Web address:** http:// www.genphysics.com. **Description:** Provides training, engineering, and technical services to clients in the aerospace, automotive, defense, government, manufacturing, utility, independent power, pharmaceutical, and process industries. **Corporate headquarters location:** Elkridge MD. **Subsidiaries include:** GP Environmental; GP Technologies.

CHARITIES AND SOCIAL SERVICES

**You can expect to find the following types of companies
in this section:**
Social and Human Service Agencies • Job Training and Vocational
Rehabilitation Services • Nonprofit Organizations

North Carolina

AMERICAN RED CROSS
P.O. Box 36507, Charlotte NC 28236. 704/376-1661. **Physical address:** 2425 Park Road, Charlotte NC 28203. **Fax:** 704/370-0244. **Contact:** Chapter Manager. **E-mail address:** beasleysa@usa.redcross.org. **World Wide Web address:** http://www.redcrosshelps.org; http://www.redcross.org. **Description:** A humanitarian organization that aids disaster victims, gathers blood for crisis distribution, trains individuals to respond to emergencies, educates individuals on various diseases, and raises funds for other charitable establishments. **NOTE:** Please visit website to see job listings. **Special programs:** Internships. **Corporate headquarters location:** Washington DC. **Other U.S. locations:** Nationwide.

AMERICAN RED CROSS
601F Country Club Drive, Greenville NC 27834-0000. 252/355-3800. **Fax:** 252/355-8831. **Contact:** Ms. Charlene Lee, Executive Director. **E-mail address:** clee@pittredcross.org. **Wide Web address:** http://www.pittredcross.org. **Description:** A humanitarian organization that aids disaster victims, gathers blood for crisis distribution, trains individuals to respond to emergencies, educates individuals on various diseases, and raises funds for other charitable establishments. **Corporate headquarters location:** Washington DC. **Other U.S. locations:** Nationwide.

DECI (DURHAM EXCHANGE CLUB INDUSTRY, INC.)
1717 Lawson Street, Durham NC 27703. 919/596-1341. **Fax:** 919/596-6380. **Recorded jobline:** 919/596-1346x501. **Contact:** Human Resources Manager. **E-mail address:** deci@deci.org. **World Wide Web address:** http://www.deci.org. **Description:** A private, nonprofit, community-based, vocational rehabilitation facility. Founded in 1966. **NOTE:** Entry-level positions are offered. **Positions advertised include:** Production Supervisor. **Special programs:** Internships; Summer Jobs. **Office hours:** Monday - Friday, 8:15 a.m. - 4:15 p.m. **Corporate headquarters location:** This location. **Listed on:** Privately held. **Number of employees at this location:** 85.

NORTH CAROLINA BIOTECHNOLOGY CENTER
P.O. Box 13547, Research Triangle Park NC 27709-3547. 919/541-9366. **Physical address:** 15 T.W. Alexander Drive, Research Triangle Park NC 27709. **Contact:** Personnel. **World Wide Web address:**

http://www.ncbiotech.org. **Description:** A nonprofit agency dedicated to supporting biotechnology research, development, and commercialization in North Carolina. **Corporate headquarters location:** This location.

PIEDMONT BEHAVIORAL HEALTH CARE
245 LePhillip Court NE, Concord NC 28025. 704/721-7000. **Fax:** 704/721-7010. **Contact:** Personnel. **E-mail address:** recruitment@pamh.com. **World Wide Web address:** http://www.piedmontbhc.org. **Description:** Provides a variety of programs and educational services for individuals with mental health needs, substance abuse issues, and developmental disabilities. **NOTE:** Please visit website to view job listings and to download application form. **Positions advertised include:** Care Coordinator; Case Manager; Child and Youth Provider Relations Manager; Community Relations Specialist – Bilingual; DD Case Management Services Administrator; Health Care Technician. **Office hours:** Monday – Friday, 8:30 a.m. – 5:00 p.m. **Corporate headquarters location:** This location. **Other area locations:** Salisbury NC; Albemarle NC; Monroe NC. **CEO:** Dan Coughlin.

PIEDMONT BEHAVIORAL HEALTH CARE
CONSUMER PLANNING AND SUPPORT SERVICES
201 North Main Street, Monroe NC 28112. 704/289-7111. **Fax:** 704/282-4602. **Contact:** Personnel. **E-mail address:** recruitment@pamh.com. **World Wide Web address:** http://www.piedmontbhc.org. **Description:** Provides a variety of programs and educational services for individuals with mental health needs, substance abuse issues, and developmental disabilities. **NOTE:** Please visit website to view job listings and to download application form. Mail application or resume to corporate office at 245 LePhillip Court NC, Concord NC 288025. **Positions advertised include:** Care Coordinator; Case Manager; Child and Youth Provider Relations Manager; Community Relations Specialist – Bilingual; DD Case Management Services Administrator; Health Care Technician. **Office hours:** Monday – Friday, 8:30 a.m. – 5:00 p.m. **Corporate headquarters location:** Concord NC. **Other area locations:** Salisbury NC; Albemarle NC. **CEO:** Dan Coughlin.

WINSTON-SALEM INDUSTRIES FOR THE BLIND
7730 North Point Drive, Winston-Salem NC 27106-3310. 336/759-0551. **Toll-free phone:** 800/242-7726. **Fax:** 336/759-0990. **Contact:** Jim Collier, Manager of Human Resources. **E-mail address:** jcollier@wsifb.com. **World Wide Web address:** http://www.wsifb.com. **Description:** Provides training and employment workshops for the blind. Founded 1936. **NOTE:** Please visit website to view job listings and apply online, **Positions advertised include:** Retail Store Cashier. **Corporate headquarters location:** This location. **President:** Daniel J. Boucher.

South Carolina

THE AMERICAN RED CROSS BLOOD SERVICES
CAROLINAS BLOOD SERVICES REGION
P.O. Box 91, Columbia SC 29202-0091. 803/251-6000. **Physical address:** 2751 Bull Street, Columbia SC 29201. **Fax:** 803/251-6191. **Recorded jobline:** 803/251-6035. **Contact:** Human Resources Manager. **World Wide Web address:** http://www.redcrossblood.org. **Description:** A nonprofit, blood collection and distribution organization serving over 100 hospitals and medical centers in an 82-county area covering North Carolina, parts of South Carolina, Georgia, and Tennessee distributing 1,500 blood products daily. **NOTE:** Entry-level positions, part-time jobs, and second and third shifts are offered. **Company slogan:** Together, We Can Save a Life. **Positions advertised include:** Collections Technicians Specialist; Lab Technician: Tele Recruiter. **Special programs:** Training. **Corporate headquarters location:** Charlotte NC. **Other U.S. locations:** Nationwide. **Parent company:** American Red Cross (Washington DC). **Operations at this facility include:** Central South Carolina Chapter. **Number of employees:** 1,050.

BERKELEY CITIZENS
1301 Old Highway 52 South, P.O. Drawer 429, Moncks Corner SC 29461. 843/761-0300. **Fax:** 843/761-0303. **Contact:** Human Resources. **E-mail address:** admin@berkeleycitizens.org **World Wide Web address:** http://www.berkeleycitizens.org. **Description:** Provides support services for people with mental retardation, head and spinal cord injuries, autism, and related disabilities. **Positions advertised include:** Conifer Associate; House Manager.

HABITAT FOR HUMANITY
CENTRAL SOUTH CAROLINA HABITAT FOR HUMANITY
P.O. Box 11502, Columbia SC 29211. 803/252-3570. **Physical address:** 209 South Sumter Street, Columbia SC 29201-4558. **Fax:** 803/252-7525. **Contact:** Director. **World Wide Web address:** http://www.habitat.org. **Office hours:** Monday – Friday, 8:00 a.m. – 5:00 p.m. **Description:** A social services organization that builds homes for the homeless. **NOTE:** The majority of this organization's staff consists of volunteers. **Special programs:** Internships. **Corporate headquarters location:** Americus GA. **Other U.S. locations:** Nationwide.

MARCH OF DIMES BIRTH DEFECTS FOUNDATION
240 Stoneridge Drive, One Graystone Building, Suite 206, Columbia SC 29210. 803/252-5200. **Fax:** 803/799-4549. **Contact:** Carryl Krohne, Human Resources. **E-mail address:** ckrohne@marchofdimes.com. **World Wide Web address:** http:// www.modimes.org. **Description:** Operates the Campaign for Healthier Babies, which includes programs of research, community services, education, and advocacy. March of Dimes chapters across the country work with their communities to determine and meet the needs of women, babies, and families. Through specially designed programs, women are provided access to prenatal

care and empowered to improve their futures and those of their children. **Positions advertised include:** Senior Community Director.

MUSCULAR DYSTROPHY ASSOCIATION
2700 Middleburgh, Suite 240, Columbia SC 29204. 803/799-7435. **Contact:** Susan Beach, District Director. **World Wide Web address:** http://www.mdausa.org. **Description:** A social services organization that provides funding for research to cure neuromuscular diseases. The group also offers support groups, summer camps, and educational programs. **Corporate headquarters location:** Tucson AZ. **Other area locations:** Charleston SC; Greenville SC. **Other U.S. locations:** Nationwide.

THE SALVATION ARMY
P.O. Drawer 2786, Columbia SC 29202-1374. 803/765-0260. **Physical address:** 2025 Main Street, Columbia SC 29201. **Fax:** 803/254-6465. **Contact:** June Bergman, Head Secretary. **World Wide Web address:** http://www.salvationarmy.org. **Description:** A nonprofit organization providing several service programs including day-care centers, programs for people with disabilities, substance abuse programs and tutoring for at-risk students. The Salvation Army targets its programs to assist alcoholics, battered women, drug addicts, the elderly, the homeless, people with AIDS, prison inmates, teenagers, and the unemployed. **Other U.S. locations:** Nationwide.

CHEMICALS, RUBBER, AND PLASTICS

**You can expect to find the following types of companies
in this section:**
Adhesives, Detergents, Inks, Paints, Soaps, Varnishes • Agricultural
Chemicals and Fertilizers • Carbon and Graphite Products • Chemical
Engineering Firms • Industrial Gases

North Carolina

BASF CORPORATION
P.O. Box 13528, Research Triangle Park NC 27709-3528. 919/547-
2000. **Physical address:** 26 Davis Drive, Research Triangle Park NC.
Fax: 919/405-2244. **Contact:** Human Resources. **World Wide Web
address:** http://www.basf.com. **Description:** Manufactures and markets
industrial chemicals, yarns, and man-made fibers. **Corporate
headquarters location:** Mount Olive NJ. **Other area locations:**
Morganton NC; Enka NC; Wilmington NC; Charlotte NC. **Other U.S.
locations:** Nationwide. **International locations:** Worldwide. **Listed on:**
New York Stock Exchange. **Stock exchange symbol:** BASF. **Parent
company:** BASF America Inc. **Number of employees worldwide:**
87,000.

CHEMICAL INDUSTRY INSTITUTE OF TOXICOLOGY (CIIT)
P.O. Box 12137, 6 Davis Drive, Research Triangle Park NC 27709.
919/558-1200. **Contact:** Rusty Bramlage, Human Resources Director. **E-
mail address:** bramlage@ciit.org. **World Wide Web address:**
http://www.ciit.org. **Description:** An independent, nonprofit research
corporation dedicated to the training of toxicologists and the scientific,
objective study of toxicological issues involved in the manufacture,
handling, use, and disposal of commodity chemicals. Founded 1974.
NOTE: Please visit website for online application form. **Positions
advertised include:** Respiratory Biologist/Toxicologist; Experimental
Pathologist; Postdoctoral Fellow – Biochemistry and Inhalation;
Postdoctoral Fellow – Bioinformatics; Postdoctoral Fellow –
Reproductive Biology; Vice President for Finance and Operations.
President: Dr. William F. Greenlee.

CRANE RESISTOFLEX COMPANY
One Quality Way, Marion NC 28752. 828/724-4000. **Fax:** 828/724-4783.
Contact: Kevin Hall, Human Resources Manager. **World Wide Web
address:** http://www.resistoflex.com. **Description:** Manufactures
thermoplastic products, including thermoplastic line pipe and flexible
hoses. **Corporate headquarters location:** Stamford CT. **Other U.S.
locations:** Jacksonville FL; Bay City MI. **International locations:**
Germany; the Netherlands; Singapore. **Parent company:** The Crane
Company manufactures and wholesales a diverse number of engineered
products for a variety of industries. Its industrial production unit
manufactures products and systems for the defense, aerospace,
construction, and transportation markets. Products include fiberglass-

reinforced panels, vending machines, water filtration and conditioning systems, pumps, valves, and coin machines. A subsidiary, Hydro-Aire, develops and manufactures brake systems, fuel pumps, and other products primarily for the aerospace industry. Crane Company's wholesaling activities are conducted through a subsidiary, Huttig Sash & Door, which operates 47 branch warehouses across the United States. This business specializes in doors, molding, trim, windows, and other construction products, and sells mostly to contractors and other larger wholesalers. **Listed on:** New York Stock Exchange. **Stock exchange symbol:** CR.

FLAMBEAU PRODUCTS CORPORATION
100 Grace Drive, Weldon NC 27890. 252/536-2171. **Fax:** 252/536-2201. **Contact:** Chinita Blaunt, Personnel Manager. **E-mail address:** hr@flambeau.com. **World Wide Web address:** http://www.flambeau.com. **Description:** A manufacturer of rigid plastic doublewall cases. Founded in 1947. **NOTE:** Please visit website to view job listings. **Corporate headquarters location:** Middlefield OH. **Other U.S. locations:** Redlands CA; Baraboo WI; Madison GA; Columbus IN. **International locations:** Mexico; England. **Subsidiaries include:** ArtBin; Duncan; Flambeau Contract Manufacturing; Flambeau Hardware; Flambeau Outdoors; Flambeau Packaging Solutions; Flambeau Premiums and Special Markets; Ornamates; Vichek Floral Containers. **Operations at this facility include:** Administration; Manufacturing; Sales. **Number of employees at this location:** 200. **Number of employees nationwide:** 3,000.

FOAM DESIGN, INC.
2425 South Alston Avenue, Durham NC 27713. 919/596-0668. **Fax:** 919/598-1761. **Contact:** Human Resources. **E-mail address:** rtp@foamdesign.com. **World Wide Web address:** http://www.foamdesign.com. **Description:** Manufactures cushioning products made of polyethylene, polyurethane, and polystyrene foams for the protection of products such as typewriters, printed circuit boards, medical instruments, and electronic components. Cushioning products are used for the packaging of consumer goods, the transport of aerospace and military missile components and related hardware, the handling and shipping of automotive parts, and the packaging of electronics components and assemblies. Foam Design also manufactures consumer products such as camping pads, bodyboards, and archery targets. **Corporate headquarters location:** Lexington KY.

INTELICOAT TECHNOLOGIES
700 Crestdale Street, Matthews NC 28105. 704/847-9171. **Toll-free phone:** 800/688-9171. **Fax:** 704/845-4307. **Contact:** Robert Thumith, Vice President of Human Resources. **E-mail address:** rthumith@intelicoat.com. **World Wide Web address:** http://www.intelicoat.com. **Description:** Specializes in custom, roll-to-roll coating and laminating of films, foils, and papers used in high-performance products. The company provides technical, pilot, and production services for companies worldwide. **NOTE:** The listed contact

is in charge of employment for the entire company. **Corporate headquarters location:** South Hadley MA. **Other U.S. locations:** Portland OR. **International locations:** United Kingdom; The Netherlands. **Parent company:** Rexam plc. **Listed on:** NASDAQ. **Stock exchange symbol:** REXMY. **President:** Robert Champigny. **Number of employees worldwide:** 750.

NORCOMP LIMITED PARTNERSHIP
P.O. Box 3867, Gastonia NC 28054-0020. 704/866-9161. **Fax:** 704/867-0577. **Contact:** Human Resources. **Description:** Engaged in the production and distribution of proprietary and custom-molded plastics for original equipment manufacturers. The company also produces and distributes interconnect devices. **Corporate headquarters location:** Minneapolis MN. **Operations at this facility include:** Administration; Manufacturing. **Listed on:** Privately held.

PARAMOUNT PAPER
953 Alma Road, Maxton NC 28364. 910/844-5293. **Contact:** Human Resources. **World Wide Web address:** http://www.paramountpaper.com. **Description:** Manufactures celluloid packaging materials for furniture companies. Founded 1958. **Office hours:** Monday – Friday, 8:00 a.m. – 5:00 p.m. **Corporate headquarters location:** Quebec Canada.

REICHHOLD CHEMICALS, INC.
P.O. Box 13582, Research Triangle Park NC 27709. 919/990-7500. **Physical address:** 2400 Elis Road, Durham NC 27703. **Toll-free phone:** 800/448-3482. **Fax:** 919/990-7711. **Contact:** Human Resources. **E-mail address:** human.resources@reichhold.com. **World Wide Web address:** http://www.reichhold.com. **Description:** Researches and develops coating resins, formulated adhesives, and several other products. **Corporate headquarters location:** This location. **Other U.S. locations:** Nationwide. **International locations:** Worldwide. **Parent company:** Dainippon Ink & Chemicals (Tokyo). **Number of employees worldwide:** 2,500.

TYCO HEALTHCARE/MALLINCKRODT
8800 Durant Road, Raleigh NC 27616. 919/878-2930. **Contact:** Human Resources. **World Wide Web address:** http://www.mallinckrodt.com. **Description:** Tyco Healthcare/Mallinckrodt, Inc. provides specialty chemicals and human and animal health products worldwide through Tyco Healthcare/Mallinckrodt and two other technology-based businesses: Mallinckrodt Chemical, Inc. and Mallinckrodt Veterinary, Inc. Mallinckrodt Chemical is a producer of pharmaceutical and specialty industrial chemicals. It is also a joint venture partner in a worldwide flavors business. The company is one of the world's largest producers of acetaminophen and a major producer of medicinal narcotics and laboratory chemicals. Mallinckrodt Veterinary is one of the world's leading animal health and nutrition companies, with approximately 1,000 products sold in more than 100 countries. Products include pharmaceuticals, livestock and pet vaccines, pesticides, surgical

supplies, anesthetics, and mineral feed ingredients. **NOTE:** Please visit website to search for jobs and apply online. **Corporate headquarters location:** Hazelwood MO. **Other U.S. locations:** Nationwide. **International locations:** Worldwide. **Operations at this facility include:** This location manufactures dyes used in CT scans. Tyco Healthcare/Mallinckrodt is a provider of technologically-advanced, cost-effective products and services to five medical specialties: anesthesiology, cardiology, critical care, nuclear medicine, and radiology. **President:** Michael J. Collins.

VITAFOAM INC.
4100 Pleasant Garden Road, Greensboro NC 27406. 336/378-9620. **Fax:** 336/273-0238. **Contact:** Human Resources. **World Wide Web address:** http://www.vitausa.com. **Description:** Manufactures urethane foam for the furniture, bedding, and automotive industries. **NOTE:** Please visit website to fill out employment inquiry form. **Corporate headquarters location:** High Point NC. **Other area locations:** Thomasville NC. **Other U.S. locations:** Chattanooga TN; Tupelo MS; Moonachie NJ. **International locations:** Worldwide. **Parent company:** British Vita plc. **President/CEO:** Bill Lucas. **Number of employees worldwide:** 9,000.

VITAFOAM INC.
2222 Surrett Drive, P.O. Box 2024, High Point NC 27263. 336/861-4433. **Fax:** 336/431-7747. **Contact:** Human Resources. **World Wide Web address:** http://www.vitausa.com. **Description:** Manufactures specialized polymer, fiber, and fabric components for the furnishing, transportation, apparel, packaging, and engineering industries. **NOTE:** Please visit website to fill out employment inquiry form. **Corporate headquarters location:** This location. **Other area locations:** Greensboro NC; Thomasville NC. **Other U.S. locations:** Chattanooga TN; Tupelo MS; Moonachie NJ. **International locations:** Worldwide. **Parent company:** British Vita plc. **President/CEO:** Bill Lucas. **Number of employees worldwide:** 9,000.

WINGFOOT COMMERCIAL TIRE SYSTEMS
3916 Highway 74 West, Monroe NC 28110. 704/238-8277. **Fax:** 704/238-8774. **Contact:** Human Resources. **World Wide Web address:** http://www.wingfootct.com. **Description:** A retail and wholesale provider of new and off-road tires. The company also provides on- and off-road truck tire retreading and repairs, as well as related on- and off-site services. **NOTE:** Please visit website to view job listings. **Corporate headquarters location:** Fort Smith AR. **Other area locations:** Candler NC; Cary NC; Charlotte NC; Greensboro NC; Salisbury NC. **Other U.S. locations:** Nationwide. **Parent company:** Goodyear.

South Carolina

DAYCO PRODUCTS INC.
108 West Street, P.O. Box 500, Williston SC 29853. 803/266-7046. **Contact:** David Hayes, Personnel Manager. **E-mail address:**

Dayco_Employment@markivanto.com. **World Wide Web address:** http://www.dayco.com. **Description:** A worldwide manufacturer and distributor of a wide range of highly engineered rubber and plastic products, many of which are used for replacement purposes. Principal markets include the agricultural, automotive, construction, energy, printing, mining, textile, and transportation industries. **Corporate headquarters location:** Dayton OH. **Parent company:** Mark IV Industries.

ENGELHARD CORPORATION
554 Engelhard Drive, Seneca SC 29678. 864/882-9841. **Fax:** 864/882-4651. **Contact:** Andy Tunstall, Human Resources. **World Wide Web address:** http:// www.engelhard.com. **Description:** Manufactures precious metal catalysts for the petrochemicals and fine chemicals industries; base metal catalysts for specialty chemical producers; catalysts for the hydrogenation of fats and oils; and separation products encompassing a wide variety of treated natural minerals for the enhancement, purification, and bleaching of chemical products. **Company slogan:** Change the Nature of Things. **Corporate headquarters location:** Iselin NJ. **Other area locations:** Duncan SC; North Charleston SC. **Other U.S. locations:** Nationwide. **Operations at this facility include:** Manufacturing of Process Catalysts; PM Salts and Solutions; Precious Metal Refining. **Listed on:** New York Stock Exchange. **Stock exchange symbol:** EC. **Chairman/President/CEO:** Barry W. Perry. **Annual sales/revenues:** $3.75 billion. **Number of employees:** 6,550.

MARTIN COLOR-FI, INC.
320 Neeley Street, Sumter SC 29150. 803/436-4200. **Fax:** 803/436-4220. **Contact:** Human Resources. **World Wide Web address:** http://www.colorfi.com. **Description:** Produces polyester fiber and pellets from recycled plastic materials such as soft drink bottles, polyester fiber waste, and film waste. The company uses low-cost waste materials to produce polyester fibers for a wide range of markets including automotive fabrics, carpet, home furnishings, industrial materials, construction reinforcement materials, and pelletized plastics for injection molding and thermoforming processes. The company also produces carpet and rug yarns and specialty carpets for the recreational vehicle and manufactured housing markets. **Positions advertised include:** Draftsperson; Electrician; Production Manager; Purchasing Agent; Systems Analyst; Traffic Specialist; Accountant. **Corporate headquarters location:** Edgefield SC.

MICHELIN NORTH AMERICA, INC.
P.O. Box 19001, Greenville SC 29602-9001. 864/458-5000. **Physical address:** One Parkway South, Greenville SC 29615. **Contact:** Human Resources. **World Wide Web address:** http://www.michelin.com. **Description:** Manufactures passenger, light truck, and high-performance tires. **Positions advertised include:** Quality Pipeline Engineer; Supply Chain Specialist; Purchasing Specialist; Senior Information Technology Auditor; Public Relations Manager; General Ledger System

Administrator. **Corporate headquarters location:** This location. **Other locations:** Nationwide. **International locations:** Algeria; Brazil; Canada; Mexico.

NAN YA PLASTICS CORPORATION, AMERICA

P.O. Box 939, Lake City SC 29560-0939. 843/389-7800. **Fax:** 843/389-6993. **Contact:** Human Resources. **World Wide Web address:** http://www.npcusa.com. **Description:** The company's products include PVC rigid film; PET sheet; PVC panel and pipe; electronic-related products (printed circuit boards, copper-clad laminates, copper foil, epoxy, BPA, and glass fiber and cloth); PP synthetic paper (a product similar in quality to wood pulp paper); and polyester fiber. Founded in 1990. **NOTE:** Entry-level positions are offered. **Positions advertised include:** Account Manager; Chemical Engineer; Civil Engineer; Electrical Engineer; Industrial Engineer; Manufacturing Engineer; Mechanical Engineer; Operations Manager; Production Manager; Project Manager; Quality Control Supervisor; Sales Representative; Systems Analyst. **Office hours:** Monday - Friday, 8:00 a.m. - 5:00 p.m. **Corporate headquarters location:** Livingston NJ. **Other locations:** Wharton TX. **Parent company:** NAPCOR (Charlotte NC). **Operations at this facility include:** Manufacturing of polyester, chip, and filament fibers.

WESTINGHOUSE ELECTRIC CORPORATION

P.O. Drawer R, Columbia SC 29205. 803/776-2610. **Physical address:** 5801 Bluff Road, Columbia SC 29250. **Contact:** Human Resources. **World Wide Web address:** http://www.westinghouse.com. **Description:** Westinghouse Electric Corporation is a diversified manufacturing company with interests in defense electronics, environmental services, broadcasting, mobile refrigeration units, office furniture, energy systems, and power generation. The company conducts operations through 791 locations in the United States and over 30 other countries. **NOTE:** Send resumes to: Westinghouse Electric Corporation, University Relations, P.O. Box 355, Energy Center Complex, Pittsburgh PA 15230-0355. **Corporate headquarters location:** Pittsburgh PA. **Operations at this facility include:** Chemical manufacturing, international headquarters for fuel marketing and contract administration, U.S. manufacturing operations, mechanical fabrication facilities, product engineering and testing laboratories. **Parent company:** British Nuclear Fuels.

COMMUNICATIONS:TELECOMMUNICATIONS AND BROADCASTING

You can expect to find the following types of companies in this section:
Cable/Pay Television Services • Communications Equipment • Radio and Television Broadcasting Stations • Telephone, Telegraph, and Other Message Communications

North Carolina

ACTERNA
1030 Swabia Court, Research Triangle Park NC 27709-3585. 919/941-5730. **Fax:** 919/941-5751. **Contact:** Human Resources. **World Wide Web address:** http://www.acterna.com. **Description:** A manufacturer of data communications and telecommunications analysis products for communications test solutions. **NOTE:** Please visit website to search for jobs. **Corporate headquarters location:** Germantown MD. **Other U.S. locations:** Brandentown FL; Indianapolis IN; Salem VA; Terre Haute IN. **International locations:** Worldwide. **Listed on:** NASDAQ. **Stock exchange symbol:** ACTR. **President/CEO:** John Peeler.

ALCATEL USA INC.
2301 Sugar Bush Road, Raleigh NC 27612. 919/850-6000. **Contact:** Human Resources Department. **E-mail address:** recruit.usa@alcatel.com. **World Wide Web address:** http://www.usa.alcatel.com. **Description:** Manufactures fiber-optic cable for the telecommunications and cable television markets. **Special programs:** Internships. **Corporate headquarters locations:** Plano TX. **Other area locations:** Concord NC; Greensboro NC; Clinton NC; Tarboro NC; Garner NC. **Other U.S. locations:** Nationwide. **International locations:** Worldwide. **Parent company:** Alcatel Alsthom (Paris, France). **Operations at this facility include:** Administration; Manufacturing; Research and Development; Service. **Listed on:** New York Stock Exchange. **Stock exchange symbol:** ALA. **Annual sales/revenues:** More than $100 million. **CEO:** Mike Quigley. **Number of employees nationwide:** 6,753.

ALCATEL USA INC.
P.O. Box 39, Claremont NC 28610. 828/459-9787. **Physical address:** 2512 Penny Road, Claremont NC 28610. **Toll-free phone:** 800/729-3737. **Fax:** 828/459-9821. **Contact:** Human Resources. **E-mail address:** recruit.usa@alcatel.com. **World Wide Web address:** http://www.usa.alcatel.com. **Description:** Manufactures fiber-optic cable for the telecommunications and cable television markets. **Other U.S. locations:** Nationwide. **Parent company:** Alcatel Alsthom (Paris, France). **Operations at this facility include:** Divisional Headquarters. **Listed on:** New York Stock Exchange. **Stock exchange symbol:** ALA. **Annual sales/revenues:** More than $100 million. **CEO:** Mike Quigley.

Number of employees at this location: 750. **Number of employees nationwide:** 6,753.

CSA WIRELESS
1500 Prodelin Drive, Newton NC 28658. 828/466-0412. **Fax:** 828-466-0413. **Contact:** Human Resources. **E-mail address:** personnel@csa-wireless.com. **World Wide Web address:** http://www.csa-wireless.com. **Description:** Manufactures antenna products and systems for the wireless and microwave markets. **International locations:** United Kingdom.

ERICSSON INC.
7001 Development Drive P.O. Box 13969, Research Triangle Park NC 27709. 919/472-7000. **Fax:** 919/472-7451. **Contact:** Human Resources. **World Wide Web address:** http://www.ericsson.com. **Description:** Provides advanced technology for wireless handset development, and sales and marketing support for North American locations. **NOTE:** Please visit http://www.ericsson.com/jobs to search for jobs and apply online. **Special programs:** Co-ops. **Corporate headquarters location:** Stockholm, Sweden. **Other U.S. locations:** CA; MD; MA; NY; TX; VA. **International locations:** Worldwide. **Parent company:** L.M. Ericsson. **Listed on:** NASDAQ. **Stock exchange symbol:** ERICY. **Annual sales/revenues:** More than $100 million. **Number of employees at this location:** 2,000. **Number of employees nationwide:** 8,000. **Number of employees worldwide:** 100,000.

JEFFERSON-PILOT COMMUNICATIONS
100 North Greene Street, P.O. Box 21008, Greensboro NC 27420. 704/374-3500. **Fax:** 704/374-3626. **Contact:** Human Resources. **E-mail address:** hired@jpc.com. **World Wide Web address:** http://www.jpc.com. **Description:** A television and radio broadcasting company. **NOTE:** Please visit website to view job listings. **Parent company:** Jefferson-Pilot Financial is a holding company whose subsidiaries include life annuity, accident and health, property and casualty, and title insurance operations. **Corporate headquarters:** This location. **Other area locations:** Charlotte NC. **Other U.S. locations:** San Diego CA; Denver CO; Miami FL; Atlanta GA; Charleston SC; Richmond VA. **Listed on:** New York Stock Exchange. **Stock exchange symbol:** JP.

LUCENT TECHNOLOGIES INC.
P.O. Box 20046, Greensboro NC 27420. 336/279-7000. **Physical address:** 5440 Millstream, McLeansville NC 27301. **Toll-free phone:** 888/4LUCENT. **Contact:** Human Resources Department. **World Wide Web address:** http://www.lucent.com. **Description:** Lucent Technologies Inc. manufactures communications products including switches, transmitters, fiber-optic cable, and wireless systems for telephone companies and other communications services providers. **NOTE:** Please visit website to search for jobs and apply online. **Corporate headquarters location:** Murray Hill NJ. **Other U.S. locations:** Nationwide. **International locations:** Worldwide. **Operations**

at this facility include: This location houses administrative offices. **Listed on:** New York Stock Exchange. **Stock exchange symbol:** LU.

MOTION MEDIA
6714 Netherlands Drive, Wilmington NC 28405. 910/395-6100. **Fax:** 910/395-6108. **Contact:** Human Resources. **E-mail address:** usrecruit@motion-media.com. **World Wide Web address:** http://www.motion-media.com. **Description:** A provider of video-conferencing technology. Founded 1993. **NOTE:** Please visit website to view job listings and apply online. **Corporate headquarters location:** This location. **International locations:** United Kingdom. **Number of employees worldwide:** 100.

NORTEL NETWORKS
4001 East Chapel Hill, Nelson Highway, Research Triangle Park NC. 919/992-5000. **Contact:** Human Resources. **World Wide Web address:** http://www.nortelnetworks.com. **Description:** Designs, produces, and supports multimedia access devices for use in building corporate, public and Internet networks. The primary focus of the company's services is the consolidation of voice, fax, video, and data and multimedia traffic into a single network link. **NOTE:** Please visit website to search for jobs and apply online. Resumes are only accepted through the website. **Corporate headquarters location:** Ontario Canada. **Other area locations:** Charlotte NC; Raleigh NC. **Other U.S. locations:** Nationwide. **International locations:** Worldwide. **Listed on:** New York Stock Exchange. **Stock exchange symbol:** NT. **President/CEO:** Frank Dunn.

SUMITOMO ELECTRIC LIGHTWAVE CORPORATION
P.O. Box 13445, Research Triangle Park NC 27709. 919/541-8100. **Physical address:** 78 Alexander Drive, Research Triangle Park NC. **Toll-free phone:** 800/358-7378. **Fax:** 919/541-8265. **Contact:** Human Resources. **E-mail address:** humanresources@sumitomoelectric.com. **World Wide Web address:** http://www.sel-rtp.com. **Description:** Develops, manufactures, and sells fiber-optic cable products. **NOTE:** Please visit website to view job listings. **Corporate headquarters location:** This location. **Listed on:** Privately held.

UNIVERSITY OF NORTH CAROLINA CENTER FOR PUBLIC TELEVISION
P.O. Box 14900, Research Triangle Park NC 27709-4900. 919/549-7000. **Contact:** Human Resources. **E-mail address:** careers@unctv.org. **World Wide Web address:** http://www.unctv.org. **Description:** This location houses administrative and fundraising offices, studios, and the technical operations center for the public television network. The station is affiliated with PBS, and was founded in 1955. **NOTE:** Please visit website to view job listings and download application form. **Special programs:** Internships.

VERIZON COMMUNICATIONS
1058 West Club Boulevard, Durham NC 27701. 919/286-7336. **Contact:** Human Resources. **World Wide Web address:** http://www.verizon.com.

Description: A full-service communications services provider. Verizon offers residential local and long-distance telephone services and Internet access; wireless service plans, cellular phones, and data services; a full-line of business services including Internet access, data services, and telecommunications equipment and services; and government network solutions including Internet access, data services, telecommunications equipment and services, and enhanced communications services. **NOTE:** Please visit website to search for jobs and apply online. Resumes are accepted online only. **Positions advertised include:** Building Services Technician. **Corporate headquarters location:** New York NY. **Other U.S. locations:** Nationwide. **Operations at this facility include:** This location is a retail service facility for Verizon Plus. **Listed on:** New York Stock Exchange. **Stock exchange symbol:** VZ. **Number of employees worldwide:** 260,000.

South Carolina

COMCAST CABLEVISION
4400 Belle Oaks Drive, North Charleston SC 29405. 843/554-4100. **Contact:** Human Resources Manager. **World Wide Web address:** http://www.comcast.com. **Description:** A cable television company. Founded in 1963. **NOTE:** Applicants may only apply for positions via the company website at http://www.careers.comcast.net. **Positions advertised include:** Customer Service Sales Supervisor; Traffic Assistant; Communications Technician. **Other area locations:** Walterboro SC. **Other U.S. locations:** Nationwide. **Parent company:** Comcast Corporation (Philadelphia PA). **Number of employees worldwide:** 20,000.

THE LIBERTY CORPORATION
135 South Main Street, P.O. Box 502, Greenville SC 29602. 864/241-5427. **Fax:** 864/241-5492. **Contact:** Mary Anne Bunton, Human Resources. **World Wide Web address:** http://www.libertycorp.com. **E-mail address:** info@libertycorp.com. **Description:** The company's Cosmos Broadcasting subsidiary owns and operates 15 network-affiliated television stations throughout the South and Midwest. It also operates and owns Take Ten, a video production company; CableVantage, a cable advertising sales company; and Broadcast Merchandising Corp, a broadcast equipment dealer. **Corporate headquarters location:** this location. **Listed on:** New York Stock Exchange. **Stock exchange symbol:** LC. **Chairman/CEO:** W. Hayne Hipp. **Annual sales/revenues:** $296 million. **Number of employees at this location:** 34. **Number of employees nationwide:** 1,300.

PIRELLI CABLE CORPORATION
700 Industrial Drive, Lexington SC 29072. 803/951-4800. **Contact:** Human Resources. **World Wide Web address:** http://www.pirelli.com. **Description:** A manufacturer of a broad range of energy cables, fiber-optic telecommunications cables, optical-electronic devices, systems for the telecommunications market, and associated accessories and services. **Positions advertised include:** Chemical Engineer; Computer

Programmer; Electrical Engineer; Production Manager; Materials Engineer; Mechanical Engineer; Operations Manager; Purchasing Agent; Quality Control Supervisor; Systems Analyst. **Corporate headquarters location:** This location. **Other area locations:** Abbeville SC. **Other U.S. locations:** Colusa CA. **Operations at this facility include:** Administration; Manufacturing; Research and Development; Sales; Service.

ROCK HILL TELEPHONE COMPANY
1969 Canterbury Glen Lane, Manchester Village, P.O. Box 470, Rock Hill SC 29731. 803/326-6025. **Fax:** 803/326-7225. **Recorded jobline:** 803/323-6565. **Contact:** Personnel Office. **E-mail address:** employment@comporium.com. **World Wide Web address:** http://www.rhtelco.com. **Description:** A local telephone company. **Office hours include:** 8:00 a.m. – 4:00 p.m. **Positions advertised include:** Call Center Attendant; Graphics Coordinator; Staff Accountant; Programmer; Systems Analyst; Computer Engineer; Technician; Construction Lineman; Engineering Associate. **Parent company:** Comporium Group (also at this location).

COMPUTER HARDWARE, SOFTWARE, AND SERVICES

You can expect to find the following types of companies in this section:
Computer Components and Hardware Manufacturers • Consultants and Computer Training Companies • Internet and Online Service Providers • Networking and Systems Services • Repair Services/Rental and Leasing • Resellers, Wholesalers, and Distributors • Software Developers/Programming Services • Web Technologies

North Carolina

AMT DATASOUTH
4216 Stuart Andrew Boulevard, Charlotte NC 28217. 704/523-8500. **Fax:** 704/525-6104. **Contact:** Human Resources. **E-mail address:** humanresources@amtdatasouth.com. **World Wide Web address:** http://www.amtdatasouth.com. **Description:** Designs, manufactures, and markets heavy-duty dot matrix and thermal printers used for high-volume print applications. The company's product lines include the XL series for medium-volume dot matrix printing applications and Documax, which has high-speed dot matrix printing capabilities. The company also manufactures a portable thermal printer, Freeliner, which is used primarily for printing one packing or shipping label at a time. **Corporate headquarters location:** Camarillo CA. **International locations:** Northampton, England. **Number of employees nationwide:** 125.

A4 HEALTH SYSTEMS
5501 Dillard Drive, Cary NC 27511. 919/851-6177. **Toll-free phone:** 888/672-3282. **Fax:** 919/851-5991. **Contact:** Human Resources. **E-mail address:** hr@A4healthsystems.com. **World Wide Web address:** http://www.a4healthsys.com. **Description:** Develops software and related hardware for hospitals. Founded 1970. **NOTE:** Please visit website to view job listings, and to find more details on applying for specific positions. **Positions advertised include:** Regional Sales Manager/Sales Representative; HealthMatics ED Project Manager; EMR Implementation Specialist; PM Ntierprise Implementation Specialist. **Corporate headquarters:** This location. **Other U.S. locations:** Novi MI; Austin TX; Nashua NH. **CEO:** John P. McConnell.

AJILON SERVICES INC.
2222 Chapel Hill, Nelson Highway, Suite 120, Durham NC 27713. 919/572-2750. **Toll-free phone:** 888/296-7575. **Fax:** 919/572-2656. **Contact:** Manager. **World Wide Web address:** http://www.ajilon.com. **Description:** Offers computer consulting services, project support, and end user services. Ajilon is also a leading Personnel and Services sources for the communications industry. **Office hours:** Monday – Friday, 8:00 a.m. – 5:00 p.m. **Corporate headquarters location:** Towson MD. **Other U.S. locations:** Nationwide. **International locations:** Worldwide. **Annual sales/revenues:** More than $100 million.

ANALYSTS INTERNATIONAL CORPORATION (AIC)
3131 RDU Center Drive, Suite 200, Morrisville NC 27560-9137. 919/460-6141. **Toll-free phone:** 800/669-2772. **Fax:** 919/460-6433. **Contact:** Recruiting Department. **World Wide Web address:** http://www.analysts.com. **Description:** An international computer consulting firm. The company assists clients in analyzing, designing, and developing systems for a variety of industries using different programming languages and software. **NOTE:** Please visit website or visit https://www.jobsatanalysts.com to register, search, and apply for jobs. **Positions advertised include:** IT&T Systems Support Analyst. **Corporate headquarters location:** Minneapolis MN. **Other U.S. locations:** Nationwide. **International locations:** Canada; Great Britain.

BLAST SOFTWARE
220 Chatham Business Drive, P.O. Box 818, Pittsboro NC 27312. 919/542-2535. **Toll-free phone:** 800/24B-LAST. **Fax:** 919/542-5955. **Contact:** Human Resources. **World Wide Web address:** http://www.blast.com. **Description:** Develops communications software that offers cross-platform file transfer, reliable terminal emulation, and error correction. **President:** Lyle Estill.

CII ASSOCIATES, INC.
7200 Falls of the Neuse Road, Suite 202, Raleigh NC 27615. 919/676-8300. **Toll-free phone:** 800/832-3443. **Fax:** 919/676-8484. **Contact:** Human Resources. **E-mail address:** hr@ciinc.com. **World Wide Web address:** http://www.ciinc.com. **Description:** Offers consulting services for software developers. **NOTE:** Contact Human Resources at Ext. 159; E-mail Recruiting at Ext. 123. Contact Sue Wadkinson, Human Resources Manager at sue.wadkinson@ciinc.com. E-mail Chris Allen, Director of Technical Recruiting at chris.allen@ciinc.com. E-mail general recruiting at recruiting@ciinc.com. **President/CEO:** Ray Allen.

CEDALION CORPORATION
401 South Sharon Amity Road, Charlotte NC 28211-2848. 704/716-1400. **Fax:** 704/716-1401. **Contact:** Bill Craemer, Human Resources. **E-mail address:** wcraemer@cedalion.net. **World Wide Web address:** http://www.cedalion.com. **Description:** Provides networking skills development training and networking expertise to companies that deploy advanced networking technologies. Founded in 1984. **NOTE:** Please visit website to download application form. **Office hours:** Monday - Friday, 8:00 a.m. - 5:00 p.m. **Listed on:** Privately held. **CEO:** Bill Thorpe.

CIBER INFORMATION SERVICES
8210 University Executive Park Drive, Suite 290, Charlotte NC 28262. 704/548-1010. **Toll-free phone:** 800/490-9230. **Fax:** 704/548-1021. **Contact:** Administrative Assistant. **World Wide Web address:** http://www.ciber.com. **Description:** Provides strategic information technology consulting, multiline ERP/EAS consulting, and professional staff supplemental services including computer network services. Founded in 1974. **NOTE:** Part-time jobs are offered. Please visit website to search for jobs and apply online. **Special programs:** Training.

Corporate headquarters location: Greenwood Village CO. **Other area locations:** Raleigh NC. **Other U.S. locations:** Nationwide. **International locations:** Worldwide. **Listed on:** New York Stock Exchange. **Stock exchange symbol:** CBR. **President:** Mac J. Slingerlend. **Listed on:** New York Stock Exchange. **Stock exchange symbol:** CBR. **Annual sales/revenues:** $21 - $50 million. **Number of employees at this location:** 50.

CISCO SYSTEMS, INC.
7025 Kit Creek Drive, Research Triangle Park NC 27709. 919/392-5000. **Fax:** 919/392-9999. **Contact:** Human Resources. **E-mail address:** apply@cisco.com. **World Wide Web address:** http://www.cisco.com. **Description:** Develops, manufactures, markets, and supports high-performance internetworking systems that enable customers to build large-scale, integrated computer networks. The company's products connect and manage communications for local and wide area networks that employ a variety of protocols, media interfaces, network topologies, and cable systems. **NOTE:** Please visit website to search for jobs and apply online. **Positions advertised include:** Solution Program Manager; Customer Support Engineer; Network Consulting Engineer; Customer Support Engineer; Design Consultant; Software/QA Engineer; AS Project Manager; IT Engineer; Manager – IT; Corporate Counsel; Human Resources Manager; Associate Inside Sales Representative. **Corporate headquarters location:** San Jose CA. **Other area locations:** Charlotte NC; Greensboro NC. **Other U.S. locations:** Nationwide. **International locations:** Worldwide. **Listed on:** NASDAQ. **Stock exchange symbol:** CSCO.

DP CONNECTIONS, INC.
348 Crompton Street, Charlotte NC 28273. 704/588-7500. **Fax:** 704/588-5420. **Contact:** Personnel. **E-mail address:** dpconnections@mindspring.com. **World Wide Web address:** http://www.dpconnections.com. **Description:** A computer reseller and acquisitions specialist. **Corporate headquarters location:** This location.

DP SOLUTIONS INC.
4905 Koger Boulevard, Suite 101, Greensboro NC 27407. 336/854-7700. **Toll-free phone:** 800/897-7233. **Fax:** 336/854-7715. **Contact:** Human Resources Department. **E-mail address:** humanresources@dpsi.com. **World Wide Web address:** http://www.dpsi.com. **Description:** Designs, develops, and supports computerized maintenance management software. Founded 1986. **NOTE:** Please visit website to view job listings, and to find more specific information on applying for positions. **Positions advertised include:** Senior Software Sales Representative. **Office hours:** Monday - Friday, 8:00 a.m. - 5:00 p.m. **Corporate headquarters location:** This location. **Other U.S. locations:** FL. **International locations:** Canada. **Listed on:** Privately held.

EDS (ELECTRONIC DATA SYSTEMS CORPORATION)
4800 Six Forks Road, Raleigh NC 27609. 919/783-8000. **Fax:** 919/783-1000. **Contact:** Marilyn Miland. **E-mail address:** careers@eds.com.

World Wide Web address: http://www.eds.com. **Description:** Provides a variety of services for the computer and telecommunications industries including global communication solutions, Internet services, gaming software, and cable television services. **Corporate headquarters:** Plano TX. **Other area locations:** High Point NC; Cary NC; Charlotte NC. **Other U.S. locations:** Nationwide. **International locations:** Worldwide. **Listed on:** New York Stock Exchange. **Stock exchange symbol:** EDS. **CEO:** Michael H. Jordan. **Number of employees nationwide:** 64,000. **Number of employees worldwide:** 130,000.

EMC CORPORATION
62 T.W. Alexander Drive, Research Triangle Park NC 27709-3968. 919/248-5970. **Contact:** Human Resources. **World Wide Web address:** http://www.emc.com. **Description:** EMC Corporation designs, manufactures, markets, and supports high-performance storage products. The company also provides related services for selected mainframe and midrange computer systems primarily manufactured by IBM and Unisys. **NOTE:** Please visit website to search for jobs and apply online. You may submit a general application for potential future opportunities. Resumes also may be mailed to the corporate office location at P.O. Box 65, Nuttling Lake MA 01865, fax is 508/435-8829. **Corporate headquarters location:** Hopkinton MA. **Other U.S. locations:** Nationwide. **International locations:** Worldwide. **Operations at this facility include:** This location performs research and development, and provides customer support. **Listed on:** New York Stock Exchange. **Stock exchange symbol:** EMC.

EPLUS TECHNOLOGY OF NORTH CAROLINA
3825 Market Street, Wilmington NC 28403. 910/763-3373. **Toll-free phone:** 888/482-1122. **Fax:** 910/762-8235. **Contact:** Human Resources. **E-mail address:** drose@eplus.com. **World Wide Web address:** http://www.eplus.com. **Description:** Leases and sells computers and other IT equipment. EPlus Technology also develops online software products that provide supply chain management solutions including electronic procurement, e-financing, and e-asset management. Founded 1990. **Corporate headquarters location:** Herndon VA. **Other area locations:** Raleigh NC; Charlotte NC. **Other U.S. locations:** Nationwide. **Listed on:** NASDAQ. **Stock exchange symbol:** PLUS. **CEO/President:** Phillip G. Norton.

FARPOINT TECHNOLOGIES, INC.
808 Aviation Parkway, Suite 1300, Morrisville NC 27560. 919/460-4551. **Fax:** 919/460-7606. **Contact:** Human Resources. **E-mail address:** hr@fpoint.com. **World Wide Web address:** http://www.fpoint.com. **Description:** Develops and manufactures custom control tools for Windows programming. FarPoint Technologies' products are used by software development companies. **NOTE:** Please visit website to view job listings. **Corporate headquarters location:** This location.

FUJITSU TRANSACTIONS SOLUTIONS
14101 Capitol Boulevard, Youngsville NC 27596. 919/556-6721. **Fax:** 919/556-7566. **Contact:** Personnel. **E-mail address:** careers@ftxs.fujitsu.com. **World Wide Web address:** http://www.ftxs.fujitsu.com. **Description:** Designs software for the banking, food, and retail industries. **Corporate headquarters location:** Frisco TX. **Other U.S. locations:** Carrolton TX. **International locations:** Canada; Caribbean. **Parent company:** Fujitsu Limited. **President/CEO:** Austen Mulinder. **Number of employee worldwide:** 1,000.

IBM CORPORATION
8501 IBM Drive, Charlotte NC 28262-8563. 704/594-1000. **Contact:** IBM Staffing Services. **World Wide Web address:** http://www.ibm.com. **Description:** IBM manufactures, sells, and markets advanced information processing products including computers and microelectronics technology, software, networking systems, and information technology-related services. **NOTE:** Please visit website to search for jobs and apply online. **Positions advertised include:** Helpdesk Support. **Special programs:** Internships; Co-ops. **Corporate headquarters location:** White Plains NY. **Other area locations:** Statewide. **Other U.S. locations:** Nationwide. **International locations:** Worldwide. **Subsidiaries include:** IBM Credit Corporation; IBM Instruments, Inc.; IBM World Trade Corporation. **Listed on:** New York Stock Exchange. **Stock exchange symbol:** IBM. **CEO:** Sam J. Palmisano.

IBM CORPORATION
3039 Cornwallis Road, P.O. Box 12195 Research Triangle Park NC 27709. 919/543-5221. **Contact:** Staffing Services. **World Wide Web address:** http://www.ibm.com. **Description:** IBM is a developer, manufacturer, and marketer of advanced information processing products including computers and microelectronics technology, software, networking systems, and information technology-related services. **NOTE:** Please visit website to search for jobs and apply online. **Positions advertised include:** Array Circuit Designer; Array Designer Engineer; Communications Professional; CSS Specialist; Engineer; Fulfillment Coordinator; Hardware Engineer; Licensing Technical Team Leader; Logic Design Engineer; Mechanical Engineer; Network Analyst; Network Management Professional; PeopleSoft Consultant; Physical Design Engineer; Program Manager; Scheduler; Software Engineer. **Special programs:** Internships; Co-ops. **Corporate headquarters location:** White Plains NY. **Other area locations:** Statewide. **Other U.S. locations:** Nationwide. **International locations:** Worldwide. **Subsidiaries include:** IBM Credit Corporation; IBM Instruments, Inc.; IBM World Trade Corporation. **Listed on:** New York Stock Exchange. **Stock exchange symbol:** IBM. **CEO:** Sam J. Palmisano.

IENTERTAINMENT NETWORK
124 Quade Drive, Cary NC 27513. 919/678-8301. **Fax:** 919/678-8302. **Contact:** Human Resources. **E-mail address:** hr@ient.com. **World Wide Web address:** http://www.ient.com. **Description:** Develops and

produces strategy and simulation computer games and online entertainment communities. **NOTE:** Please visit website to view job listings. **Corporate headquarters location:** This location. **Listed on:** NASDAQ. **Stock exchange symbol:** IENT. **CEO:** J.W. Stealey.

KNOWLEDGE SYSTEMS CORPORATION

1143 Executive Circle, Suite G, Cary NC 27511. 919/789-8549. **Toll-free phone:** 800/348-8323. **Fax:** 919/789-8615. **Contact:** Recruiting Manager. **World Wide Web address:** http://www.ksccary.com. **Description:** Develops educational software and provides computer consulting services. Founded 1985.

KYRUS CORPORATION

7500 East Independence Boulevard, Suite 100, Charlotte NC 28227. 704/567-8203. **Toll-free phone:** 888/833-2106. **Fax:** 704/567-9468. **Contact:** Human Resources. **E-mail address:** hrkyrus@kyrus.com. **World Wide Web address:** http://www.kyrus.net. **Description:** Writes programs, resells computer hardware and software, and offers technical support. Founded 1974. **NOTE:** Please visit website to view job listings. Send resumes to the corporate office location at 5 Artillery Road, Taylors SC 29687. **Corporate headquarters location:** Taylors SC. **Other area locations:** Arden NC. **Other U.S. locations:** Kingsport TN; Knoxville TN. **Parent company:** Agilysys, Inc.

LEAD TECHNOLOGIES, INC.

1201 Greenwood Cliff, Suite 400, Charlotte NC 28204. 704/332-5532. **Toll-free phone:** 800/637-4699. **Fax:** 704/372-8161. **Contact:** Human Resources. **E-mail address:** jobs@leadtools.com. **World Wide Web address:** http://www.leadtools.com. **Description:** Develops image file format, processing, and compression tool kits. **Positions advertised include:** Technical Writer; Senior Programmer. **Corporate headquarters location:** This location.

LEVEL 8 SYSTEMS

8000 Regency Parkway, Suite 542, Cary NC 27511. 919/380-5000. **Fax:** 919/380-5121. **Contact:** Personnel. **E-mail address:** careers@level8.com. **World Wide Web address:** http://www.level8.com. **Description:** Develops business applications software. **Corporate headquarters location:** Princeton NJ. **Other U.S. locations:** Wilmington DE, Dulles VA. **International locations:** London, England; Paris, France; Milan, Italy. **Listed on:** NASDAQ. **Stock exchange symbol:** LVEL.

MCNC - RESEARCH & DEVELOPMENT INSTITUTE

P.O. Box 13910, Research Triangle Park NC 27709-3910. 919/990/2000. **Physical address:** 3021 Cornwallis Road, Research Triangle Park NC. **Fax:** 919/248-1923. **Contact:** Personnel. **E-mail address:** hr@mcnc.org. **World Wide Web address:** http://www.mcnc-rdi.org. **Description:** A nonprofit company that researches and develops software for electronic and information technologies. **NOTE:** Please visit website to view job listings and download application form. No phone calls regarding employment. Student positions are also available. **Positions advertised include:** Research Engineer. **Corporate headquarters location:** This location. **President/CEO:** David P. Rizzo.

MANAGEMENT INFORMATION SYSTEMS GROUP, INC.
10 Laboratory Drive, P.O. Box 13966, Research Triangle Park NC 27709-3966. 919/549-8700. **Fax:** 919/549-8733. **Contact:** Human Resources. **E-mail address:** techjobs@misg.com. **World Wide Web address:** http://www.misg.com. **Description:** Offers EDI (Electronic Data Interchange) services that help process business documents over networks. **Corporate headquarters location:** This location.

McKESSON INFORMATION SOLUTIONS
10735 David Taylor Drive, Charlotte NC 28262. 704/549-7000. **Contact:** Tracy Schweikert, Human Resources. **World Wide Web address:** http://infosolutions.mckesson.com. **Description:** McKesson Information Solutions provides technology to health care enterprises including hospitals, integrated delivery networks, and managed care organizations. McKessonHBOC's primary products are Pathways 2000, a family of client/server-based applications that allow the integration and uniting of health care providers; STAR, Series, and HealthQuest transaction systems; and TRENDSTAR decision support system. The company also offers outsourcing services that include strategic information systems planning, data center operations, receivables management, business office administration, and major system conversions. **NOTE:** Please submit your resume via McKesson's resume builder Website at http://jobs.infosolutions.mckesson.com. **Positions advertised include:** Receptionist; Route Sales Representative; Enterprise Vice President – New Business; Regional Vice President; Account Manager. **Corporate headquarters location:** Alpharetta GA. **Other U.S. locations:** Nationwide. **International locations:** Canada; France; Netherlands; United Kingdom; Puerto Rico. **Operations at this facility include:** This location offers sales and technical support. **President:** Pamela Pure.

MISYS, INC.
8529 Six Forks Road, Raleigh NC 27615. 919/847-8102. **Fax:** 919/848-5770. **Contact:** Human Resources. **E-mail address:** recruiter@misyshealthcare.com. **World Wide Web address:** http://www.misyshealthcare.com. **Description:** Misys develops health care management software. Products include +Medic Vision, +Medic PM, Auto Chart, AutoImage, and FasTracker. **NOTE:** Please visit website to register, search for jobs, and apply online. Online applications are preferred. **Positions advertised include:** Administrative Assistant; Application Product Specialist; Client Support Analyst; Corporate Receptionist; Director – Customer Call Center; EMR Template Care Analyst; Human Factors Engineer; Inside Sales Representative; Internal Auditor; Manager – Client Implementation Services; Product Line Director; Sales Development Executive; Sales Executive Assistant; Test Engineer. **Corporate headquarters location:** This location. **Other U.S. locations:** Nationwide. **International locations:** United Kingdom; Denmark; Ireland; Middle East. **Operations at this facility include:** This

location provides sales, training, and support. **Parent company:** Misys plc. **CEO:** Tom Skelton.

NEXUS SOFTWARE, INC.
8024 Glenwood Road, Suite 305, Raleigh NC 27612.. 919/788-8665. **Fax:** 919/788-8733. **Contact:** Human Resources. **World Wide Web address:** http://www.nexussoft.com. **Description:** Manufactures software for the financial industry. **Corporate headquarters location:** This location.

OPSWARE, INC.
11000 Regency Parkway, Suite 301, Cary NC 27511. 919/653-6000. **Contact:** Human Resources. **E-mail address:** jobs@opsware.com. **World Wide Web address:** http://www.tangram.com. **Description:** Manufactures information center automation software. **NOTE:** Please visit website to view job listings. **Special programs:** Internships. **Corporate headquarters location:** Sunnyvale CA. **Other U.S. locations:** Novi MI; New York NY; Bethesda MD. **International locations:** United Kingdom. **Listed on:** NASDAQ. **Stock exchange symbol:** OPSW. **CEO:** Ben Horowitz.

ORACLE
2550 West Tyvola, Suite 200, Charlotte NC 28217. 704/357-3155. **Fax:** 704/423-1307. **World Wide Web address:** http://www.oracle.com. **Description:** Provides technology for managing database systems. **NOTE:** Please visit https://irecruitment.oracle.com to search for jobs. **Positions advertised include:** Technology Sales Representative. **Corporate headquarters location:** Redwood Shores CA. **Other area locations:** Morrisville NC. **Other U.S. locations:** Nationwide. **International locations:** Worldwide. **Number of employees worldwide:** 40,000.

PROGRESSIVE COMPUTER SYSTEMS, INC.
615 Eastowne Drive, Chapel Hill NC 27514. 919/929-3080. **Fax:** 919/929-3087. **Contact:** Lisa Mitchell, Human Resources Manager. **E-mail address:** hr@pc-net.com. **World Wide Web address:** http://www.pc-net.com. **Description:** A computer firm providing hardware assembly, sales, and service. **NOTE:** Contact Human Resources at 919/929-3087. **Corporate headquarters location:** This location.

RED HAT SOFTWARE, INC.
P.O. Box 13588, Research Triangle Park NC 27709. 919/754-3700. **Physical address:** 1801 Varsity Drive, Raleigh NC 27606. **Fax:** 919/754-3701. **Contact:** Personnel. **E-mail address:** careers@redhat.com. **World Wide Web address:** http://www.redhat.com. **Description:** Develops software for Linux systems and offers technical support. **Positions advertised include:** Lead Generation Representative; Programmer/Analyst; Database Administrator; Web Engineer; Technical Writer; Senior Corporate Communications Specialist; Legal Administrative Assistant; Product

Marketing Manager; Global Account Director; Telephony Engineer; Financial Analyst; Order Entry Administrator. **Other U.S. locations:** Huntsville AL; Mountain View CA; Westford MA; Minneapolis MN; Vienna VA. **International locations:** Worldwide. **Operations at this facility include:** Regional headquarters. **Listed on:** NASDAQ. **Stock exchange symbol:** RHAT. **CEO:** Matthew Szulik. **Number of employees worldwide:** 600.

SAS INSTITUTE INC.
100 SAS Campus Drive, Cary NC 27513-2414. 919/677-8000. **Toll-free phone:** 800/727-0025. **Fax:** 919/677-4444. **Contact:** Personnel. **World Wide Web address:** http://www.sas.com. **Description:** Designs a variety of software programs including those used for warehouse management, statistics, and inventory control. **NOTE:** Please visit website to search for jobs and apply online. **Positions advertised include:** Account Executive; Analytical Consultant; Applications Developer; Administrative Support Student; Data Architect; Development Tester; Food Service Associate; Human Factors Engineer; Industry Strategist; Java Development Applications Engineer; Pricing Optimization Tester; Research Statistician; Staff Assistant; Technical Writer. **Corporate headquarters location:** This location. **Other U.S. locations:** Nationwide. **International locations:** Worldwide. **President/CEO:** Jim Goodnight. **Number of employees at this location:** 3,989. **Number of employees nationwide:** 5,085. **Number of employees worldwide:** 9,227.

SIMCLAR NORTH AMERICA INC.
810 South Church Street, Winterville NC 28950. 252/355-3443. **Fax:** 252/355-3144. **Contact:** Human Resources. **World Wide Web address:** http://www.simclar.com. **Description:** Manufactures parts for the large appliances industries, including makers of photocopiers, and ATMs. **NOTE:** Entry-level positions and second and third shifts are offered. **Office hours:** Monday - Friday, 8:00 a.m. - 4:30 p.m. **Corporate headquarters location:** Scotland. **Other U.S. locations:** Hialeah FL; Dayton OH; North Attleboro MA; Kenosha WI; Round Rock TX. **International locations:** Tianjin, China; Tamps, Mexico. **Parent company:** Simclar Group. **Listed on:** NASDAQ. **Stock exchange symbol:** SIMC. **Number of employees worldwide:** 2,500.

SLICKEDIT, INC.
3000 Aerial Center Parkway, Suite 120, Morrisville NC 27560. 919/473-0070. **Toll-free phone:** 800/934-EDIT. **Fax:** 919/473-0080. **Contact:** Personnel. **E-mail address:** careers@slickedit.com. **World Wide Web address:** http://www.slickedit.com. **Description:** Develops graphical programmers' editing software including Visual SlickEdit and SlickEdit text-mode version. **Positions advertised include:** Software Engineer. **Office hours:** Monday – Friday, 9:00 a.m. – 6:00 p.m. **Corporate headquarters location:** This location. **CEO:** Jill Maurer.

SOURCE TECHNOLOGIES, INC.

2910 White Hall Park Drive, Charlotte NC 28273. 704/696-7500. **Toll-free phone:** 800/922-8501. **Contact:** Human Resources Department. **World Wide Web address:** http://www.sourcetech.com. **Description:** A reseller of computer printers and printer equipment. Source Technologies also offers a wide variety of printing solutions. **Corporate headquarters location:** This location. **Other U.S. locations:** GA; SC; MN; WA; CA; NY.

STRATEGIC TECHNOLOGIES

301 Gregson Drive, Cary NC 27511. 919/379-8000. **Fax:** 919/379-8100. **Contact:** Human Resources. **E-mail address:** info@stratech.com. **World Wide Web address:** http://www.stratech.com. **Description:** Provides network integration services. **NOTE:** Please visit website to view job listings and apply online. **Positions advertised include:** Oracle Technical Trainer. **Corporate headquarters location:** This location. **Other area locations:** Charlotte NC; Greensboro NC. **Other U.S. locations:** AL; CT; FL; GA; NY; SC; TN; VA. **Listed on:** Privately held. **President/CEO:** Mike Shook.

SUMMUS LIMITED

434 Fayetteville Street Mall, Suite 600, Raleigh NC 27601. 919/807-5600. **Fax:** 919/807-5601. **Contact:** Human Resources. **E-mail address:** info@summus.com. **World Wide Web address:** http://www.summus.com. **Description:** Develops compression technology software for image and video data transmissions over the Internet and other networks. **Corporate headquarters location:** This location. **Other U.S. locations:** Boston MA; Kansas City KS; Chicago IL. **International locations:** Gothenburg Sweden; Split Croatia. **CEO:** Bjorn Jawerth.

SYNOPSYS, INC.

1101 Slater Road, Suite 300, Durham NC 27703. 919/941-6600. **Fax:** 919/941-6700. **Contact:** Director of Human Resources. **E-mail address:** jobs@avanticorp.com. **World Wide Web address:** http://www.synopsys.com. **Description:** Develops, markets, and supports software products that assist IC design engineers in performing automated design, layout, physical verification, and analysis of advanced integrated circuits. **Corporate headquarters location:** Mountain View CA. **Other U.S. locations:** Nationwide. **International locations:** Worldwide. **Listed on:** NASDAQ. **Stock exchange symbol:** SNPS. **CEO:** Aart De Geus. **Number of employees at this location:** 4,362.

THALES COMPUTERS

3100 Spring Forest Road, Raleigh NC 27616. 919/231-8000. **Toll-free phone:** 800/848-2330. **Fax:** 919/231-8001. **Contact:** Personnel. **World Wide Web address:** http://www.thalescomputers.com. **Description:** A designer and manufacturer of computer boards for use in harsh environments. **NOTE:** Please visit website to view job listings. **Corporate headquarters location:** France. **Other U.S. locations:** Jamestown RI; Moorpark CA. **International locations:** France; United Kingdom.

Operations at this facility include: This location serves as the U.S. Headquarters.

TOUCHPOINT SOLUTIONS
Prosperity Place, 10200 Mallard Creek Road, Charlotte NC 28262. 704/943-7242. **Contact:** Recruiting Manager. **E-mail address:** dana.stephens@fnf.com. **World Wide Web address:** http://www.touchpoint-solutions.com. **Description:** Develops software for banks and other financial institutions. **Corporate headquarters location:** Atlanta GA. **Other U.S. locations:** Little Rock AR; **Parent company:** Fidelity Information Services. **President:** Jim Szyperski.

TRANSBOTICS CORPORATION
3400 Latrobe Drive, Charlotte NC 28211. 704/362-1115. **Fax:** 704/364-4039. **Contact:** Human Resources. **E-mail address:** careers@transbotics.com. **World Wide Web address:** http://www.transbotics.com. **Description:** Supplies hardware and software that are incorporated into and used to control automatic guided vehicle systems (AGVS), which are used by customers to transport materials between various locations within a manufacturing or distribution facility. **Corporate headquarters location:** This location. **Other U.S. locations:** Fraser MI. **President/CEO:** Claude Imbleau.

TROY GROUP
501 West John Street, Matthews NC 28105. 704/847-1210. **Contact:** Human Resources. **World Wide Web address:** http://www.troygroup.com. **Description:** Manufactures internal and external hardware to interface with computer printers, primarily intended for use with IBM mainframes. **Corporate headquarters location:** Santa Ana CA. **Other U.S. locations:** Irvine CA; Meridian ID. **International locations:** Herrenberg, Germany. **Listed on:** NASDAQ. **Stock exchange symbol:** TROY. **President/CEO:** Patrick J. Dirk.

ULTIMUS
15200 Weston Parkway, Suite 106, Cary NC 27513. 919/678-0900. **Fax:** 919/678-0901. **Contact:** Office Manager. **E-mail address:** admin@ultimus.com. **World Wide Web address:** http://www.ultimus.com. **Description:** Offers workflow automation software through client/server Windows applications, allowing users to design, simulate, implement, monitor, and measure workflow for various administrative business processes. Founded in 1994. **Company slogan:** Workflow on the Web. **Positions advertised include:** Regional Sales Manager; Senior Workflow Consultant; Technical Support Specialist; Technical Trainer; Technical Training Manager; Workflow Consultant. **Office hours:** Monday - Friday, 9:00 a.m. - 5:30 p.m. **Corporate headquarters location:** This location. **International locations:** Worldwide. **Listed on:** Privately held. **CEO:** Rashid Khan.

VERBATIM CORPORATION
1200 West W.T. Harris Boulevard, Charlotte NC 28262. 704/547-6500. **Contact:** Human Resources Manager. **World Wide Web address:**

http://www.verbatimcorp.com. **Description:** Develops data storage products including computer disks and CD ROMs. **Corporate headquarters location:** This location. **Parent company:** Mitsubishi Chemical Corporation.

XEROX
P.O. Box 4006 Greenville NC 27836. 252/321-7994. **Physical address:** 1706-D East Arlington Boulevard, Greenville NC 27858. **Fax:** 252/353-0690. **Contact:** Personnel. **World Wide Web address:** http://www.xerox.com. **Description:** Provides printing and publishing services as well as network printer, copiers, and fax machines. **NOTE:** Please visit website to search for jobs and apply online. **Corporate headquarters location:** Stamford CT. **Other area locations:** Winston-Salem NC; Charlotte NC; Greensboro NC; Matthews NC; Rocky Mount NC. **Other U.S. locations:** Nationwide. **International locations:** Worldwide. **Operations at this facility include:** Sales. **Listed on:** New York Stock Exchange. **Stock exchange symbol:** XRX.

South Carolina

BLACKBAUD, INC.
2000 Daniel Island Drive, Charleston SC 29492-7541. 800/468-8996. **Fax:** 843/216-6100. **Contact:** Laura Kennedy, Personnel Coordinator. **E-mail address:** recruiting@blackbaud.com. **World Wide Web address:** http://www.blackbaud.com. **Description:** Provides computer programming services for nonprofit companies and designs software that helps companies with a wide variety of activities including fundraising, administration, and organization. Founded in 1981. **NOTE:** Submit resumes online through the company Website. **Positions advertised include:** Customer Service Representative; Staff Accountant; Division Controlling Associate; Blackbaud Director; Prospect Researcher; Consulting Representative; Corporate Revenue Analyst; Customer Support Analyst; Application Developer; Software Instructor; High Tech Recruiters; Corporate Para legal; Product Marketing Manager; Sales Manager; System Administrator. **Special programs:** Internships. **Corporate headquarters location:** This location. **Other locations:** Glasgow, Scotland; Sydney, Australia. **Listed on:** Privately held. **CEO:** Robert (Bob) J. Sywolski. **Annual sales/revenues:** $105.2 million. **Number of employees:** 700.

CAMBAR SOFTWARE, INC.
2387 Clements Ferry Road, Charleston SC 29492. 843/856-2822. **Toll-free phone:** 800/756-4402. **Fax:** 842/881-4893. **Contact:** Human Resources. **E-mail address:** recruiting@cambarsoft.com. **World Wide Web address:** http://www.cambarsoftware.com. **Description:** Develops order and warehouse system software used by large distributors and manufacturers. **Corporate headquarters location:** This location. **Other locations:** Bohemia NY. **Parent company:** Supply Chain Holdings, LLC (Charleston SC).

DATASTREAM SYSTEMS, INC.
50 Datastream Plaza, Greenville SC 29605. 864/422-5001. **Fax:** 800/905-8980. **Contact:** Gary Craft, Human Resources. **E-mail address:** datastream@rpc.webhire.com. **World Wide Web address:** http://www.dstm.com. **Description:** Develops maintenance management software. Datastream serves many major industries including government, health care, hospitality, manufacturing, and transportation. Founded in 1996. **NOTE:** Human Resources phone: 864/422-5305. **Positions advertised include:** Corporate Accounting Manager; Tax Compliance Manager; Systems Administrator; Account Manager; Technical Writer; Product Engineer; Project Manager; Billable Consultant; Senior Consultant; Software Developer. **Special programs:** Internships. **Corporate headquarters location:** This location. **Other locations:** GA; IL; NJ; PA; TX. **International locations:** Canada; China; Japan; Singapore. **Listed on:** NASDAQ. **Stock exchange symbol:** DSTM. **Chairman/President/CEO:** Larry G. Blackwell. **Annual sales/revenues:** $90 million. **Number of employees:** 713.

MODIS IT RESOURCE MANAGEMENT
1122 Lady Street, Suite 640, Columbia SC 29201. 803/227-3010. **Fax:** 803/227-3020. **Contact:** Human Resources. **E-mail address:** columbia@modisit.com. **World Wide Web address:** http://www.modisit.com. **Description:** A provider of information technology resource management services and solutions. **Positions advertised include:** Web Tester; Business Objects Server Administrator. **Corporate headquarters location:** Jacksonville FL. **Other area locations:** Greenville SC. **Other U.S. locations:** Nationwide. **Parent company:** MPS Group.

SOLUTIENCE
25 East Court Street, Suite 203, Greenville SC 29601. 864/242-6302. **Fax:** 864/242-6303. **Contact:** Human Resources. **World Wide Web address:** http://www.solutience.com. **E-mail address:** jobs@solutience.com. **Description:** Develops, markets, and supports software for banks and insurance companies. Founded in 1971. **Positions advertised include:** Warehouse Manager; Console Consultant; Quality Management Consultant; Functional Consultant. **Corporate headquarters location:** This location. **Other U.S. locations:** Alpharetta GA; Birmingham AL; Jersey City NJ; Orangeburg SC; Southfield MI. **Parent company:** The BMW Group Munich, Germany).

SYNNEX INFORMATION TECHNOLOGIES, INC.
39 Pelham Ridge Drive, Greenville SC 29615. 864/289-4000. **Toll-free phone:** 800/756-9888. **Fax:** 864/289-4284. **E-mail address:** hr@synnex.com. **Contact:** Human Resources. **World Wide Web address:** http://www.synnex.com. **Description:** Formerly Gates Arrow Distributors, Synnex distributes microcomputers, networking software, and computer peripheral equipment including monitors, hard-disk drives, and modems. The company also packages computer systems, offers

systems integration services, and provides technical support services. **NOTE:** Resumes for openings at this facility may be sent to the above fax or e-mail, or to: Human Resources, SYNNEX Information Technologies, Inc., 1041 East Butler Road, Suite 1200, Greenville SC 29607. Applicants may fill out applications online. **Positions advertised include:** Computer Operator; Computer Programmer; Customer Service Representative; Services Sales Representative. **Corporate headquarters location:** Fremont CA. **Operations at this facility include:** Administration; Sales.

EDUCATIONAL SERVICES

You can expect to find the following types of companies in this section:
Business/Secretarial/Data Processing Schools •
Colleges/Universities/Professional Schools • Community
Colleges/Technical Schools/Vocational Schools • Elementary and
Secondary Schools • Preschool and Child Daycare Services

North Carolina

APPALACHIAN STATE UNIVERSITY
504 Dauph Blan Street, First Floor, Boone NC 28608. 828/262-3186.
Fax: 828/262-6489. **Recorded jobline:** 828/262-6488. **Contact:** Human
Resources. **World Wide Web address:** http://www.appstate.edu.
Description: A four-year state university. **NOTE:** You must complete an
application form to be considered for employment. Please visit the
website to search for jobs and download an application form, or visit the
office to pick one up. Applications are kept on file for one year. You may
also call the automated line at 828/262-6624 and leave your name and
contact information. You can reach a Personnel Assistant at 828/262-
6520. **Positions advertised include:** Office Assistant; Student Center
Technical Director; Sales Manager; Maintenance Mechanic; Food
Service Assistant; Chairperson – Various Departments; Assistant
Professor – Various Departments; Dean – College of Arts and Sciences;
GIS Lab Supervisor; Adjunct Faculty – Various Departments; Lecturer –
Psychology; Collection Development Librarian. **Special programs:**
Internships. **Operations at this facility include:** Administration;
Research and Development; Service. **Number of employees at this
location:** 2,034.

ASHEBORO CITY SCHOOLS
P.O. Box 1103, Asheboro NC 27204-1103. 336/625-5104. **Physical
address:** 1126 South Park Street, Asheboro NC 27203. **Fax:** 336/625-
9238. **Contact:** Timothy Allgood, Assistant Superintendent of Human
Resources Department. **E-mail address:** tallgood@asheboro.k12.nc.us.
World Wide Web address: http://www.asheboro.k12.nc.us.
Description: Operates the public school system in Asheboro for
students in kindergarten through grade 12. The curriculum includes both
a vocational and college preparatory program. **NOTE:** Entry-level
positions are offered. **Positions advertised include:** Custodian;
Teacher Assistant; Bus Driver; Occupational Therapist; School
Psychologist; Speech/Language Pathologist; Pre-Kindergarten Teacher;
ESL Teacher; Technology Education Teacher; Elementary Teacher;
Media Personnel. **Corporate headquarters location:** This location.
Number of employees at this location: 592.

BREVARD COLLEGE
400 North Broad Street, Brevard NC 28712. 828/883-8292. **Contact:**
Employment. **World Wide Web address:** http://www.brevard.edu.

Description: A four-year liberal arts college offering education services to more than 650 students. Founded 1853. **NOTE:** Please visit website to view job listings and for more information on applying for specific positions. **Positions advertised include:** Director – Center for Career, Service, and Learning; Director of Student Activities; Director of First Year Programs; Admissions Counselor; Director of the Academic Enrichment Center; Head Women's Soccer Coach; Assistant Professor; Athletic Director; Business and Organizational Leadership. **President:** Drew L. Van Horn.

CALDWELL COUNTY SCHOOL DISTRICT
1914 Hickory Boulevard SW, Lenoir NC 28645. 828/728-8407. **Recorded jobline:** 828/728-2800. **Fax:** 828/728-0012. **Contact:** Pat Mitchell Personnel. **E-mail address:** pmitchell@caa.k12.nc.us. **World Wide Web address:** http://www.caa.k12.nc.us. **Description:** Administrative offices of the public school district. **NOTE:** Please visit website to view job listings and apply online. You may apply online at http://schooljobs.dpi.state.nc.us. **Positions advertised include:** Wrap Around Lead Assistant; Principal; Assistant Principal; Media Coordinator; Career Development Coordinator; Rising Stars Coordinator; Exceptional Teacher Assistant – Temporary; Transportation Director.

CHARLOTTE-MECKLENBURG SCHOOL SYSTEM
P.O. Box 30035, Charlotte NC 28230-0035. 980/343-3000. **Physical address:** 701 East Second Street, Charlotte NC 28202. **Fax:** 704/343-3124. **Contact:** Human Resources. **E-mail address:** hr@cms.k12.nc.us. **World Wide Web address:** http://www.cms.k12.nc.us. **Description:** Administrative offices of the public school system. **NOTE:** Please visit website to search for jobs and apply online. Applications are kept on file for one year. **Positions advertised include:**Bus Driver; ASEP Associate; Site Coordinator; Science/Chemistry Teacher; Office Coordinator; Preschool Psychologist; Administrative Secretary; HVAC Mechanic; Grounds Worker; ISS Assistant; Early Reading First Coach; Custodian; Administrative Student Intervention Assistant; Bilingual Resource Assistant; Senior Administrative Secretary; Band Teacher; Keyboarding Teacher; Business Analyst; Technician; Talent Development Compliance Teacher. **Office hours:** Monday – Friday, 8:00 a.m. – 5:00 p.m. **Corporate headquarters location:** This location.

DAVIDSON COLLEGE
Box 7163, Davidson NC 28035-7163. 704/894-2212. **Physical address:** 431 Concord Road, #11 Jackson Court, Davidson NC. **Fax:** 704/894-2638. **Contact:** Human Resources. **E-mail address:** jobs@davidson.edu. **World Wide Web address:** http://www2.davidson.edu. **Description:** An independent liberal arts college enrolling more than 1,500 students. Founded 1837. **NOTE:** Please visit website to view job listings, register, and apply online. **Positions advertised include:** Assistant Professor – Biology; ITS Widows System Administrator; Prospect Researcher; Union Café Cook; Area Coordinator – Residence Life; Head Women's Soccer Coach; Union Café Manager; Police Officer; Communications Assistant;

Research Coordinator; Research Technician; International Student Advisor; Laundry Production Assistant.

DUKE UNIVERSITY
P.O. Box 90496 Durham NC 27708. 919/684-5600. **Physical address:** 2024 West Main Street, Durham NC. **Contact:** Human Resources Center. **Fax:** 919/668-0386. **E-mail address:** hr@mc.duke.edu. **World Wide Web address:** http://www.duke.edu. **Description:** A research university operating four campuses. Duke enrolls 5,300 undergraduates in its Trinity College of Arts and Sciences; 1,000 students in its School of Engineering; and 4,500 graduate and professional students in a variety of other programs. The university also operates the Duke University Art Museum, the Duke University Marine Laboratory, and the Duke Primate Center. Duke University Community Service Center (CSC) provides support to various groups including the Duke Cancer Patient Support Group and the Durham County Youth Home. Founded in 1892. **NOTE:** Please visit http://www.hr.duke.edu to search for jobs and apply online. **Positions advertised include:** Associate Dean of External Affairs; Musician; Administrative Secretary; Utility Worker; Research and Development Engineer; Research Technician; Program Coordinator; Steam Plant Operator; Security Officer; Public Relations Specialist; Major Gifts Officer; Senior Family/School Program Specialist; Housekeeper; Office Coordinator; Postal Clerk; Departmental Business Manager; Veterinary Technician; General Maintenance Mechanic. **President:** Nannerl O. Keohane.

DURHAM PUBLIC SCHOOLS
511 Cleveland Avenue, P.O. Box 30002, Durham NC 27702. 919/560-2000. **Contact:** Human Resources. **World Wide Web address:** http://www.dpsnc.com. **Description:** Operators of the public schools in Durham. **NOTE:** Please visit website to search for jobs and to access online application form. **Positions advertised include:** Child Nutrition Assistant; School Bus Driver; Lead Translator; Painter; Elementary Literacy Specialist; Energy Management Coordinator; Group Leader – Various Schools; Assistant Manager – Before School Care; Internal Control and Risk Manager; Heavy Equipment Operator; Electrician; Computer Programmer; Preschool Facilitator; Plumber; Wellness Specialist; Coordinator of Arts Education.

EAST CAROLINA UNIVERSITY
210 East First Street, Greenville NC 27858-4353. 252/328-6352. **Fax:** 252/328-4191. **Recorded jobline:** 252/328-4851. **Contact:** Human Resources. **World Wide Web address:** http://www.ecu.edu. **Description:** A university offering undergraduate, graduate, and medical programs. **NOTE:** Please download and submit an ECU application form with your resume. **Positions advertised include:** Administrative Assistant; Office Assistant; Accounting Clerk; Clinical Pharmacist; ECU Staff Nurse; Nursing Assistant; Research Technician; Facility Architect; Enrollment Services Officer; Electronics Technician; Laboratories Mechanic; Housekeeper; Computing Consultant; Research Assistant; Assistant Professor – Various Departments; Student Employment

Administrator; Faculty Position – Various Departments. **Corporate headquarters location:** This location.

FORSYTH TECHNICAL COMMUNITY COLLEGE
2100 Silas Creek Parkway, Winston-Salem NC 27103-5197. 336/723-0371. **Fax:** 336/761-2399. **Contact:** Gregory M. Chase, Director of Human Resources. **World Wide Web address:** http://www.forsyth.tec.nc.us. **Description:** A community college. **NOTE:** There are five office locations in Winston-Salem, and campuses at the following locations – Kernersville NC; Danbury NC. Please visit website to view job listings and to download application form. You must submit an application to be eligible for employment. Contact Human Resources at 336/734-7246. **Positions advertised include:** Program Coordinator – Emergency Medical Science; Program Coordinator BLET & Instructor – Criminal Justice; Dean – Business Information Technologies; Coordinator – Cooperative Education; Director – Shugart Women's Center; Switchboard Operator. **Corporate headquarters location:** This location. **Operations at this facility include:** Administration; Research and Development. **Number of employees at this location:** 310.

MEREDITH COLLEGE
3800 Hillsborough Street, Raleigh NC 27607. 919/760-8600. **Fax:** 919/760-2828. **Description:** A women's college offering undergraduate and graduate programs. **NOTE:** Please visit website to view job listings. **Positions advertised include:** Director of Financial Assistance; French Instructor – Part-time; Latin Instructor – Part-time; Assistant Director of the Learning Center; Director of Human Resources; Italian Instructor – Part-time; Spanish Instructor – Part-time.

NORTH CAROLINA AGRICULTURAL & TECHNICAL STATE UNIVERSITY
1601 East Market Street, Greensboro NC 27411. 336/334-7500. **Recorded jobline:** 336/334-7292. **Contact:** Personnel. **World Wide Web address:** http://www.ncat.edu. **Description:** A state university offering graduate and undergraduate programs in agriculture, business, engineering, and other disciplines. **NOTE:** You must complete a North Carolina State Government Application for Employment. You can download one at http://www.osp.state.nc.us/jobs/gnrlinfo.htm#app. Please mail applications to 1020 East Wendover Avenue, Greensboro NC 27411. Human Resources phone is 336/334-7862. **Positions advertised include:** Residence Administrator; Processing Assistant; Police Officer; Administrative Secretary; Student Services Manager; Housekeeper; Research Technician; Director of Human Resources; Special Assistant to the Vice Chancellor for Research; Director of Research Services; Director of Development for Athletics; Professor – Various Departments; Tenure Tract Position – Various Departments; University Physician; Assistant/Associate Professor – Various Departments; Staff Psychiatrist;. **Office Hours:** Monday – Friday, 8:00 a.m. – 5:00 p.m. **Corporate headquarters location:** This location.

NORTH CAROLINA CENTRAL UNIVERSITY
1801 Fayetteville Street, Durham NC 27707. 919/530-6100. **Fax:** 919/530-7984. **Contact:** Director of Human Resources. **World Wide Web address:** http://www.nccu.edu. **Description:** A university offering graduate and undergraduate programs in business, education, law, library science, and other disciplines. **NOTE:** Please visit website to view job listings and for more specific information on applying for specific jobs. **Positions advertised include:** Accounting Clerk; Accounting Technician; Administrative Secretary; Data Entry Specialist; Information Processing Technician; Mail Clerk; Office Assistant; Processing Assistant; Word Processor; Warehouse Manager; Internal Auditor; Administrative Officer; Attorney; Official Court Reporter; Reimbursement Officer.

NORTH CAROLINA SCHOOL OF THE ARTS
P.O. Box 12189, Winston-Salem NC 27117-2189. **Physical address:** 1533 South Main Street, Administrative Building Room 105, Winston-Salem NC 27127-2188. 336/770-3399. **Fax:** 336/770-1462. **Contact:** Mack Greer, Director of Human Resources. **E-mail address:** greerm@ncarts.edu. **World Wide Web address:** http://www.ncarts.edu. **Description:** A college offering specialized programs in the fine arts, including dance, drama, filmmaking, music, design and production, and visual arts. **NOTE:** Please visit website to view job listings. **Positions advertised include:** Program Assistant; Assistant Manager – Fitness Center; Faculty – Various Departments; Vice Chancellor of Development and Public Relations; Dean of School of Music. **Office hours:** Monday – Friday, 8:00 a.m. – 5:00 p.m.; *Summer office hours* – Monday – Thursday, 7:30 a.m. – 5:20 p.m.; Friday, 7:30 a.m. – 11:30 p.m. **Number of employees at this location:** 500.

NORTH CAROLINA STATE UNIVERSITY
2711 Sullivan Drive, Box 7210, Raleigh NC 27695-7210. 919/515-2011. **Fax:** 919/515-7543. **Contact:** Human Resources. **World Wide Web address:** http://www.ncsu.edu. **Description:** A state university offering graduate and undergraduate programs in agriculture, design, engineering, and other disciplines. **NOTE:** Please visit website to search for jobs and to download employment application. **Positions advertised include:** Associate Dean for Academic Affairs and Interdisciplinary Program; Associate General Counsel; Director – Centennial Campus Development; Executive Director of Development; Career Counselor; Costume Designer; Director – Software Systems; Grant Proposal Developer; Research Assistant; Assistant Professor – Various Departments; Lecturer – Various Departments; Housekeeper; Accountant; Groundskeeper; Laboratory Mechanic; Veterinary Technician. **Number of employees at this location:** 7,000.

OMEGA PERFORMANCE INC.
8701 Red Oak Boulevard, Suite 450, Charlotte NC 28217-3972. 704/672-1400. **Fax:** 704/525-4852. **Contact:** Human Resources. **E-mail address:** jobs@omega-performance.com. **World Wide Web address:** http://www.omega-performance.com. **Description:** Trains personnel in

financial services, telecommunications, transportation, and other industries using interactive, multimedia teaching methods along with traditional classroom instruction. **Positions advertised include:** Financial Services Training – Product Development/Instructional Designer; Executive Consultant; Regional Sales Manager; Account Manager; Relationship Manager. **Corporate headquarters location:** This location. **International locations:** Sydney, Australia; Toronto, Canada; London, England; Wellington, New Zealand; Singapore. **President/CEO:** Juan Gutierrez.

RUTHERFORD COUNTY SCHOOLS
382 West Main Street, Forest City NC 28043-3027. 828/245-0252. **Recorded jobline:** 828/245-0252 x603. **Fax:** 828/245-4151. **Contact:** Personnel Director. **E-mail address:** rcs_eo@rutherford.k12.nc.us. **World Wide Web address:** http://www.rutherford.k12.nc.us. **Description:** Operates the Rutherford County public school system. **NOTE:** Please visit website to view job listings and access application form. **Positions advertised include:** Literacy Lead Teacher; Interim Media Coordinator; Interim Social Studies Teacher; Assistant Superintendent for Curriculum and Instruction; Business Manager; Elementary Principal; Assistant Principal.

SALEM COLLEGE
SALEM ACADEMY
P.O. Box 10548, Winston-Salem NC 27108-0548. 336/721-2600. **Physical address:** 601 South Church Street, Winston –Salem NC 27101. **Fax:** 336/721-2785. **Recorded jobline:** 336/917-5522. **Contact:** Human Resources. **World Wide Web address:** http://www.salem.edu. **Description:** A women's liberal arts college offering both undergraduate and graduate programs of study. Salem Academy (also at this location) is a private, college preparatory boarding and day school for girls in grades 9 through 12. **NOTE:** Please visit website to view job listings and download employment application. **Positions advertised include:** Assistant Dean of Continuing Studies; Faculty – Various Departments. **Corporate headquarters location:** This location. **Operations at this facility include:** Administration; Service. **Listed on:** Privately held.

UNIVERSITY OF NORTH CAROLINA AT CHAPEL HILL
725 Airport Road, Campus Box 1045, Chapel Hill NC 27599-1045. 919/962-2991. **Fax:** 919/962-2658. **Contact:** Human Resources. **E-mail address:** employment@unc.edu. **World Wide Web address:** http://www.unc.edu. **Description:** A campus of the state university which offers graduate and undergraduate programs in education, dentistry, law, public health, journalism, nursing, and other disciplines. **NOTE:** Jobseekers should submit both an application and a resume. Please visit website to view job listings and for more specific information on applying for positions. **Positions advertised include:** Dean – Various Schools/Departments; Vice Chancellor of Student Affairs; University Librarian; Professor – Various Departments; Assistant Professor – Various Departments; Tenure-track Faculty – Various Departments; Clinical Instructor; Accountant; Administrative Assistant; Art Museum

Registrar; Customer Network Coordinator; Computing Consultant; Grounds Worker; Housekeeper; Laboratory Research Specialist; Maintenance Mechanic; Office Assistant; Nurse Clinician; Processing Assistant; Research Analyst. **Number of employees at this location:** 8,000.

UNIVERSITY OF NORTH CAROLINA AT CHARLOTTE
9201 University City Boulevard, Charlotte NC 28223-0001. 704/687-2000. **Physical address:** King Building, Room 222, University of North Carolina, Charlotte NC 28223. **Fax:** 704/687-3239. **Contact:** Human Resources. **World Wide Web address:** http://www.uncc.edu. **Description:** A campus of the state university. The university has an enrollment of approximately 15,600 students. **NOTE:** Please visit website to view job listings. Human Resources phone is 704/687-2276. For information on staff positions, please e-mail mismith@email.uncc.edu. **Positions advertised include:** Housekeeping Assistant – Part-time; Library Clerk; Greenhouse Manager; Processing Assistant; Office Assistant; Accounting Clerk; Administrative Assistant; Residence Administrator; Computing Consultant; Faculty Engineering Specialist; Director of Purchasing; Manuscript Librarian; Senior Program Manager. **Office hours:** Monday – Friday, 8:00 a.m. – 5:00 p.m. **Number of employees at this location:** 2,500.

UNIVERSITY OF NORTH CAROLINA AT GREENSBORO
P.O. Box 26170, Greensboro NC 27402-6170. 336/334-5009. **Physical address:** 1000 Spring Garden Street, Greensboro NC 27403. **Fax:** 336/334-5585. **Recorded jobline:** 336/334-5023. **Contact:** Human Resources. **World Wide Web address:** http://www.uncg.edu. **Description:** A campus of the state university offering a number of different academic programs ranging from accounting to women's studies. **NOTE:** Please visit website to download application form. You can also receive an application form by contacting the Greensboro Employment Security Commission. **Positions advertised include:** Director of Employee Services; Administrative Manager; Physician Extender; Processing Assistant; Administrative Secretary; Security Officer; Social Research Assistant. **Office hours:** Monday – Friday, 8:00 a.m. – 4:00 p.m. **Number of employees at this location:** 2,000.

UNIVERSITY OF NORTH CAROLINA AT WILMINGTON
University Center, 601 South College Road, Wilmington NC 28403. 910/962-3160. **Physical address:** 5051 New Centre Drive, Wilmington NC 28403-5960. **Fax:** 910/962-3840. **Recorded jobline:** 910/962-3791. **Contact:** Human Resources. **E-mail address:** hrsearch@uncw.edu. **World Wide Web address:** http://www.uncwil.edu. **Description:** A campus of the state university enrolling approximately 9,200 students. **NOTE:** Please visit website to view job listings. **Positions advertised include:** Dean – College of Arts and Sciences; Art Historian; Director of Student Life Assessment; Counselor; Director of Leadership Education Programs; Vice Chancellor – Public Service and Continuing Studies; Assistant Professor – Marine Biochemist; Director of Athletic Training; Lecturer in Athletic Training; Tenure Track Faculty – Nursing; Office

Assistant; Assistant Manager – Printing Services; Assistant Director – Alumni Relations.

WATTS NURSING SCHOOL
3643 North Roxboro Road, Durham NC 27704. 919/470-7348. **Contact:** Human Resources. **E-mail address:** wattsson@drh.duhs.duke.edu. **World Wide Web address:** http://dukehealth1.org/watts/index.asp. **Description:** The oldest nursing school in North Carolina. **Parent company:** Duke University Health System.

WAYNE COUNTY PUBLIC SCHOOLS
P.O. Drawer 1797, Goldsboro NC 27533-1797. 919/731-5900. **Contact:** Personnel Director. **E-mail address:** gwhitley@wcps.org. **World Wide Web address:** http://www.waynecountyschools.org. **Description:** Offices of the Wayne County public school district. **NOTE:** Human Resources phone is 919/705-6179. Please visit website to download application form. **Positions advertised include:** Director – Summer Focus Intervention Program; Clerical Assistant – Summer Focus Intervention Program.

WELDON CITY SCHOOL DISTRICT
301 Mulberry Street, Weldon NC 27890. 252/536-4821. **Fax:** 252/536-3062. **Contact:** Personnel Director. **World Wide Web address:** http://www.weldoncityschools.k12.nc.us. **Description:** A public school district. **Special programs:** Training. **Office hours:** Monday – Friday, 8:00 a.m. – 5:00 p.m. **Corporate headquarters location:** This location. **Number of employees at this location:** 225.

WESTERN CAROLINA UNIVERSITY
220 HFR Administration, Western Carolina University, Cullowhee NC 28723. 828/227-7218. **Fax:** 828/227-7007. **Contact:** Human Resources. **World Wide Web address:** http://www.wcu.edu. **Description:** A university offering programs in business, education, and other disciplines. **Positions advertised include:** Assistant Professor – Various Departments; Assistant Women's Basketball Coach; Director of Enrollment Support; Professor – Various Departments; Reference Librarian; Administrative Assistant; Electrician; Electric Meter Reader; Enrollment Services Officer; Floor Maintenance Assistant; Grounds Worker; Housekeeper; Library Assistant; Occupational Therapist; Speech and Language Pathologist.

South Carolina

ANDERSON COUNTY SCHOOL DISTRICT 1
P.O. Box 99, Williamston SC 29697. 864/847-7344. **Fax:** 864/847-3543. **Contact:** Personnel. **E-mail address:** jobopportunities@.anderson1.k12.sc.us. **World Wide Web address:** http://www.anderson1.k12.sc.us. **Description:** Administrative offices for the public school district. **NOTE:** As of February 2003 there is a temporary hiring freeze due to state budget cuts and most positions are

on hold. **Positions advertised include:** Elementary Education Director; Bus Driver Assistant; Custodian; School Nurse.

COASTAL CAROLINA UNIVERSITY
P.O. Box 261954, Conway SC 29528-6054. 843/347-3161. **Contact:** Human Resources. **World Wide Web address:** http://www.coastal.edu. **Description:** A private four-year university offering both Graduate and Undergraduate programs that currently enrolls 6,780 students. **Positions advertised include:** Athletic Training Instructors; Director of Counseling Services; Security Officer. **Office Hours:** Monday – Friday, 8:30 a.m. – 4:30 p.m.

ORANGEBURG CONSOLIDATED SCHOOL DISTRICT 5
578 Ellis Avenue, Orangeburg SC 29115. 803/534-7936. **Contact:** Dr Charles G. Spell. Assistant Superintendent of Human Resources/Support Services. **E-mail address:** cgs45@orangeburg5.k12.sc.us. **World Wide Web address:** http://www.orangeburg5.k12.sc.us. **Description:** A public school district comprised of eight elementary schools, five middle schools, and three high schools. **Positions advertised include:** Elementary School Principal; Educable Mentally Disabled Learning Teacher; Emotionally Disabled Teacher; Social Studies Teacher; Occupational Therapist; Registered Nurse; Adult Bus Driver; Building Fund Management Specialist; Guidance Counselor; Mechanic.

UNIVERSITY OF SOUTH CAROLINA
508 Assembly Street, Columbia SC 29208. 803/777-3821. **Physical address:** USC Employment Office 1600 Hampton Street, Columbia SC 29208. **Fax:** 803/777-0302. **Contact:** Loretta Poston, Employment Office. **E-mail address:** loretta@gwm.sc.edu. **Note:** Do not e-mail applications. **World Wide Web address:** http://www.sc.edu. **Description:** A four-year, state university. The university awards bachelors, masters, and doctoral degrees and enrolls over 25,000 students per year. The University of South Carolina also has campuses in Spartanburg and Aiken. Founded in 1801. **Positions advertised include:** Administrative Coordinator; Lab Technician; Technical Medical Associate; Administrative Specialist; Research Technician; Public Information Coordinator; Data Entry & Control Clerk. **Corporate headquarters location:** This location. **Operations at this facility include:** Administration; Research and Development; Service.

WILLIAMSBURG COUNTY SCHOOL DISTRICT
423 School Street, P.O. Box 1067, Kingstree SC 29556. 843/354-5571. **Fax:** 843/355-0804. **Contact:** Mr. Francis Burrows, Director of Human Resources. **E-mail address:** wcsd@hotmail.com. **World Wide Web address:** http:// www. wcsd.k12.sc.us. **Description:** Early Childhood Education Teacher; Family Consulting Services; Heating and Air Mechanic; Music Teacher; Language Arts Teacher; Mathematics Teacher; Physical Education Teacher; Science Teacher; Special Education Teacher. **Number of employees:** 450.

ELECTRONIC/INDUSTRIAL ELECTRICAL EQUIPMENT AND COMPONENTS

You can expect to find the following types of companies in this section:
Electronic Machines and Systems • Semiconductor Manufacturers

North Carolina

ACME ELECTRIC CORPORATION
4815 West Fifth Street, Lumberton NC 28358-0499. 910/738-1121. **Toll-free phone:** 800/334-5214. **Fax:** 910/739-0024. **Contact:** Human Resources. **World Wide Web address:** http://www.acmepowerdist.com. **Description:** Manufactures dry-type industrial distribution transformers and related products. **Corporate headquarters location:** This location. **International locations:** Monterrey Mexico. **Parent company:** Key Components Inc. **Operations at this facility include:** Administration; Divisional Headquarters; Management Consulting; Sales.

AMETEK, INC.
1210 North Carolina Highway 61, Whitsett NC 27377. 336/449-3400. **Contact:** Human Resources. **E-mail address:** corp.jobs@ametek.com. **World Wide Web address:** http://www.ametek.com. **Description:** AMETEK, Inc. is a global manufacturing company that serves a variety of industrial and commercial markets. The company produces and sells its products through its Electromechanical, Precision Instruments, and Industrial Materials groups. The Electromechanical Group has a leading market share in the production of electric motors for vacuum cleaners and floor care products. The company operates 32 manufacturing facilities. **NOTE:** Please mail resumes to the corporate office location at 37 North Valley Road Building 4, P.O. Box 1764, Paoli PA 19301. Phone is 610/647-2121, fax is 610/296-3412. Please visit website to link to jobsearch, or visit http://hotjobs.yahoo.com to search. **Corporate headquarters location:** Paoli PA. **International locations:** Denmark; England; Italy; Mexico. **Listed on:** New York Stock Exchange. **Stock exchange symbol:** AME. **Operations at this facility include:** This location is part of Ametek's Technical Motor Division. **Number of employees worldwide:** 7,600.

ANALOG DEVICES, INC.
7910 Triad Center Drive, Greensboro NC 27409. 336/668-9511. **Contact:** Human Resources Manager. **World Wide Web address:** http://www.analog.com. **Description:** Designs, manufactures, and markets a broad line of high-performance linear, mixed-signal, and digital integrated circuits (ICs) that address a wide range of real-world signal processing applications. The company's principal products include system-level ICs and general purpose, standard linear ICs. Analog's system-level ICs are used primarily in communications and computer applications. Analog's core technologies are required for all of the emerging communications standards, providing the company numerous

new product opportunities for ICs used in the wireless, fiber-optic, coaxial cable, and twisted pair applications that will be part of the new information infrastructure. Analog sells its products worldwide through a direct sales force, third-party industrial distributors, and independent sales representatives. The company has direct sales offices in 17 countries including the United States. **NOTE:** Please visit website to search for jobs. **Positions advertised include:** Senior IC Design Engineer. **Special programs:** Internships; Co-ops. **Corporate headquarters location:** Norwood MA. **Other U.S. locations:** WA; OR; CA; TX; GA; NJ; NH; MA. **International locations:** Worldwide. **Listed on:** New York Stock Exchange. **Stock exchange symbol:** ADI. **CEO:** Jerry Fishman. **Number of employees worldwide:** 8,600.

CEM CORPORATION
P.O. Box 200, Matthews NC 28106. 704/821-7015. **Physical address:** 3100 Smith Farm Road, Matthew NC 28105. **Toll-free phone:** 800/726-3331. **Fax:** 704/821-0491. **Contact:** Molly Rogers, Human Resources. **E-mail address:** human.resources@cem.com. **World Wide Web address:** http://www.cem.com. **Description:** CEM Corporation develops, manufactures, markets, and services microwave-based instrumentation for testing and analysis in the industrial and analytical laboratory markets. The company's products include microwave digestion systems, moisture/solids analyzers, fat analyzer systems, microwave extraction systems, microwave ashing systems, and SpectroPrep systems. **NOTE:** Please visit website to search for jobs. **Corporate headquarters location:** This location. **Subsidiaries include:** CEM (France); CEM GmbH (Kamp-Linfort, Germany); CEM Ltd. (Buckingham, England); CEM S.r.l. (Cologno al Serio, Italy). **CEO:** Michael Collins. **Number of employees nationwide:** 175.

COOPER BUSSMANN INC.
1000 Craigmont Road, Black Mountain NC 28711. 828/669-6482. **Contact:** Human Resources Manager. **E-mail address:** blkmtn.recruit@buss.com. **World Wide Web address:** http://www.bussmann.com. **Description:** The Bussmann Division of Cooper Industries manufactures electrical protection devices, such as fuses, fuse holders, and fuse boxes. The division's major markets include secondary electrical power distribution, construction, and electronic signal transmission and control. Its products are distributed for use in general construction, plant maintenance, utilities, process and energy applications, shopping centers, parking lots, sports facilities, and data processing and telecommunications systems; through distributors and direct to manufacturers for use in electronic equipment for consumer, industrial, government, and military applications; and directly to original equipment manufacturers of appliances, tools, machinery, and electronic equipment. **NOTE:** Please visit website to search for jobs and apply online. **Corporate headquarters location:** St. Louis MO. **Other area locations:** Apex NC; Burlington NC; Charlotte NC; Goldsboro NC; LaGrange NC; Monroe NC; Raleigh NC. **Other U.S. locations:** Nationwide. **Parent company:** Cooper Industries Inc. (Houston TX) is a diversified company engaged in three primary areas of manufacturing:

tools and hardware, electrical and electronic products, and automotive products. **Listed on:** New York Stock Exchange. **Stock exchange symbol:** CBE. **Number of employees at this location:** 500. **Number of employees nationwide:** 45,000.

CREE INC.

4600 Silicon Drive, Durham NC 27703. 919/313-5300. **Fax:** 919/313-5453. **Contact:** Human Resources. **E-mail address:** hr@cree.com. **World Wide Web address:** http://www.cree.com. **Description:** Develops, manufactures, and markets electronic devices made from silicon carbide (SiC), a semiconductor material. The company manufactures a commercialized, super bright blue light-emitting diode based on a combination of SiC and gallium nitride. Cree Inc. markets its SiC wafers to corporate, government, and university research laboratories. Other devices developed by the company include SiC radio frequency and microwave power devices, and high-temperature semiconductors. **NOTE:** Please visit website to search for jobs. **Positions advertised include:** Cost Accountant; Credit Manager; EH&S Manager; Employee Relations Representative; Manufacturing Equipment Maintenance Technician; Manager Manufacturing Engineer; Packaging Engineer; Process Development Engineer; Process Engineer Sustaining; Program Manager; Research Scientist; SiC Power Device Scientist; Semiconductor Production Worker; SemiFab Scientist; Supply Chain Manager; Test Engineer. **Corporate headquarters location:** This location. **Listed on:** NASDAQ. **Stock exchange symbol:** CREE. **Number of employees nationwide:** 1,121.

EATON ELECTRICAL

221 Heywood Road, Arden NC 28704. 828/684-2381. **Contact:** Human Resources. **World Wide Web address:** http://www.eatonelectrical.com. **Description:** Eaton Electrical produces industrial and commercial controls (electromechanical and electronic controls; motor starters, contractors, overloads, and electric drives; programmable controllers, counters, man/machine interface panels, and push buttons; photoelectric, proximity, temperature, and pressure sensors; circuit breakers; load centers; safety switches; panelboards; switchboards; dry type transformers; busway; meter centers; portable tool switches; commercial switches; relays; illuminated panels; annunciator panels; and electrically actuated valves and actuators); automotive and appliance controls (electromechanical and electronic controls; convenience, stalk, and concealed switches; knock sensors; climate control components; speed controls; timers; pressure switches; water valves; range controls; thermostats; gas valves; infinite switches; and temperature and humidity sensors); and specialty controls (automated material handling systems, automated guided vehicles, stacker cranes, ion implanters, engineered fasteners, golf grips, and industrial clutches and brakes). These products are sold, either directly by the company or indirectly through distributors and manufacturers' representatives, to industrial, commercial, automotive, appliance, aerospace, and government customers. **NOTE:** Resumes are only accepted when applying for specific positions. Please visit http://www.eatonjobs.com to search for jobs and apply online.

Corporate headquarters location: Pittsburgh PA. International locations: Worldwide. Parent company: Eaton Corporation (Cleveland OH) has operations in vehicle components (truck components, passenger car components, and off-highway vehicle components, which are usually sold directly from the company's plants to original equipment manufacturers of trucks, passenger cars, and off-highway vehicles) and defense systems (strategic countermeasures, tactical jamming systems, electronic intelligence, and electronic support measures for the federal government). Listed on: New York Stock Exchange. Stock exchange symbol: ETN. Number of employees nationwide: 51,000.

KEARFOTT GUIDANCE & NAVIGATION CORPORATION
Asheville, Route 70, Black Mountain NC 28711. 828/686-3811. Contact: Denise Thomas, Human Resources. E-mail address: humanresources@kearfott.com. World Wide Web address: http://www.kearfott.com. Description: Manufactures precision electromechanical and electronic components used to generate, sense, control, and display motion such as synchros, resolvers, cant angle sensors, and servo motors. Founded in 1917. NOTE: Entry-level positions and second and third shifts are offered. Please visit website to fill out Personnel application. Special programs: Apprenticeships; Training. Corporate headquarters location: Wayne NJ. Other U.S. locations: Little Falls NJ. International locations: Mexico. Parent company: Astronautics Corporation of America. Listed on: Privately held. Annual sales/revenues: $21 - $50 million.

MOOG COMPONENTS GROUP
POLY-SCIENTIFIC
1995 NC Highway, Murphy NC 28906-6864. 828/837-5115. Toll-free phone: 800/577-8685. Fax: 828/837-0846. Contact: Human Resources. E-mail address: staylor2@moog.com. World Wide Web address: http://www.polysci.com. Description: Moog Components Group designs and manufactures technology components. NOTE: Please visit website to view job listings. Other U.S. locations: Blacksburg VA; Springfield PA. Operations at this facility include: This location manufactures brush and brushless DC motors, drives and integrated motion systems.

NETWORK CONTROLS INTERNATIONAL INC.
9 Woodlawn Green, Suite 120, Charlotte NC 28217-2202. 704/527-4357. Fax: 704/523-3502. Contact: Human Resources. E-mail address: hrdept@nci-inc.com. World Wide Web address: http://www.nci-inc.com. Description: Manufactures circuit boards to integrate computer systems in banks. Positions advertised include: Active Server Page Developer; Database Developer; C++ Developer; Quality Assurance Lead Programmer. International locations: London, England. Parent company: IFS International Holdings, Inc. Listed on: NASDAQ. Stock exchange symbol: IFSH.

POWERWARE CORPORATION
8609 Six Forks Road, Raleigh NC 27615. 919/872-3020. Toll-free phone: 800/554-3448. Fax: 919/870-3100. Contact: Human Resources

Manager. **World Wide Web address:** http://www.powerware.com. **Description:** Manufactures and markets uninterruptible power supplies, power control and energy storage products, and backup power management solutions. **NOTE:** Entry-level positions are offered. Please visit website to search for jobs and apply online. **Positions advertised include:** Customer Service Representative. **Corporate headquarters location:** This location. **International locations:** Worldwide. **Parent company:** Invesys plc (London, England). **Annual sales/revenues:** More than $100 million.

RF MICRO DEVICES INC.
7628 Thorndike Road, Greensboro NC 27409-9421. 336/664-1233. **Fax:** 336/931-7454. **Contact:** Human Resources. **World Wide Web address:** http://www.rfmd.com. **Description:** Manufactures semiconductors. **NOTE:** Please visit website to view job listings and submit resume online. **Positions advertised include:** Database Administrator; E-systems Developer; MBE Equipment Technician; Reliability Engineer; SAP Basis Administrator; Staff Systems Engineer. **Corporate headquarters location:** This location. **Other area locations:** Charlotte NC. **Other U.S. locations:** Phoenix AZ; Irvine CA; Scotts Valley CA; San Jose CA; Cedar Rapids IA; Boston MA. **International locations:** Worldwide. **Listed on:** NASDAQ. **Stock exchange symbol:** RFMD. **President/CEO:** Robert A. Bruggeworth. **Annual sales/revenues:** More than $100 million. **Number of employees worldwide:** 1,800.

TRION, INC.
101 McNeill Road, Sanford NC 27330. 919/775-2201. **Toll-free phone:** 800/884-0002. **Fax:** 919/777-6399. **Toll-free fax:** 800/458-2379. **Contact:** Director of Human Resources. **World Wide Web address:** http://www.trioninc.com. **Description:** Manufactures electronic indoor air cleaners for home, office, and industrial use. Founded in 1947. **NOTE:** Please visit website to view job listings. **Corporate headquarters location:** This location. **Parent company:** Fedders Corporation. **Operations at this facility include:** Administration; Engineering and Design; Manufacturing; Research and Development; Sales. **Listed on:** New York Stock Exchange. **Stock exchange symbol:** FJC.

TROXLER ELECTRONIC LABORATORIES, INC.
3008 Cornwallis Road, P.O. Box 12057, Research Triangle Park NC 27709. 919/549-8661. **Toll-free phone:** 877/TROXLER. **Fax:** 919/485-2257. **Contact:** Human Resources. **E-mail address:** troxlerjobs@troxlerlabs.com. **World Wide Web address:** http://www.troxlerlabs.com. **Description:** Develops electronic products for measuring characteristics in engineering materials. **NOTE:** Please visit website to view job listings and apply online. **Corporate headquarters location:** This location. **Other U.S. locations:** Rockville MD; Lakewood WA; Rancho Cordova CA; Arlington TX; Nashville TV; Downers Grove IL; Lakewood CO. **International locations:** Germany; Hong Kong; Canada. **CEO:** Billy Troxler.

VISHAY MICRO-MEASUREMENTS

P.O. Box 27777, Raleigh NC 27611-7777. 919/365-3800. **Physical address:** 951 Wendall Boulevard, Wendall NC 27591. **Fax:** 919/365-5043. **Contact:** Personnel. **World Wide Web address:** http://www.vishay.com. **Description:** Develops, manufactures, and markets stress analysis products for measurement of mechanical strains. **Office hours:** Monday – Friday, 8:30 a.m. – 5:30 p.m. **Corporate headquarters location:** Malvern PA. **Parent company:** Vishay is engaged in the manufacture and sale of precision stress-analysis systems and services, as well as high-precision resistive systems. In addition to Vishay Measurements Group, Vishay also operates in two other business segments: Resistive Systems Group, which develops, manufactures, and markets resistive products; and Medical Systems Group, which develops, manufactures, and markets dental products. **Listed on:** New York Stock Exchange. **Stock exchange symbol:** VSH.

South Carolina

ABB POWER T&D COMPANY, INC.

P.O. Box 100524, Florence SC 29501-0524. 843/665-4144. **Physical address:** 2300 Mechanicsville Road, Florence SC 29501. **Contact:** Human Resources. **World Wide Web address:** http://www.abb.com/us. **Description:** Manufactures medium- and low-voltage circuit breakers and kirk lock (interlock) systems. **Corporate headquarters location:** Norwalk CT. **Other U.S. locations:** Nationwide. **Parent company:** ABB Group (Zurich, Switzerland). **Operations at this facility include:** Manufacturing; Research and Development; Sales. **Number of employees nationwide:** 10,000.

AVX CORPORATION

801 17th Avenue South, P.O. Box 867, Myrtle Beach SC 29578-0867. 843/448-9411. **Fax:** 843/448-7662. **Contact:** Dennis Overfield, Human Resources. **E-mail address:** doverfield@avxus.com. **World Wide Web address:** http://www.avxcorp.com. **Description:** A worldwide manufacturer and supplier of a broad line of passive electronic components and related products, operating 12 manufacturing facilities in 12 countries. Passive electronic components include ceramic and tantalum capacitors, both in leaded and surface-mount versions. AVX Corporation's customers include original equipment manufacturers in industries such as telecommunications, computers, automotive electronics, medical devices and instrumentation, industrial instrumentation, military and aerospace electronic systems, and consumer electronics. The company also manufactures and sells electronic connectors and distributes and sells certain components and connectors manufactured by its parent company. **Positions advertised include:** Internal Auditor; Compliance Manager. **Corporate headquarters location:** This location. **Other U.S. locations:** Nationwide. **International locations:** Northern Ireland; England; France; Israel. **Parent company:** Kyocera Corporation (Kyoto, Japan). **Listed on:** New York Stock Exchange. **Stock exchange symbol:** AVX.

Chairman: Benedict P. (Dick) Rosen. **Annual sales/revenues:** $1.25 billion. **Number of employees:** 12,900.

ACTARIS METERING SYSTEMS
dba ACTARIS NEPTUNE DIVISION
1310 Emerald Road, Greenwood SC 29646. 864/223-1212. **Fax:** 864/942-2204. **Contact:** Joseph Askew, Human Resources. **E-mail address:** jaskew@ greenwood.actaris.com. **World Wide Web address:** http://www.actaris.com. **Description:** Manufactures measurement equipment and systems for various energy applications, including petroleum meters, with 60 facilities in 30 countries. Founded in 1892. **NOTE:** Human Resources phone: 864/942-2274. **Positions advertised include:** Project Manager; Electrical Engineer; Mechanical Engineer. **Special programs:** Internships. **Annual sales/revenues:** $750 million. **Number of employees worldwide:** 7,000.

CUTLER-HAMMER, INC.
P.O. Box 1406, Greenwood SC 29648. 864/229-3006. **Contact:** Rick McLain, Human Resources Manager. **World Wide Web address:** http://www.cutler-hammer.com. **Description:** Part of the electrical and electronic controls segment of Eaton Corporation that produces industrial and commercial controls (electromechanical and electronic controls; motor starters, contractors, overloads, and electric drives; programmable controllers, counter, man-to-machine interface panels, and push buttons; photoelectric, proximity, temperature, and pressure sensors; circuit breakers; load centers; safety switches; panelboards; switchboards; dry tape transformers; busway; meter centers; portable tool switches; commercial switches; relays; illuminated panels; annunciator panels; and electrically-actuated valves and actuators); automotive and appliance controls (electromechanical and electronic controls; convenience, stalk, and concealed switches; knock sensors; climate control components; speed controls; timers; pressure switches; water valves; range controls; thermostats; gas valves; infinite switches; and temperature and humidity sensors); and specialty controls (automated material handling systems, automated guided vehicles, stacker cranes, ion implanters, engineered fasteners, golf grips, and industrial clutches and brakes). These products are sold directly by the company or indirectly through distributors and manufacturers' representatives to industrial, commercial, automotive, appliance, aerospace, and government customers. **Positions advertised include:** Lean Coordinator; Mechanical Drafting Engineer; Manufacturing Engineer; Network Administrator. **Corporate headquarters location:** Pittsburgh PA. **Parent company:** Eaton Corporation (Cleveland OH).

KINGS ELECTRONICS COMPANY INC.
1685 Overview Drive, Rock Hill SC 29730. 803/909-5000. **Fax:** 803/909-5029. **Contact:** Charles Robinson, Director of Human Resources. **E-mail address:** hrinfo@kingselectronics.com. **World Wide Web address:** http:// www.kingselectronics.com. **Description:** Manufactures, sells, and distributes a large line of specialized RF coaxial connectors for various

electronics and aerospace industry applications. **NOTE:** Human Resources phone: 803/909-5042.

NEWARK ELECTRONICS
217 Wilcox Avenue, Gaffney SC 29340-8650. 864/487-1900. **Contact:** Human Resources. **World Wide Web address:** http://www.newark.com. **Description:** Distributes electronic parts and products through sales offices in North America and Europe. **Positions advertised include:** Order Processor; Export Specialist; Operations Supervisor; Sales Associate; Customer Service Representative. **Other U.S. locations:** Nationwide. **Parent company:** Premier Farnell PLC is a broad line distributor of electronic components used in the production and maintenance of equipment; a supplier of maintenance products for industrial, commercial, and institutional applications; and a manufacturer of fire-fighting equipment.

PROGRESS LIGHTING, INC.
P.O. Box 989, Cowpens SC 29330. 864/463-3274. **Fax:** 864/599-6153. **Contact:** Vice President for Human Resources. **E-mail address:** jobs@progresslighting.com. **World Wide Web address:** http://www.progresslighting.com. **Description:** A manufacturer of home and commercial lighting systems and fixtures. **Positions advertised include:** Sales Representative.

SCANSOURCE, INC.
6 Logue Court, Greenville SC 29615. 864/288-2432. **Fax:** 864/288-1165. **Contact:** Human Resources. **E-mail address:** jobs@scansource.com. **World Wide Web address:** http://www.scansource.com. **Description:** A reseller and distributor of barcode, automatic data capture, and point-of-sale equipment as well as voice, data, and telephony products through its subsidiary, Catalyst Telecom. Since 1992. **Positions advertised include:** Product Asset Manager; Product Manager; Marketing Manager; Business Development Specialist; Financial Analyst; Credit Vice President. **Corporate headquarters location:** This location. **Other locations:** Worldwide. **Subsidiaries include:** Catalyst Telecom; Paracon. **Listed on:** NASDAQ. **Stock exchange symbol:** SCSC. **Chairman:** Steven H. Owings. **Annual sales/revenues:** $842 million. **Number of employees:** 700.

SQUARE D COMPANY
1990 Sandifer Boulevard, Seneca SC 29678. 864/882-2414. **Contact:** Russ Karpick, Human Resources Director. **E-mail address:** uwb@schneiderelectricjobs.com. **World Wide Web address:** http://www.squared.com. **Description:** A manufacturer of electrical distribution products for the construction industry. The company's products are used in commercial and residential construction, industrial facilities, and machinery and original equipment manufacturers products. Residential building products feature circuit breakers with an exclusive quick-open mechanism that isolates potential dangers quickly, and a complete home wiring system connecting multiple telephone lines, audio signals, VCR, cable, or closed circuit television. Square D also

manufactures a Home Power System that reduces installation times and cuts labor costs. In office developments, hotels and restaurants, retail shops, and other businesses, Square D Company provides products ranging from parking lot gate controls and uninterrupted power systems for personal computers to space-saving remote-controlled lighting and custom circuit breaker panel boards. Square D Company also equips public buildings such as schools, stadiums, museums, hospitals, prisons, military bases, and wastewater treatment plants with electrical distribution systems. **Positions advertised include:** Application Engineer. **Corporate headquarters location:** Palatine IL. **Other U.S. locations:** AZ; CA; KY; MO; NE; OH; TN. **Parent company:** Schneider Electric.

SUPERIOR ESSEX
P.O. Box 640, Chester SC 29706. 803/581-9200. **Physical address:** 995 Old York Road, Chester SC 29706. **Contact:** Human Resources. **World Wide Web address:** http://www.superioressex.com. **E-mail address:** career_ops@superior.essex.com. **Description:** A manufacturer and distributor of electrical wire and cable and electrical insulation products including magnetic wire, building wire, telephone cable, and other related products operating 30 facilities nationwide. **Positions advertised include:** District Operator; Customer Service Representative; Accounting Associate; Manufacturing Supervisor; Distribution Administrator; Manufacturing Engineer. **Corporate headquarters location:** Fort Wayne IN. **Parent company:** Superior TeleCom Inc. (East Rutherford NJ). **Listed on:** Privately held. **Number of employees:** 4,000.

WOVEN ELECTRONICS CORPORATION
P.O. Box 189, Mauldin SC 29662. 864/963-5131. **Physical address:** Old Stage Road, Simpsonville SC 29680. **Contact:** Human Resources. **World Wide Web address:** http://www.wovenelectronics.com. **Description:** Manufactures cable harness systems and electrical wiring. The company also offers electrical engineering services. Founded in 1924. **Corporate headquarters location:** Greenville SC. **Other locations:** Charleston SC; China; Great Britain; Merrimack NH. **Subsidiaries include:** Woven Electronics, Ltd. **Parent company:** Southern Weaving Corporation. **Number of employees:** 400.

ENVIRONMENTAL & WASTE MANAGEMENT SERVICES

You can expect to find the following types of companies in this section:
Environmental Engineering Firms • Sanitary Services

North Carolina

MANTECH ENVIRONMENTAL TECHNOLOGY, INC.
P.O. Box 12313, Research Triangle Park NC 27709. 919/549-0611. **Contact:** Human Resources. **E-mail address:** jobs@mantech.com. **World Wide Web address:** http://www.mantech.com. **Description:** An environmental engineering firm offering analytical research services and environmental information services. **NOTE:** Please visit website to search for jobs and apply online. **Positions advertised include:** Secretary/Administrative Assistant; Environmental Scientist. **Office hours:** Monday – Friday, 8:00 a.m. – 5:00 p.m. **Corporate headquarters location:** Fairfax VA. **Other area locations:** Fort Bragg NC; Havelock NC. **Other U.S. locations:** Nationwide. **International locations:** Worldwide. **Listed on:** NASDAQ. **Stock exchange symbol:** MANT. **President/CEO:** George J. Pederson. **Number of employees worldwide:** 5,000.

SHAMROCK ENVIRONMENTAL SERVICES
503 Patton Avenue, P.O. Box 14987, Greensboro NC 27406. 336/375-1989. **Toll-free phone:** 800/881-1098. **Fax:** 336/375-1801. **Contact:** Human Resources. **World Wide Web address:** http://www.shamrockenviro.com. **Description:** Provides hazardous and nonhazardous material collection and disposal services. **NOTE:** Please visit website to view job listings and download employment application. **Positions advertised include:** Project Manager; Site Supervisor; Field Technician; Equipment Operator; CDL Driver. **CEO:** Gail B. McGroarty.

URS CORPORATION
P.O. Box 769, Morrisville NC 27560. 919/461-1100. **Physical address:** 1600 Perimeter Park Drive, Suite 100, Morrisville NC 27560. **Fax:** 919/461-1415. **Contact:** Human Resources. **World Wide Web address:** http://www.urscorp.com. **Description:** Develops solutions to technical problems for government and corporate clients. Specific technical services provided include regulatory compliance support, site investigation and remediation, air pollution controls, VOC and air toxin control, biotreatment, waste management, ambient and source monitoring, risk management, information management, project chemistry, specialty chemicals, remote sensing services, materials and machinery analysis, and electronic services. **NOTE:** Please visit website to search for jobs and apply online. **Positions advertised include:** Geologist; Project Environmental Engineer; Senior Geologist; Assistant Programmer; Civil Engineer; Environmental Scientist; Graduate Environmental Engineer; Project Civil Engineer;

Structural/Facility/Foundation Engineer. **Corporate headquarters location:** San Francisco CA. **Other area locations:** Charlotte NC. **Other U.S. locations:** Nationwide. **International locations:** Worldwide. **Listed on:** New York Stock Exchange. **Stock exchange symbol:** URS.

WASTE MANAGEMENT, INC.
P.O. Box 16148, Winston-Salem NC 27115. 336/723-5744. **Physical address:** 3303 North Glenn Avenue, Winston-Salem NC 27105. **Fax:** 336/725-3113. **Contact:** Human Resources. **World Wide Web address:** http://www.wm.com. **Description:** Provides garbage removal services for residential and commercial locations. **NOTE:** Please visit website to search for jobs. **Corporate headquarters location:** Houston TX. **Other U.S. locations:** Nationwide. **International locations:** Canada. **Listed on:** New York Stock Exchange. **Stock exchange symbol:** WMI. **CEO:** David P. Steiner. **Number of employees worldwide:** 51,700.

South Carolina

GENERAL ENGINEERING LABORATORIES, LLC
P.O. Box 30712, Charleston SC 29417. 843/556-8171. **Physical address:** 2040 Savage Road, Charleston SC 29407. **Fax:** 843/769-1176. **Recorded jobline:** 843/769-7376 ext4798. **Contact:** Rosemary Keikow, Human Resources Director. **E-mail address:** hr@gel.com. **World Wide Web address:** http://www.gel.net. **Description:** Provides environmental testing on soil, air, water, and sludge for private industry and the government. This location also hires seasonally. Founded in 1981. **NOTE:** Entry-level positions, part-time jobs, and second and third shifts are offered. **Positions advertised include:** Laboratory Technician; Senior Civil Engineer; Chemical Engineer; Computer Support Technician; Draftsperson; Environmental Engineer; Industrial Engineer; Project Manager. **Special programs:** Internships. **Affiliates include:** General Engineering & Environmental, LLC; General Engineering Geophysics, LLC. **Parent company:** The GEL Group, Inc.

SAFETY-KLEEN CORPORATION
1301 Gervais Street, Columbia SC 29201. 803/933-4200. **Contact:** Human Resources. **World Wide Web address:** http://www.safety-kleen.com. **E-mail address:** info@safety-kleen.com. **Description:** A landfill company that accepts mainly nonhazardous waste from companies. **Corporate headquarters location:** Plano TX. **Other locations:** Nationwide.

FABRICATED METAL PRODUCTS AND PRIMARY METALS

You can expect to find the following types of companies in this section:
Aluminum and Copper Foundries • Die-Castings • Iron and Steel Foundries • Steel Works, Blast Furnaces, and Rolling Mills

North Carolina

ALLVAC
P.O. Box 5030, Monroe NC 28111-5030. 704/289-4511. **Physical address:** 2020 Ashcroft Avenue, Monroe NC 28110. **Toll-free phone:** 800/841-5491. **Fax:** 704/282-1577. **Contact:** Human Resources. **E-mail address:** hr@allvac.com. **World Wide Web address:** http://www.allvac.com. **Description:** Wholesalers of titanium and nickel alloys, as well as assorted metal and wire products. **Positions advertised include:** Inside Sales Representative; Manager – Business Process Development. **Corporate headquarters location:** This location. **Other U.S. locations:** Albany OR; Lockport NY; Richburg SC; Richland WA. **International locations:** Sheffield England. **Parent company:** Allegheny Technologies. **Operations at this facility include:** Administration; Manufacturing; Research and Development; Sales; Service. **Listed on:** New York Stock Exchange. **Stock exchange symbol:** ATI.

FMC LITHIUM
449 North Cox Road, Gastonia NC 28054. 704/868-5300. **Toll-free phone:** 888/LITHIUM. **Fax:** 704/868-5370. **Contact:** Don Taylor, Human Resources. **E-mail address:** lithium-info@fmc.com. **World Wide Web address:** http://www.fmclithium.com. **Description:** Provides solutions for companies specializing in industries including air treatment, fine chemicals, construction, glass and ceramics; and pool water treatment. **NOTE:** Contact Human Resources at 704/868-5455, fax is 704/868-0822. **Corporate headquarters location:** This location. **Other area locations:** Bessemer City NC. **Parent company:** FMC Corporation. **Listed on:** New York Stock Exchange. **Stock exchange symbol:** FMC.

FMC LITHIUM
P.O. Box 795, Highway 161, Bessemer City NC 28016. 704/868-5300. **Fax:** 704/868-5486. **Contact:** Don Taylor, Human Resources. **E-mail address:** lithium_hr@fmc.com **World Wide Web address:** http://www.fmclithium.com. **Description:** Provides solutions for companies specializing in industries including air treatment, fine chemicals, construction, glass and ceramics; and pool water treatment. **NOTE:** Contact Human Resources at 704/868-5455, fax is 704/868-0822. **Corporate headquarters location:** Gastonia NC. **Parent company:** FMC Corporation. **Operations at this facility include:** This

location manufactures lithium-based compounds. **Listed on:** New York Stock Exchange. **Stock exchange symbol:** FMC.

GOODYEAR TIRE & RUBBER COMPANY
890 Pineview Road, Asheboro NC 27203. 336/495-2240. **Contact:** Warren Thacker, Human Resources Manager. **World Wide Web address:** http://www.goodyear.com. **Description:** Goodyear Tire & Rubber Company's principal business is the development, manufacture, distribution, and sale of tires. Goodyear also manufactures and sells a broad spectrum of rubber products and rubber-related chemicals for various industrial and consumer markets and provides auto repair services. The company operates 32 plants in the United States, 42 plants in 29 other countries, and more than 1,800 retail tire and service centers and other distribution facilities around the globe. Strategic business units of Goodyear Tire & Rubber include North American Tire, Kelly-Springfield, Goodyear Europe, Goodyear Latin America, Goodyear Asia, Engineered Products, Chemicals, Celeron, and Goodyear Racing. **NOTE:** Please visit website to search for jobs. **Corporate headquarters location:** Akron OH. **Other U.S. locations:** Nationwide. **International locations:** Worldwide. **Operations at this facility include:** This location manufactures steel tire cord. **Listed on:** New York Stock Exchange. **Stock exchange symbol:** GT. **Number of employees worldwide:** 92,000.

INDALEX INC.
600 North Metcalf Street, Winton NC. 252/358-5811. **Toll-free phone:** 800/334-8731. **Fax:** 252/358-5683. **Contact:** Gail Miller, Human Resources. **World Wide Web address:** http://www.indalex.com. **Description:** Manufactures extruded aluminum and related products. **NOTE:** Please visit website to view job listings and post resume online. **Corporate headquarters location:** Girard OH. **Other area locations:** Burlington NC. **Other U.S. locations:** CA; CT; GA; IA; OH; PA. **International locations:** Canada. **Parent company:** Novar plc. **Number of employees at this location:** 500.

INDALEX INC.
1507 Industry Drive, P.O. Box 2437, Burlington NC 27216. 336/227-8826. **Toll-free phone:** 800/334-6825. **Fax:** 336/228-9813. **Contact:** Human Resources. **World Wide Web address:** http://www.indalex.com. **Description:** Manufactures extruded aluminum and related products. **NOTE:** Please visit website to view job listings and post resume online. **Corporate headquarters location:** Girard OH. **Other area locations:** Winton NC. **Other U.S. locations:** CA; CT; GA; IA; OH; PA. **International locations:** Canada. **Parent company:** Novar plc.

INSTEEL INDUSTRIES, INC.
1373 Boggs Drive, Mount Airy NC 27030. 336/719-9000. **Contact:** Human Resources. **E-mail address:** humanresources@insteel.com. **World Wide Web address:** http://www.insteel.com. **Description:** Produces industrial wire, galvanized fencing products, nails, specialty wire fabrics, concrete reinforcing products, and Insteel 3-D. **NOTE:**

Human Resources phone is 336/719-9000 Ext. 3165. Please visit website to view job listings. **Corporate headquarters location:** This location. **Other U.S. locations:** DE; FL; KY; SC; TN; TX; VA. **Operations at this facility include:** Administration; Sales. **Number of employees nationwide:** 700.

NUCOR CORPORATION
2100 Rexford Road, Charlotte NC 28211. 704/366-7000. **Fax:** 704/362-4208. **Contact:** Personnel. **World Wide Web address:** http://www.nucor.com. **Description:** Manufactures steel and steel products including hot-rolled and cold-finished steel shapes, girders, joists, and beams. The company also recycles more than 14 million tons of scrap steel every year. **Corporate headquarters location:** This location. **Other U.S. locations:** Nationwide. **Subsidiaries include:** Nucor Steel produces angles, bars, light structural, sheet, and specialty steel products. **Listed on:** New York Stock Exchange. **Stock exchange symbol:** NUE.

ORO MANUFACTURING COMPANY
P.O. Box 5018, Monroe NC 28111-5018. 704/283-2186. **Physical address:** 5000 Stitt Street, Monroe NC 28110. **Fax:** 704/283-0269. **Contact:** Human Resources. **World Wide Web address:** http://www.oromfg.com. **Description:** Light metal fabricators operating complete facilities for fabrication and finishing operations. **Corporate headquarters location:** This location.

South Carolina

ALCOA (ALUMINUM COMPANY OF AMERICA)
3575 US Highway 52, P.O. Box 1000, Goose Creek SC 29445. 843/572-3700. **Fax:** 843/572-5297. **Contact:** Human Resources. **World Wide Web address:** http://www.alcoa.com. **Description:** Engaged in all aspects of the aluminum industry including mining, refining, smelting, fabricating, and recycling. ALCOA also manufactures ceramic packaging for the semiconductor industry, alumina chemicals, plastic bottle closures, vinyl siding, packaging machinery, and electrical distribution systems for automobiles. **Positions advertised include:** Maintenance; Brick Mason; Mechanic; Machinist. **Corporate headquarters location:** Pittsburgh PA. **Other area locations:** Gaffney SC (Home Exteriors/Building Products); McBee SC (Southern Graphic Systems/Digital Services); Spartanburg SC (Alcoa Fujikura, Ltd/Telecommunications). **Other U.S. locations:** Nationwide. **International Locations:** Worldwide. **Subsidiaries include:** Alcoa Fujikura Ltd.; Howmet Castings; Integris Metals, Inc.; Ivex Packaging Corp. **Operations at this facility include:** The Mt. Holly Works in Goose Creek is a primary aluminum production facility and foundry producing billet, rolling slab, tee-pure/foundry, standard ingot-pure/foundry. **Listed on:** New York Stock Exchange. **Stock exchange symbol:** AA. **Chairman/President/CEO:** Alain J. P. Belda. **Annual sales/revenues:** $20.3 billion. **Number of employees worldwide:** 129,000.

CERAMTEC NORTH AMERICA
P.O. Box 89, Highway 14, Laurens SC 29360-0089. 864/682-3215. **Physical address:** One Technology Place, Laurens SC 29360-1669. **Fax:** 864/682-1140. **Contact:** Employment Manager. **E-mail address:** hr@ceramtec.com. **World Wide Web address:** http://www.ceramtech.com. **Description:** Manufactures ceramic products made out of alumina, zirconia, and titania. **Positions advertised include:** Field Sales Representative; Ceramics Engineer; Mechanical Engineer; Marketing Representative. **Corporate headquarters location:** This location. **Other locations:** New Lebanon NY. **Parent company:** CeramTec AG (Germany). **Operations at this facility include:** Laurens Operations – Ceramic Products; Corporate Offices.

HYDRO ALUMINUM
117 Blake Dairy Road, P.O. Box 627, Belton SC 29627. 864/338-8000. **Contact:** Human Resources. **World Wide Web address:** http://www.hydroaluminuma.com. **Description:** Engaged in aluminum extrusion operations. **Positions advertised include:** Manufacturing Manager; Draftsperson; Mechanical Engineer; Operations Manager. **Parent company:** Hydro Aluminum North America (Linthicum MD). **Operations at this facility include:** Belton Operations, advanced extrusion, fabrication, and finishing services using three extrusion presses. **Number of employees at this location:** 200.

NUCOR STEEL
300 Steel Mill Road, P.O. Box 525, Darlington SC 29540. 843/393-5841. **Fax:** 843/895-8708. **Contact:** Human Resources. **World Wide Web address:** http://www.nucor.com. **Description:** Nucor Steel manufactures carbon and alloy steel in bar, sheet, and structural forms, steel joist and joist girders, steel deck, cold finished steel, steel grinding balls, steel fasteners, metal building systems, and steel bearing products. **Corporate headquarters location:** Charlotte NC. **Other area locations:** Florence SC; Swanson SC. **Other U.S. locations:** AZ; NE; TX; UT. **Parent company:** Nucor Corporation is a manufacturer of steel products, with other divisions that include Vulcraft, one of the nation's largest producers of steel joists and joist girders; Nucor Cold Finish, which produces cold-finished steel bars used extensively for shafting and machined precision parts; Nucor Grinding Balls, which produces steel grinding balls for the mining industry; Nucor Fastener, a steel bolt-making facility; Nucor Bearing Products, Inc., which produces steel bearings and machined steel parts; and Nucor Building Systems, which produces metal buildings and components. **Operations at this facility include:** Production of carbon steel angles, bars, light structural, sheet, and special steel products.

OWEN STEEL COMPANY
727 Mauney Drive, P.O. Box 18, Columbia SC 29201. 803/251-7680. **Fax:** 803/251-7613. **Contact:** Deloris Walters, Human Resources. **E-mail address:** information@owensteel.com or deloris.walters@ownsteel.com. **World Wide Web address:**

http://www.owensteel.com. **Description:** Manufactures structural and reinforcing steel used in large-scale construction. Founded in 1936. **Positions advertised include:** Structural Steel Detailer; Draftsperson; Electrician; Structural Engineer. **Operations at this facility include:** Administration; Manufacturing; Sales. **Parent company:** ADF Group Inc. (Terrebonne, Quebec, Canada).

THE SHAW GROUP, INC.
dba B.F. SHAW, INC.
366 Old Airport Road, Laurens SC 29360. 864/682-4000. **Fax:** 864/683-4771. **Contact:** Human Resources. **World Wide Web address:** http://www.alloypipingproducts.com. **Description:** A union shop fabricator of piping components for both new construction and the maintenance of existing systems. **Positions advertised include:** Project Administrator; Draftsperson; Pipe Fitter; Welder. **Corporate headquarters location:** Baton Rouge LA. **Other area locations:** Greenville SC. **Other locations:** Worldwide. **Operations at this facility include:** Manufacturing. **Number of employees worldwide:** 20,000.

SPARTANBURG STEEL PRODUCTS INC.
1290 New Cut Road, P.O. Box 6428, Spartanburg SC 29304. 864/585-5211. **Fax;** 864/583-5641. **Contact:** Human Resources. **World Wide Web address:** http://www.ssprod.com. **E-mail address:** info@ssprod.com. **Description:** Manufactures a variety of steel products including automotive stampings, beverage containers, and beer kegs. **Positions advertised include:** Draftsperson; Electrical Engineer; Industrial Designer; Industrial Engineer; Mechanical Engineer. **Corporate headquarters location:** This location. **Parent company:** The Reserve Group (Akron OH). **Operations at this facility include:** Manufacturing; Research and Development; Sales.

FINANCIAL SERVICES

You can expect to find the following types of companies in this section:
Consumer Financing and Credit Agencies • Investment Specialists • Mortgage Bankers and Loan Brokers • Security and Commodity Brokers, Dealers, and Exchanges

North Carolina

AMERICAN GENERAL FINANCE
1724 Winkler Street, Wilkesboro NC 28697-2251. 336/838-5157. **Fax:** 336/838-7881. **Contact:** Human Resources. **World Wide Web address:** http://www.agfinance.com. **Description:** A consumer lending company with over 1,300 branches in 41 states. The company's subsidiaries are engaged in the consumer finance, credit card, and insurance businesses. Founded in 1920. **NOTE:** Please visit website to view job listings. **Positions advertised include:** Management Trainee; Customer Account Administrator; Customer Account Specialist. **Corporate headquarters location:** Evansville IN. **Other area locations:** Statewide. **Other U.S. locations:** Nationwide. **Parent company:** American General Corporation. **Number of employees nationwide:** 8,700.

SCOTT & STRINGFELLOW, INC.
2626 Glenwood Avenue, Raleigh NC 27608. 919/571-1893. **Toll-free phone:** 800/763-1893. **Contact:** Hiring Manager. **E-mail address:** resume@scottstringfellow.com. **World Wide Web address:** http://www.scottstringfellow.com. **Description:** A full-service regional brokerage and investment banking firm. Services of Scott & Stringfellow include investment advice and brokerage for individual and institutional clients, investment banking and securities underwriting for corporations and municipalities, and a wide array of other investment-related financial services including investment advisory services through its affiliate, Scott & Stringfellow Capital Management, Inc. Founded 1893. **NOTE:** Please visit website to search for jobs. **Corporate headquarters location:** Richmond VA. **Other area locations:** Statewide. **Other U.S. locations:** SC; VA. **Parent company:** BB&T Corporation. **Listed on:** New York Stock Exchange. **Stock exchange symbol:** BBT.

South Carolina

AMERICAN GENERAL FINANCE
412 Bells Highway, Walterboro SC 29488. 843/549-5536. **Fax:** 843/549-6543. **Contact:** Human Resources. **World Wide Web address:** http://www.agfinance.com. **Description:** A consumer lending company with over 1,300 branches nationwide engaged in consumer finance, credit card, and insurance. Founded in 1920. **NOTE:** Jobseekers should send resumes to the corporate headquarters location at: 601 NorthWest Second Street, Evansville IN 47701. **Positions advertised include:** Management Trainee; Customer Account Administrator; Customer

Account Specialist. **Corporate headquarters location:** Evansville IN. **Parent company:** American International Group, Inc. (New York NY).

HAWTHORNE CORPORATION
P.O. Box 61000, Charleston SC 29419. 843/797-8484. **Fax:** 843/797-5258. **Physical address:** 6543 Fair Street, Charleston SC 29419. **E-mail address:** Info@hawthornecorp.com. **Contact:** Human Resources. **World Wide Web address:** http://www.hawthornecorp.com. **Description:** A holding company whose subsidiaries are engaged in a wide variety of industries including aviation (operating airports); real estate operations that develop land for fixed base operations; and investor services. **Corporate headquarters location:** This location.

MERRILL LYNCH & CO., INC.
One Chamber of Commerce Drive, P.O. Box 5607, Hilton Head SC 29938. 843/785-9620. **Contact:** Human Resources. **World Wide Web address:** http:// www.ml.com. **Description:** One of the largest securities brokerage firms in the world, Merrill Lynch provides financial services in securities, financial planning, insurance, estate planning, mortgages, and related areas. The company also brokers commodity futures and options, is a major underwriter of new securities issues, and is a dealer in corporate and municipal securities. **Positions advertised include:** Financial Advisor; Underwriter; Investment Officer; Auditor; Cash Flow Director; Real Estate Team Leader; Account Executive; Credit Officer. **Corporate headquarters location:** New York NY. **Other locations:** Worldwide. **Listed on:** New York Stock Exchange. **Stock exchange symbol:** MER. **Number of employees worldwide:** 50,900.

SALOMON SMITH BARNEY
P.O. Box 2628, Spartanburg SC 29304. 864/585-7761. **Contact:** Fran Godshall, Human Resources. **World Wide Web address:** http://www.salomonsmithbarney.com. **Description:** An investment banking and securities broker. Salomon Smith Barney also provides related financial services including stocks, bonds, and money market accounts. **Parent company:** Citigroup.

SECURITY FINANCE CORPORATION
P.O. Box 811, Spartanburg SC 29304. 864/582-8193. **Contact:** Human Resources. **E-mail address:** careers@security-finance.com. **World Wide Web address:** http://www.securityfinancecorp.com. **Description:** A credit institution providing commercial and personal loans.

WASHINGTON MUTUAL HOME LOANS
1333 Main Street, Columbia SC 29201. 803/929-7900. **Contact:** Human Resources. **World Wide Web address:** http://www.wamuhomeloans.com. **Description:** A servicer of single-family residential mortgages and one of the nation's largest originators of home loans. **Positions advertised include:** Loan Specialist; Home Loan Manager; Support Specialist; Mortgage Underwriter. **Office hours:** Monday – Friday, 8:00 a.m. – 5:00 p.m. **Other area locations:** Florence SC; Greenville SC. **Parent company:** Washington Mutual, Inc.

FOOD AND BEVERAGES/AGRICULTURE

You can expect to find the following types of companies in this section:
Crop Services and Farm Supplies • Dairy Farms • Food Manufacturers/Processors and Agricultural Producers • Tobacco Products

North Carolina

CAROLINA TURKEYS
P.O. Box 589, Mount Olive NC 28365. 919/658-6743. **Physical address:** 1628 Garner Chapel Road, Mount Olive NC. **Toll-free phone:** 800/523-4559. **Fax:** 919/658-5865. **Contact:** Human Resources. **World Wide Web address:** http://www.carolinaturkey.com. **Description:** A turkey processing company. Carolina Turkeys processes more than 22 million birds annually. The company is a fully integrated operation that includes diagnostic labs, research and breeder farms, hatcheries, and feed mills. The company's line of turkey meats is distributed across the country to restaurants, delis, hospitals, schools, and retail markets. Products include Just Perfect Turkey Breasts, Premium Turkey Breasts, Classic and Legend Turkey Breasts, Deluxe and Deli Turkey Breasts, and Cured Deli Meats & Franks. Founded in 1986. **NOTE:** Second and third shifts are offered. **Special programs:** Internships; Training. **Office hours:** Monday - Friday, 8:00 a.m. - 6:00 p.m. **Corporate headquarters location:** This location. **Parent company:** Goldsboro Milling. **CEO:** C. Daniel Blackshear. **Number of employees at this location:** 2,150.

CASE FARMS, INC.
P.O. Box 308, Morganton NC 28680. 828/438-6900. **Physical address:** 121 Rand Street Morganton NC 28655-3925. **Fax:** 828/437-5205. **Contact:** Human Resources. **Description:** Processes chicken for sale to retailers and sells chicken parts to manufacturers of pet foods.

COCA-COLA BOTTLING COMPANY CONSOLIDATED
4100 Coca-Cola Plaza, Charlotte NC 28211-3481. 704/557-4000. **Fax:** 704/551-4646. **Contact:** Personnel. **World Wide Web address:** http://www.cokebottling.com. **Description:** A bottling company packaging Coca-Cola, Barq's, and Dr. Pepper. **NOTE:** Interested jobseekers should send a scannable resume. **Positions advertised include:** Forklift Operator; Supply Chain Network Analyst; Route Supervisor; Corporate Mail Center Assistant; Sales Unit Analyst; Bulk Merchandiser; Express Checker; Diesel Mechanic; Interactive Marketing Assistant. **Corporate headquarters location:** This location. **Other area locations:** Statewide. **Other U.S. locations:** Southeast U.S. **Parent company:** The Coca-Cola Company (Atlanta GA) is one of the world's largest marketers, distributors, and producers of bottled and canned products. Coca-Cola Enterprises, part of The Coca-Cola Company, is in the liquid nonalcoholic refreshment business, which includes traditional

carbonated soft drinks, still and sparkling waters, juices, isotonics, and teas. The company operates in 38 states, the District of Columbia, the U.S. Virgin Islands, the Islands of Tortola and Grand Cayman, and the Netherlands. Coca-Cola Enterprises franchise territories encompass a population of over 154 million people, representing 54 percent of the population of the United States. Coca-Cola Enterprises operates 268 facilities, approximately 24,000 vehicles, and over 860,000 vending machines, beverage dispensers, and coolers used to market, distribute, and produce the company's products. **Listed on:** NASDAQ. **Stock exchange symbol:** COKE. **CEO:** J. Frank Harrison. **Annual sales/revenues:** More than $100 million. **Number of employees nationwide:** 5,500.

CONAGRA SPECIALTY SNACKS
4851 Jones Sausage Road, Garner NC 27529. 919/772-1511. **Fax:** 919/779-9369. **Contact:** Personnel. **World Wide Web address:** http://www.conagra.com. **Description:** A producer and marketer of meat snacks. ConAgra's principal meat snack brands include Slim Jim, Penrose, Pemmican, and Smokey Mountain. The company also produces an extruded grain snack under the Andy Capp's brand name, and produces and sells packaged meats under the Jesse Jones brand name. **NOTE:** Mail resumes to corporate office location at One ConAgra Drive, Omaha NE 68102-5001. Please visit http://www.conagrafoods.com/careers to search for jobs and apply online. **Corporate headquarters location:** Omaha NE. **Parent company:** ConAgra Foods. **Listed on:** NASDAQ. **Stock exchange symbol:** CAG. **Number of employees worldwide:** 47,000.

FLOWERS BAKING COMPANY
P.O. Box 819, Jamestown NC 27282. 336/841-8840. **Physical address:** 801 West Main Street, Jamestown NC. **Contact:** Employment. **World Wide Web address:** http://www.flowersfoods.com. **Description:** Flowers Baking operates more than 20 bakeries, which produce a wide variety of products including bread, buns, rolls, and donuts for retail sale to food stores, restaurants, and institutions. **NOTE:** This location does not accept resumes, you must apply through a temporary employment service. **Corporate headquarters location:** Thomasville GA. **Parent company:** Flowers Foods. **Operations at this facility include:** This location of Flowers Baking Company produces sandwich bread and hot dog rolls. **Listed on:** New York Stock Exchange. **Stock exchange symbol:** FLO. **President/CEO:** George E. Deese.

GOLD KIST, INC.
484 Zimmerman Road, P.O. Box 3668, Sanford NC 27330. 919/774-7333. **Contact:** John Williams, Human Resources. **E-mail address:** nc.jobs@goldkist.com. **World Wide Web address:** http://www.goldkist.com. **Description:** A processing plant for poultry. Retail products are marketed under the Young 'n Tender label or under the customers' private labels and are sold primarily in Florida, Georgia, the Mid-Atlantic states, the Northeast, and the Midwest. The company also purchases and resells processed chicken, turkey, beef, pork,

seafood, dairy, and other food products. Customers include a retail chain in the Southeast, major fast-food companies, and many other retail, institutional, and restaurant accounts. **Positions advertised include:** Division Safety Coordinator; Broiler Field Representative; Unit Manager. **Corporate headquarters location:** Atlanta GA. **Other area locations:** Bear Creek NC; Siler City NC; Staley NC. **Subsidiaries include:** AgraTrade Financing; Luker Inc. **Number of employees nationwide:** 16,000.

LANCE, INC.
P.O. Box 32368, Charlotte NC 28232. 704/554-1421. **Physical address:** 8600 South Boulevard, Charlotte NC 28273. **Fax:** 704/556-5636. **Contact:** Ray Silinski, Human Resources. **E-mail address:** fresh@lance.com. **World Wide Web address:** http://www.lance.com. **Description:** Produces snack products under the Home-pak, Club-pak, Snack-Right, and Vista brand names. The company also operates Midwest Biscuit (Burlington IA) and Caronuts (Boykins VA). Founded in 1913. **Positions advertised include:** Records Retention Specialist. **Corporate headquarters location:** This location. **Other area locations:** Charlotte NC. **Other U.S. locations:** Burlington IA; Hyannis MA. **Listed on:** NASDAQ. **Stock exchange symbol:** LNCE.

MERCHANTS DISTRIBUTORS INC. (MDI)
P.O. Box 2148, Hickory NC 28603. 828/323-4100. **Physical address:** 5005 Alex Lee Boulevard, Hickory NC 28601. **Fax:** 828/323-4527. **Contact:** Human Resources. **World Wide Web address:** http://www.merchantsdistributors.com. **Description:** A wholesaler of groceries. **NOTE:** Please visit website to register, search for jobs, and apply online. **Special programs:** Internships. **Corporate headquarters location:** This location. **Other U.S. locations:** SC; GA; TN; VA; WV; KY. **Operations at this facility include:** Administration; Sales. **Listed on:** Privately held. **Number of employees at this location:** 1,260.

PERDUE FARMS, INC.
P.O. Box 1357, Rockingham NC 28345. 910/997-8600. **Contact:** Human Resources. **World Wide Web address:** http://www.perdue.com. **Description:** Perdue Farms is one of the largest suppliers of fresh poultry products in the United States. The company's products are sold in supermarkets, small groceries, and butcher shops from Maine to Georgia and as far west as Chicago. The company is a fully integrated operation, from breeding and hatching to delivering packaged goods to market. **NOTE:** Please visit website to search for jobs and apply online. **Corporate headquarters location:** Salisbury MD. **Other U.S. locations:** Nationwide. **Listed on:** Privately held. **Number of employees nationwide:** 20,000.

PERDUE FARMS, INC.
P.O. Box 460, Lewiston NC 27849. 252/348-4200. **Contact:** Human Resources. **World Wide Web address:** http://www.perdue.com. **Description:** Perdue Farms is one of the largest suppliers of fresh poultry products in the United States. The company's products are sold

in supermarkets, small groceries, and butcher shops from Maine to Georgia and as far west as Chicago. The company is a fully integrated operation, from breeding and hatching to delivering packaged goods to market. **NOTE:** Please visit website to search for jobs and apply online. **Corporate headquarters location:** Salisbury MD. **Other U.S. locations:** Nationwide. **Listed on:** Privately held. **Number of employees nationwide:** 20,000.

R.J. REYNOLDS TOBACCO HOLDINGS, INC.

401 North Main Street, Winston-Salem NC 27101. 336/741-5500. **Fax:** 336/741-4238. **Contact:** Human Resources. **World Wide Web address:** http://www.rjrt.com. **Description:** A holding company. **Office hours:** Monday – Friday, 8:00 a.m. – 4:30 p.m. **Corporate headquarters location:** This location. **Subsidiaries include:** R.J. Reynolds Tobacco Company manufactures tobacco products, including the Camel, Winston, Salem, and Doral brands. Santa Fe Natural Tobacco Company, Inc. produces American Spirit brand cigarettes. **Listed on:** New York Stock Exchange. **Stock exchange symbol:** RJR.

SMITHFIELD PACKING COMPANY, INC.

2602 West Vernon Avenue, Kinston NC 28504. 252/522-4777. **Contact:** Human Resources. **E-mail address:** humanresources@smithfieldpacking.com. **World Wide Web address:** http://www.smithfield.com. **Description:** Processes and sells ham under the brand name Smithfield Hams. The company's products are distributed nationwide. Founded 1936. **Corporate headquarters location:** Smithfield VA. **Other area locations:** Benson NC; Tarheel NC; Wilson NC. **Other U.S. locations:** VA; FL. **Parent company:** Smithfield Foods. **Listed on:** New York Stock Exchange. **Stock exchange symbol:** SFD. **Number of employees nationwide:** 9,330.

STANDARD COMMERCIAL CORPORATION

2201 Miller Road, P.O. Box 450, Wilson NC 27894-0450. 252/291-5507. **Fax:** 252/237-0018. **Contact:** Human Resources Director. **World Wide Web address:** http://www.sccgroup.com. **Description:** Buys and processes a variety of tobaccos for sale to domestic and international makers of cigarettes, cigars, and pipe tobaccos in 85 countries. Standard Commercial Corporation also purchases, processes, and markets wool to international customers. The company operates three tobacco processing plants in the United States and 17 other plants throughout the world; and eight wool manufacturing and storage plants in eight countries. The company is also involved in importing-exporting in Eastern Europe and operates a building supply company. **Corporate headquarters location:** This location. **Other area locations:** King NC. **International locations:** Worldwide. **Listed on:** New York Stock Exchange. **Stock exchange symbol:** STW. **President/CEO:** Robert E. Harrison.

TYSON FOODS INC.

P.O. Box 88, Wilkesboro NC 28697. 336/838-2171. **Contact:** Division Personnel Manager. **World Wide Web address:**

http://www.tysonfoodsinc.com. **Description:** Tyson Foods Inc. is one of the world's largest fully-integrated producers, processors, and marketers of poultry-based food products. **NOTE:** The hiring center is located at 704 Factory Street, Wilkesboro NC 28697. **Corporate headquarters location:** Springdale AR. **International locations:** Worldwide. **Operations at this facility include:** Poultry processing and packaging. **Listed on:** New York Stock Exchange. **Stock exchange symbol:** TSN.

South Carolina

GOLD KIST, INC.
2050 Highway 15 South, Sumter SC 29150-8799. 803/481-8555. **Contact:** Human Resources. **E-mail address:** jobs@goldkist.com. **World Wide Web address:** http://www.goldkist.com. **Description:** Processes and markets whole and cut chicken throughout the Northeast and the Midwest operating nine integrated poultry divisions in Alabama, Georgia, Florida, North Carolina and South Carolina. Founded in 1933. **NOTE:** Resumes should be sent to the company's headquarters address: Gold Kist Inc., Corporate Employment, P.O. Box 2210, Atlanta GA 30301. **Positions advertised include:** Breeder Field Representative; Yield Processing Supervisor. **Number of employees nationwide:** 16,000.

LOUIS RICH COMPANY
3704 Louis Rich Drive, Newberry SC 29108. 803/276-5015. **Fax:** 803/321-7254. **Contact:** Natalie Marzan, Human Resources Manager. **World Wide Web address:** http://www.louisrich.com. **Description:** A poultry processor. **Positions advertised include:** Production Supervisor; Maintenance Technician; Sanitation Technician; Production Manager; Support Mechanic; Project Engineer. **Parent company:** Kraft Foods North America (Northfield IL).

NESTLE USA
P.O. Box 1419, Gaffney SC 29342. 864/487-7111. **Physical address:** 2132 Old Georgia Highway, Gaffney SC 29340. **Contact:** Human Resources. **World Wide Web address:** http://www.nestleusa.com. **Description:** Manufactures prepared frozen food products. **Positions advertised include:** Retail Sales Representative; Pediatric Nutrition Representative. **Parent company:** Nestle S.A. (Vevey, Switzerland). **Number of employees worldwide:** 16,000.

U.S. FOODSERVICE
P.O. Box 1328, Greenville SC 29602. 864/676-8600. **Contact:** Personnel. **World Wide Web address:** http://www.usfoodservice.com. **Description:** A leading foodservice distributor with over 100 distribution centers nationwide. **NOTE:** Employment applications and resumes should be directed to the Human Resources office at the company's headquarters, attention of: Jodie Manning. Fax: 410/910-2225. E-mail: jmanning@usfood.com. **Positions advertised include:** Dispatcher; Dispatcher Trainee. **Corporate headquarters location:** Columbia MD. **Other locations:** Nationwide.

GOVERNMENT

You can expect to find the following types of companies in this section:
Courts • Executive, Legislative, and General Government • Public Agencies (Firefighters, Military, Police) • United States Postal Service

North Carolina

CARY, TOWN OF
P.O. Box 8005, Cary NC 27512-8005. 919/469-4070. **Physical address:** 100 Charlie Gaddy Lane, Cary NC 27511. **Fax:** 919/319-4567. **Recorded jobline:** 919/319-4500x283. **Contact:** Valiria Willis, Director of Human Resources. **E-mail address:** valiria.willis@ci.cary.nc.us. **World Wide Web address:** http://www.townofcary.org. **Description:** Municipal government for one of the 10 largest cities in North Carolina. **NOTE:** Please visit website to view job listings and download an application form. You must complete an application in order to be considered for employment. Human Resources direct contact phone numbers are 919/469-4070 and 919/469-4072. Do not fax resumes. **Positions advertised include:** Police Project Manager; Operations, Construction and Fleet Management; Wastewater System Worker; Solid Waste Collector; Special Events Team Member; Utility Maintenance Worker; Engineer; Arts Director; Center Aide; Cultural Arts Teaching Assistant; Park Attendant; Recreation Program Instructor. **Number of employees at this location:** 750.

CHARLOTTE, CITY OF
600 East Fourth Street, Charlotte NC 28202. 704/336-2285. **Fax:** 704/336-3236. **Recorded jobline:** 704/336-3968. **Contact:** City Human Resources Department. **E-mail address:** vacancyresumes@ci.charlotte.nc.us. **World Wide Web address:** http://www.charmeck.nc.us. **Description:** Administrative offices for the city of Charlotte and the Mecklenburg County Government. **Positions advertised include:** Administrative Officer; Animal Control Bureau Manager; Assistant Corporate Communications Director; Print Production Coordinator; Procurement Officer; Wellness Program Administrator; Assistant Project Manager; Engineering Project Manager; Planning/Design Engineer; Watershed Manager; Director of Planning; Transportation Planner; Management Analyst; Accounting Clerk; Office Assistant; Airport Law Enforcement Officer; Police Officer; Electrician; Street Maintenance Crew Member. **Corporate headquarters location:** This location. **Operations at this facility include:** Administration; Service. **Number of employees at this location:** 5,700.

DURHAM POLICE DEPARTMENT
505 West Chapel Hill Street, Durham NC 27713. 919/560-4569. **Contact:** Officer T. Hodge, Recruiting. **E-mail address:** thodge@ci.durham.nc.us. **World Wide Web address:**

http://www.durhampolice.com. **Description:** Provides law enforcement services for the city of Durham. **NOTE:** For information on civilian jobs with the Durham City Police Department, please visit the Durham City employment page at http://www.ci.durham.nc.us/employment.

NORTH CAROLINA DEPARTMENT OF AGRICULTURE & CONSUMER SERVICES
P.O. Box 27647, Raleigh NC 27611. 919/733-2243. **Physical address:** 2 West Edenton Street, Agriculture Building, Room 302, Raleigh NC 27601. **Fax:** 919/715-4295. **Contact:** Rosilyn McNair, Recruiting Specialist. **E-mail address:** rosilyn.mcnair@ncmail.net. **World Wide Web address:** http://www.agr.state.nc.us. **Description:** Oversees the agricultural industries of North Carolina. **Positions advertised include:** Internal Marketing Specialist; Veterinary Laboratory Director; Assistant to Farmers Market Manager; Administrative Secretary; Processing Assistant; Standards Inspector; Chemistry Technician; Processing Assistant; Chemistry Manager.

NORTH CAROLINA DEPARTMENT OF CORRECTION
4202 Mail Service Center, Raleigh NC 27699-4202. 919/716-3700. **Fax:** 919/716-3955. **World Wide Web address:** http://www.doc.state.nc.us. **Description:** Oversees the maintenance and hiring of North Carolina's prisons. **NOTE:** Please visit website for a listing of jobs statewide.

NORTH CAROLINA DEPARTMENT OF TRANSPORTATION
1500 Mail Service Center, Raleigh NC 27699-1500. 919/733-2520. **Physical address:** 1 South Wilmington Street, Raleigh NC 27611. **Toll-free phone:** 877/DOT-4YOU. **Fax:** 919/733-9150. **World Wide Web address:** http://www.ncdot.org. **Description:** Operates and maintains a transportation system that includes aviation, ferry, rail, highway, and public transportation systems. **NOTE:** Please visit website to view job listings. Contact Diane Strickland with any questions regarding employment, at 919/715-9836 Ext. 205.

RALEIGH, CITY OF
222 West Hargett Street, Room 101, P.O. Box 590, Raleigh NC 27602. 919/890-3315. **Fax:** 919/890-3845. **Recorded jobline:** 919/890-3305. **Contact:** Personnel Recruitment. **World Wide Web address:** http://www.raleigh-nc.org. **Description:** Provides municipal services including law enforcement, fire services, building code enforcement, water/sewer services, transportation, planning, engineering, and administration services for the city of Raleigh. **NOTE:** Entry-level positions, part-time jobs, and second and third shifts are offered. Please visit website to search for jobs and to download an application form. Please be sure to include the job number you're your application. Volunteer positions are also available. **Positions advertised include: Police** Officer; Assistant Planning Director; Systems Analyst; Administrative Assistant; Accounts Receivable Specialist; Staff Support Specialist; Code Enforcement Inspector; Site Review Specialist; Computer Operator; Traffic Signs and Marketing Technician; Senior Survey Technician; Fire Equipment Mechanic; Treatment Plant Operator;

Equipment Operator; Laborer; Utility Service Field Technician; Parks and Recreation Temporary Workers. **Special programs:** Training; Summer Jobs. **Office hours:** Monday – Friday, 8:00 a.m. – 5:15 p.m. **Operations at this facility include:** Administration. **Number of employees at this location:** 2,600.

U.S. DEPARTMENT OF AGRICULTURE FOREST SERVICE SOUTHERN RESEARCH STATION
3041 Cornwallis Road, P.O. Box 12254, Research Triangle Park NC 27709. 919/549-4000. **Fax:** 919/549-4047. **Contact:** Human Resources. **E-mail address:** fsjobs@fs.fed.us. **World Wide Web address:** http://www.srs.fs.usda.gov. **Description:** Researches a variety of topics including forest health, global climate change, and soils. **NOTE:** All hiring is conducted through the Asheville location. Interested jobseekers should direct resumes to Human Resources, U.S. Department of Agriculture, Forest Service, Southern Research Station, 200 Weaver Boulevard, Asheville NC 28804. **Other U.S. locations:** Nationwide.

U.S. ENVIRONMENTAL PROTECTION AGENCY (EPA)
109 T.W. Alexander Drive, Research Triangle Park NC 27711. 919/541-2201. **Fax:** 919/541-2186. **Recorded jobline:** 800/433-9633. **Contact:** Human Resources Director. **World Wide Web address:** http://www.epa.gov/rtp. **Description:** The EPA is dedicated to improving and preserving the quality of the environment, both nationally and globally, and protecting human health and the productivity of natural resources. The agency is committed to ensuring that federal environmental laws are implemented and enforced effectively; U.S. policy, both foreign and domestic, fosters the integration of economic development and environmental protection so that economic growth can be sustained over the long term; and public and private decisions affecting energy, transportation, agriculture, industry, international trade, and natural resources fully integrate considerations of environmental quality. **NOTE:** Please visit http://www.epa.gov/ezhire to search for jobs and apply online. Resumes are not accepted when mailed to the office. **Positions advertised include:** Financial Technician; Epidemiologist. **Corporate headquarters location:** Washington DC. **Other U.S. locations:** Nationwide. **Operations at this facility include:** This location of the EPA is a research and development laboratory. **Number of employees nationwide:** 18,000.

WINSTON-SALEM, CITY OF
101 North Main Street, Suite 53, Winston-Salem NC 27101. 336/747-6800. **Fax:** 336/748-3053. **Recorded jobline:** 336/631-6496. **Contact:** Human Resources. **World Wide Web address:** http://www.cityofws.org. **Description:** Responsible for hiring town employees for the city of Winston-Salem. **NOTE:** Please visit website to view job listings and download application form. **Positions advertised include:** Senior Utilities Plant Mechanic; Assistant Recreation Center Supervisor; Associate Engineering Technician; Casual Laborer; Custodian; Police Officer; Recreation Center Supervisor; Senior Crew Coordinator; Trades Helper; Utilities Plant Operator; Vehicle Operator.

South Carolina

CHARLESTON COUNTY GOVERNMENT
Lonnie Hamilton III Public Services Building, 4045 Bridge View Drive, North Charleston SC 29405-7464. 843/958-4700. **Fax:** 843/958-4720. **Recorded jobline:** 843/958-4719. **Contact:** Joyce Moseley, Charleston County Human Resources. **E-mail address:** job@charlestoncounty.org. **World Wide Web address:** http://www.charlestoncounty.org. **Description:** Provides a broad range of services including public safety (law enforcement, emergency medical services, emergency preparedness, detention facilities, and fire protection); engineering services; economic development; street and drainage maintenance; waste disposal; recycling; planning and zoning administration; grants administration; criminal prosecution services; criminal, civil, probate, and family court administration; document recording services; tax assessment; collection and dispersal; alcohol and other drug abuse services; library services; veteran's assistance; and voter registration. **Positions advertised include:** Paramedic (pool); Human Resources Generalist; County Service Representative; Civil Structural Engineer; Equipment Operator; Emergency Service Dispatcher. **Number of employees:** 2,000.

DISABILITIES BOARD OF CHARLESTON COUNTY
995 Morrison Drive, P.O. Box 22708, Charleston SC 29413-2708. 843/805-5800. **Fax:** 843/805-5805. **Contact:** Human Resources. **World Wide Web address:** http://www.dsncc.com. **Description:** Provides a variety of services for people with disabilities including early intervention, residential living assistance, and supportive employment programs. **Positions advertised include:** Early Interventionist; Community Training Home Coordinator; Rehabilitative Support Specialist; Job Coach. **Executive Director:** Karolyn Elliot.

SOUTH CAROLINA DEPARTMENT OF AGRICULTURE
Wade Hampton Building, Fifth Floor, P.O. Box 11280, Columbia SC 29211-1280. 803/734-2199. **Contact:** Clarissa Adams, Administrative and Human Resources Manager. **World Wide Web address:** http://www.state.sc.us/scda. **Description:** This location of the Department of Agriculture provides services that include working with farmers to market their produce and testing products (produce and gasoline) in a laboratory. **NOTE:** Human Resources phone: 803/734-2196.

U.S. POSTAL SERVICE
1900B North Main Street, Anderson SC 29621. 864/226-1595. **Contact:** Human Resources. **World Wide Web address:** http://www.usps.com. **Description:** One of the 38,000 locations of the U.S. postal service. **NOTE:** For all positions at the post office, applicants must apply in person to South Carolina Employment Security Commission, 309 West Whitner Street, Anderson SC 29621. 864/226-6273. **Number of employees nationwide:** 800,000.

HEALTH CARE SERVICES, EQUIPMENT, AND PRODUCTS

You can expect to find the following types of companies in this section:
Dental Labs and Equipment • Home Health Care Agencies • Hospitals and Medical Centers • Medical Equipment Manufacturers and Wholesalers • Offices and Clinics of Health Practitioners • Residential Treatment Centers/Nursing Homes • Veterinary Services

North Carolina

ALPHA OMEGA HEALTH INC.
6036 Six Forks Road, Raleigh NC 27609. 919/844-1008. **Toll-free phone:** 800/525-5293. **Fax:** 919/844-0042. **Contact:** Personnel. **E-mail address:** twadford@aohealth.com. **World Wide Web address:** http://www.aohealth.com. **Description:** A home health care agency that also offers nurse-staffing services. Founded 1989. **NOTE:** Please visit website to search for jobs and to access online application form. **Positions advertised include:** Residential Habitation Technician; Qualified Professional. **Office hours:** Monday – Friday, 8:00 a.m. – 5:00 p.m. **Corporate headquarters location:** This location. **Other area locations:** Boone NC; Burnsville NC; Chapel Hill NC; Greenville NC; Lenoir NC; Smithfield NC; Wilmington NC; Winston-Salem NC.

CENTRAL PRISON HOSPITAL
1300 Western Boulevard, Raleigh NC 27606. 919/733-0800x411. **Contact:** Personnel. **World Wide Web address:** http://www.doc.state.nc.us/DOP/prisons/Central.htm. **Description:** A prison hospital. **NOTE:** Please visit website to search for jobs and download application form. You must complete an application to be considered for employment. Specific contact information is available with listed jobs. **Positions advertised include:** Dentist; RN; LPN; Staff Psychologist; Correctional Officer. **Operations at this facility include:** Service. **Number of employees at this location:** 500.

MOSES CONE HEALTH SYSTEM
1200 North Elm Street, Greensboro NC 27401-1020. 336/832-7400. **Toll-free phone:** 800/476-6737. **Fax:** 336/832-2999. **Contact:** Corporate Recruitment. **E-mail address:** recruitment@mosescone.com. **World Wide Web address:** http://www.mosescone.com. **Description:** A nonprofit hospital system operating the Moses H. Cone Memorial Hospital (547 beds), the Women's Hospital of Greensboro (130 beds), and Wesley Long Community Hospital. Moses Cone Memorial Hospital is a Level II trauma center as well as a teaching hospital and referral center. The hospital operates five centers specializing in neuroscience, cardiology, cancer, rehabilitation, and trauma. **NOTE:** Please visit website to search for jobs and apply online. **Positions advertised include:** Certified Medical Assistant; Clinical Nutritionist; CRNA; Development Coordinator; LPN; Physical Therapist Assistant; Physician

Practice Administrator; RN. **Office hours:** Monday - Friday, 8:30 a.m. - 5:00 p.m. **Corporate headquarters location:** This location. **Operations at this facility include:** Administration. **Number of employees at this location:** 6,800.

DAVIS REGIONAL MEDICAL CENTER
P.O. Box 1823, Statesville NC 28687. 704/873-0281. **Physical address:** 218 Old Marksville Road, Statesville NC 28625. **Fax:** 704/838-7114. **Recorded jobline:** 704/838-7500. **Contact:** Alison Kay, Human Resources. **E-mail address:** alison.kay@drmc.hma-corp.com. **World Wide Web address:** http://www.davisregional.com. **Description:** A 149-bed, state-of-the-art, acute care medical center. **NOTE:** Please visit website to search for jobs. Human Resources phone is 704/838-7110. Applications are kept on file for one year. **Positions advertised include:** Licensed Physical Therapy Assistant; Medical Technologist; MRI Technologist; RN – Various Departments; Telemetry Technician. **Special programs:** Internships. **Corporate headquarters location:** This location. **Parent company:** Health Trust, Inc. **Operations at this facility include:** Administration; Service. **Number of employees at this location:** 540.

DURHAM REGIONAL HOSPITAL
3643 North Roxboro Road, Durham NC 27704. 919/470-4000. **Toll-free phone:** 888/275-3853. **Fax:** 919/470-7376. **Recorded jobline:** 919/470-JOBS; 800/233-3313. **Contact:** Human Resources. **World Wide Web address:** http://www.durhamregional.org. **Description:** A full-service hospital. **Positions advertised include:** Clerk; Health Unit Coordinator; Chief Operating Officer; Clinical Speech Pathologist; Dietitian Clinician; Director of Radiology; Financial Management Analyst; Laboratory Supervisor; Manager CSR; Occupational Therapist; Physical Therapist; Senior Physicians Assistant; Security Captain; Clinical Nurse – Various Departments; Nurse Practitioner; Nursing Care Assistant; Food Services Supervisor; Patient Transporter; Computer Operator; Interventional Technologist; Pharmacy Technician; Radiologic Technician; Respiratory Care Practitioner; Surgical Technician. **Parent company:** Duke University Health System.

GOOD HOPE HOSPITAL
410 Denim Drive, Erwin NC 28339. 910/897-6151 Ext. 152. **Fax:** 910/897-4050. **Contact:** Michelle Baker, Human Resources. **E-mail address:** mbaker@goodhopehospital.org. **World Wide Web address:** http://www.goodhopehospital.org. **Description:** A 72-bed, nonprofit, acute care, community hospital. Affiliated physicians' offices are located in three surrounding communities. **NOTE:** Please visit website to search for jobs and to complete a pre-employment application. **Positions advertised include:** House Coordinator; RN – Various Departments; Radiologic Technologist; Surgical Services Manager; Pharmacist; Pharmacy Technician; Physical Therapist; MT/MLT; Echo Cardiographer Technician; Respiratory Therapist; Patient Financial Counselor. **Office hours:** Monday - Friday, 8:00 a.m. - 4:30 p.m. **Corporate headquarters**

location: This location. **Parent company:** Quorum Health Resources. **Number of employees at this location:** 300.

GRACE HOSPITAL
2201 South Sterling Street, Morganton NC 28655. 828/580-5000. **Fax:** 828/580-5609. **Contact:** Human Resources. **World Wide Web address:** http://www.blueridgehealth.org/our_facilities/grace_hospital.html. **Description:** A nonprofit, full-service hospital. **NOTE:** Second and third shifts are offered. Please visit website to search for jobs and download application form. **Positions advertised include:** Admitting Nurse; Aerobic/Aquatic/Pilates Instructor; Catering Supervisor; CNA; RN – Various Departments; Chief Radiologic Technologist; Coder; Director of Maternal Child Health Services; Exercise Physiologist; Food Service Assistant; Front Desk Clerk; Housekeeper; LPN; Materials Manager; Psychiatric Technician; Social Worker; Secretary. **Special programs:** Internships; Apprenticeships; Summer Jobs. **Parent company:** BlueRidge Health Care System. **Number of employees at this location:** 800.

MEDCATH INC.
10720 Sikes Place, Suite 300, Charlotte NC 28277. 704/708-6610. **Contact:** Human Resources. **World Wide Web address:** http://www.medcath.com. **Description:** Develops and manages cardiovascular care hospitals and catheterization laboratories. **Positions advertised include:** Senior Coding Consultant. **Corporate headquarters location:** This location. **Other area locations:** Greensboro NC; Raleigh NC; Wilmington NC. **Other U.S. locations:** Nationwide. **Listed on:** NASDAQ. **Stock exchange symbol:** MDTH.

MISSION ST. JOSEPH'S HOSPITAL
509 Biltmore Avenue, Ashville NC 28801. 828/213-1111. **Recorded jobline:** 828/213-4400. **Contact:** Human Resources. **World Wide Web address:** http://www.msj.org. **Description:** A hospital licensed for over 800 beds and bassinets. The hospital has been ranked as a top 50 hospital for heart and heart surgery services, and a top 100 for breast cancer research, among other awards. **NOTE:** Contact Human Resources directly at 828/213-5600. Please visit website to search or jobs and apply online. To apply for clerical temp-to-hire positions, please go through Kelly Services. Volunteer positions are also available. Applications will remain active for 90 days. **Positions advertised include:** Nuclear Medicine Technologist; Lead Physicist; Clinical Trials Manager; Pharmacy Manager; Respiratory Therapist. **Corporate headquarters location:** This location. **Number of employees at this location:** 5,600.

NORTHERN HOSPITAL
P.O. Box 1101, Mount Airy NC 27030. 336/719-7000. **Physical address:** 830 Rockford Street, Suite 6, Mount Airy NC 27030. **Contact:** Human Resources. **World Wide Web address:** http://www.northernhospital.com. **Description:** A hospital that offers home health care services in addition to in-hospital services. **Positions**

advertised include: Speech Therapist; Occupational Therapist; PRN; CRNA; RN – Home Care; RN – Various Departments; Coding Specialist; Security Officer; Spanish Interpreter; Project Manager; Patient Registration Representative; Mechanic – HVAC; Infection Control/Quality Review Practitioner. **Corporate headquarters location:** This location. **Other U.S. locations:** Cana VA. **Listed on:** Privately held. **Number of employees at this location:** 200.

ONSLOW MEMORIAL HOSPITAL
317 Western Boulevard, Jacksonville NC 28541. 910/577-2345. **Recorded jobline:** 910/577-2250. **Contact:** Human Resources. **E-mail address:** employment@onslowmemorial.org. **World Wide Web address:** http://www.onslowmemorial.org. **Description:** A hospital equipped with 162 beds, treating more than 37,000 patients every year. **Positions advertised include:** Occupational Therapist; Transcriptionist Coordinator; Radiologic Technician; RN – Various Departments; PC Technician; Sterile Processing and Distribution Technician; Speech/Language Pathologist; MRI Technician; Lab Assistant. **Special programs:** Internships. **Office hours:** Monday – Friday, 8:00 a.m. – 4:30 p.m. **Number of employees at this location:** 1000.

MARGARET R. PARDEE MEMORIAL HOSPITAL
800 North Justice Street, Hendersonville NC 28791. 828/696-1000. **Fax:** 828/696-1208. **Recorded jobline:** 828/696-4700. **Contact:** Jeanette Moody, Human Resources. **E-mail address:** human.resources@pardeehospital.org. **World Wide Web address:** http://www.pardeehospital.org. **Description:** A 262-bed, acute care hospital. **NOTE:** Contact Human Resources directly at 828/696-4209. Please visit website to view job listings, apply online, or download application. **Positions advertised include:** Director of Rehab Services; ER Registration Clerk; Switchboard Relief; File Room Receptionist; RN – Various Departments; CNA – Various Departments; Phlebotomist; Clinical Dietician; Certified Surgical Technician; Pharmacist; Radiation Therapist; Registered Respiratory Therapist; Trayline Supervisor; Nutrition Assistant; Supply Technician.

PITT COUNTY MEMORIAL HOSPITAL
UNIVERSITY HEALTH SYSTEMS OF EASTERN CAROLINA
2100 Statonsburg Road, P.O. Box 6028, Greenville NC 27835-6028. 252/816-4556. **Toll-free phone:** 800/346-4307. **Fax:** 252/847-8225. **Contact:** Manager of Employment. **World Wide Web address:** http://www.uhseast.com. **Description:** A 725-bed, Level I, regional medical center and constituent of the University Health Systems of Eastern Carolina. This location also serves as the teaching facility for the East Carolina University School of Medicine, Nursing, and Allied Health. **NOTE:** Human Resources phone is 252/847-4130. Please visit website to view job listings and apply online. **Positions advertised include:** RN – Various Departments; Accounting Clerk; Administrative Secretary; Assistant Patient Counselor; Community Resource Center Supervisor; Coordinator – Medical Staff; Credentialing Specialist; File Clerk; Medical Transcriptionist; Patient Access Representative; Vehicle Technician;

Groundskeeper; Administrator – Cost Report; Manager – HIMS; Patient Care Coordinator; Central Service Technician; Electrician; Advanced Level Practitioner; Annual Fund Coordinator; Assistant Nursing Manager; Call Center Nurse Consultant; Clinical Analyst; Child Life Specialist; Contract Behavioral Health Triage; Exercise Physiologist; Home Health Nurse; Neonatal Nurse Practitioner; Pharmacist; Physical Therapist; Area Technician; Operating Room Assistant; Cytotechnologist; LPN; Paramedic. **Number of employees at this location:** 4,000.

PREMIER, INC.
2320 Cascade Pointe Boulevard, Charlotte NC 28208. 704/357-0022. **Contact:** Human Resources. **World Wide Web address:** http://www.premierinc.com. **Description:** Operates hospitals and provides healthcare. **Positions advertised include:** Clinical Analyst; Manager – Environmentally Preferred Purchasing; Senior Director – Alternate Site HealthCare; Vice President – Clinical Programs; Contract Recruiter; Application Quality Engineer; Clinical Advisor; Director – Analytics & Research; ETL Development and Applications Engineer; Perspective Analyst; Product Manager; Senior Unix Systems Administrator. **Other U.S. locations:** San Diego CA; Chicago IL; Washington D.C.

RANDOLPH HOSPITAL
P.O. Box 1048, Asheboro NC 27204-1048. 336/625-5151. **Physical address:** 364 White Oaks Street, Asheboro NC 27203. **Fax:** 336/633-7749. **Recorded jobline:** 336/629-8842. **Contact:** Employee Relations and Staffing. **E-mail address:** dvernon@randolphhospital.org. **World Wide Web address:** http://www.randolphhospital.org. **Description:** A 145-bed general hospital. **NOTE:** Please visit website to view job listings and to download an application form. **Positions advertised include:** Registered Respiratory Therapist; Senior Director – Clinical Services; Diabetic Educator; Clinical Educator; ED Patient Representative; ED Technician; Dining Commons Manager; Food Server; Home Health Aide; Occupational Therapist; Physical Therapist; Rehab Coordinator; Unit Secretary; OB Technician; RN – Various Departments. **Number of employees at this location:** 560.

U.S. DEPARTMENT OF VETERANS AFFAIRS
DURHAM VETERANS ADMINISTRATION MEDICAL CENTER
508 Fulton Street, Durham NC 27705. 919/286-0411. **Fax:** 919/286-6825. **Contact:** Human Resources. **World Wide Web address:** http://www.va.gov. **Description:** A medical center operated by the U.S. Department of Veterans Affairs. From 54 hospitals in 1930, the VA health care system has grown to include 171 medical centers; more than 364 outpatient, community, and outreach clinics; 130 nursing home care units; and 37 domiciliary residences. The VA operates at least one medical center in each of the 48 contiguous states, Puerto Rico, and the District of Columbia. With approximately 76,000 medical center beds, the VA treats nearly one million patients in VA hospitals, 75,000 in nursing home care units, and 25,000 in domiciliary residences. The VA's outpatient clinics register approximately 24 million visits per year. **NOTE:**

Please visit http://www.va.gov/jobs to search for jobs. **Corporate headquarters location:** Washington DC. **Other U.S. locations:** Nationwide.

JOHN UMSTEAD HOSPITAL
1003 12th Street, Butner NC 27509. 919/575-7943. **Fax:** 919/575-7550. **Recorded jobline:** 919/575-7680. **Contact:** Recruitment Specialist. **Description:** A psychiatric hospital providing mental health treatment and psycho-educational rehabilitation. The hospital also operates the Butner Adolescent Treatment Center, which is composed of BATC, a locked residential facility, and Oakview Residential Treatment Program, a nonsecure apartment facility. Each of these facilities can accommodate 12 male residents ages 13 to 17. **NOTE:** Please visit http://www.dhhs.state.nc.us to search for jobs and apply online. **Positions advertised include:** Health Care Technician; LPN; RN; Clinical Pharmacist; Clinical Social Worker; Cook; Food Service Assistant; Internal Escort; Housekeeper; Occupational Therapist; Painter; Physician; Quality Assurance Specialist; Substance Abuse Counselor; Teacher. **Office hours:** Monday - Friday, 8:00 a.m. - 5:00 p.m. **Number of employees at this location:** 1,400.

WAKE FOREST UNIVERSITY-BAPTIST MEDICAL CENTER
Medical Center Boulevard, Winston-Salem NC 27157. 336/716-3367. **Toll-free phone:** 800/323-9777. **Fax:** 336/716-5656. **Contact:** Human Resources. **E-mail address:** erecruit@wfubmc.edu. **World Wide Web address:** http://www.wfubmc.edu. **Description:** One of the country's leading hospitals, offering a wide variety of services. The medical center has 20 subsidiary or affiliate hospitals and 87 satellite clinics throughout the surrounding areas. **NOTE:** Please visit website to view job listings and apply online. For nursing positions, please call 336/716-3339, and email to nrsrecrt@wfubmc.edu. **Positions advertised include:** Assistant Unit Manager; Clinical Documentation Consultant; Manager – Abdominal Transplant Program; Neonatal Nurse Practitioner; OR Service Coordinator; Palliative Care Coordinator; Quality Improvement Coordinator; Staff Nurse – Various Departments; CRNA – Various Departments; Dental Assistant; Clinical Nutritionist; Histologic Technician; MRI Technologist; Physical Therapist; Respiratory Therapist; Pharmacist; Database Specialist; Community Health Program Coordinator; Assistant Manager – Best Health; Social Worker; Assistant Teacher; Dietetic Clerk; Housekeeping Technician; Carpenter; Electrician. **Corporate headquarters location:** This location. **Number of employees at this location:** 5,500.

THE WOMEN'S HOSPITAL OF GREENSBORO
801 Green Valley Road, Greensboro NC 27408. 336/832-6500. 7000. **Contact:** Human Resources. **E-mail address:** recruitment@mosescone.com. **World Wide Web address:** http://www.mosescone.com. **Description:** A family-centered, 115-bed facility, dedicated exclusively to the care of women and newborns. The hospital offers ultrasound, mammography, surgery, and outpatient treatment. In addition, an entire floor is dedicated to a Level III neonatal

intensive care unit. The hospital also specializes in the area of perinatology. **NOTE:** Resumes should be sent to: Moses Cone Health System Recruitment Department, 1200 Elm Street, Greensboro NC 27401-1020. Phone is 336/832-7400, or 800/476-6737. Fax is 336/832-2999. Please visit website to search for jobs and apply online. **Positions advertised include:** Assistant Director – Nursing Leadership; Food Service Technician; Laundry Technician; Nursing Secretary; Nursing Technician; Phlebotomist; RN – Various Departments; Scheduler; Ultrasound Technician. **Parent company:** Moses Cone Health System. **Number of employees nationwide:** 6,900.

South Carolina

ANDERSON AREA MEDICAL CENTER
800 North Fant Street, Anderson SC 29621. 864/261-1000. **Fax:** 864/261-1952. **Recorded jobline:** 800/423-2172. **Contact:** Human Resources. **E-mail address:** sblakene@anmed.com. **World Wide Web address:** http://www.anmed.com. **Description:** A 567-bed, acute care, regional medical center. **Positions advertised include:** Compliance Auditor; Counselor; Certified Registered Nursing Assistant; Nursing Director; Food Service Worker; Histotechnologist; Licensed Practical Nurse; Nurse Assistant; Office Clerk.

BAUSCH & LOMB INCORPORATED
8507 Pelham Road, Greenville SC 29615. 864/297-5500. **Contact:** Human Resources Manager. **World Wide Web address:** http://www.bausch.com. **Description:** Manufactures eye care products, pharmaceuticals, and surgical equipment including contact lenses; lens care solutions; premium sunglasses (sold under Ray-Ban and Revo brands) prescription and over-the-counter ophthalmic drugs; and equipment used for cataract and ophthalmic surgery. **NOTE:** Apply online through the company Website. **Positions advertised include:** Transportation Specialist; Chemistry Technician III. **Special programs:** Summer Internships. **Corporate headquarters location:** Rochester NY. **Other area locations:** Columbia SC. **Other U.S. locations:** Nationwide. **Operations at this facility include:** Manufacturing. **Listed on:** New York Stock Exchange. **Stock exchange symbol:** BOL. **Chairman/CEO:** Ronald L. Zarrella. **Annual sales/revenues:** $1.8 billion. **Number of employees:** 11,600.

BECTON DICKINSON AND COMPANY (BD)
P.O. Box 2128, Sumter SC 29151-2128. 803/469-8010. **Contact:** Human Resources Department. **World Wide Web address:** http://www.bd.com. **Description:** A medical and pharmaceutical company engaged in the manufacture of health care products, medical instrumentation, a line of diagnostic products, and industrial safety equipment. Becton Dickinson's major product lines for medical equipment include hypodermics, intravenous equipment, operating room products, thermometers, gloves, and specialty needles. The company also offers contract packaging services. **NOTE:** Human Resources extension: x1610. **Positions advertised include:** Project Engineer;

Product Development Engineer; Manufacturing Process Engineer; Equipment Technician; Electrical Engineer; Industrial Engineer; Mechanical Engineer; Operations Manager. **Special programs:** Internships; Coops. **Company Slogan:** Helping all people live healthy lives. **Corporate headquarters location:** Franklin Lakes NJ. **Other area locations:** Seneca SC. **Other U.S. locations:** Nationwide. **International locations:** Worldwide. **Operations at this facility include:** Manufacturing of blood collection supplies. **Listed on:** New York Stock Exchange. **Stock exchange symbol:** BDX. **Chairman/President/CEO:** Edward J. Ludwig. **Annual sales/revenues:** $4 billion. **Number of employees:** 25,250.

EAST COOPER MEDICAL CENTER

1200 Johnnie Dodds Boulevard, Mount Pleasant SC 29464. 843/881-0100. **Fax:** 843/881-4396. **Contact:** Human Resources Department. **World Wide Web address:** http://www.eastcoopermedcntr.com. **Description:** Offering a comprehensive range of services with the patient in mind first. **Positions advertised include:** Registered Nurse; Physical Therapist; Admit Communications Representative; Imaging Assistant; Assistant Nurse.

GE MEDICAL SYSTEMS

3001 West Radio Drive, Florence SC 29501. 843/667-9799. **Contact:** Personnel. **World Wide Web address:** http://www.gemedicalsystems.com. **Description:** Manufactures superconducting magnets for magnetic resonance imaging. **Positions advertised include:** Field Service Engineer; Process Engineer; X-ray Engineer; Regional Manager; Field Solutions Engineer; Program Coordinator; Electrical Engineer; Mechanical Engineer; Physicist. **Other area locations:** Anderson SC; Charleston SC. **Other U.S. locations:** Nationwide. **Parent company:** General Electric Company (Fairfield CT) is a diversified manufacturer operating in the following areas: aircraft engines (jet engines, replacement parts, and repair services for commercial, military, executive, and commuter aircraft); appliances; broadcasting (NBC); industrial (lighting products, electrical distribution and control equipment, transportation systems products, electric motors and related products, a broad range of electrical and electronic industrial automation products, and a network of electrical supply houses); materials (plastics, ABS resins, silicones, superabrasives, and laminates); power systems (products for the generation, transmission, and distribution of electricity); technical products and systems (medical systems and equipment, as well as a full range of computer-based information and data interchange services for both internal use and external commercial and industrial customers); and capital services (consumer services, financing, and specialty insurance). **Operations at this facility include:** Manufacturing; Research and Development.

GREENVILLE HOSPITAL SYSTEM

701 Grove Road, Greenville SC 29605. 864/455-8976. **Fax:** 864/455-1799. **Recorded jobline:** 864/455-8799. **Contact:** Human Resources. **World Wide Web address:** http://www.ghs.org. **Description:** A

multihospital system that provides health care services to several communities and major tertiary referral services for the upstate area. **NOTE:** Applicants are required to submit a completed "Authorization for Release of Information for Employment Purposes" form to be considered for any position. Forms are available on the company Website and should be sent to: Greenville Hospital System, 701 Grove Road, Greenville SC 29605; or faxed to GHS: 864/455-6218. **Office hours:** Monday – Friday, 8:00 a.m. – 5:00 p.m. **Positions advertised include:** Nurse Supervisor; Registered Nurse; Pediatrician; Chief Technician; Radiology; Physical Therapy. **Number of employees at this location:** 6,500.

KERSHAW COUNTY MEDICAL CENTER
1315 Roberts Street, P.O. Box 7003, Camden SC 29020. 803/432-4311. **Fax:** 803/425-6369. **Contact:** Human Resources. **E-mail address:** info@kcmc.org. **World Wide Web address:** http://www.kcmc.org. **Description:** A 121-bed acute care facility and 88-bed long term care facility operating facilities in Camden and Lugoff South Carolina. **NOTE:** Apply online. **Positions advertised include:** Licensed Practical Nurse; Registered Nurse; Community Health Educator; Physical Therapist; Recruiter; Speech Therapist; CT Scan Diagnostic Technologist; Polysonographer; Respiratory Therapist.

LEXINGTON MEDICAL CENTER
2720 Sunset Boulevard, West Columbia SC 29169. 803/791-2000. **Fax:** 803/359-2267. **Recorded jobline:** 803/739-3562. **Contact:** Betsy Brooks, Employment Coordinator. **E-mail address:** bsbrooks@lexhealth.org. **World Wide Web address:** http://www.lexmed.com. **Description:** A 292-bed metropolitan medical complex, which includes six community medical centers serving Lexington County, an occupational health center and 16 affiliated physician practices. **NOTE:** For physician opportunities contact: Crystal Smith, 2720 Sunset Boulevard, West Columbia SC 29169; Phone: 803/791-2958; E-mail address: csmith@lexhealth.org. For all other opportunities contact: LMC Extended Care, Human Resources, 815 Old Cherokee Road, Lexington SC 29072. Employment Coordinator phone: 803/996-6240. **Positions advertised include:** Nursing Supervisor; Registered Nurse; Licensed Practical Nurse; Certified Nurses Aide; Ward Clerk; Occupational Manager; Social Worker.

LORIS HEALTHCARE SYSTEM
LORIS COMMUNITY HOSPITAL
3655 Mitchell Street, Loris SC 29569. 843/716-7000. **Fax:** 843/716-7254. **Recorded jobline:** 843/716-7000, ext5320. **Contact:** Theresa Pougnaud, Director of Human Resources, or Wendy Harrelson. **E-mail address:** wharrels@sccoast.net. **World Wide Web address:** http://www.lorishealthcaresystem.com. **Description:** A general, acute care hospital. **NOTE:** Application materials should be sent to: Employment Coordinator, Loris Healthcare System, 3655 Mitchell System Box 690001, Loris SC 29569-9601. Human Resources phone: 843/716-7196. **Positions advertised include:** Carpenter; Cashier;

Executive Physiologist; Licensed Practical Nurse; Nuclear Medical Technician; Pharmacist; Physical Therapist; Radiological Technician; Receptionist; Registered Nurse; Transcriptionist; Utility Aide.

PALMETTO HEALTH

P.O. Box 2266, Columbia SC 29202. 803/434-7000. **Physical address:** 5 Richland Medical Park Drive, Columbia SC 29203. **Fax:** 803/296-5928. **Contact:** Human Resources. **World Wide Web address:** http://www.palmettohealth.org. **Description:** A locally-owned, non-profit healthcare system operating several hospitals and medical centers with a total of 1,247 beds. **NOTE:** Human Resources phone: 803/296-2100. **Positions advertised include:** Administrative Associate; Business Analyst; Communications Coordinator; Communications Advocate; Information Technology Business Analyst; Network Engineer; Manager; Nurse Practitioner; Planning Analyst; Project Manager; Workers Compensation Manager. **Office hours:** Monday – Friday, 9:00 a.m. – 4:00 p.m. **Corporate headquarters location:** Columbia SC. **Subsidiaries include:** Palmetto Health Baptist; Palmetto Health Richland; Palmetto Health South Carolina Cancer Center; Palmetto Health South Carolina Comprehensive Breast Center; Gamma Knife Center of the Carolinas; CareForce; Palmetto Health Hospice. **Number of employees:** 7,000.

PROVIDENCE HOSPITALS

2709 Laurel Street, Columbia SC 29204. 803/256-5410. **Fax:** 803/256-5838. **Recorded jobline:** 803/256-5627. **Contact:** Human Resources. **E-mail address:** hr@providencehospitals.com. **World Wide Web address:** http://www.provhosp.com. **Description:** The Sisters of Charity Providence Hospitals is a non-profit organization operating three facilities with a total of 311 beds: Providence Hospital, Providence Heart Institute, and Providence Hospital Northeast serving the Midlands region of South Carolina. **Positions advertised include:** Office Coordinator; Executive Secretary; Collections Specialist; Environmental Services Technician; Assembly Analyst; Phlebotomist; Registered Nurse; Sleep Lab Technician; Affairs Vice President; Medical Lab Student; Pharmacy Specialist. **Parent company:** Sisters of Charity of Saint Augustine Health System. **Number of employees statewide:** 1,500.

RICHLAND MEMORIAL HOSPITAL

5 Richland Medical Park, Columbia SC 29203. 803/434-7733. **Contact:** Employment Services Department. **World Wide Web address:** http://www.rmh.edu. **Description:** A 626-bed, regional, community teaching hospital. Richland Memorial Hospital's facilities include a Children's Hospital; the Center for Cancer Treatment and Research; the Heart Center; the Midlands Trauma Center; and Richland Springs, a free-standing psychiatric hospital. Specialty services include a partially matched bone marrow transplantation program, high-risk obstetrics, orthopedics, psychiatry, cardiology, oncology, nephrology, neonatology, neurology, neurosurgery, and medical and surgical services. The hospital is affiliated with the University of South Carolina and other universities. **Positions advertised include:** Physician Office Manager;

Assistant Nurse Manager; Clinical Nurse Specialist; Licensed Practical Nurse; Neonatal Nurse Practitioner; Nurse Manager; Registered Nurse; Certified Occupational Therapist; Clinical Engineering Manager; Dietician; Magnetic Resonance Imaging Technician; Pharmacist; Physical Therapist; Radiology Technician; Research Assistant; Respiratory Therapist; Health Information Assistant Accounting Specialist; Collector; Data Processor; Dental Assistant; Laboratory Assistant; Linen Technician; Mechanical Engineer; Mental Health Assistant; Emergency Department Nurse; Phlebotomist; Cardiac Care Technician. **Special programs:** Internships. **Parent company:** Palmetto Health.

SPAN-AMERICA MEDICAL SYSTEMS, INC.
P.O. Box 5231, Greenville SC 29606. 864/288-8877. **Toll-free phone:** 800/888-6752. **Fax:** 864/288-8692. **Contact:** Human Resources. **E-mail address:** employment@spanamerica.com. **World Wide Web address:** http://www. spanamerica.com. **Description:** Manufactures and distributes a variety of polyurethane foam products for the health care, consumer, and industrial markets. The company's principal health care products consist of polyurethane foam mattress overlays including its Geo-Matt overlay, therapeutic replacement mattresses, patient positioners, and single-use flexible packaging products. These products are marketed primarily to hospitals but are also marketed to long-term care facilities in the United States. Span-America's specialty products are sold under the trademark Span-Aids, which consists of over 300 different foam items that relieve the basic patient positioning problems of elevation, immobilization, muscle contraction, foot drop, and foot or leg rotation. Founded in 1970. **Corporate headquarters location:** This location. **Other locations:** Norwalk CA. **Listed on:** NASDAQ. **Stock exchange symbol:** SPAN. **Number of employees:** 225.

TUOMEY HEALTHCARE SYSTEM
129 North Washington Street, Sumter SC 29150. 803/778-9000. **Fax:** 803/778-9494. **Contact:** Employment Supervisor. **E-mail address:** ptruluck@tuomey.com. **World Wide Web address:** http://www.tuomey.com. **Description:** A non-profit medical system, which includes the 266-bed Tuomey Regional Medical Center and a staff of over 150 physicians. Facilities include a 36-bed nursery, expanded ICU, 10 operating suites and a satellite medical park as well as diagnostic and treatment capabilities with a Cancer Treatment Center, cardiac catheterization and updated HiSpeed Computed Tomography. Transitional care is provided via Home Services and a Subacute Skilled Care program. **NOTE:** Human Resources phone: 803/778-8760 or 800/648-1195. For Nursing/Allied Health Recruiter: 803/778-8762. **Positions advertised include:** Echo Vascular Technologist; Licensed Practical Nurse; Mammography Technician; Medical Lab Assistant; Medical Technician; Nurse Technician Extern; Occupational Therapist; Physical Therapist; Registered Nurse; Surgical Technician.

TYCO HEALTHCARE
dba KENDALL HEALTHCARE COMPANY
525 North Emerald Road, Greenwood SC 29646. 864/223-4281.
Contact: Human Resources. **World Wide Web address:**
http://www.tycohealthcare.com. **Description:** Manufactures and
distributes disposable incontinence products. **NOTE:** Entry-level
positions and second and third shifts are offered. **Positions advertised
include:** Production Superintendent. **Special programs:** Internships.
Corporate headquarters location: Mansfield MA. **Other area
locations:** Camden SC; Seneca SC. **Other U.S. locations:** Nationwide.
International locations: Worldwide. **Parent company:** Tyco
International (Portsmouth NH). **Operations at this facility include:**
Administration; Divisional Headquarters; Manufacturing; Sales.

HOTELS AND RESTAURANTS

You can expect to find the following types of companies in this section:
Casinos • Dinner Theaters • Hotel/Motel Operators • Resorts • Restaurants

North Carolina

BLOCKADE RUNNER HOTEL
P.O. Box 555, 275 Waynick Boulevard, Wrightsville Beach NC 28480. 910/256-2251. **Contact:** Personnel. **E-mail address:** blockade@bellsouth.net. **World Wide Web address:** http://www.blockade-runner.com. **Description:** A full-service hotel with 150 rooms.

CAROLINA INN
211 Pittsboro Street, Chapel Hill NC 27514. 919/933-2001. **Fax:** 919/918-2763. **Recorded jobline:** 919/918-2769. **Contact:** Cheryl Wendel, Human Resources. **E-mail address:** hr@carolinainn.com. **World Wide Web address:** http://www.carolinainn.com. **Description:** A 194-room hotel with conference facilities and banquet staff. The hotel has been rated with Four Diamonds on the National Register of Historic Places. **NOTE:** For management positions, please visit http://www.aramarkcareers.com to search for jobs and apply online.

CHARLOTTE MARRIOTT CITY CENTER
100 West Trade Street, Charlotte NC 28202. 704/333-9000. **Toll-free phone:** 800/4-MARRIOTT. **Fax:** 704/342-3419. **Contact:** Nancy McNeill, Director of Human Resources. **World Wide Web address:** http://www.marriottcitycenter.com. **Description:** A 421-guest room hotel featuring an indoor pool, a health club, and two restaurants. **NOTE:** Please visit website to search for jobs and apply online. **Positions advertised include:** Director of Sales; Chief Engineer. **Corporate headquarters location:** Washington D.C. **Other U.S. locations:** Nationwide. **Listed on:** New York Stock Exchange. **Stock exchange symbol:** MAR. **CEO:** J. Marriott. **Number of employees worldwide:** 128,000.

GOLDEN CORRAL CORPORATION
P.O. Box 29502, Raleigh NC 27626-0502. 919/781-9310. **Physical address:** 5151 Glenwood Avenue, Raleigh NC 27612. 800/284-5673. **Fax:** 919/881-4577. **Contact:** Human Resources. **World Wide Web address:** http://www.goldencorralrest.com. **Description:** Operates a chain of family steakhouses. Founded in 1973. **NOTE:** Entry-level positions are offered. Please visit website to search for jobs and apply online. If you are looking for a field position, please contact the location in your area. **Company slogan:** Making pleasurable dining affordable. **Corporate headquarters location:** This location. **Other U.S. locations:**

Nationwide. **Operations at this facility include:** Administration; Research and Development; Service. **Listed on:** Privately held. **President:** Ted Fowler. **Annual sales/revenues:** More than $100 million. **Number of employees at this location:** 170. **Number of employees nationwide:** 3,700.

WINSTON HOTELS, INC.
2626 Glenwood Avenue, Suite 200, Raleigh NC 27608. 919/510-6010. **Fax:** 919/510-6832. **Contact:** Patti Belle, Human Resources. **World Wide Web address:** http://www.winstonhotels.com. **Description:** Owns 16 hotels, including 11 Hampton Inns in Georgia, North Carolina, South Carolina, and Virginia; and 5 Comfort Inns in North Carolina and Virginia. **Corporate headquarters location:** This location. **Listed on:** New York Stock Exchange. **Stock exchange symbol:** WXH. **CEO:** Robert W. Winton.

South Carolina

CARAVELLE RESORT INC.
6900 North Ocean Boulevard, Myrtle Beach SC 29572. 843/918-8000. **Toll-free phone:** 800/785-4460. **Fax:** 843/918-7036. **Contact:** Grace Andrews, Personnel. **World Wide Web address:** http://www.thecaravelle.com. **Description:** A resort with 590 rooms and villas. **Parent company:** Caravelle Properties Ltd Partnership (also at this location). **Affiliates include:** Santa Maria Restaurant; Saint Johns.

THE CLUB GROUP, LTD.
71 Lighthouse Road, Suite 300, Hilton Head SC 29938. 843/363-5699. **Contact:** Christiana G. Martin, Controller. **Description:** Operates a resort. **Positions advertised include:** Cook; Hotel Manager; Food Service Manager. **Subsidiaries include:** Harbour Town Resorts; National Liability & Fire Insurance Company.

CROWNE PLAZA RESORT
130 Shipyard Drive, Hilton Head Island SC 29928. 843/842-2400. **Fax:** 843/785-4879. **Contact:** Melissa Love, Assistant Director of Human Resources. **World Wide Web address:** http://www.crowneplazaresort.com. **Description:** A 340-room hotel located in Shipyard Plantation. This location also hires seasonally. **NOTE:** Entry-level positions, part-time jobs, and second and third shifts are offered. **Positions advertised include:** Part Time PM Line Cook; Loss Preventing Associate; Part Time Night Auditor; Mini Bar Attendant; Bartender; Restaurant Servers; Restaurant Supervisor. **Special programs:** Internships; Training; Summer Jobs. **International locations:** Worldwide. **Parent company:** Six Continents PLC (London, United Kingdom).

RYAN'S FAMILY STEAK HOUSES, INC.
P.O. Box 100, Greer SC 29652. 864/879-1011. **Fax:** 864/894-0256. **Contact:** Kim Lynch, Human Resources. **World Wide Web address:**

http://www.ryansinc.com. **Description:** Owns and franchises over 250 restaurants in 21 states. **NOTE:** Contact the company's recruiter in South Carolina, Kim Lynch at: 864/879-1011 ext3572. Fax: 828/894-0256. For restaurant positions, contact local restaurants directly. **Positions advertised include:** Manager Trainee; Cook; Server; Cashier; Host/Hostess; Utility Worker; Restaurant/Food Service Manager. **Corporate headquarters location:** This location. **Listed on:** NASDAQ. **Stock exchange symbol:** RYAN. **Annual sales/revenues:** $774 million. **Number of employees nationwide:** 21,300.

SANDS RESORTS
P.O. Box 2968, Myrtle Beach SC 29578. 843/445-2623. **Physical address:** 3015 Church Street, Myrtle Beach SC 29577. **Fax:** 843/445-2737. **Contact:** Ms. Sandi Madorno, Director of Human Resources. **World Wide Web address:** http:// www.sandsresorts.com. **Description:** Owns and manages several resorts in Myrtle Beach and one resort in North Carolina. **Positions advertised include:** Customer Service Representative; Human Resources Manager. **Corporate headquarters location:** This location. **Listed on:** Privately held.

SEA PINES ASSOCIATES, INC.
32 Greenwood Drive, Hilton Head Island SC 29928. 843/785-3333. **Fax:** 843/842-1412. **Contact:** Monica Nash, Director of Human Resources. **World Wide Web address:** http://www.seapines.com. **Description:** A holding company. **NOTE:** Human Resources phone: 843/842-1882. **Special programs:** Internships. **Corporate headquarters location:** This location. **Subsidiaries include:** Sea Pines Company, Inc. (also at this location) operates resort assets including three golf courses, a 28-court racquet club, a home and villa rental management business, retail sales outlets, food services operations, and other resort recreational facilities. Sea Pines Real Estate Company, Inc. is an independent real estate brokerage firm with 18 offices. Sea Pines Country Club, Inc. owns and operates a full-service private country club providing golf, tennis, and clubhouse facilities for approximately 1,500 club members.

INSURANCE

You can expect to find the following types of companies in this section:
Commercial and Industrial Property/Casualty Insurers • Health Maintenance Organizations (HMO's) • Medical/Life Insurance Companies

North Carolina

BLUE CROSS AND BLUE SHIELD OF NORTH CAROLINA
P.O. Box 2291, Durham NC 27702-2291. 919/489-7431. **Physical address:** 1830 US 15-501 North, Chapel Hill NC 27514. **Toll-free phone:** 800/250-3630. **Contact:** Personnel. **World Wide Web address:** http://www.bcbsnc.com. **Description:** A nonprofit health care insurance organization providing managed health care plans to both individuals and groups. Blue Cross and Blue Shield offers Point-of-Service, individual health, and HMO plans, as well as life insurance, dental insurance, accidental death and dismemberment, and short- and long-term disability. **NOTE:** Please visit website to search for jobs and apply online. **Corporate headquarters location:** This location. **Other area locations:** Winston-Salem NC; Hickory NC; Charlotte NC; Morrisville NC; Greensboro NC; Wilmington NC; Greenville NC.

GMAC INSURANCE
P.O. Box 3199, Winston-Salem NC 27102-3199. 336/770-2000. **Physical address:** 500 West Fifth Street, Winston-Salem NC 27152. **Fax:** 336/7702190. **Contact:** Human Resources. **World Wide Web address:** http://www.gmacinsurance.com. **Description:** An insurance company operating in 22 states through more than 11,000 independent agents. The company's East Division primarily underwrites nonstandard auto insurance in Alabama, Florida, Georgia, North Carolina, Ohio, and Virginia. The division also underwrites preferred auto, homeowners, and mobile home insurance in North Carolina. The North Division underwrites nonstandard auto insurance in Connecticut, Illinois, Indiana, Maine, Maryland, New Hampshire, New York, Pennsylvania, Rhode Island, and Vermont. The South Division underwrites nonstandard auto insurance in Kentucky, Louisiana, Mississippi, Tennessee, and Texas. The Specialty Auto division underwrites insurance for business autos and motorcycles. **NOTE:** Please visit website to search for jobs and apply online. **Positions advertised include:** Application System Analyst; Claim Service Consultant Trainee; Customer Sales Agent; Customer Service Consultant; Director of Accounting; Human Representative; Human Resources Representative; Infrastructure Project Manager; Pricing/Product Manager; Regional Marketing Manager. **Corporate headquarters location:** Southfield MI. **Number of employees worldwide:** 3,800.

INVESTORS TITLE INSURANCE COMPANY

P.O. Drawer 2687, Chapel Hill NC 27515. 919/968-2200. **Physical address:** 121 North Columbia Street, Chapel Hill NC 27514 **Toll-free phone:** 800/326-4842. **Fax:** 919/968-2235. **Contact:** Human Resources. **E-mail address:** humanresources@invtitle.com. **World Wide Web address:** http://www.invtitle.com. **Description:** Investors Title Insurance Company, through its two title insurance subsidiaries, Investors Title Insurance Company and Northeast Investors Title Insurance Company, writes title insurance in Florida, Georgia, Illinois, Indiana, Kentucky, Maryland, Michigan, Minnesota, Mississippi, Nebraska, New York, North Carolina, Pennsylvania, South Carolina, Tennessee, and Virginia. A third subsidiary, Investors Title Exchange Corporation, serves as a qualified intermediary in tax-deferred exchanges of real property. Founded in 1972. **NOTE:** Please visit website to view job listings and apply online. **Positions advertised include:** Agency Underwriting and Operations Support Coordinator; Sales Executive; Senior Vice President of Finance; Underwriter; Vice President of Vendor Management Operations. **Corporate headquarters location:** This location. **Other area locations:** Statewide. **Other U.S. locations:** Lansing MI; Columbia SC; Pittsford NY. **Listed on:** NASDAQ. **Stock exchange symbol:** ITIC. **Annual sales/revenues:** $21 - $50 million. **Number of employees at this location:** 50. **Number of employees nationwide:** 180.

NORTH CAROLINA MUTUAL LIFE INSURANCE COMPANY

411 West Chapel Hill Street, Mutual Plaza, Durham NC 27701. 919/682-9201. **Toll-free phone:** 800/626-1899. **Fax:** 919/682-1685. **Contact:** Human Resources. **E-mail address:** askhr@ncmututallife.com. **World Wide Web address:** http://www.ncmutuallife.com. **Description:** A life insurance company. The company is licensed to operate in 23 states and Washington D.C. Founded 1898. **NOTE:** Human Resources is at Ext. 318. **Corporate headquarters location:** This location. **Other area locations:** Charlotte NC; Greenville NC; Raleigh NC. **Other U.S. locations:** GA; IL; MI; PA; VA; MD. **Operations at this facility include:** Administration. **Number of employees at this location:** 145. **Number of employees nationwide:** 560. **President:** Bert Collins.

ROYAL & SUNALLIANCE USA

P.O. Box 1000, Charlotte NC 28201-1000. 704/522-2000. **Physical address:** 9300 Arrow Point Boulevard, Charlotte NC 28273-8135. **Contact:** Human Resources. **World Wide Web address:** http://www.royalsunalliance-usa.com. **Description:** Provides commercial property and casualty insurance as well as personal and specialty insurance. **Corporate headquarters location:** This location. **Other area locations:** Goldsboro NC. **Other U.S. locations:** Nationwide. **Parent company:** Royal & SunAlliance Insurance Group plc (London, England). **President/CEO:** John Tighe. **Number of employees nationwide:** 3,500.

STERLING HEALTHCARE

P.O. Box 15309, Durham NC 27704. 919/383-0355. **Physical address:** 2828 Croasdaile Drive, Suite 100, Durham NC 27705. **Toll-free phone:**

800/476-4587. **Fax:** 919/382-3257. **Contact:** Carolyn Carle, Recruitment and Staff Development. **E-mail address:** carolyn.carle@phyamerica.com. **World Wide Web address:** http://www.phyamerica.com. **Description:** A national provider of physician practice management services to hospitals, government entities, managed care organizations, and other health care institutions. Under contract with its clients, the company identifies and organizes physician practices for credentialing and privileging, and coordinates the ongoing scheduling of health care professionals who provide clinical coverage in designated areas of primary care, mainly in the areas of emergency care. Sterling Healthcare also assists the client's administrative and medical staff in such areas as quality assurance, risk management, practice accreditation, and marketing, as well as in the documentation, billing, and collection of professional charges. **Positions advertised include:** Compliance Officer; Legal Assistant/Hospital Contracting Coordinator. **Corporate headquarters location:** This location. **Other U.S. locations:** Nationwide. **President/CEO:** Stephen J. Dresnick.

South Carolina

CANAL INSURANCE COMPANY
P.O. Box 7, Greenville SC 29602. 864/242-5365. **Physical address:** 400 East Stone Avenue, Greenville SC 29601. **Contact:** Office/Personnel Manager. **E-mail address:** hr@canal-ins.com. **World Wide Web address:** http://www.canal-ins.com. **Description:** An insurance company that specializes in commercial vehicle insurance. Founded in 1933.

COLONIAL LIFE & ACCIDENT INSURANCE COMPANY
P.O. Box 1365, Columbia SC 29202. 803/798-7000. **Fax:** 803/731-2618. **Recorded jobline:** 803/750-0088. **Contact:** Don Montgomery, Human Resources. **World Wide Web address:** http://www.coloniallife.com. **Description:** An accident and health insurance company specializing in supplemental insurance offered to employees at their worksite, as well as underwriting lines such as accident, disability, life, and cancer insurance. Founded in 1939. **Positions advertised include:** Sales Director; Atraus Consultant; Account Service Representative; Independent Contractor. **Corporate headquarters location:** This location. **Parent company:** UNUMProvident Corporation (Portland ME). **Number of employees:** 900.

KANAWHA INSURANCE COMPANY, INC.
South White Street, P.O. Box 610, Lancaster SC 29721. 803/283-5300. **Fax:** 803/283-5676. **Contact:** Human Resources. **E-mail address:** lbranham@kanawha.com. **World Wide Web address:** http://www.kanawha.com. **Description:** An insurance company specializing in health, life, supplemental, and long-term care insurance. **Positions advertised include** Account Manager; Assistant Counsel Associate; Claims Examiner; Medical Claims Review Registered Nurse.

Corporate headquarters location: This location. **Other area locations:** Statewide. **Other U.S. locations:** IA; NC.

LIBERTY INSURANCE SERVICES CORPORATION

P.O. Box 789, Greenville SC 29602-0789. 864/609-8334. **Fax:** 864/609-3120. **Contact:** Human Resources. **E-mail address:** recruiters@lisinfo.com. **World Wide Web address:** http://www.rbclibertyinsurance.com. **Description:** Provides a broad range of insurance services. **NOTE:** Jobseekers are encouraged to apply via the Website. **Positions advertised include:** Accountant; Customer Service Representative; Department Manager; Insurance Agent; Broker; Marketing Specialist; Underwriter; Assistant Underwriter. **Corporate headquarters location:** This location. **Parent company:** RBC Insurance (Canada). **Subsidiaries/affiliates include:** Genelco Software. New York Stock Exchange. **Stock exchange symbol:** RY.

THE SEIBELS BRUCE GROUP, INC.

P.O. Box One, Columbia SC 29202-0001. 803/748-2000. **Physical address:** 1501 Lady Street, Columbia SC 29201. **Fax:** 803/748-8394. **Contact:** Recruiter. **E-mail address:** recruiter@seibels.com. **World Wide Web address:** http://www.seibels.com. **Description:** An automobile, flood, property and casualty insurance company. Founded in 1869. **Positions advertised include:** Associate Underwriter; Commercial Lines Rater. **Corporate headquarters location:** This location. **Other locations:** Winston-Salem NC. **Subsidiaries include:** Agency Specialty of Kentucky, Inc.; Agency Specialty, Inc.; Catawba Insurance Company; Consolidated American Insurance Company; FLT Plus, Inc.; Forest Lake Travel Service, Inc.; Investors National Life Insurance Company of South Carolina; Kentucky Insurance Company; Policy Finance Company; Seibels Bruce Service Corporation; Seibels, Bruce & Company; South Carolina Insurance Company. **Number of employees at this location:** 329.

LEGAL SERVICES

You can expect to find the following types of companies in this section:
Law Firms • Legal Service Agencies

North Carolina

BROOKS, PIERCE, McLENDON, HUMPHREY & LEONARD, L.L.P.
P.O. Box 26000, Greensboro NC 27420. 336/373-8850. **Physical address:** 2000 Renaissance Plaza, 230 North Elm Street, Greensboro NC 27401. **Fax:** 336/378-1001. **Contact:** Ms. Mary Beth McCausland, Recruiting Coordinator. **E-mail address:** mmccausland@brookspierce.com **World Wide Web address:** http://www.brookspierce.com. **Description:** A corporate law firm. Founded 1897. **Positions advertised include:** Attorney. **Special programs:** Summer Associate Program. **Other area locations:** Raleigh NC. **Other U.S. locations:** Washington D.C. **Number of employees at this location:** 135.

KENNEDY COVINGTON LOBDELL & HICKMAN
Hearst Tower, 47th Floor, 214 North Tryon Street, Charlotte NC 28202. 704/331-7400. **Fax:** 704/331-7598. **Contact:** Human Resources. **E-mail address:** humanresources@kennedycovington.com. **World Wide Web address:** http://www.kennedycovington.com. **Description:** A law firm that specializes in employee benefits, estate litigation, real estate, taxes, and wills for corporate clients. **NOTE:** Please visit website or contact an office for more information on the application process for attorney positions. **Special programs:** Summer Associate Program. **Other area locations:** Raleigh NC; Morrisville NC. **Other U.S. locations:** Rock Hill SC; Columbia SC.

PARKER POE ADAMS & BERNSTEIN
3 Wachovia Center, 401 South Tryon Street, Suite 3000, Charlotte NC 28202. 704/372-9000. **Fax:** 704/334-4706. **Contact:** Joann L. Enos, Director of Human Resources Manager. **E-mail address:** joannenos@parkerpoe.com. **World Wide Web address:** http://www.parkerpoe.com. **Description:** A law firm with 140 attorneys that primarily serves corporate clients. **NOTE:** For attorney positions or law student hiring, contact John W. Francisco (johnfrancisco@parkerpoe.com). Caryn A. Johnson (carynjohnson@parkerpoe.com) also handles law student hiring. **Corporate headquarters location:** This location. **Other area locations:** Raleigh NC. **Other U.S. locations:** Columbia SC; Spartanburg SC; Charleston SC.

PERRY, PERRY & PERRY
P.O. Drawer 1475, Kinston NC 28501. 252/523-5107. **Physical address:** 518 Plaza Boulevard, Kinston NC 28503. **Contact:** Office

Manager. **Description:** A law firm with five attorneys who specialize in criminal, social security and disability, and real estate law. **Number of employees at this location:** 500.

WOMBLE CARLYLE SANDRIDGE & RICE, PLLC
P.O. Box 831, Raleigh NC 27602. 919/755-2100. **Physical address:** 150 Fayetteville Street Mall, Suite 2100, Raleigh NC 27601. **Fax:** 919/755-2150. **Contact:** Professional Development and Recruiting. **E-mail address:** jbeavers@wcsr.com. **World Wide Web address:** http://www.wcsr.com. **Description:** One of the largest law firms in the Southeastern and mid-Atlantic U.S. Founded 1876. **NOTE:** For staff positions, contact John Turlington at 919/755-2117. **Special programs:** Summer Associate Program. **Other area locations:** Charlotte NC; Greensboro NC; Research Triangle Park NC; Winston-Salem NC. **Other U.S. locations:** Washington D.C.; Tyson's Corner VA; Atlanta GA.

South Carolina

HAYNSWORTH SINKLER BOYD, P.A.
P.O. Box 2048, Greenville SC 29602. 864/240-3200. **Fax:** 864/240-3300. **Physical address:** 75 Beattie Place, Two Liberty Square, 11th Floor, Greenville SC 29601. **E-mail address:** cgantt@hsblawfirm.com. **Contact:** Office Manager. **World Wide Web address:** http://www.hsblawfirm.com **Description:** A law firm with approximately 50 attorneys that specializes in different areas of the law including bond, corporate, insurance, and real estate. **Special programs:** Summer employment program.

LEATHERWOOD WALKER TODD & MANN P.C.
P.O. Box 87, Greenville SC 29602. 864/242-6440. **Contact:** Margaret Watson, Human Resources Manager. **E-mail address:** mwatson@lwtm.com. **World Wide Web address:** http://www.lwtmlaw.com. **Description:** A law firm with over 50 lawyers that has a variety of specialties including tax and bankruptcy litigation.

McNAIR LAW FIRM
P.O. Box 11390, Columbia SC 29211. 803/799-9800. **Physical address:** Bank of America Tower, 1301 Gervais Street, Columbia SC 29201. **Fax:** 803/799-9804. **Contact:** Risa Hudson, Personnel Manager. **World Wide Web address:** http:// www.mcnair.net. **Description:** A law firm with approximately 55 attorneys who have broad ranges of specializations in the fields of corporate and civil law. Founded in 1971. **NOTE:** For summer associate program contact Bonnie Nelson, Recruiting Coordinator by e-mail: bnelson@mcnair.net. **Positions advertised include:** Associate Lawyer; Law Clerk; Summer Associate. **Special programs:** Summer Associate program. **Corporate headquarters location:** This location. **Other locations:** Anderson SC; Charleston SC; Charlotte NC; Georgetown SC; Greenville SC; Hilton Head Island SC; Myrtle Beach SC; Raleigh NC.

NEXSEN PRUET JACOBS & POLLARD, LLC

P.O. Drawer 2426, Columbia SC 29202-2426. 803/771-8900. **Physical address:** 1441 Main Street, Suite 1500, Columbia SC 29201. **Fax:** 803/253-8277. **Contact:** Human Resources. **World Wide Web address:** http://www.npjp.com. **Description:** A law firm with a wide variety of specialties including real estate, corporate law, banking and finance, securities, tax and estate planning, health care, employee benefits, construction, labor and employment, environmental law, communications, patents and intellectual property, international, regulatory, administrative and legislative law. **Positions advertised include:** Attorney; Litigation Software Support Specialist; File Clerk; Paralegal; Litigation Paralegal; Legal Secretary; Records Clerk. **Corporate headquarters location:** This location. **Other locations:** Charleston SC; Greenville SC; Hilton Head SC; Myrtle Beach SC; Charlotte NC.

STEINBERG LAW FIRM

61 Broad Street, Charleston SC 29402. 843/720-2800. **Fax:** 843/722-1190. **Contact:** Human Resources Director. **E-mail address:** tprior@steinberglawfirm.com. **World Wide Web address:** http://www.steinberglawfirm.com. **Description:** A law firm. **Positions advertised include:** Runners.

TURNER PADGET GRAHAM & LANEY

P.O. Box 1473, Columbia SC 29202. 803/254-2200. **Physical address:** Bank of America Plaza, 17th Floor, 1901 Main Street, Columbia SC 29201. **Fax:** 803/799-3957. **Contact:** Mimi Love, Human Resources Manager. **E-mail address:** mwl@tpgl.com. **World Wide Web address:** http://www.tpgl.com. **Description:** A law firm specializing in a variety of legal areas including corporate, insurance defense, medical malpractice, and tax. **NOTE:** Human Resources phone: 803/227-4211. For summer internships contact Recruitment Committee Chairman, Drew Williams by e-mail: daw@tpgl.com. **Positions advertised include:** Attorney; Law Clerk; Paralegal; Secretary; Administrative Assistant. **Corporate headquarters location:** This location. **Other locations:** Charleston SC; Florence SC.

MANUFACTURING: MISCELLANEOUS CONSUMER

You can expect to find the following types of companies in this section:
Art Supplies • Batteries • Cosmetics and Related Products • Household Appliances and Audio/Video Equipment • Jewelry, Silverware, and Plated Ware • Miscellaneous Household Furniture and Fixtures • Musical Instruments • Tools • Toys and Sporting Goods

North Carolina

BSH HOME APPLIANCES
120 Bosch Boulevard, New Bern NC 28562-6997. 252/636-4454. **Contact:** Chuck Dale, Manager of Human Resources. **Description:** A manufacturer of electrical industrial power tools for woodworking and concrete applications. **Special programs:** Internships. **Corporate headquarters location:** Chicago IL. **Other U.S. locations:** Heber Springs AK; Walnut Ridge AR. **Operations at this facility include:** Manufacturing. **Number of employees at this location:** 350. **Number of employees nationwide:** 2,300.

BASSETT FURNITURE INDUSTRIES, INC.
1111 East 20th Street, Newton NC 28658. 828/465-7700. **Contact:** Human Resources Department. **E-mail address:** bassett@bassettfurniture.com. **World Wide Web address:** http://www.bassettfurniture.com. **Description:** Manufactures and sells a full line of furniture for the home, such as bedroom and dining suites; accent pieces; occasional tables; wall and entertainment units; upholstered sofas, chairs, and love seats; recliners; and mattresses and box springs. **Corporate headquarters location:** Bassett VA. **Operations at this location include:** This location is part of Bassett's Upholstery Division. **Listed on:** NASDAQ. **Stock exchange symbol:** BSET. **President/CEO:** Rob Spilman. **Number of employees nationwide:** 7,800.

CAROLINA MIRROR COMPANY
P.O. Box 548, North Wilkesboro NC 28659-0548. 336/838-2151. **Physical address:** 201 Elkin Highway, North Wilkesboro NC. **Toll-free phone:** 800/334-7245. **Fax:** 336/838-9734. **Contact:** Human Resources Department. **E-mail address:** jkilby@carolinamirror.com. **World Wide Web address:** http://www.carolinamirror.com. **Description:** Manufactures mirrors. **Corporate headquarters location:** This location. **Operations at this facility include:** Administration; Manufacturing; Sales. **Listed on:** Privately held. **Number of employees at this location:** 575.

CARSONS INC.
4200 Cheyenne Drive, P.O. Box 14186, Archdale NC 27263. 336/431-1101. **Contact:** Kathy Proctor, Human Resources Manager. **World Wide Web address:** http://www.carsonsofhp.com. **Description:** Carsons Inc. manufactures upholstered furniture. The company wholesales its furniture to retail stores. **Corporate headquarters location:** This location.

DREXEL HERITAGE FURNITURE
1925 Eastchester Drive, High Point NC 27265. 336/888-4800. **Fax:** 336/888-4815. **Contact:** Human Resources. **World Wide Web address:** http://www.drexelheritage.com. **Description:** A furniture manufacturer. **NOTE:** Job candidates are advised to contact The North Carolina Employment Security Office for available positions with the company. **Special programs:** Internships. **Corporate headquarters location:** This location. **Other area locations:** Hickory NC; Marion NC. **Other U.S. locations:** Lititz PA; Clearwater FL. **Parent company:** Masco Corporation (Taylor MI). **Operations at this facility include:** Divisional Headquarters; Manufacturing. **President/CEO:** Jeff Young. **Number of employees at this location:** 500. **Number of employees nationwide:** 1,300.

ELECTROLUX HOME PRODUCTS
4850 West Vernon Avenue, Kinston NC 28504. 252/527-5100. **Fax:** 252/527-4848. **Contact:** Human Resources. **World Wide Web address:** http://www.frigidaire.com. **Description:** Manufactures household appliances including washing machines, ranges, dishwashers, refrigerators, freezers, air conditioners, and disposals. **NOTE:** Resumes should be sent to: 250 Bobby Jones Expressway, Martinez GA 30907. **Corporate headquarters location:** Augusta GA. **International locations:** Canada; Mexico. **Parent company:** AB Electrolux has four business areas: Household Appliances, Commercial Appliances, Outdoor Products, and Industrial Products. The main operation in Household Appliances is white goods, which account for 70 percent of sales. Other operations include floor-care products, absorption refrigerators for caravans and hotel rooms, room air-conditioners, and sewing machines, as well as kitchen and bathroom cabinets. The main operations in Commercial Appliances are food-service equipment for restaurants and institutions, and equipment for apartment-house laundry rooms and commercial laundries. Other operations include refrigeration equipment and freezers for shops and supermarkets, as well as vacuum cleaners and wet/dry cleaners for commercial use. Outdoor Products include garden equipment, chain saws, and other equipment for forestry operations. Industrial Products comprise the group's second-largest business area. Other main operations include car safety belts and other products for personal safety in cars as well as materials-handling equipment. **Number of employees worldwide:** 18,000.

FOUNTAIN POWERBOAT INDUSTRIES INC.
1653 Whichards Beach Road, P.O. Drawer 457, Washington NC 27889. 252/975-2000. **Fax:** 252/975-6793. **Contact:** Carol Price, Director of

Human Resources. **E-mail address:** humanresources@fountainpowerboats.com. **World Wide Web address:** http://www.fountainpowerboats.com. **Description:** Designs, manufactures, and sells sport boats, sport cruisers, and sport fishing boats. **NOTE:** Contact Human Resources directly at 252/975-7017. **Positions advertised include:** Mechanic; Cabinet Builder; Carpenter; Gel Detailer; Laminator; Service Mechanic; Welder; Machinist; Painter; Screen Printer; Engine Rigger; Assembly Cabin Rigger; Assembly Cockpit Rigger; Electrical Engineering Technician; Pre-Rigger; Plexi-Glass Fabricator. **Corporate headquarters location:** This location. **Listed on:** NASDAQ. **Stock exchange symbol:** FPWR. **President/CEO:** R.M. Fountain Jr. **Number of employees at this location:** 353.

HAMILTON BEACH/PROCTOR-SILEX, INC.
261 Yadkin Road, Southern Pines NC 28387. 910/692-7676. **Toll-free phone:** 800/851-8900. **Contact:** Human Resources Administrator. **World Wide Web Address:** http://www.hamiltonbeach.com. **Description:** Manufactures small appliances including blenders, can openers, coffeemakers, food processors, irons, mixers, steamers, and toasters. **NOTE:** Please visit http://www.monster.com to search for jobs. **International locations:** Canada; Mexico. **Parent company:** NACCO Industries, Inc. **President/CEO:** Michael J. Morecroft.

HAMMARY FURNITURE COMPANY
P.O. Box 760, Lenoir NC 28645. 828/728-3231. **Physical address:** 2464 Norwood Street SW, Lenoir NC 28645. **Contact:** Human Resources. **World Wide Web address:** http://www.hammary.com. **Description:** Manufactures tables, wall units, couches, loveseats, and chairs. **Office hours:** Monday – Friday, 8:00 a.m. – 5:00 p.m. **Parent company:** La-Z-Boy Inc.

HENREDON FURNITURE INDUSTRIES, INC.
641 West Ward Avenue, High Point NC 27260. 336/885-9141. **Fax:** 336/888-2951. **Contact:** Human Resources Manager. **World Wide Web address:** http://www.henredon.com. **Description:** Manufactures and designs upholstered furniture and case goods. **Office hours:** Monday – Friday, 8:00 a.m. – 5:00 p.m. **Corporate headquarters location:** Morganton NC. **Other area locations:** Spruce Pine NC. **Parent company:** Furniture Brands International, Inc. **Operations at this facility include:** Administration; Divisional Headquarters; Manufacturing; Sales. **Listed on:** New York Stock Exchange. **Stock exchange symbol:** FBN. **Number of employees at this location:** 420.

HICKORY CHAIR COMPANY
P.O. Box 2147, Hickory NC 28603. 828/328-1802. **Fax:** 828/326-4223. **Contact:** Personnel Director. **World Wide Web address:** http://www.hickorychair.com. **Description:** A manufacturer of 18th-century style furniture. Founded in 1911. **NOTE:** Contact Human Resources directly at Ext. 7315. **Special programs:** Internships. **Corporate headquarters location:** Altavista VA. **Parent company:** The

Lane Company Inc. **Operations at this facility include:** Administration; Divisional Headquarters; Manufacturing; Sales. **Number of employees at this location:** 1,000.

HOOKER FURNITURE CORPORATION
P.O. Box 617, Maiden NC 28650. 828/428-9978. **Physical address:** 2900 US Highway 321, Maiden NC 28650. **Contact:** Denise Campbell, Personnel. **World Wide Web address:** http://www.hookerfurniture.com. **Description:** Manufactures home and home office furniture. The company recently acquired Bradington-Young, and has begun developing upholstered and leather furniture. Founded 1924. **Corporate headquarters location:** Martinsville VA. **Number of employees nationwide:** 2,200.

KING HICKORY FURNITURE COMPANY
P.O. Box 1179, Hickory NC 28603. 828/322-6025. **Physical address:** 1820 Main Avenue SE, Hickory NC 28603. **Toll-free phone:** 800/337-8827. **Contact:** Human Resources. **World Wide Web address:** http://www.kinghickory.com. **Description:** Manufactures sofas, sleepers, loveseats, settees, ottomans, and other furniture. All furniture has hardwood frames and hand-tied springs. Founded 1958. **Corporate headquarters location:** This location.

LA-Z-BOY CHAIR COMPANY
1164 Burris Boulevard, Lincolnton NC 28092. 704/735-0441. **Fax:** 704/748-6559. **Contact:** Human Resources. **World Wide Web address:** http://www.la-z-boy.com. **Description:** A manufacturer of upholstered seating, and one of the nation's largest manufacturers of residential furniture. La-Z-Boy is best known for its upholstered recliners. The company also manufactures furniture for family rooms, living rooms, bedrooms, and dining rooms. The company operates in five divisions: La-Z-Boy Residential produces stationary chairs, sofas and loveseats, recliners, reclining sofas, sleeper sofas, and modular seating groups, which it sells in a national network of La-Z-Boy proprietary stores, and in department stores, furniture stores, and regional furniture chains; La-Z-Boy Canada manufactures residential seating and markets La-Z-Boy residential products in Canada; Hammary produces occasional tables, living room cabinets, wall entertainment units, and upholstered furniture sold in furniture and department stores, as well as CompaTables occasional tables, which are featured in La-Z-Boy proprietary stores; Kincaid makes solid-wood bedroom, dining room, and occasional furniture sold through in-store Kincaid Galleries, and select La-Z-Boy Furniture Galleries nationwide; La-Z-Boy Contract Furniture Group includes La-Z-Boy Business Furniture, La-Z-Boy Healthcare Furniture (hospital chairs, recliners, and special mobile recliners, marketed through contract dealers and medical sales companies), and La-Z-Boy Hospitality Furniture (specially engineered La-Z-Boy recliners that are sold directly to major hotel and motel chains and through hospitality sales companies). **Office hours:** Monday – Thursday, 7:00 a.m. – 4:30 p.m.; Friday – 7:00 a.m. 11:00 a.m. **Corporate headquarters location:** Monroe MI. **Other U.S. locations:** Nationwide. **Subsidiaries include:**

Bauhaus USA Furniture; Centurion Furniture; Clayton Marcus; Hammary Furniture; Kincaid Furniture. **Listed on:** New York Stock Exchange. **Stock exchange symbol:** LZB. **Number of employees worldwide:** 17,000.

LEA INDUSTRIES
P.O. Box 26777, Greensboro NC 27417. 336/294-5233. **Physical address:** 4620 Grandover Parkway, Greensboro NC 27407. **Fax:** 336/315-4380. **Contact:** Personnel. **E-mail address:** leaindustries@leaindustries.com. **World Wide Web address:** http://www.leafurniture.com. **Description:** Manufactures a variety of styles of furniture for children. Looks vary from country to 18th Century-style to contemporary pieces, and products include bunk beds, dual sleep beds, canopy beds, and desks. Some of their featured collections are the Jessica McClintock Collection, Grant Hill Collection, Dennis Connor Collection, Youth Collection, and Master Bedroom Collection. **Corporate headquarters location:** This location. **Parent company:** La-Z-Boy Inc.

LEVOLOR HOME FASHIONS
4110 Premier Drive, High Point NC 27265. 336/812-8181. **Toll-free phone:** 800/538-6567. **Contact:** Human Resources Director. **E-mail address:** career.opportunities@levolor.com. **World Wide Web address:** http://www.levolor.com. **Description:** Manufactures drapery hardware, window blinds, and shades. **Corporate headquarters location:** This location.

LEXINGTON HOME BRANDS
P.O. Box 1008, Lexington NC 27293. 336/236-5300. **Toll-free phone:** 800/LEX-INFO. **Contact:** Human Resources. **World Wide Web address:** http://www.lexington.com. **Description:** A manufacturer of upholstered furniture. Lexington Upholstery is best known for its Bob Timberlake and Arnold Palmer collections. **CEO:** Bob Stec. **Number of employees at this location:** 220.

MILLER DESK INC.
Drawer HP-11, Hight Point NC 27261. 336/819-6400. **Physical address:** 1212 Lincoln Drive, High Point NC 27261. **Toll-free phone:** 800/438-4324. **Fax:** 800/756-9715. **Contact:** Human Resources. **World Wide Web address:** http://www.millerdesk.com. **Description:** A manufacturer of office furniture including both ergonomic and traditional seating.

RAUCH INDUSTRIES
P.O. Box 609, Gastonia NC 28053-0609. 704/867-5333. **Physical address:** 2408 Forbes Road Gastonia NC 28056. **Toll-free phone:** 800/313-1830. **Fax:** 704/864-2081. 865-8260. **Contact:** Personnel Manager. **Description:** Manufactures and imports Christmas and holiday decorations. **Corporate headquarters location:** This location.

RUDDICK CORPORATION
301 South Tryon Street, Suite 1800, Charlotte NC 28202. 704/372-5404. **Fax:** 704/372-6409. **Contact:** Human Resources. **World Wide Web address:** http://www.ruddickcorp.com. **Description:** A holding company. The company oversees Harris Teeter, Inc., which operates a supermarket chain; and American & Efird, Inc., a manufacturer of both industrial and consumer sewing thread. **Listed on:** New York Stock Exchange. **Stock exchange symbol:** RDK. **President/CEO:** Thomas W. Dickson.

ST. TIMOTHY CHAIR COMPANY
P.O. Box 2427, Hickory NC 28613. 828/322-7125. **Physical address:** Highway 70-A East, Hickory NC 28601. **Contact:** Personnel Manager. **World Wide Web address:** http://www.sttimothychair.com. **Description:** Manufactures case goods, chairs, and other home and office furnishings. **Parent company:** Classic Leather.

SEALY, INC.
One Office Parkway, Trinity NC 27370. 336/861-3500. **Fax:** 336/861-3715. **Contact:** Joe Taylor, Human Resources. **World Wide Web address:** http://www.sealy.com. **Description:** One of the largest mattress and furniture manufacturers in North America. **NOTE:** Please visit website to search for jobs. **Corporate headquarters location:** This location. **Other U.S. locations:** Nationwide. **International locations:** Canada. **Operations at this facility include:** Administration. **Listed on:** Privately held. **CEO:** David McIlquham. **Number of employees nationwide:** 6,562.

SOUTHERN FURNITURE COMPANY
1099 Second Avenue Pl SE, P.O. Box 307, Conover NC 28613. 828/464-0311. **Contact:** Personnel & Human Resources Director. **Description:** A manufacturer of upholstery goods and case goods. The company has plants located throughout North Carolina. **NOTE:** You may mark your resume attention to Emily, post number 8284640460. **Corporate headquarters location:** This location.

South Carolina

THE COLEMAN COMPANY, INC.
P.O. Box 1119, Lake City SC 29560. 843/394-8893. **Contact:** Personnel Director. **E-mail address:** careers@coleman.com. **World Wide Web address:** http://www.colemancareers.com. **Description:** The Coleman Company manufactures, markets, and distributes outdoor recreation gear such as sleeping bags, lanterns, flashlights, coolers, backpacks, camp stoves, canoes and fishing boats, water ski boats, sleeping bags, fuel, and hot tubs. Nationally, the company manufactures the following brands: Coleman, Campingaz, Peak 1, Outing Sports Products; Hobie Cat and O'Brien Marine Products; Coleman Camping Trailers; Home Heating and Air Conditioning Products; and Recreational Vehicle Products. Its Coleman Powermate division produces portable generators, fuel cell generators, and compressors. The company

operates internationally through Coleman Canadian Sales and Coleman Foreign Sales. **NOTE:** Resumes accepted through the company Website. **Positions advertised include:** Project Analyst; Design Engineer. **Corporate headquarters location:** Wichita KS. **Other area locations:** Statewide. **Other U.S. locations:** AR; FL; KS; OK; TX. **International locations:** Worldwide. **Subsidiaries include:** Coleman Powermate, Inc. **Parent company:** American Household (formerly Sunbeam). **Chairman:** Jerry W. Levin. **Annual sales/revenues:** $1 billion. **Number of employees at this location:** 100. **Number of employees nationwide:** 2,000.

ELECTROLUX HOME PRODUCTS OF NORTH AMERICA
2500 Saint Matthews Road, North, SC. 803/534-1685. **Physical address:** 172 Old Elloree Road, Orangeburg SC 29115. **Contact:** Betty Johnson-Pringle, Human Resources. **World Wide Web address:** http://na.electrolux.com. **Description:** Formerly Frigidaire Home Products, Electrolux manufactures household appliances including washing machines, ranges, dishwashers, refrigerators, freezers, air conditioners, and disposals at 14 manufacturing locations in North America. **NOTE:** Resumes may be sent to the company's headquarters address: 250 Bobby Jones Expressway, Martinez GA 30907. **Positions advertised include:** Process Owner Customer Service; Electrical Control Engineer; Electrical Engineer; Quality Engineer; Project Manager; Information Technology Support Analyst; Mechanical Engineer. **Corporate headquarters location:** Martinez GA. **Other area locations:** Anderson SC. **Other U.S. locations:** Nationwide. **International locations:** Canada; Mexico. **Subsidiaries/affiliates include:** Frigidaire; White Westinghouse; Tappan; Gibson. **Parent company:** AB Electrolux (Stockholm, Sweden). **Operations at this facility include:** Manufacturing/Engineering. **Annual sales/revenues:** $4 billion. **Number of employees:** 19,000.

ELLETT BROTHERS, INC.
267 Columbia Avenue, P.O. Box 128, Chapin SC 29036. 803/345-3751. **Contact:** Human Resources. **World Wide Web address:** http://www.ellettbrothers.com. **Description:** Manufacturers leisure products focusing on outdoor recreational sports such as hunting and shooting, marine activities, camping, and archery. Founded in 1933. **Positions advertised include:** Sales Representative; Business Unit Manager. **Corporate headquarters location:** This location. **Other locations:** Newbury SC; Taylorsville NC; Houston MO; Monroe MI. **Subsidiaries include:** Evans Sports, Inc.; Vintage Editions, Inc.; Archery Center International. **Parent company:** Tuscarora Incorporated (New Brighton PA). **Operations at this facility include:** Distribution; Product Sourcing; Teleservicing Operations. **Listed on:** Privately held. **President/CEO:** Bob McBeth. **Annual sales/revenues:** $150 million. **Number of employees nationwide:** 411.

INTERTAPE POLYMER GROUP
2000 South Beltline Boulevard, Columbia SC 29201-5110. 803/799-8800. **Contact:** Sandra Rivers, Human Resources Manager. **E-mail**

address: info@tape.com. **World Wide Web address:** http://www.intertapepolymer.com. **Description:** Manufactures a variety of pressure-sensitive tape products and polyolefin plastic products. The company's products include duct tape and masking tape. **Positions advertised include:** Accountant; Chemist; Controls Engineer; Electrical Engineer; Electrician; Industrial Engineer; Mechanical Engineer; Production Manager; Process Engineer. **Corporate headquarters location:** Montreal, Canada. **Other U.S. locations:** Nationwide. **Operations at this facility include:** Administration; Manufacturing; Research and Development; Sales; Service. **Listed on:** New York Stock Exchange. **Stock exchange symbol:** ITP. **Chairman/CEO:** Melbourne F. Yull. **Annual sales/revenues:** $595 million. **Number of employees nationwide:** 2,900.

SPRINGS INDUSTRIES, INC.
P.O. Box 70, Fort Mill SC 29716. 803/547-1500. **Physical address:** 205 North White Street, Fort Mill SC 29715. **Contact:** Human Resources. **World Wide Web address:** http://www.springs.com. **Description:** A producer of home furnishings, finished fabrics, and other fabrics for industrial uses. Products include bedroom accessories, bath products, novelties, window treatments, and specialty fabrics for the apparel, home furnishing, home sewing, and sporting good industries. Brand names include Wamsutta, Springmaid, Nanik, Graber, Bali, Springs Baby, Daisy Kingdom, and Regal Rugs operating 40 facilities in North America. Founded in 1887. **Positions advertised include:** Process Engineer; Field Sales Representative. **Corporate headquarters location:** This location. **Other locations:** Nationwide. **International locations:** Canada; Mexico. **Listed on:** Privately held. **Chairman:** Crandall Bowles. **Annual sales/revenues:** $2.1 billion. **Number of employees:** 12,000.

3M COMPANY
1400 Perimeter Road, Greenville SC 29605. 864/277-8270. **Contact:** Human Resources. **World Wide Web address:** http://www.3m.com. **Description:** The company manufactures products in three sectors: industrial and consumer; information, imaging, and electronic; and life sciences. The industrial and consumer sector includes a variety of products under brand names including 3M, Scotch, Post-it, Scotch-Brite, and Scotchgard. The information, imaging, and electronic sector is a leader in several high-growth global industries including telecommunications, electronics, electrical, imaging, and memory media. The life sciences sector serves two broad market categories: health care, and traffic and personal safety. In the health care market, 3M is a leading provider of medical and surgical supplies, drug delivery systems, and dental products. In traffic and personal safety, 3M is a leader in products for transportation safety, worker protection, vehicle and sign graphics, and out-of-home advertising. Founded in 1929. **Corporate headquarters location:** St. Paul MN. **Operations at this facility include:** Tape manufacturing. **Listed on:** New York Stock Exchange. **Stock exchange symbol:** MMM. **Number of employees nationwide:** 71,600.

WILSON SPORTING GOODS COMPANY

206 Georgia Street, Fountain Inn SC 29644. 864/862-4416. **Fax:** 864/862-6150. **Contact:** Personnel. **World Wide Web address:** http://www.wilson.com. **Description:** The company manufactures sports-related products for golf, tennis, and team sports operating eight domestic manufacturing plants and 11 other facilities located outside the United States. Wilson Sporting Goods Company has been affiliated with the National Football League since 1941, has produced the official baseball of the National Collegiate Athletic Association championships since 1986 and the official ball of many of professional baseball's minor league teams. The company also manufactures and supplies uniforms to the National Football League, Major League Baseball, and the National Basketball Association, as well as many colleges, universities, and high schools throughout the United States. **NOTE:** Application materials and resumes may be sent to the attention of Corporate Human Resources at: Wilson Sporting Goods Co., 8700 West Bryn Mawr Avenue, Chicago IL 60631. **Positions advertised include:** Chemical Engineer; Chemist; Draftsperson; Electrical Engineer; Electrician; Industrial Engineer; Mechanical Engineer; Operations Manager. **Corporate headquarters location:** Chicago IL. **Other U.S. locations:** Nationwide. **Parent company:** Amer Group, Ltd. (Helsinki, Finland) is an international, highly diversified conglomerate also involved in the marketing of motor vehicles, paper, communications, and tobacco. **Operations at this facility include:** Tennis ball and racquetball manufacturing. **Listed on:** Privately held. **Number of employees worldwide:** 3,062.

MANUFACTURING: MISCELLANEOUS INDUSTRIAL

You can expect to find the following types of companies in this section:
Ball and Roller Bearings • Commercial Furniture and Fixtures • Fans, Blowers, and Purification Equipment • Industrial Machinery and Equipment • Motors and Generators/Compressors and Engine Parts • Vending Machines

North Carolina

A.G. INDUSTRIES INC.
376 Pine Street Extension, Forest City NC 28043. 828/245-9871. **Fax:** 828/248-4848. **Contact:** Gray Webber, Human Resources Manager. **World Wide Web address:** http://www.agischutz.com. **Description:** Manufactures display cabinets and display racks for wholesalers and stores.

ALTEC INDUSTRIES, INC.
1550 Aerial Avenue, Creedmoor NC 27522. 919/528-2535. **Contact:** Human Resources. **E-mail address:** webcreedmoor@altec.com. **World Wide Web address:** http://www.altec.com. **Description:** Altec Industries, Inc. manufactures a wide variety of products including utility trucks, overhead traveling cranes, hoists, and monorail systems. **NOTE:** Please visit website for online application form. **Special programs:** Internships. **Corporate headquarters location:** Birmingham AL. **Other U.S. locations:** Nationwide. **International locations:** Canada. **Operations at this facility include:** Manufacturing; Service. **Number of employees at this location:** 220. **Number of employees worldwide:** 2,500.

BORG WARNER EMISSIONS/THERMAL SYSTEMS
P.O. Box 1509, Fletcher NC 28732. 828/684-3501. **Physical address:** 40 Cane Creek Industrial Park, Fletcher NC 23732. **Fax:** 828/687-5325. **Contact:** Human Resources. **World Wide Web address:** http://www.cs.bwauto.com. **Description:** Borg Warner is a worldwide manufacturer of hydraulic products, fluid connectors, electrical power distribution equipment, engine components, and truck drive train systems. The company serves a variety of industries including automotive, aerospace, industrial, and semiconductor. Founded 1928. **NOTE:** Please send resume to corporate office location at 3800 Automation Avenue, Suite 200, Auburn Mills MI 48326. **Special programs:** Internships. **Corporate headquarters location:** Auburn Hills MI. **International locations:** Brazil; United Kingdom; Germany; Korea; Japan; China; India. **Parent company:** BorgWarner Engine Group. **Operations at this facility include:** This location manufactures viscous fan drives. **Listed on:** New York Stock Exchange. **Stock exchange symbol:** BWA. **Number of employees at this location:** 500. **Number of employees worldwide:** 14,000.

BOSTON GEAR
701 North Interstate 85 Service Road, Charlotte NC 28216. 704/588-5610. **Contact:** Human Resources Department. **E-mail address:** hr@bostongear.com. **World Wide Web address:** http://www.bostongear.com. **Description:** Boston Gear manufactures speed-reducers used for conveyor belts including those used at retail checkout counters. **NOTE:** Please visit website to search for jobs. **Corporate headquarters location:** Quincy MA. **Parent company:** Colfax Power Transmission Group. **Operations at this facility include:** Manufacturing.

COPELAND CORPORATION
4401 East Dixon Boulevard, Shelby NC 28152. 704/484-3011. **Contact:** Human Resources Manager. **E-mail address:** corpresume@copeland-corp.com. **World Wide Web address:** http://www.copeland-corp.com. **Description:** A manufacturer of compressors and condensing units for the commercial, industrial, and residential air conditioning and refrigeration industries. **NOTE:** Please visit website to search for jobs and apply online. **Corporate headquarters location:** Sidney OH. **International locations:** Worldwide. **Parent company:** Emerson Electric.

DANA CORPORATION
P.O. Box 1967, Gastonia NC 28053-1967. 704/864-6711. **Physical address:** One Wix Way, Gastonia NC 28054. **Fax:** 704/853-6143. **Contact:** Human Resources. **World Wide Web address:** http://www.dana.com. **Description:** Dana Corporation is a global leader in engineering, manufacturing, and marketing of products and systems for the worldwide vehicular, industrial, and mobile off-highway original equipment markets and is a major supplier to related aftermarkets. Dana is also a leading provider of lease financing services in selected markets. The company's products include drive train components, such as axles, driveshafts, clutches, and transmissions; engine parts, such as gaskets, piston rings, seals, pistons, and filters; chassis products, such as vehicular frames and cradles and heavy duty side rails; fluid power components, such as pumps, motors, and control valves; and industrial products, such as electrical and mechanical brakes and clutches, drives, and motion control devices. Dana's vehicular components and parts are used on automobiles, pickup trucks, vans, minivans, sport utility vehicles, medium and heavy trucks, and off-highway vehicles. The company's industrial products include mobile off-highway and stationary equipment applications. Founded in 1904. **NOTE:** Please visit website to search for jobs and apply online. **Special programs:** Internships; Co-ops. **Corporate headquarters location:** Toledo OH. **Other area locations:** Asheboro NC; Raleigh NC; Morganton NC; West End NC; Whitsett NC. **Other U.S. locations:** Nationwide. **International locations:** Worldwide. **Operations at this facility include:** This location manufactures air, oil, and specialty filters. **Listed on:** New York Stock Exchange. **Stock exchange symbol:** DCN. **Number of employees worldwide:** 45,000.

DOUGLAS BATTERY MANUFACTURING COMPANY
P.O. Box 12159, Winston-Salem NC 27117. 336/650-7000. **Physical address:** 500 Battery Drive, Winston-Salem NC 27107. **Toll-free phone:** 800/368-4527. **Fax:** 336/650-7057. **Contact:** Manager of Employment. **World Wide Web address:** http://www.douglasbattery.com. **Description:** A manufacturer of lead-acid batteries for industrial, automotive, lawn and garden, marine, and specialty applications. Founded 1921. **Corporate headquarters location:** This location. **Other U.S. locations:** Temple TX; Rocky Hill CT. **Operations at this facility include:** Administration; Manufacturing; Research and Development; Sales; Service. **Listed on:** Privately held. **CEO:** Wilson Douglas, Jr.

FLOWSERVE PUMP COMPANY
264 Wilson Park Road, Statesville NC 28625. 704/872-2468. **Fax:** 704/872-2467. **Contact:** Personnel. **World Wide Web address:** http://www.flowserve.com. **Description:** Produces multistage, submersible pumps with directly coupled water-lubricated motors for municipal, industrial, and agricultural water supply; large capacity axial flow pumps for water level control systems, flood control, dewatering applications, and power plants; maneuvering equipment for ships; and thruster equipment for dynamic positioning of ships. The company also produces submersible motors for marine technology applications. **Corporate headquarters location:** Irving TX. **Parent company:** Dresser Industries, Inc. **Operations at this facility include:** Manufacturing. **Listed on:** New York Stock Exchange. **Stock exchange symbol:** FLS. **Number of employees worldwide:** 14,000.

HON INDUSTRIES
7966 NC 56 Highway West, Louisburg NC 27549. 919/496-5701. **Fax:** 919/496-2389. **Contact:** Christine Whitaker, Human Resources. **World Wide Web address:** http://www.honi.com. **Description:** A diversified manufacturer and marketer of office furniture, workspace accessories, and home-building products, comprised of nine operating companies with offices, showrooms, distribution centers, and manufacturing plants nationwide. Six operating companies, marketing under various brand names (The Hon Company, Gunlocke Company, XLM, Chandler Attwood, BPI, and Holga), participate in the office furniture industry. Ring King Visibles manufactures and markets workspace accessories to improve productivity and ergonomic comfort; Heatilator, Inc. manufactures and markets factory-built fireplaces, fireplace inserts, heating stoves, and accessories; and Hon Export Limited markets the corporation's products worldwide. Founded 1944. **Corporate headquarters location:** Muscatine IA. **Listed on:** New York Stock Exchange. **Stock exchange symbol:** HNI. **President:** Stan A. Akren. **CEO:** Jack D. Michaels.

HONEYWELL NYLON INC. (HNI)
4824 Parkway Plaza Boulevard Suite 300 Charlotte NC 28817-9730. 704/423-2000. **Contact:** Human Resources. **World Wide Web address:** http://www.honeywell.com/sites/sm/nylon.htm. **Description:** Creates

high-performance nylon fabrics. **Corporate headquarters location:** This location. **Other U.S. locations:** SC; VA. **International locations:** Canada; China. **Parent company:** Honeywell. **Number of employees worldwide:** 4,000.

JACOBSEN
3800 Arco Corporate Drive, Suite 310, Charlotte NC 28273. 704/504-6600. **Contact:** Human Resources. **E-mail address:** jobs@textron.com. **World Wide Web address:** http://www.jacobsen.com. **Description:** Manufactures equipment for lawn and turf maintenance, including the brand name products Bob-Cat, Brouwer, and Ransomes. **NOTE:** Please visit website to search for jobs. **Positions advertised include:** Lead Purchasing Analyst; Purchasing Engineer; Value Engineer; Value Group Manager; Manager – Service Parts Warehouse; Senior Financial Analyst; Senior Buyer; Service Parts Buyer; Human Resources Executive Assistant. **Parent company:** Textron, Inc. is a diversified company with manufacturing and financial services operations. The company is one of the U.S. government's largest defense contractors. Products include helicopters; gas turbine engines; combat vehicles; air cushion landing craft; missile re-entry systems; aircraft wing structures; and aerospace materials, controls, and electronics. The remainder of manufacturing primarily consists of automotive parts, outdoor products, and specialty fasteners. Financial and other services segments include Avco Financial Services, Textron Financial Corporation, Avco Insurance Services/Balboa Life and Casualty, and Paul Revere Insurance Group. **Corporate headquarters location:** This location. **Other US. Locations:** Johnson Creek WI; Augusta GA. **International locations:** United Kingdom; Asia. **Listed on:** New York Stock Exchange. **Stock exchange symbol:** TXT. **President/CEO:** Lewis B. Campbell. **Number of employees worldwide:** 49,000.

KABA ILCO CORPORATION
2941 Indiana Avenue, Winston-Salem NC 27105. 336/725-1331. **Toll-free phone:** 800/849-8324. **Fax:** 336/722-8814. **Contact:** Human Resources. **E-mail address:** cv@kaba-ilco.com. **World Wide Web address:** http://www.kaba-ilco.com. **Description:** Manufactures key blanks, key machines, and two types of locks (mechanical push-button and electronic access control). **NOTE;** Please visit website to view job listings. **Other area locations:** Rocky Mount NC. **International locations:** Montreal, Canada. **Number of employees worldwide:** 300.

LONG AGRI-BUSINESS
P.O. Box 1139, Tarboro NC 27886. 252/823-4151. **Physical address:** 111 Fairview Street, Tarboro NC 27886. **Fax:** 252/823-4576. **Contact:** Human Resources Director. **World Wide Web address:** http://www.longagri.com. **Description:** Develops, manufactures, and markets a broad range of farm and industrial equipment including tractors, tillers, harrows, unloading equipment, elevators, backhoes, storage bins, furnaces, and wood-burning stoves. Founded 1941. **Office hours:** Monday – Friday, 8:00 a.m. – 5:00 p.m. **Corporate headquarters location:** This location. **Operations at this facility**

include: Administration; Manufacturing; Research and Development; Sales; Service. **Listed on:** Privately held. **Number of employees at this location:** 325.

MOOG COMPONENTS GROUP
POLY-SCIENTIFIC
1995 NC Highway, Murphy NC 28906-6864. 828/837-5115. **Toll-free phone:** 800/577-8685. **Fax:** 828/837-0846. **Contact:** Human Resources. **E-mail address:** staylor2@moog.com. **World Wide Web address:** http://www.polysci.com. **Description:** Moog Components Group designs and manufactures technology components. **NOTE:** Please visit website to view job listings. **Other U.S. locations:** Blacksburg VA; Springfield PA. **Operations at this facility include:** This location manufactures brush and brushless DC motors, drives and integrated motion systems.

MURATA MACHINERY USA
2120 I-85 South Charlotte NC 28208. 704/875-9280. **Toll-free phone:** 800/428-8469. **Contact:** Human Resources. **World Wide Web address:** http://www.muratec.net. **Description:** Develops, manufactures, and sells computer-controlled fabrication equipment, accessories, and systems, which provide flexibility and productivity for nonmass producers of parts made from flat materials (primarily sheet metal) in the world markets. Products include CNC Punch Press, Laser Contouring Equipment, Panel Bender, Plasma Arc, Right Angle Shears, and Twin Spindle Lathes. **NOTE:** Entry-level positions and part-time jobs are offered. **Special programs:** Internships; Co-ops; Summer Jobs. **Office hours:** Monday – Friday, 8:00 a.m. – 5:00 p.m. **Corporate headquarters location:** Kyoto, Japan. **International locations:** China; Germany; Singapore; Switzerland. **Operations at this facility include:** Administration; Manufacturing; Sales; Service. **Listed on:** Privately held. **Annual sales/revenues:** $21 - $50 million.

POWERWARE CORPORATION
8609 Six Forks Road, Raleigh NC 27615. 919/872-3020. **Toll-free phone:** 800/554-3448. **Fax:** 919/870-3100. **Contact:** Human Resources Manager. **World Wide Web address:** http://www.powerware.com. **Description:** Manufactures and markets uninterruptible power supplies, power control and energy storage products, and backup power management solutions. **NOTE:** Entry-level positions are offered. Please visit website to search for jobs and apply online. **Positions advertised include:** Customer Service Representative. **Corporate headquarters location:** This location. **International locations:** Worldwide. **Parent company:** Invesys plc (London, England). **Annual sales/revenues:** More than $100 million.

SAFT AMERICA INC.
313 Crescent Street, Valdese NC 28690. 828/874-4111. **Fax:** 828/874-2431. **Contact:** Staff Services Manager. **World Wide Web address:** http://www.saftbatteries.com. **Description:** A manufacturer of industrial aviation batteries and numerous other storage batteries for industrial use. **Corporate headquarters location:** Bagnolet, France. **Other U.S.**

locations: Cockeysville MD; Valdosta GA. **International locations:** Worldwide. **Operations at this facility include:** Manufacturing. **Number of employees worldwide:** 4,000.

TARHEEL ROLLER & BRAYER
2156 Lewisville-Clemmons Road, P.O. Box 773, Clemmons NC 27012. 336/766-9823. **Fax:** 336/766-4286. **Contact:** Human Resources. **E-mail address:** hau6118@aol.com. **NOTE:** Phone number will connect you directly with the company's owner. **World Wide Web address:** http://www4.ncsu.edu/~bdhauser/tarheelroller.htm. **Description:** Manufactures composition printer rollers and paper cutter blades for paper cutting machines. **Owner:** David H. Hauser.

TESA TAPE, INC.
5825 Carnegie Boulevard, Charlotte NC 28209. 704/554-0707. **Toll-free phone:** 800/426-2181. **Fax:** 800/852-8831. **Contact:** Human Resources. **World Wide Web address:** http://www.tesatape.com. **Description:** Engaged in the production and sale of an extensive line of masking, cellophane, electrical, cloth, and other pressure-sensitive tape products for business, industrial, and household use. **Corporate headquarters location:** This location. **Other U.S. locations:** Carbondale IL; Sparta MI; Middletown NY. **International locations:** Worldwide. **Parent company:** Tesa AG (Hamburg Germany). **Operations at this facility include:** Research and Development.

WEAVEXX
P.O. Box 471, Wake Forest NC 27588. 919/556-7235. **Physical address:** 11120 Capital Boulevard, Wake Forest NC 27587. **Toll-free phone:** 800/932-8399. **Contact:** Human Resources. **World Wide Web address:** http://www.weavexx.com. **Description:** Manufactures forming fabrics, press felt, dryer fabrics, and wet-end drainage equipment for paper manufacturers. **NOTE:** For information about employment, call the Xerium offices at 508/616-9468. **Other U.S. locations:** Starkville MS; Greenville TN; Farmville VA; Huntington Beach CA. **International locations:** Canada; Mexico. **Parent company:** Xerium Companies.

South Carolina

COOPER INDUSTRIES INC.
COOPER TOOLS DIVISION
P.O. Box 1410, Lexington SC 29071-1410. 803/359-1200. **Contact:** Human Resources. **E-mail address:** lexington.recruit@coopertools.com. **World Wide Web address:** http://www.cooperindustries.com. **Description:** Manufactures pneumatic hand tools, air motors, air feed drills, and hoists. Overall, Cooper Industries Inc. is engaged in three primary areas of manufacturing: tools and hardware, electrical and electronic products, and automotive products. **Positions advertised include:** Draftsperson; Industrial Designer; Production Engineer; Mechanical Engineer; Quality Control Supervisor. **Corporate headquarters location:** Houston TX. **Other area locations:** Cherow

SC; Georgetown SC; Greenwood SC; Sumter SC. **Other U.S. locations:** Nationwide. **Listed on:** New York Stock Exchange. **Stock exchange symbol:** CBE. **Chairman/President/CEO:** H. John Riley Jr. **Annual sales/revenues:** $4 billion. **Number of employees nationwide:** 28,500.

CROWN HOLDINGS, INC.
100 Evans Row, P.O. Box 759, Cheraw SC 29020. 843/537-9794. **Fax:** 843/537-4382. **Contact:** Personnel Manager. **World Wide Web address:** http://www.crowncork.com. **Description:** A worldwide manufacturer and distributor of a wide range of crowns, seals, and aluminum/steel cans including aerosol and beverage cans. The company also manufactures bottling equipment. **NOTE:** The company requests resumes to be submitted online. **Positions advertised include:** Corporate Trainer; Production Engineer; Manufacturing Supervisor; Production Foreman. **Corporate headquarters location:** Philadelphia PA. **Other area locations:** Spartanburg SC. **Other U.S. locations:** Nationwide. **International locations:** Worldwide. **Subsidiaries include:** Crown Cork & Seal Company. **Operations at this location include:** Beverage Division. **Listed on:** New York Stock Exchange. **Stock exchange symbol:** CCK. **Chairman/President/CEO:** John W. Conway. **Annual sales/revenues:** $7.2 billion. **Number of employees:** 33,050.

KENNAMETAL INC.
P.O. Box 872, Clemson SC 29633-0872. 864/654-4922. **Contact:** Human Resources. **World Wide Web address:** http://www.kennametal.com. **Description:** Manufactures and markets tools, services, related supplies, and specially engineered products for metalworking, mining, construction, and other industrial applications with operations in over 60 countries and specializes in cemented tungsten carbide, high-speed steel tools, and wear-resistant carbide components. **Positions advertised include:** Human Resources Generalist; Administrative Support Associate; Administrator; Industrial Engineer; Information Technology Administrator; Inside Sales; Outside Sales; Project Manager; Attorney; General Counsel. **Corporate headquarters location:** Latrobe PA. **Other locations:** Worldwide. **Subsidiaries include:** Greenfield Industries Inc.; JLK Direct Distribution Inc.; Widia Group. **Listed on:** New York Stock Exchange. **Stock exchange symbol:** KMT. **Chairman/President/CEO:** Markos I. Tanbakeras. **Annual sales/revenues:** $1.6 billion. **Number of employees worldwide:** 14,000.

SACO LOWELL, INC.
P.O. Box 2327, Greenville SC 29602. 864/850-4400. **Fax:** 864/859-2908. **Contact:** Gene Dunlap, Human Resources. **World Wide Web address:** http://www.sacolowell.com. **E-mail address:** bkhaleghi@sacolowell.com. **Description:** Saco Lowell, Inc. designs and manufactures textile machinery including parts, attachments, and accessories. The company's primary customers are textile mills. **Positions advertised include:** Computer-assisted Design Operator; Draftsperson; Electrical Engineer; Industrial Engineer; Production Manager; Machinist; Mechanical Engineer; Sheet-Metal Worker; Tool and Die Maker.

SCOTSMAN ICE SYSTEMS

Industrial Park, P.O. Box 890, Fairfax SC 29827. 803/632-2511. **Contact:** Human Resources. **World Wide Web address:** http://www.scotsman-ice.com. **Description:** A manufacturer of commercial ice machines. **Office hours:** Monday – Friday, 7:00 a.m. – 4:00 p.m. **Positions advertised include:** Industrial Engineer; Management Trainee; Production Manager; Quality Control Supervisor. **Corporate headquarters location:** Vernon Hills IL. **Parent company:** Enodis.

SONOCO PRODUCTS

One North Second Street, Hartsville SC 29550. 843/383-7000. **Fax:** 843/383-3334. **Contact:** Lisa Spears, Human Resources. **E-mail address:** Lisa.Spears@sonoco.com. **World Wide Web address:** http://www.sonoco.com. **Description:** Manufactures paper and plastic cones, tubes, cores and spools; composite cans and containers; plastic bottles; plastic meter boxes and underground enclosures; specialties; partitions and pads; paperboard; aluminum and steel textile beams; machinery products; hardwood lumber; plastic grocery bags; metal, plastic, and wood reels; adhesives; fiber and plastic drums; and dual oven trays operating over 300 facilities in 32 countries. **Positions advertised include:** Auditor; Commercial Analyst; Corporate Accountant; Corporate Fleet Manager; Financial Analyst; IPD Quality Manager; Operations Manager; Senior Sourcing Specialist; Timber Procurement Forester; Segment Services Quality Manager. **Corporate headquarters location:** This location. **Other area locations:** Union SC. **Other U.S. locations:** Nationwide. **International locations:** Worldwide. **Listed on:** New York Stock Exchange. **Stock exchange symbol:** SON. **Number of employees worldwide:** 18,000

SPIRAX SARCO INC.

1150 Northpoint Boulevard, Blythewood SC 29016. 803/714-2000. **Fax:** 803/714-2222. **Contact:** Human Resources. **World Wide Web address:** http://www.spiraxsarco-usa.com. **Description:** A leading supplier of steam system solutions. The company manufactures regulators, controls, steam traps, strainers, pumps, and other steam specialty products operating 39 facilities in 28 countries including 12 manufacturing locations. **Positions advertised include:** Draftsperson; Electrician; Environmental Engineer; Materials Engineer; Mechanical Engineer; Operations/Production Manager. **Corporate headquarters location:** This location. **Parent company:** Spirax Sarco Engineering PLC. **Operations at this facility include:** Administration; Manufacturing; Research and Development; Sales; Service. **Number of employees worldwide:** 3,900.

MINING, GAS, PETROLEUM, ENERGY RELATED

You can expect to find the following types of companies in this section:
Anthracite, Coal, and Ore Mining • Mining Machinery and Equipment • Oil and Gas Field Services • Petroleum and Natural Gas

North Carolina

CHEMETALL FOOTE MINERAL COMPANY
348 Holiday Inn Drive, Kings Mountain NC 28086. 704/739-2501. **Fax:** 704/734-0208. **Contact:** Human Resources. **E-mail address:** human-resources@chemetall.com. **World Wide Web address:** http://www.chemetall.com. **Description:** One of the world's largest producers of lithium carbonide, which is used in aluminum melting, synthetic rubber, specialty glass greases, batteries, and pharmaceuticals. **Corporate headquarters location:** This location. **Other U.S. locations:** New Johnsonville TN; Silver Peak NV; Duffield VA; Berkeley Heights NJ; La Marida CA; Romulus MI. **International locations:** Worldwide. **Parent company:** Dynamit Nobel AG. **Operations at this facility include:** Administration; Research and Development; Sales. **Number of employees at this location:** 75. **Number of employees worldwide:** 2,514.

COGENTRIX ENERGY, INC.
9405 Arrowpoint Boulevard, Charlotte NC 28273-8110. 704/525-3800. **Fax:** 704/529-5313. **Contact:** Personnel. **E-mail address:** hr@cogentrix.com. **World Wide Web address:** http://www.cogentrix.com. **Description:** Develops, constructs, and operates nonutility electricity generating facilities. The company has 10 operating facilities. **Corporate headquarters location:** This location. **Other U.S. locations:** Nationwide. **International locations:** Singapore. **Listed on:** Privately held. **CEO:** James E. Lewis. **Number of employees nationwide:** 500.

GILBARCO
P.O. Box 22087, Greensboro NC 27420. 336/547-5000. **Physical address:** 7300 West Friendly Avenue, Greensboro NC 27410. **Fax:** 336/547-5549. **Contact:** Human Resources. **World Wide Web address:** http://www.gilbarco.com. **Description:** A manufacturer of electronic fuel dispensing equipment and peripheral devices for the petroleum industry. **NOTE:** Please visit website to search for jobs, apply online, or download application form. **Special programs:** Internships. **Corporate headquarters location:** This location. **Other U.S. locations:** Glendale CA. **International locations:** Argentina; Australia; Canada; China; Germany; Italy; New Zealand; Thailand; United Kingdom. **Parent company:** Donaher Corporation. **Listed on:** New York Stock Exchange. **Stock exchange symbol:** DHR. **Number of employees at this location:** 1,600. **Number of employees worldwide:** 4,000.

South Carolina

KASHO GOLD COMPANY, INC.
2526 Mineral Mining Road, P.O. Box 458, Kershaw SC 29067. 803/285-3965. **Contact:** Human Resources. **Description:** Formerly Mineral Mining Company, the company specializes in the mining of gold and mineralite mica. **Affiliates include:** Piedmont Gold Company, Inc.; Haile Mine Properties. **Parent company:** Piedmont Mining Co. (Charlotte NC).

SCHLUMBERGER RESOURCE MANAGEMENT SERVICES
313 North Highway 11, West Union SC 29696. 864/638-8300. **Contact:** Sue Gray, Personnel Supervisor. **World Wide Web address:** http://www.slb.com. **Description:** A global technology services company with operations in 100 countries divided into two business segments: Schlumberger Oilfield Services and SchlumbergerSema. The company provides services for utilities, energy service providers, and industry worldwide through consulting, meter deployment and management, data collection and processing, and information analysis in all utility sectors including water, gas, electricity, and heat. **Positions advertised include:** Field Engineer; Field Specialist; Account Manager; Assistant Accountant; Web Developer; Data Architect; Chemical Product Developer; Chemical Engineer; Compensation & Compliance Specialist; Electrical Development Engineer; Electrical Engineer; Oilfield Services Electronic Technician; Field Marketing Manager; GeoScientist; Applications Engineer; Design Engineer; Sales Engineer; Software Engineer. **Corporate headquarters location:** New York NY. **Other locations:** Worldwide. **Parent company:** Schlumberger Ltd. manufactures measurement, electronics, and testing products and provides well site exploration and computer aided design.

PAPER AND WOOD PRODUCTS

You can expect to find the following types of companies in this section:
Forest and Wood Products and Services • Lumber and Wood Wholesalers • Millwork, Plywood, and Structural Members • Paper and Wood Mills

North Carolina

ATLANTIC VENEER CORPORATION
P.O. Box 660, Beaufort NC 28516. 252/728-3169. **Physical address:** 2457 Lennoxville Road, Beaufort NC 28516. **Fax:** 252.728-4203. **Contact:** Human Resources. **E-mail address:** atlanticveneer@coastalnet.com. **Description:** Manufactures, produces, and sells veneer, hardwood lumber, and plywood. **Special programs:** Internships. **Corporate headquarters location:** This location. **Operations at this facility include:** Administration; Manufacturing; Research and Development; Sales; Service. **Number of employees at this location:** 700.

INTERNATIONAL PAPER COMPANY
100 Gaston Road, Roanoke Rapids NC 27870. 252/533-6000. **Toll-free phone:** 800/223-1268. **Contact:** Human Resources Manager. **World Wide Web address:** http://www.internationalpaper.com. **Description:** International Paper is a manufacturer of pulp and paper, packaging, and wood products, as well as a range of specialty products. Millions of acres of timberland are controlled by International Paper, making it one of the largest private landowners in the United States. The company is organized into five business segments: Printing Papers, which includes uncoated papers, coated papers, bristles, and pulp; Packaging, which includes industrial packaging, consumer packaging, and kraft and specialty papers; Distribution, which includes printing papers, graphic arts equipment and supplies, packaging materials, industrial supplies, and office products; Specialty Products, which includes imaging products, specialty panels, nonwovens, chemicals, and minerals; and Forest Products, which includes logs and wood products. **Special programs:** Internships; Co-ops. **Office hours:** Monday – Friday, 8:00 a.m. – 4:30 p.m. **Corporate headquarters location:** Stamford CT. **U.S. locations:** Nationwide. **International locations:** Worldwide. **Listed on:** New York Stock Exchange. **Stock exchange symbol:** IP. **Number of employees worldwide:** 83,000.

INTERNATIONAL PAPER COMPANY
865 John L. Riegel Road, Riegelwood NC 28456. 910/655-3856. **Toll-free phone:** 800/672-3866. **Fax:** 800/553-1914. **Contact:** Human Resources Manager. **World Wide Web address:** http://www.internationalpaper.com. **Description:** International Paper is a manufacturer of pulp and paper, packaging, and wood products, as well as a range of specialty products. Millions of acres of timberland are

controlled by International Paper, making it one of the largest private landowners in the United States. The company is organized into five business segments: Printing Papers, which includes uncoated papers, coated papers, bristles, and pulp; Packaging, which includes industrial packaging, consumer packaging, and kraft and specialty papers; Distribution, which includes printing papers, graphic arts equipment and supplies, packaging materials, industrial supplies, and office products; Specialty Products, which includes imaging products, specialty panels, nonwovens, chemicals, and minerals; and Forest Products, which includes logs and wood products. **Corporate headquarters location:** Stamford CT. **U.S. locations:** Nationwide. **International locations:** Worldwide. **Operations at this facility include:** This location is a paper mill. **Listed on:** New York Stock Exchange. **Stock exchange symbol:** IP. **Number of employees worldwide:** 83,000.

JORDAN LUMBER & SUPPLY, INC.
P.O. Box 98, Mount Gilead NC 27306. 910/439-6121. **Physical address:** 1939 Highway 109 South, Mount Gilead NC 27306. **Fax:** 910/439-6105. **Contact:** Personnel Director. **World Wide Web address:** http://www.jordanlumber.com. **Description:** A distributor of southern yellow pine lumber, wood chips, sawdust, bark, and related products. Founded 1939. **Corporate headquarters location:** This location. **Number of employees at this location:** 150. **President:** Bob Jordan.

ORACLE PACKAGING
2221 JR Kennedy Drive, Wilmington NC 28405. 910/763-2921. **Fax:** 910/343-9875. **Contact:** James Hummer, Plant Manager. **E-mail address:** jameshummer@oraclepkg.com. **World Wide Web address:** http://www.oraclepackaging.com. **Description:** The United States' largest supplier of private label butter packaging. The company also produces doughnut and cream cheese packaging, as well as other bakery cartoning. **Other U.S. locations:** Toledo OH; Thomaston GA. **Number of employees nationwide:** 425

SMURFIT-STONE CONTAINER CORPORATION
2606 Wilco Boulevard, Wilson NC 27895-3124. 252/237-7121. **Toll-free phone:** 877/772-2999. **Contact:** Human Resources. **World Wide Web address:** http://www.smurfit-stone.com. **Description:** Smurfit-Stone Container Corporation is one of the world's leading paper-based packaging companies. The company's main products include corrugated containers, folding cartons, and multiwall industrial bags. The company is also one of the world's largest collectors and processors of recycled products that are then sold to a worldwide customer base. Smurfit-Stone Container Corporation also operates several paper tube, market pulp, and newsprint production facilities. **Corporate headquarters location:** Chicago IL. **Other area locations:** Lexington NC; Raleigh NC; Shelby NC; Statesville NC; Winston-Salem NC; Greensboro NC. **Other U.S. locations:** Nationwide. **International locations:** Canada; Mexico; China. **Operations at this facility include:** This location manufactures corrugated boxes. **Listed on:** NASDAQ. **Stock exchange symbol:** SSCC. **Number of employees worldwide:** 38,600.

WEYERHAEUSER COMPANY

NC Highway 149 North, P.O. Box 787, Plymouth NC 27962-0787. 252/793-8111. **Contact:** Human Resources Manager. **E-mail address:** careers@weyerhaeuser.com. **World Wide Web address:** http://www.weyerhaeuser.com. **Description:** Weyerhaeuser Company's principal businesses are the growing and harvesting of timber; the manufacture, distribution, and sale of forest products including logs, wood chips, and building products; real estate development and construction; and financial services. Weyerhaeuser is one of the world's largest private owners of marketable softwood timber and one of the largest producers of softwood lumber and pulp. The company is also one of North America's largest producers of forest products and recyclers of office wastepaper, newspaper, and corrugated boxes. Weyerhaeuser Company also sells electricity to utility companies generated from its 15 trash-to-energy plants and 6 small cogeneration and recycling plants. The Water Division manufactures and operates facilities and systems for water purification, water treatment, and managed by-products. The Air Division designs, manufactures, and integrates air pollution emission control and measurement systems and related equipment. **NOTE:** Please visit website to view job listings and apply online. **Special programs:** Internships. **Corporate headquarters location:** Federal Way WA. **Other area locations:** Statewide. **Other U.S. locations:** Nationwide. **International locations:** Worldwide. **Operations at this facility include:** This location manufactures pulp and paper. **Listed on:** New York Stock Exchange. **Stock exchange symbol:** WY. **President/CEO:** Steven R. Rogel. **Number of employees worldwide:** 57,000.

WEYERHAEUSER COMPANY

5419 Hovis Road, Charlotte NC 28206-1241. 704/392-4141. **Contact:** Human Resources Manager. **World Wide Web address:** http://www.weyerhaeuser.com. **Description:** Weyerhaeuser Company's principal businesses are the growing and harvesting of timber; the manufacture, distribution, and sale of forest products including logs, wood chips, and building products; real estate development and construction; and financial services. Weyerhaeuser is one of the world's largest private owners of marketable softwood timber and one of the largest producers of softwood lumber and pulp. The company is also one of North America's largest producers of forest products and recyclers of office wastepaper, newspaper, and corrugated boxes. Weyerhaeuser Company also sells electricity to utility companies generated from its 15 trash-to-energy plants and 6 small cogeneration and recycling plants. The Water Division manufactures and operates facilities and systems for water purification, water treatment, and managed by-products. The Air Division designs, manufactures, and integrates air pollution emission control and measurement systems and related equipment. **NOTE:** Please visit website to view job listings and apply online. **Special programs:** Internships. **Corporate headquarters location:** Federal Way WA. **Other area locations:** Statewide. **Other U.S. locations:** Nationwide. **International locations:** Worldwide. **Listed on:** New York Stock Exchange. **Stock exchange symbol:** WY. **President/CEO:**

Steven R. Rogel. **Number of employees at this location:** 90. **Number of employees worldwide:** 57,000.

WEYERHAEUSER COMPANY
1525 Mount Olive Church Road, P.O. Box 408 Newton NC 28658. 828/464-3841. **Fax:** 828/465-4615. **Contact:** General Manager. **World Wide Web address:** http://www.weyerhaeuser.com. **Description:** Weyerhaeuser Company's principal businesses are the growing and harvesting of timber; the manufacture, distribution, and sale of forest products including logs, wood chips, and building products; real estate development and construction; and financial services. Weyerhaeuser is one of the world's largest private owners of marketable softwood timber and one of the largest producers of softwood lumber and pulp. The company is also one of North America's largest producers of forest products and recyclers of office wastepaper, newspaper, and corrugated boxes. Weyerhaeuser Company also sells electricity to utility companies generated from its 15 trash-to-energy plants and 6 small cogeneration and recycling plants. The Water Division manufactures and operates facilities and systems for water purification, water treatment, and managed by-products. The Air Division designs, manufactures, and integrates air pollution emission control and measurement systems and related equipment. **NOTE:** Please visit website to view job listings and apply online. **Special programs:** Internships. **Corporate headquarters location:** Federal Way WA. **Other area locations:** Statewide. **Other U.S. locations:** Nationwide. **International locations:** Worldwide. **Listed on:** New York Stock Exchange. **Stock exchange symbol:** WY. **President/CEO:** Steven R. Rogel. **Number of employees worldwide:** 57,000.

WEYERHAEUSER COMPANY
306 Corinth Road, P.O. Box 230, Moncure NC 27559. 919/542-2311. **Contact:** Human Resources. **World Wide Web address:** http://www.weyerhaeuser.com. **Description:** Weyerhaeuser Company's principal businesses are the growing and harvesting of timber; the manufacture, distribution, and sale of forest products including logs, wood chips, and building products; real estate development and construction; and financial services. Weyerhaeuser is one of the world's largest private owners of marketable softwood timber and one of the largest producers of softwood lumber and pulp. The company is also one of North America's largest producers of forest products and recyclers of office wastepaper, newspaper, and corrugated boxes. Weyerhaeuser Company also sells electricity to utility companies generated from its 15 trash-to-energy plants and 6 small cogeneration and recycling plants. The Water Division manufactures and operates facilities and systems for water purification, water treatment, and managed by-products. The Air Division designs, manufactures, and integrates air pollution emission control and measurement systems and related equipment. **NOTE:** Please visit website to view job listings and apply online. **Special programs:** Internships. **Corporate headquarters location:** Federal Way WA. **Other area locations:** Statewide. **Other U.S. locations:** Nationwide. **International locations:** Worldwide. **Listed on:** New York

Stock Exchange. **Stock exchange symbol:** WY. **President/CEO:** Steven R. Rogel. **Number of employees worldwide:** 57,000.

South Carolina

BOWATER INC.
P.O. Box 7, Catawba SC 29704. 803/981-8000. **Fax:** 803/981-8031. **Contact:** Barry Baker, Personnel Manager. **World Wide Web address:** http:// www.bowater.com. **Description:** Produces three million tons of newsprint annually manufacturing coated and uncoated groundwood papers, bleached kraft pulp, and lumber products at 12 pulp and paper mills and 12 sawmills supported by 1.5 million acres of timberland in the U.S. and Canada with timber-cutting rights of 33 million acres in Canada. The company is one of the largest users of recycled newspapers and magazines. **NOTE:** Personnel Office phone: 803/981-8110. **Positions advertised include:** Chemical Engineer; Chemist; Production Engineer; Forester/Conservation Scientist; Mechanical Engineer. **Corporate headquarters location:** Greenville SC. **Other U.S. locations:** AL; MI; MS; SC; TN. **International locations:** throughout Canada; South Korea. **Operations at this facility include:** Coated & Specialty Papers Division manufacturing coated paper, market pulp, newsprint, and uncoated groundwood paper. **Listed on:** New York Stock Exchange; London Stock Exchange; Toronto Stock Exchange. **Stock exchange symbol:** BOW; BDX. **Chairman/President/CEO:** Arnold M. Nemorow. **Annual sales/revenues:** $2.6 billion. **Number of employees worldwide:** 8,600.

BOWATER INC.
P.O. Box 1028, Greenville SC 29602. 864/271-7733. **Physical address:** 55 East Camperdown Way, Greenville SC 29602-1028. **Fax:** 864/282-9482. **Contact:** James T. Wright, Human Resources. **World Wide Web address:** http:// www.bowater.com. **Description:** Produces three million tons of newsprint annually manufacturing coated and uncoated groundwood papers, bleached kraft pulp, and lumber products at 12 pulp and paper mills and 12 sawmills supported by 1.5 million acres of timberland in the U.S. and Canada with timber-cutting rights of 33 million acres in Canada. The company is one of the largest users of recycled newspapers and magazines. **Positions advertised include:** Accountant/Auditor; Financial Analyst; Human Resources Manager; Marketing Specialist; Mechanical Engineer; Sales Representative. **Corporate headquarters location:** This location. **Other U.S. locations:** AL; MI; MS; SC; TN. **International locations:** throughout Canada; South Korea. **Operations at this facility include:** Corporate Administration. **Listed on:** New York Stock Exchange; London Stock Exchange; Toronto Stock Exchange. **Stock exchange symbol:** BOW; BDX. **Chairman/President/CEO:** Arnold M. Nemorow. **Annual sales/revenues:** $2.6 billion. **Number of employees worldwide:** 8,600.

INTERNATIONAL PAPER COMPANY
700 South Kaminski Street, Georgetown SC 29440. 843/546-6111. **Fax:** 843/545-2695. **Contact:** Personnel. **World Wide Web address:** http:// www.internationalpaper.com. **Description:** International Paper Company

manufactures pulp and paper, packaging, wood products, and a range of specialty products. The company is organized into five business segments: Printing Papers, with principal products that include uncoated papers, coated papers, bristles, and pulp; Packaging, which includes industrial packaging, consumer packaging, and kraft and specialty papers; Distribution, including the sale of printing papers, graphic arts equipment and supplies, packaging materials, industrial supplies, and office products; Specialty Products, which includes imaging products, specialty panels, nonwovens, chemicals, and minerals; and Forest Products which includes logging and wood products. **Positions advertised include:** Mill Communications Manager. **Note:** Applicants may apply for jobs at the company website under people category. **Corporate headquarters location:** Stamford CT. **Other locations:** Worldwide. **Listed on:** New York Stock Exchange. **Stock exchange symbol:** IP. **Chairman/CEO:** John Dillon. **Annual sales/revenues:** $25 billion. **Number of employees worldwide:** 83,000.

SMURFIT-STONE CONTAINER CORPORATION
Paper Mill Road, P.O. Box 100544, Florence SC 29501-0544. 843/662-0313. 843/772-2932. **Contact:** Bill Flynn, Director of Human Resources. **World Wide Web address:** http://www.smurfit-stone.com. **Description:** A paper-based packaging company specializing in corrugated containers, folding cartons, and multiwall industrial bags. The company is also one of the world's largest collectors and processors of recycled products that are then sold to a worldwide customer base. Smurfit-Stone Container Corporation also operates several paper tube, market pulp, and newsprint production facilities. **Corporate headquarters location:** Chicago IL. **Other area locations:** Columbia SC; Latta SC; Spartanburg SC. **Other U.S. locations:** CO; FL; MO; OH; PA; TN. **Operations at this facility include:** The Florence Mill manufactures containerboard, paperboard and linerboard for cardboard boxes. **Listed on:** NASDAQ. **Stock exchange symbol:** SSCC. **Annual sales/revenues:** $7.5 billion. **Number of employees worldwide:** 38,600.

WEYERHAEUSER COMPANY
300 Northpark Drive, Rock Hill SC 29730. 803/328-3800. **Fax:** 803/328-3085. **Contact:** Human Resources. **World Wide Web address:** http://www.weyerhaeuser.com. **Description:** An integrated forest products company with offices and operations in 18 countries, Weyerhaeuser is principally engaged in the growing and harvesting of timber; the manufacture, distribution, and sale of forest products; and real estate construction, development and related activities. Founded in 1900. **NOTE:** Applications materials and resumes should be sent to the company's headquarters address: Recruiting, Staffing & Diversity, P.O. Box 9777, Federal Way WA 98063-9777; or by fax: 206/374-2210. The company prefers resumes posted to the company Website. **Positions advertised include:** Operations Manager; Mill Supply Representative; Finance and Planning Manager. **Corporate headquarters location:** Federal Way WA. **Other locations:** Worldwide. **Operations at this facility include:** Manufacturing of continuous stock computer forms. **Listed on:** New York Stock Exchange. **Stock exchange symbol:** WY.

Chairman/President/CEO: Steven R Rogel. **Annual sales/revenues:** $18.5 billion. **Number of employees worldwide:** 58,000.

WEYERHAEUSER COMPANY
1445 Lancaster Highway, P.O. Box 1110, Chester SC 29706. 803/581-7164. **Fax:** 803/581-4036. **Contact:** Regional Manager. **World Wide Web address:** http://www.weyerhaeuser.com. **Description:** An integrated forest products company with offices and operations in 18 countries, Weyerhaeuser is principally engaged in the growing and harvesting of timber; the manufacture, distribution, and sale of forest products; and real estate construction, development and related activities. Founded in 1900. **NOTE:** Applications materials and resumes should be sent to the company's headquarters address: Recruiting, Staffing & Diversity, P.O. Box 9777, Federal Way WA 98063-9777; or by fax: 206/374-2210. The company prefers resumes posted to the company Website. **Positions advertised include:** Technical Service Representative; Green End Night Shift Coordinator; Instrumentation Journeyman; Account Manager; Retail Marketing Manager; Electrician; Sales Representative; Outside Sales Representative; Products Supervisor; Mill Supply Representative. **Corporate headquarters location:** Federal Way WA. **Other locations:** Worldwide. **Operations at this facility include:** Plywood manufacturing. **Listed on:** New York Stock Exchange. **Stock exchange symbol:** WY. **Chairman/President/CEO:** Steven R Rogel. **Annual sales/revenues:** $18.5 billion. **Number of employees worldwide:** 58,000.

WEYERHAEUSER COMPANY
191 West Main Street, P.O. Box 219, Tatum SC 29594. 843/523-5058. **Contact:** Donnie Culbertson, Plant Manager. **World Wide Web address:** http://www.weyerhaeuser.com. **Description:** An integrated forest products company with offices and operations in 18 countries, Weyerhaeuser is principally engaged in the growing and harvesting of timber; the manufacture, distribution, and sale of forest products; and real estate construction, development and related activities. Founded in 1900. **NOTE:** Application materials and resumes should be sent to the company's headquarters address: Recruiting, Staffing & Diversity, P.O. Box 9777, Federal Way WA 98063-9777; or by fax: 206/374-2210. The company prefers resumes posted to the company Website. **Positions advertised include:** Technical Service Representative; Green End Night Shift Coordinator; Instrumentation Journeyman; Account Manager; Retail Marketing Manager; Electrician; Sales Representative; Outside Sales Representative; Products Supervisor; Mill Supply Representative. **Corporate headquarters location:** Federal Way WA. **Other locations:** Worldwide. **Operations at this facility include:** A paper conversion plant. **Listed on:** New York Stock Exchange. **Stock exchange symbol:** WY. **Chairman/President/CEO:** Steven R Rogel. **Annual sales/revenues:** $18.5 billion. **Number of employees worldwide:** 58,000.

WEYERHAEUSER COMPANY

P.O. Box 636, Bennettsville SC 29512. 843/479-3002. **Fax:** 842/479-2711. **Contact:** Cynthia Carruth, Human Resource Manager. **World Wide Web address:** http://www.weyerhaeuser.com. **Description:** An integrated forest products company with offices and operations in 18 countries, Weyerhaeuser is principally engaged in the growing and harvesting of timber; the manufacture, distribution, and sale of forest products; and real estate construction, development and related activities. Founded in 1900. **NOTE:** Application materials and resumes should be sent to the company's headquarters address: Recruiting, Staffing & Diversity, P.O. Box 9777, Federal Way WA 98063-9777; or by fax: 206/374-2210. The company prefers resumes posted to the company Website. **Positions advertised include:** Technical Service Representative; Green End Night Shift Coordinator; Instrumentation Journeyman; Account Manager; Retail Marketing Manager; Electrician; Sales Representative; Outside Sales Representative; Products Supervisor; Mill Supply Representative. **Corporate headquarters location:** Federal Way WA. **Other locations:** Worldwide. **Operations at this facility include:** Fiberboard manufacturing. **Listed on:** New York Stock Exchange. **Stock exchange symbol:** WY. **Chairman/President/CEO:** Steven R Rogel. **Annual sales/revenues:** $18.5 billion. **Number of employees worldwide:** 58,000.

WEYERHAEUSER COMPANY

581 Willamette Highway, P.O. Box 678, Bennettsville SC 29512-0678. 843/479-0200. **Fax:** 843/479-2985. **Contact:** Donald Newton, Director of Human Resources. **E-mail address:** resume@weyerhaeuser.com. **World Wide Web address:** http://www.weyerhaeuser.com. **Description:** An integrated forest products company with offices and operations in 18 countries, Weyerhaeuser is principally engaged in the growing and harvesting of timber; the manufacture, distribution, and sale of forest products; and real estate construction, development and related activities. Founded in 1900. **NOTE:** Application materials and resumes should be sent to the company's headquarters address: Recruiting, Staffing & Diversity, P.O. Box 9777, Federal Way WA 98063-9777; or by fax: 206/374-2210. The company prefers resumes posted to the company Website. **Positions advertised include:** Technical Service Representative; Green End Night Shift Coordinator; Instrumentation Journeyman; Account Manager; Retail Marketing Manager; Electrician; Sales Representative; Outside Sales Representative; Products Supervisor; Mill Supply Representative. **Corporate headquarters location:** Federal Way WA. **Other locations:** Worldwide. **Operations at this facility include:** Marlboro Facility, produces papergrade pulps, market pulp, uncoated papers, and copy machine paper. **Listed on:** New York Stock Exchange. **Stock exchange symbol:** WY. **Chairman/President/CEO:** Steven R Rogel. **Annual sales/revenues:** $18.5 billion. **Number of employees worldwide:** 58,000.

PRINTING AND PUBLISHING

You can expect to find the following types of companies in this section:
Book, Newspaper, and Periodical Publishers • Commercial Photographers • Commercial Printing Services • Graphic Designers

North Carolina

AMERICAN CITY BUSINESS JOURNALS
120 West Morehead Street, Suite 200, Charlotte NC 28202. 704/973-1000. 375-7404. **Fax:** 704/973-1001. **Contact:** Human Resources. **World Wide Web address:** http://www.bizjournals.com. **Description:** Publishes 27 business newspapers, a legal newspaper, and the *Winston Cup Scene,* which is devoted to coverage of NASCAR motor sports racing. **Corporate headquarters locations:** This location. **Other U.S. locations:** Nationwide. **Subsidiaries include:** The Network of City Business Journals is a national advertising representation firm. Circulation of the business weeklies is 313,000. **CEO:** Ray Shaw.

BELLSOUTH ADVERTISING AND PUBLISHING CORPORATION
9144 Arrowpoint Boulevard, Suite 100, Charlotte NC 28273. 704/522-5894. **Contact:** Employment Office. **World Wide Web address:** http://www.bellsouth.com/bapco. **Description:** Publishes print telephone directories in the southeastern United States, Brazil, and Peru. **NOTE:** Please visit website to search for jobs and apply online. **Positions advertised include:** Account Executive; Network Manager; Directory Advertising; Directory Telephone Sales Representative. **Corporate headquarters location:** Atlanta GA. **Other area locations:** Statewide. **Subsidiaries include:** Stevens Graphics; The Berry Company. **Parent company:** BellSouth Corporation. **Operations at this facility include:** Administration; Regional Headquarters; Sales; Service. **Listed on:** New York Stock Exchange. **Stock exchange symbol:** BLS. **CEO:** F. Duane Ackerman.

BLAIR PUBLISHING
1406 Plaza Drive, Winston-Salem NC 27103. 336/768-1374. **Toll-free phone:** 800/222-9796. **Fax:** 336/768-9194. **Contact:** Human Resources. **E-mail address:** blairpub@blairpub.com. **World Wide Web address:** http://www.blairpub.com. **Description:** A general trade publisher of specialty regional titles including history, travel, folklore, and biographies. The company publishes 15 - 20 books per year. Founded in 1954. **Special programs:** Internships. **Corporate headquarters location:** This location. **President:** Carolyn Sakowski.

RR DONNELLEY
LITHO INDUSTRIES, A MOORE WALLACE COMPANY
One Litho Way, Page Pointe Centre, Research Triangle Park, Durham NC 27703. 919/596-7000. **Contact:** Human Resources Manager. **World Wide Web address:** http://www.rrdonnelley.com. **Description:** A full-service commercial printer specializing in business forms. **Corporate headquarters location:** Chicago IL. **Other area locations:** Wilson NC. **Other U.S. locations:** Nationwide. **International locations:** Worldwide. **Operations at this facility include:** Commercial Printing. **Listed on:** New York Stock Exchange. **Stock exchange symbol:** RRD. **Number of employees worldwide:** 50,000.

FAYETTEVILLE OBSERVER TIMES
458 Whitfield Street, P.O. Box 849, Fayetteville NC 28302. 910/323-4848. **Toll-free phone:** 800/682-3476. **Contact:** John Holmes, Personnel Director. **E-mail address:** holmesj@fayettevillenc.com. **World Wide Web address:** http://www.fayettevillenc.com. **Description:** Publishes a daily newspaper with a circulation of approximately 70,000. **NOTE:** Contact Personnel directly at 910/486-3508.

FUTURA CREATIVE
4711 Hope Valley Road, #419, Durham NC 27707. 919/933-2150. **Fax:** 919/942-0041. **Contact:** Human Resources. **World Wide Web address:** http://www.futuracreative.com. **Description:** Offers graphic design services including corporate identity development, logos, letterhead, brochures, annual reports, and other printed media. The company also offers Website design and multimedia services. **Corporate headquarters location:** This location.

HINSHAW MUSIC, INC.
P.O. Box 470, Chapel Hill NC 27514. 919/933-1691. **Fax:** 919/967-3399. **Contact:** Manager. **World Wide Web address:** http://www.hinshawmusic.com. **Description:** A printer and publisher of choral music. Founded in 1975. **Corporate headquarters location:** This location.

HUNTER TEXTBOOKS, INC.
701 Shallowford Street, Winston-Salem NC 27101. 336/725-0608. **Toll-free phone:** 800/367-4159. **Fax:** 336/722-0530. **Contact:** Human Resources. **E-mail address:** hunter@rbdc.com. **World Wide Web address:** http://www.huntertextbooks.com. **Description:** Specializes in the publication of college textbooks and laboratory manuals in the areas of physical education, biology, geology, and the humanities. Founded in 1976. **Corporate headquarters location:** This location.

METRO PRODUCTIONS
6005 Chapel Hill Road, Raleigh NC 27607. 919/851-6420. **Fax:** 919/851-6418. **Contact:** Human Resources. **World Wide Web address:** http://www.metroproductions.com. **Description:** Provides graphic design, Web offset printing, and video production services.

THE NEWS & OBSERVER
P.O. Box 191, Raleigh NC 27602. 919/829-4500. **Physical address:**
215 South McDowell Street, Raleigh NC 27601. **Fax:** 919/829-8990.
Contact: Personnel Director. **E-mail address:**
hrresume@newsobserver.com. **World Wide Web address:**
http://www.news-observer.com. **Description:** A daily newspaper with a
Sunday circulation of 273,000 and a daily circulation of 152,000.
Corporate headquarters location: This location.

NEWS & RECORD
P.O. Box 20848, Greensboro NC 27420-0848. 336/373-7000. **Toll-free
phone:** 800/553-6880. **Fax:** 336/373-7183. **Contact:** Director of Human
Resources. **World Wide Web address:** http://www.news-record.com.
Description: A daily newspaper with weekday circulation of 90,000,
Saturday circulation of 115,000, and Sunday circulation of 123,000.
Founded in 1890. **NOTE:** Second and third shifts are offered. **Positions
advertised include:** Inside Sales Representative; Interactive Account
Executive; Sports Copy Editor – Part-time; Newspaper Rack
Maintenance Representative – Part-time; Advertising Sales Account
Executive. **Special programs:** Internships. **Corporate headquarters
location:** Norfolk VA. **Parent company:** Landmark Communications,
Inc. **Listed on:** Privately held. **Number of employees at this location:**
820.

OPUS ONE GRAPHIC DESIGN
715 West Johnson Street, Suite 200, Raleigh NC 27603. 919/834-9441.
Contact: Human Resources. **Description:** Offers graphic design
services that assist clients in advertising their products.

PCA INTERNATIONAL, INC.
P.O. Box 1393, Matthews NC 28106. 704/847-8011. **Physical address:**
815 Matthews-Mint Hill Road, Matthews NC 28105. **Toll-free phone:**
800/438-8868. **Contact:** Personnel. **E-mail address:**
careers@pcaintl.com. **World Wide Web address:**
http://www.pcaintl.com. **Description:** Provides family portrait
photography through retailers. The exclusive operator of children's
portrait photography services in over 1,400 Wal-Mart stores. Adult and
family portraits are marketed through the Institutional Division, which
works primarily through church promotions. **NOTE:** Please visit website
to submit resume online. For employment information, dial 800/438-8868
Ext. 2410. **Corporate headquarters location:** This location. **Other U.S.
locations:** Nationwide. **International locations:** Canada; Mexico;
Puerto Rico; Virgin Islands. **President/CEO:** Barry J. Feld. **Annual
sales/revenues:** More than $100 million. **Number of employees
nationwide:** 3,300.

QUALEX, INC.
3404 North Duke Street, Durham NC 27704. 919/383-8535. **Contact:**
Human Resources. **Description:** Manufactures, markets, and services
photo finishing equipment. Qualex also establishes one-hour photo labs.
Office hours: Monday – Friday, 8:30 a.m. – 5:00 p.m. **Corporate**

headquarters location: This location. **Other U.S. locations:** Tuscany CA. **Parent company:** Eastman Kodak. **Number of employees at this location:** 275. **Number of employees nationwide:** 7,500.

UNIVERSITY OF NORTH CAROLINA PRESS
P.O. Box 2288, Chapel Hill NC 27515-2288. 919/966-3561. **Physical address:** 116 South Boundary Street, Chapel Hill NC 27514-3808. **Fax:** 919/966-3829. **Contact:** Human Resources. **E-mail address:** uncpress@unc.edu. **World Wide Web address:** http://uncpress.unc.edu. **Description:** Publishes nonfiction history, sociology, and related books as well as journals. Founded in 1922. **NOTE:** Please visit website to find a specific staff contact for your employment enquiries. Resumes and applications are preferred by mail. Unsolicited applications sent via e-mail and fax may not receive a response. Full-time and freelance work is generally available. **Corporate headquarters location:** This location.

WINSTON-SALEM JOURNAL
P.O. Box 3159, Winston-Salem NC 27102. 336/727-7211. **Physical address:** 418 North Marshall Street, Winston-Salem NC 27101. **Toll-free phone:** 800/642-0925. **Fax:** 336/727-4331. **Contact:** Gina Wingfield, Human Resources. **E-mail address:** gwingfield@wsjournal.com. **World Wide Web address:** http://www.journalnow.com. **Description:** A daily newspaper. **NOTE:** In order to be considered for employment, you must submit a signed employment application. For newsroom opportunities, address your resume and application to the editor of the department you are interested in. Please visit website to view job listings. Contact Human Resources directly at 336/727-7331. **Position advertised include:** Account Executive – Retail Advertising. **Special programs:** Internships. **Corporate headquarters location:** This location. **Parent company:** Media General, Inc. **Listed on:** New York Stock Exchange. **Stock exchange symbol:** MEG. **Annual sales/revenues:** $51 - $100 million. **Number of employees at this location:** 480. **Number of employees nationwide:** 9,000.

South Carolina

AIKEN STANDARD
P.O. Box 456, Aiken SC 29802. 803/648-2311. **Fax:** 830/648-6052. **Contact:** Judy Randall, Executive Secretary. **E-mail address:** editorial@duesouth.net. **World Wide Web address:** http://www.aikenstandard.com. **Description:** Publishes *Aiken Standard*, a daily newspaper with a circulation of 15,000. **Positions advertised include:** Lead Pressman; Press Operator; Circulation District Manager; Route Carrier; Route Driver. **Office hours:** Monday – Friday, 8:30 a.m. – 5:30 p.m. **Parent company:** Aiken Communications, Inc.

ARCADIA PUBLISHING

420 Wando Park Boulevard, Mount Pleasant SC 29464. 843/853-2070. **Fax:** 843/853-8044. **Contact:** Jane Elliot, Human Resources. **E-mail address:** jelliot@arcadiapublishing.com. **World Wide Web address:** http://www.arcadiapublishing.com. **Description:** The largest local and regional history publisher in the U.S. **Note:** Intern applications are always accepted. **Positions advertised include:** Marketing Manager. **Corporate headquarters location:** This location. **Other U.S. locations:** San Francisco CA; Chicago IL; Portsmouth NH.

R.R. DONNELLEY & SONS COMPANY

300 Jones Road, Spartanburg SC 29307. 864/579-6000. **Contact:** Doug Winslow, Human Resources Manager. **E-mail address:** rrdonnelley@hiresystems.com. **World Wide Web address:** http://www. rrdonnelley.com. **Description:** The company is engaged in managing, reproducing, and distributing print and digital information for publishing, merchandising, and information technology customers. The company is one of the largest commercial printers in the world, producing catalogs, inserts, magazines, books, directories, computer documentation, and financial printing. R.R. Donnelley & Sons Company has more than 180 sales offices and production facilities. Principal services offered by the company are conventional and digital prepress operations, computerized printing and binding, and sophisticated pool shipping and distribution services for printed products; information repackaging into multiple formats (print, magnetic, and optical media); database management, list rental, list enhancement, and direct mail production services; turnkey computer documentation services (outsourcing, translation, printing, binding, diskette replication, kitting, licensing, republishing, and fulfillment); reprographics and facilities management; creative design and communication services; and digital and conventional map creation and related services. Founded in 1864. **Positions advertised include:** Safety Technician; Process Engineer. **Corporate headquarters location:** Chicago IL. **Other U.S. locations:** Nationwide. **International locations:** Worldwide. **Subsidiaries include:** Lakeside Press. **Operations at this facility include:** Commercial printing of catalogues and newspaper inserts. **Listed on:** New York Stock Exchange. **Stock exchange symbol:** RRD.

EVENING POST PUBLISHING COMPANY

134 Columbus Street, Charleston SC 29403-4800. 843/577-7111. **Contact:** Paul Sharry, Personnel Department. **E-mail address:** jobs@postandcourier.com. **World Wide Web address:** http://www.evepost.net. **Description:** An umbrella corporation for several newspaper publishing companies throughout South Carolina. The Evening Post Publishing Company owns *The Post Courier*, which has a daily circulation of 115,000 and a Sunday circulation of 125,000. Evening Post Publishing Company's business holdings include: several television stations in Arizona, Colorado, Kentucky, Louisiana, Montana, and Texas; daily and weekly newspapers in South Carolina, North Carolina, and Texas; an English-language daily newspaper in Buenos Aires, Argentina; a Florida-based feature article subsidiary; and a Southern pine

timberlands management company. Founded in 1803. **NOTE:** The company prefers resumes sent by mail; or by e-mail with job title in the subject line; but does not accept faxed resumes. **Positions advertised include:** Press Operator; Packaging and Distribution Helper; Classified Advertising Clerk; Graphic Designer; Marketing Associate; Data Entry Operator; Advertising Production Graphic Designer. **Subsidiaries include:** *Moultrie News*; *The Salisbury Post*; *The Georgetown Times*; *The* (Kingstree) *News*; *Aiken Standard*; *Buenos Aires Herald*; Editors Press Service, Inc.; KRIS-TV Channel 6; KVOA-TV Channel 4; KOAA-TV Channels 5/30; KPAX-TV Channel 8; KTVQ-TV Channel 2; KXLF-TV Channel 4; KRTV-TV Channel 3; KBZK-TV Channel 7; WLEX-TV Channel 13; KATC-TV Channel 3; *Summerville Journal-Scene*; *Davie County Enterprise*; *The Clemmons Courier*. **Other locations:** Black Eagle MT; Corpus Christi TX; Tucson AZ; Pueblo/Colorado Springs CO; Missoula MT; Billings MT; Butte MT; Great Falls MT; Bozeman MT; Lexington KY; Lafayette LA. **Chairman:** Peter Manigault.

FREY MEDIA
2 Park Lane, Suite H, Hilton Head Island SC 29928. 843/842-7878. **Fax:** 843/842-5743. **Contact:** Personnel. **E-mail address:** fminfo@hargray.com. **World Wide Web address:** http://www.freymedia.com. **Positions advertised include:** Regional Publisher Associate. **Description:** Publishes regional magazines including *Golfer's Guide* and *Home Resource Book*. **NOTE:** Contact regional publishers for open positions. **Other locations:** Kennesaw GA.

THE GREENVILLE NEWS
305 South Main Street, P.O. Box 1688, Greenville SC 29602-1688. 864/298-4006. **Fax:** 864/298-4063. **Contact:** Ms. Elgin, Human Resources Specialist. **E-mail address:** resumehr@greenvillenews.com. **World Wide Web address:** http://www.greenvilleonline.com. **Description:** Publishes *The Greenville News*, a daily newspaper with a circulation of over 100,000 on weekends and slightly less on weekdays. The company also operates an online service. Founded in 1874. **NOTE:** Entry-level positions and second and third shifts are offered. Human Resources phone: 864/298-4452. **Positions advertised include:** Advertising Sales Representative; Automotive Sales Representative; Senior Advertising Sales Representative; Consumer Marketing Manager; Computer Programmer; Customer Service Representative; Graphic Artist; Reporter. **Special programs:** Internships. **Parent company:** Gannett, Inc. (Arlington VA).

INTERNATIONAL EMPLOYMENT GAZETTE
423 Townes Street, Greenville SC 29601. 864/235-4444. **Toll-free phone:** 800/882.9138. **Fax:** 864/235-3369. **Contact:** Del Hymen, General Manager. **E-mail address:** info@intemployment.com. **World Wide Web address:** http://www.intemployment.com. **Description:** Publishes *International Employment Gazette*, a bi-monthly magazine with over 400 international job listings per issue. Job listings are primarily in the areas of science/technology, public/social services, computer science, construction and trades, and education. Founded in 1990.

THE STATE NEWSPAPER

P.O. Box 1333, Columbia SC 29202. 803/771-8350. **Recorded jobline:** 803/771-8562. **Contact:** Holly Rogers, Human Resources Director. **World Wide Web address:** http://www.thestate.com. **Description:** Publishes *The State*, a daily newspaper with a weekday circulation exceeding 145,000. **NOTE:** Human Resources phone: 803/771-8350. **Positions advertised include:** Retail Account Executive; Lake Murray Sales Representative; Field Service Assistant. **Corporate headquarters location:** This location. **Parent company:** Knight-Ridder, Inc., a major newspaper publishing company, owns 28 dailies in 15 states, and three nondailies. The company also publishes larger papers including the *Miami Herald*, *Philadelphia Inquirer*, *Philadelphia Daily News*, *Detroit Free Press*, and *San Jose Mercury News*. Knight-Ridder also has interests in the information distribution market through Business Information Services, with subsidiaries Knight-Ridder Information, Inc., Knight-Ridder Financial, and Technimetrics. Knight Ridder's online information retrieval serves the business, scientific, technology, medical and education communities in more than 100 countries. Knight-Ridder Financial provides real-time financial news and pricing information through primary products MoneyCenter, Digital Datafeed, ProfitCenter, and TradeCenter. Knight-Ridder also has interests in cable television and other businesses. Other interests include partial ownership of the Seattle Times Company, two paper mills, a newspaper advertising sales company, and SCI Holdings.

REAL ESTATE

You can expect to find the following types of companies in this section:
Land Subdividers and Developers • Real Estate Agents, Managers, and Operators • Real Estate Investment Trusts

North Carolina

CB RICHARD ELLIS
201 South College Street, Suite 1900, Charlotte NC 28244. 704/376-7979. **Fax:** 704/331-1259. **Contact:** Human Resources. **E-mail address:** cbrejobs@cbre.com. **World Wide Web address:** http://www.cbrichardellis.com. **Description:** A real estate services company offering property sales and leasing, property and facility management, mortgage banking, and investment management services. **NOTE:** Please visit website to search for jobs and apply online. Online job listings are updated every business day. **Corporate headquarters location:** Los Angeles CA. **Other area locations:** Raleigh NC. **Other U.S. locations:** Nationwide. **International locations:** Worldwide. **CEO:** Raymond Wirta. **Number of employees nationwide:** 9,600. **Number of employees worldwide:** 13,500.

CB RICHARD ELLIS
1201 Edwards Mill Road, Suite 100, Raleigh NC 27607. 919/831-8200. **Fax:** 919/856-2530. **Contact:** Human Resources. **E-mail address:** cbrejobs@cbre.com. opps@cbre.com. **World Wide Web address:** http://www.cbrichardellis.com. **Description:** A real estate services company offering property sales and leasing, property and facility management, mortgage banking, and investment management services. **NOTE:** Please visit website to search for jobs and apply online. Online job listings are updated every business day. **Corporate headquarters location:** Los Angeles CA. **Other area locations:** Charlotte NC. **Other U.S. locations:** Nationwide. **International locations:** Worldwide. **CEO:** Raymond Wirta. **Number of employees nationwide:** 9,600. **Number of employees worldwide:** 13,500.

PRUDENTIAL CAROLINAS REALTY
380 Knollwood Street, Suite 420, Winston-Salem NC 27103. 336/725-1970. **Contact:** Sales Manager. **World Wide Web address:** http://www.prudential-carolinas.com. **Description:** A real estate company specializing in residential properties. **Corporate headquarters location:** This location. **Other area locations:** Statewide. **Other U.S. locations:** Rock Hill SC. **President/CEO:** Robert E. Helms.

WESTMINSTER HOMES
2706 North Church Street, Greensboro NC 27405. 336/375-6200. **Fax:** 336/375-6355. **Contact:** Human Resources. **World Wide Web address:**

http://www.greensboro.com/westminster. **Description:** A real estate and construction company. Westminster Homes specializes in single-family home development and sales in North Carolina. **Corporate headquarters location:** This location. **Other U.S. locations:** Cary NC. **Parent company:** Washington Homes, Inc. **Operations at this facility include:** Administration; Sales; Service. **Number of employees at this location:** 60. **Number of employees nationwide:** 100.

South Carolina

AMERICAN INVESTMENT AND MANAGEMENT COMPANY (AIMCO)
P.O. Box 1089, Greenville SC 29602. 864/239-1000. **Physical address:** 55 Beattie Place, Third Floor, Greenville SC 29601. **Fax:** 864/239-5819. **Contact:** Martin Haider, Human Resources. **E-mail address:** martin.haider@aimco.com. **World Wide Web address:** http://www.aimco.com. **Description:** A real estate investment trust, management and mortgage banking company managing over 300,000 apartments nationwide. **NOTE:** Human Resources phone for corporate opportunities: 864/239-2678. For site opportunities fax Sherry Riddle: 864/239-0710 or e-mail: sherry.riddle@aimco.com. **Positions advertised include:** Reporting Accountant Associate; Real Estate Accountant; Payroll Processing Representative. **Corporate headquarters location:** Denver CO. **Other area locations:** Statewide. **Other U.S. locations:** Nationwide. **Subsidiaries include:** Amreal Corporation; Coventry Properties, Inc.; Dalcap Management, Inc.; First Piedmont Mortgage Company, Inc.; IFGP Corporation; Insignia Commercial Group, Inc.; Insignia Management Corporation; Shelter Realty Corporation. **Listed on:** New York Stock Exchange. **Stock exchange symbol:** AIV. **Annual sales/revenues:** $1.6 billion. **Number of employees nationwide:** 7,800.

DUNES PROPERTIES OF CHARLESTON, INC.
1400 Palm Boulevard, P.O. Box 524, Isle of Palms SC 29451. 843/886-5600. **Toll-free phone**: 800/476-8444. **Fax:** 843/886-4953. **Contact:** Human Resources. **World Wide Web address**: http://www.dunesproperties.com. **Description:** Rental agent for resort and vacation properties. **Positions advertised include:** Administrative Assistant; Front Desk Sales Agent; Property and Real Estate Manager. **Corporate headquarters location:** This location. **Other locations:** Folley Beach SC; Johns Island SC. **Listed on:** Privately held

KIAWAH ISLAND REAL ESTATE
P.O. Box 12001, Charleston SC 29422. 843/768-3400. **Tpll-free phone:** 888/559-9024. **Contact:** Patrick McKinney, Broker-in-Charge. **E-mail address:** karla_story@kiawahisland.com. **World Wide Web address:** http:// www.kiawahisland.com. **Description:** A real estate company specializing in residential properties. **NOTE:** Those interested in support staff positions (including secretarial) should direct resumes to Michelle Canaday, Office Manager. **Office Hours:** Monday – Friday, 9:00 a.m. – 5:30 p.m.

SOUTHEASTERN COMMERCIAL SERVICES
P.O. Box 6958, Hilton Head Island SC 29938. 843/342-2007. **Physical address:** 8 Lafayette Place, Hilton Head Island SC 29926. **Office Hours:** Monday – Friday, 9:00 a.m. – 5:00 p.m. **Fax:** 843/342-3428. **Contact:** Susan Underwood, Office Manager. **Description:** A commercial property real estate company.

ZIFF PROPERTIES
70 East Bay Street, Charleston SC 29403. 843/724-3500. **Contact:** Human Resources. **E-mail address:** email@spi.net. **World Wide Web address:** http://www.zpi.net. **Description:** Specializing in acquisition of shopping centers, office buildings and light industrial properties in the South East. **Positions advertised include:** Accountant; Accounts Payable Supervisor. **Number of employees:** 30.

RETAIL

You can expect to find the following types of companies in this section:
Catalog Retailers • Department Stores, Specialty Stores • Retail Bakeries • Supermarkets

North Carolina

BELK STORES SERVICES INC.
P.O. Box 1099, Charlotte NC 28201-1099. **Physical address:** 2801 West Tyvola Road, Charlotte NC 28217-4500. 704/357-1000. **Toll-free phone:** 866/235-5443. **Fax:** 704/357-1876. **Contact:** Human Resources. **World Wide Web address:** http://www.belk.com. **Description:** Operates 260 department stores located in 14 southeastern states. **Special programs:** Internships. **Corporate headquarters location:** This location. **Other U.S. locations:** East and Southeast U.S. **CEO:** John M. Belk. **Number of employees nationwide:** 17,800.

CVS
297 East 22nd Street, Kannapolis NC 28083. 704/939-6000. **Contact:** Jeannene Allen, Employee Relations Manager. **World Wide Web address:** http://www.cvs.com. **Description:** CVS operates a chain of drugstores throughout the United States. Pharmacy operations make up a large portion of the company's business, offering both brand name and generic prescription drugs. CVS stores also offer a broad range of health and beauty aids, cosmetics, greeting cards, convenience foods, photo finishing services, and other general merchandise. **Office hours:** Monday – Friday, 8:00 a.m. 5:00 p.m. **Corporate headquarters location:** Woonsocket RI. **Operations at this facility include:** This location serves as an area business office. **Listed on:** New York Stock Exchange. **Stock exchange symbol:** CVS. **Number of employees nationwide:** 110,000.

CATO CORPORATION
8100 Denmark Road, Charlotte NC 28273-5975. 704/554-8510. **Fax:** 704/551-7246. **Contact:** Paula Sanders, Recruiter. **E-mail address:** catjobs@catcorp.com. **World Wide Web address:** http://www.catocorp.com. **Description:** Owns and operates over 500 stores in 22 states. The stores operate under the names Cato, Cato Fashions, and Cato Plus, and feature women's apparel for junior, misses, and large-sized customers. The company also has an off-price division that operates 67 stores under the Its Fashion! name, featuring primarily sportswear and accessories. **Positions advertised include:** Executive Administrative Assistant; Payroll Clerk; Payroll Director; Tax Manager; Vice President – Internal Audit; Human Resources File Clerk; Programmer Analyst; Store Development Coordinator; Store Analyst; Jewelry Buyer; Technical Specialist. **Corporate headquarters location:**

This location. **Other U.S. locations:** Southeast, South, East, and Middle U.S. **Number of employees nationwide:** 2,800.

FAMILY DOLLAR STORES, INC.
P.O. Box 1017, Charlotte NC 28201-1017. 704/847-6961. **Fax:** 704/845-0582. **Contact:** Mary D. Lauzon, Corporate Recruiter. **E-mail address:** mlauzon@familydollar.com. **World Wide Web address:** http://www.familydollar.com. **Description:** Owns and operates a chain of more than 5,000 discount stores. The company provides merchandise for family and home needs. Stores are located in 43 states, as far northwest as South Dakota, northeast to Maine, southeast to Florida, and southwest to New Mexico. Founded in 1959. **NOTE:** Entry-level positions and second and third shifts are offered. Please visit website to search for jobs and apply online. **Positions advertised include:** Corporate Attorney; Paralegal; Assistant Lease Administrator; Personnel Data Processing Clerk; Security Officer; Director of Merchandise Planning; Project Manager; Data Integrity Analyst; Accounts Payable Clerk; Human Resources Customer Services Center Representative; Store Planner; Maintenance Assistant; Division Recruiter – Store Operations; Construction Secretary; Claims Consultant; Buyer; Web Developer. **Corporate headquarters location:** This location. **Listed on:** New York Stock Exchange. **Stock exchange symbol:** FDO. **Number of employees nationwide:** 37,000.

FOOD LION, INC.
P.O. Box 1330, Salisbury NC 28145-1330. 704/633-8250. **Physical address:** 2110 Executive Drive, Salisbury NC 28147. **Contact:** Recruiting Manager. **World Wide Web address:** http://www.foodlion.com. **Description:** Owns a chain of discount retail food stores. Food Lion, Inc. is comprised of approximately 1,200 stores operating throughout the Eastern United States. Founded in 1957. **NOTE:** Please visit website to search for jobs and apply online. **Positions advertised include:** Produce Sales Manager; Corporate Recruiter; FT Grocery Associate; Physical Security Systems Technician; Service Associate. **Corporate headquarters location:** This location. **Other U.S. locations:** East and Southeast U.S. **Parent company:** Delhaize America Inc. **Listed on:** New York Stock Exchange. **Stock exchange symbol:** DEG. **Number of employees nationwide:** 84,000.

HARRIS TEETER, INC.
P.O. Box 10100, Matthews NC 28106-0100. 704/844-3100. **Physical address:** 701 Crestdale Drive, Matthews NC 28105. **Toll-free phone:** 800/432-6111. **Contact:** Director of Personnel. **E-mail address:** jfranklin@harristeeter.com. **World Wide Web address:** http://www.harristeeter.com. **Description:** Operates a regional supermarket chain with over 140 stores in five southeastern states. **NOTE:** All hiring for Harris Teeter is done at this location. **Corporate headquarters location:** This location. **Other U.S. locations:** FL; GA; SC; TN; VA. **Parent company:** Ruddick Corporation (Charlotte NC) is a diversified holding company operating through wholly-owned subsidiaries American & Efird, Inc.; and Ruddick Investment Company. American &

Efird (Mount Holly NC) manufactures and distributes sewing thread for worldwide industrial and consumer markets and handles its own hiring. **Listed on:** New York Stock Exchange. **Stock exchange symbol:** RDK. **Number of employees nationwide:** 13,900.

INGLES MARKETS, INC.
P.O. Box 6676, Asheville NC 28816. 828/669-2941. **Physical address:** 2913 US Highway 70 West, Black Mountain NC 28711. **Fax:** 828/669-3678. **Contact:** Human Resources/Recruiting. **E-mail address:** recruit@ingles-markets.com. **World Wide Web address:** http://www.ingles-markets.com. **Description:** Operates over 200 supermarkets in North Carolina, South Carolina, Georgia, Tennessee, Virginia, and Alabama. In conjunction with its supermarket activities, the company owns and operates neighborhood shopping centers. Ingles Markets also owns and operates a milk processing and packaging plant. **Positions advertised include:** Retail Pharmacist. **Corporate headquarters location:** This location. **Listed on:** NASDAQ. **Stock exchange symbol:** IMKTA. **Number of employees nationwide:** 6,512.

JC PENNEY
246 North New Hope Road, Eastridge Mall, Gastonia NC 28054. 704/867-0781. **Contact:** Store Manager. **World Wide Web address:** http://www.jcpenney.com. **Description:** A nationwide chain of retail department stores. Founded 1902. **NOTE:** Please visit website for more information on career opportunities and to apply online. **Corporate headquarters location:** Plano TX. **Other area locations:** Statewide. **Other U.S. locations:** Nationwide. **Operations at this facility include:** Sales; Customer Service. **Listed on:** New York Stock Exchange. **Stock exchange symbol:** JCP. **Number of employees nationwide:** 147,000.

LOWE'S COMPANIES, INC.
P.O. Box 1111, North Wilkesboro NC 28656. 336/658-4000. **Fax:** 336/658-4766. **Contact:** Human Resources. **World Wide Web address:** http://www.lowes.com. **Description:** A discount retailer of consumer durables, building supplies, and home products for the do-it-yourself and home improvement markets. The company conducts operations over 900 retail stores in 45 states, primarily in the south central and southeastern regions of the United States. Products sold include tools, lumber, building materials, heating, cooling, and water systems, and specialty goods. **NOTE:** Please visit website to search for jobs and apply online. **Positions advertised include:** Accountant; Applied Design Manager; Applied Trend Manager; Commercial Marketing Manager; Career Development Specialist; Corporate Counsel; Customer Care Associate; Designer; Director – Various Departments; Engagement Manager; Forecast Analyst; Human Resources Manager. **Company slogan:** Lowe's knows. **Special programs:** Internships. **Corporate headquarters location:** This location. **Listed on:** New York Stock Exchange. **Stock exchange symbol:** LOW. **CEO:** Robert L. Tillman. **Annual sales/revenues:** More than $100 million. **Number of employees nationwide:** 153,000.

LOWE'S FOODS
P.O. Box 24908, Winston-Salem NC 27714. 336/659-0180. **Physical address:** 1381 Old Mill Circle, Suite 200, Winston-Salem NC 27103. **Fax:** 336/768-4702. **Contact:** Manager of Human Resources Department. **E-mail address:** donna.johnson@lowesfoods.com. **World Wide Web address:** http://www.lowesfood.com. **Description:** Operates a food store chain. **NOTE:** Please visit website to view job listings. **Parent company:** Alex Lee. **Corporate headquarters:** This location.

OFFICE DEPOT
BUSINESS SERVICES DIVISION
5809 Long Creek Park Drive, Charlotte NC 28269. 704/597-8501. **Fax:** 704/598-2873. **Contact:** Human Resources. **E-mail address:** jobs@officedepot.com. **World Wide Web address:** http://www.officedepot.com. **Description:** Office Depot is a wholesale and retail dealer of office supplies. Both Wilson Office Products (a division of Office Depot) and Office Depot offer over 11,000 different business products from basic supplies such as copy and printer paper to high-tech business furniture. Product categories include furniture; desk accessories; office essentials; computers; business machines; visual communications; safety and maintenance supplies; personal organizers and dated goods; writing instruments; business cases and binders; filing and storage units; paper, envelopes and business forms; and labels and mailing supplies. **NOTE:** Please visit website to search for jobs and apply online. **Positions advertised include:** Business Development Manager; Consultant Service; Account Manager. **Corporate headquarters location:** Delray Beach FL. **Other U.S. locations:** Nationwide. **International locations:** Worldwide. **Operations at this facility include:** This location supplies office products to contract customers. **Listed on:** New York Stock Exchange. **Stock exchange symbol:** ODP. **CEO:** Bruce Nelson.

SONIC AUTOMOTIVE INC.
6415 Idlewild Road, Suite 109, Charlotte NC 28212. 704/566-2400. **Fax:** 704/536-4665. **Contact:** Human Resources. **World Wide Web address:** http://www.sonicautomotive.com. **Description:** Operates a nationwide car dealership chain. Sonic Automotive also provides parts and services. **NOTE:** Please visit website to search for jobs. **Corporate headquarters location:** This location. **Listed on:** New York Stock Exchange. **Stock exchange symbol:** SAH. **CEO:** O. Bruton Smith.

VARIETY WHOLESALER
218 South Garnet Street, P.O. Drawer 947, Henderson NC 27536. 252/430-2600. **Fax:** 252/430-2499. **Contact:** Francis Winslow, Director of Human Resources. **Description:** Operates a chain of retail variety stores. **Corporate headquarters location:** This location. **Other area locations:** Raleigh NC.

WELCOME HOME, INC.
309 Raleigh Street, Wilmington NC 28412. 910/791-4312. **Toll-free phone:** 800/348-4088. **Fax:** 910/791-4945. **Contact:** Human Resources.

World Wide Web address: http://www.welchome.com. **Description:** A retailer of giftware and home decor including fragrances, candles, framed art, furniture, and seasonal gifts. The company operates over 100 stores in 36 states. **Corporate headquarters location:** This location. **Other U.S. locations:** Nationwide.

South Carolina

BABIES 'R US
605 Haywood Road, Greenville SC 29607. 864/297-9444. **Contact:** Human Resources. **E-mail address:** bruregion3@toysrus.com. **World Wide Web address:** http://www5.toysrus.com/our/bru. **Description:** A retailer of baby and young children's products including infant and toddler apparel, furniture, and feeding supplies at over 165 stores nationwide. Founded in 1996. **NOTE:** Resumes are requested to be sent by e-mail. **Positions advertised include:** Assistant Manager; Cashier; Management; Sales Executive; Services Sales Representative; Stock Clerk. **Other area locations:** Augusta SC; Columbia SC; Greenville SC; North Charleston SC. **Other U.S. locations:** Nationwide. **Parent company:** Toys "R" Us, Inc. (Paramus NJ).

BI-LO, INC.
P.O. Drawer 99, Mauldin SC 29662. 864/234-1600. **Physical address:** 208 Industrial Boulevard, Greenville SC 29607. **Fax:** 864/234-6999. **Contact:** Scott Santos, Employment Office. **E-mail address:** BILOHR@aholdusa.com. **World Wide Web address:** http://www.bi-lo.com. **Description:** Operates a supermarket chain with stores in South Carolina, North Carolina, Georgia, and Tennessee. **NOTE:** Second shifts offered. Resumes should be submitted online via the company Website. **Positions advertised include:** Perishable Management Auditor. **Corporate headquarters location:** This location. **Parent company:** Ahold USA. **President/CEO:** Dean Cohagan. **Annual sales/revenues:** $3.6 billion. **Number of employees:** 26,000.

CALE YARBOROUGH HONDA/MAZDA
2723 West Palmetto Street, Florence SC 29501. 843/669-5556. **Fax:** 843/667-0964. **Contact:** William Howell, Services Manager. **Description:** An automobile dealership that sells new and used Hondas and Mazdas as well as other vehicles. Cale Yarborough Honda/Mazda also offers automobile repair services. **Positions advertised include:** Automotive Mechanic.

HAMRICK'S, INC.
742 Peachoid Road, Gaffney SC 29341. 864/489-6095. **Fax:** 864/489-8734. **E-mail address:** jobs@hamricks.com. **Contact:** Greg Burnett, Director of Personnel. **World Wide Web address:** http://www.hamricks.com. **Description:** Operates a chain of men's clothing stores. These stores are located in the southeastern United States at 20 different locations. **Positions advertised include:** Assistant Store Manager; District Manager; Retail Management Trainee.

Corporate headquarters location: This location. **Other U.S. locations:** GA; NC; TN.

ONE PRICE CLOTHING STORES, INC.
P.O. Box 2487, Spartanburg SC 29304. 864/433-8888. **Physical address:** 1875 East Main Street, Duncan SC 29334. **Fax:** 864/433-9584. **Contact:** Human Resources. **E-mail address:** human-resources@oneprice.com. **World Wide Web address:** http://www.oneprice.com. **Description:** Operates over 600 specialty off-price stores in 30 states featuring a wide variety of contemporary women's apparel. **Positions advertised include:** Operations Manager; Regional Manager; District Manager; Store Manager; Sales Representative; Loss Prevention Associate; Field Auditor; Financial Officer; Merchandise Buyer; Distribution Supervisor. **Listed on:** NASDAQ. **Stock exchange symbol:** ONPR. **Chairman/CEO:** Leonard M. Snyder. **Annual sales/revenues:** $340 million. **Number of employees nationwide:** 4,200.

STONE, CLAY, GLASS, AND CONCRETE PRODUCTS

You can expect to find the following types of companies in this section:
Cement, Tile, Sand, and Gravel • Crushed and Broken Stone • Glass and Glass Products • Mineral Products

North Carolina

APAC – BARRUS CONSTRUCTION COMPANY
669 Bell Fork Road, Jacksonville NC 28541. 910/577-5659. **Contact:** Human Resources. **World Wide Web address:** http://www.apac.com. **Description:** A contracting company that handles a variety of construction projects and activities including asphalt, concrete, curbing, gutters, and the construction of highways, streets, and parking lots.

APAC – COASTAL CAROLINA DIVISION
P.O. Box 399, Kinston NC 28502. 252/527-8021. **Physical address:** 604 East New Bern Road, Kinston NC 28504. **Toll-free phone:** 800/849-1400. **Fax:** 252/527-4739. **Contact:** Bill Earp, Human Resources Manager. **World Wide Web address:** http://www.apac.com. **Description:** A contracting company that handles a variety of construction projects and activities including asphalt, concrete, curbing, gutters, and the construction of highways, streets, and parking lots.

BARNHILL CONTRACTING COMPANY
P.O. Box 35376, Fayetteville NC 28303-5376. 910/488-1319. **Physical address:** 1134 Shaw Mill Road, Fayetteville NC. **Fax:** 910/488-5673. **Contact:** S. James Hughes, Jr., Vice President of Human Resources. **E-mail address:** jhughes@barnhillcontracting.com. **World Wide Web address:** http://www.barnhillcontracting.com. **Description:** Barnhill Contracting Company is a construction company operating in two divisions. The Building Division is engaged in nonresidential building construction, such as schools and public buildings. The Paved Roads Division is involved in heavy highway construction and driveway paving. **NOTE:** Please visit website to search for jobs. If there is no specific contact listed for the position you are interested in, send your resume to the above contact at P.O. Box 1529, Tarboro NC 27886. Phone is 252/823-1021, fax is 252/823-0137. **Positions advertised include:** Pipe Foreman; Asphalt Paving Machine Screed Operator; Asphalt Distributor Truck Driver; Asphalt Laborer; Scraper Operator. **Other area locations:** Elizabeth City NC; Kitty Hawk NC; Raleigh NC; Tarboro NC; Rocky Mount NC; Wilmington NC. **Other U.S. locations:** VA. **Operations at this facility include:** This location produces asphalt. **Listed on:** Privately held. **President/CEO:** Robert E. Barnhill ,Jr.

NATIONAL GYPSUM COMPANY
2001 Rexford Road, Charlotte NC 28211. 704/365-7300. **Fax:** 800/329-6421. **Contact:** Human Resources. **E-mail address:** ng@nationalgypsum.com. **World Wide Web address:** http://www.national-gypsum.com. **Description:** One of the largest manufacturers of gypsum wallboard in the United States, as well as a major producer of joint treatment products. National Gypsum Company operates eight mines and quarries, and its manufacturing operations include nine joint treatment, 18 gypsum wallboard, and three paper facilities. **NOTE:** Please visit website to search for jobs. **Corporate headquarters location:** This location. **Other U.S. locations:** Nationwide. **Listed on:** Privately held. **CEO:** Tom Nelson. **Number of employees at this location:** 260. **Number of employees nationwide:** 2,500.

VULCAN MATERIALS COMPANY
P.O. Box 4239, Winston-Salem NC 27115-4239. 336/767-0911. **Physical address:** 4401 North Patterson Avenue Winston-Salem NC 27105. **Fax:** 336/744-2978. **Contact:** Human Resources. **E-mail address:** mideastresumes@vmcmail.com. **World Wide Web address:** http://www.vulcanmaterials.com. **Description:** The company primarily produces crushed stone and aggregates for the highway and construction markets. Vulcan Materials Company has 21 plant locations throughout the Southeast (14 in Georgia and seven in South Carolina). **Positions advertised include:** Staff Accountant Land and Lease. **Corporate headquarters location:** Birmingham AL. **Other area locations:** Charlotte NC. **Operations at this facility include:** Headquarters of the Mideast Division. **Listed on:** New York Stock Exchange. **Stock exchange symbol:** VMC. **CEO:** Donald M. James. **Number of employees nationwide:** 8,500.

South Carolina

APAC-CAROLINA INC.
805 Mineral Springs Road, P.O. Box 521, Darlington SC 29540. 843/393-2837. **Contact:** Human Resources. **World Wide Web address:** http://www.apac.com. **E-mail address:** apac@Ashland.com. **Description:** The Apac group of construction companies operates in 14 Southern and Midwestern states providing highway construction, road paving, and bridge construction services. The companies operate 36 quarries, 61 production facilities, 67 ready-mix concrete plants, and 242 asphalt plants. **NOTE:** Human Resources extension: x3029. **Positions advertised include:** Dozer Operator; Grader Operator; Concrete Mixer Truck Driver. **Corporate headquarters location:** Kinston NC. **Other area locations:** Statewide. **Other U.S. locations:** AL; AR; FL; GA; KS; MS; NC; OK; TN; TX; VA; WV. **Parent company:** Ashland Inc. (Covington KY). **Operations at this facility include:** Coastal Carolina Division. **President:** Charles F. Potts. **Number of employees nationwide:** 11,000.

COMPOSITES ONE LLC

467 Lakeshore Parkway, Rock Hill SC 29732-8212. 803/328-3862. **Fax:** 803/327-8089. **Contact:** Ann Ward, Distribution Manager. **World Wide Web address:** http://www.compositesone.com. **E-mail address:** info@CompositeOne.com. **Description:** A wholesale distributor of fiberglass, chemicals and related composite materials including additives, adhesives, gel coats, pigments, putties, polyester, and vinyl ester resins. **Positions advertised include:** Software Engineer; Production Manager; Chemicals Scientist. **Corporate headquarters location:** Arlington Heights IL. **Other U.S. locations:** Nationwide.

GUARDIAN INDUSTRIES CORPORATION

610 LNC Railway Distribution Park, State Highway 9, Richburg SC 29729. 803/789-6100. **Fax:** 803/789-6859. **Contact:** Tom Monzitta, Human Resources Representative. **E-mail address:** tom_monzitta@guardian.com. **World Wide Web address:** http://www.guardian.com. **Description:** Guardian Industries Corporation is an international manufacturer of glass including tempered glass, reflective coatings, and insulated glass. **Positions advertised include:** Production Manager; Ceramics Engineer; Materials Engineer; Mechanical Engineer; Metallurgical Engineer. **Corporate headquarters location:** Auburn Hills MI. **Other U.S. locations:** Nationwide. **Operations at this facility include:** Float Glass Plant/Manufacturing. **Number of employees nationwide:** 19,000.

OWENS CORNING

P.O. Box 1367, Anderson SC 29622. 864/296-4000. **Contact:** Human Resources Manager. **World Wide Web address:** http://www.owenscorning.com. **Description:** Manufactures and sells thermal and acoustical insulation products including insulation for appliances, glass-fiber roofing shingles, and roof insulation and industrial asphalt. Other products of the company include windows, glass-fiber textile yarns, wet process chopped strands and specialty mats, and polyester resins. Founded in 1938. **NOTE:** Second and third shifts offered, as well as on-call/24-hour positions. Human Resources phone: 864/296-4055. **Positions advertised include:** Concrete Process Engineer; Health Specialist; Operations Leader; Plant Leader. **Corporate headquarters location:** Toledo OH. **Other area locations:** Aiken SC; Chester SC; Duncan SC. **Other locations:** Worldwide. **Subsidiaries include:** Advanced Glassfiber Yarns LLC. **Operations at this facility include:** Composite materials manufacturing. **Listed on:** Over The Counter. **Stock exchange symbol:** OWENQ. **Chairman/CEO:** Michael H. Thaman. **Annual sales/revenues:** $4.8 billion. **Number of employees nationwide:** 19,000.

TRANSPORTATION AND TRAVEL

You can expect to find the following types of companies in this section:
Air, Railroad, and Water Transportation Services • Courier Services • Local and Interurban Passenger Transit • Ship Building and Repair • Transportation Equipment • Travel Agencies • Trucking • Warehousing and Storage

North Carolina

HATTERAS YACHTS
110 North Glenburnie Road, New Bern NC 28560-2799. 252/633-3101. **Contact:** Human Resources. **World Wide Web address:** http://www.hatterasyachts.com. **Description:** Hatteras Yachts builds, sells, and repairs fiberglass yachts. **NOTE:** Please visit http://sh.webhire.com/public/250 to search for jobs and apply online. **Positions advertised include:** Customer Service Process Representative; Director of Quality and Process Improvement; Fiberglass Application Engineer; Industrial Designer/Class A Surfacer; Interior Designer; Lean Six Sigma Black Belt. **Corporate headquarters location:** This location. **Parent company:** Brunswick Corporation. **Listed on:** New York Stock Exchange. **Stock exchange symbol:** BC. **Number of employees nationwide:** 21,000.

LANDSTAR EXPRESS AMERICA, INC.
1901-A1 Associates Lane, Suite A1, Charlotte NC 28217. 704/424-9912. **Contact:** Human Resources. **E-mail address:** employment@landstar.com. **World Wide Web address:** http://www.landstar.com. **Description:** Performs expedited and emergency air and truck freight services. **Corporate headquarters location:** Jacksonville FL. **Other U.S. locations:** Rockford IL. **Listed on:** NASDAQ. **Stock exchange symbol:** LSTR. **CEO:** Jeffrey C. Crowe.

TRIANGLE TRANSIT AUTHORITY
P.O. Box 13787, Research Triangle Park NC 27709. 919/549-9999. **Fax:** 919/485-7441. **Contact:** Human Resources Administrator. **E-mail address:** jobs@ridetta.org. **World Wide Web address:** http://www.ridetta.org. **Description:** Offers access to various methods of transportation including bus services, vanpooling, and carpooling to the Triangle Park area The TTA is currently planning to expand their services to include a railway system. **NOTE:** Please visit website to view job listings. **Positions advertised include:** Mechanic; Bus Operator; Dispatcher/Supervisor; Service Attendant.

UTILITIES: ELECTRIC, GAS, AND WATER

You can expect to find the following types of companies in this section:
Gas, Electric, and Fuel Companies • Other Energy-Producing Companies • Public Utility Holding Companies • Water Utilities

North Carolina

DUKE ENERGY CORPORATION
P.O. Box 1244, Charlotte NC 28201-1244. 704/594-6200. 0887. **Physical address:** 526 South Church Street, Charlotte NC 28202-1904. **Toll-free phone:** 800/873-3853. **Fax:** 704/382-3781. **Contact:** Corporate Staffing. **World Wide Web address:** http://www.duke-energy.com. **Description:** Provides electric service to about 2 million customers, operates natural gas pipelines, and is a leading producer of electricity, natural gas, and natural gas liquids. Founded in 1904. **NOTE:** Please visit website to search for jobs and submit electronic interest form. **Positions advertised include:** Accounting Assistant; Accountant; Customer Services Specialist; Hangar Attendant; Leasing Associate; Nuclear Maintenance Specialist; Technical Specialist; Web Specialist. **Special programs:** Internships; Summer Jobs. **Corporate headquarters location:** This location. **Subsidiaries include:** Church Street Capital Corporation; Crescent Resources, Inc.; Duke Energy Group, Inc.; Duke Engineering & Services, Inc.; Duke Merchandising; Duke Power Electric Operation; Duke Water Operations; Duke/Fluor Daniel; DukeNet Communications, Inc.; Nantahala Power and Light Company. **Listed on:** New York Stock Exchange. **Stock exchange symbol:** DUK. **CEO:** Paul M. Anderson. **Number of employees nationwide:** 17,000. **Number of employees worldwide:** 23,800.

PIEDMONT NATURAL GAS CO., INC.
1915 Rexford Road, P.O. Box 33068, Charlotte NC 28233. 704/364-3120. **Contact:** Personnel. **E-mail address:** corporate.recruiter@piedmontng.com. **World Wide Web address:** http://www.piedmontng.com. **Description:** Sells and transports natural gas and propane to over 625,000 commercial, industrial, and residential customers in North Carolina, South Carolina, and Tennessee. Founded in 1951. **Positions advertised include:** Rate Analyst; Senior Auditor; Customer Service Representative; Major Account Services Representative; Drafter; Environmental Engineer; Senior Service Specialist. **Special programs:** College Co-op. **Corporate headquarters location:** This location. **Other U.S. locations:** SC; TN. **Listed on:** New York Stock Exchange. **Stock exchange symbol:** PNY. **Annual sales/revenues:** More than $100 million. **Number of employees at this location:** 400. **Number of employees nationwide:** 2,100.

PROGRESS ENERGY
P.O. Box 1551, Raleigh NC 27602-1551. 919/508-5400. **Fax:** 919/546-7784. **Contact:** Corporate Employment. **World Wide Web address:**

http://www.progress-energy.com. **Description:** Provides electricity to approximately 1.2 million customers in North and South Carolina. Progress Energy owns and operates a network of 18 power plants throughout the region. The company also provides natural gas service to approximately 166,000 customers in North Carolina through its wholly-owned subsidiary, North Carolina Natural Gas. **NOTE:** Please visit website to search for jobs and apply online. **Positions advertised include:** Associate Communications Specialist; Associate Financial Specialist; Business Financial Analyst; Credit Analyst; Financial Specialist; Financial Auditor; Human Resources Representative; IT Analyst; Lead Business Financial Analyst; Operations and Strategic Planning Analyst; Senior Engineer; Supervisor – Disbursement Services. **Special programs:** Internships. **Corporate headquarters location:** This location. **Other U.S. locations:** FL; GA; SC. **Listed on:** New York Stock Exchange. **Stock exchange symbol:** PGN. **President/CEO:** Robert B. McGehee. **Number of employees nationwide:** 15,300.

PUBLIC SERVICE COMPANY OF NORTH CAROLINA, INC.
P.O. Box 1398, Gastonia NC 28053-1398. 704/864-6731. **Contact:** Human Resources. **World Wide Web address:** http://www.psnc.com. **Description:** Delivers natural gas products and services to residential, commercial, industrial, transportation, and electric power generation customers, and also to other local distribution companies. Public Service Company of North Carolina's products and services include natural gas distribution; interstate and intrastate pipeline services; supply and capacity brokering; natural gas vehicle fueling; and natural gas appliance sales, installation, and service. **NOTE:** Please visit website to apply online. **Corporate headquarters location:** This location. **Parent company:** SCANA.

South Carolina

CUMMINGS OIL COMPANY, INC.
P.O. Box 186, Hampton SC 29924. 803/943-3921. **Contact:** Human Resources. **Description:** Sells gas, diesel fuel, and propane primarily to residential customers. **Corporate headquarters location:** This location. **Other area locations:** Walterboro SC. **Other U.S. locations:** Nationwide.

SOUTH CAROLINA ELECTRIC AND GAS COMPANY
1115 East Main Street, Lake City SC 29560. 843/394-8043. **Contact:** Human Resources. **World Wide Web address:** http://www.sceg.com. **Description:** A public service organization that produces and distributes electricity and natural gas. **NOTE:** Send resumes to Human Resources, South Carolina Electric and Gas, Columbia SC 29218. Each department is responsible for its own hiring. Jobseekers should address inquiries to a particular area of interest. **Positions advertised include:** Maintenance Mechanic; Right of Way Agent; Apprentice Mechanic; Customer Service Support Associate; Technical Assistant; Safe Guard; Contract Analyst; Remittance Processor; Copy Writer; Line Man. **Corporate headquarters location:** Columbia SC. **Parent company:** SCANA Corporation.

MISCELLANEOUS WHOLESALING

You can expect to find the following types of companies in this section:
Exporters and Importers • General Wholesale Distribution Companies

North Carolina

BRADY DISTRIBUTING
P.O. Box 19269, Charlotte NC 28219. 704/357-6284. **Physical address:** 2708 Yorkmont Road, Charlotte NC 28208. **Fax:** 704/357-1243. **Contact:** Sue Ballard, Human Resources Manager. **World Wide Web address:** http://www.bradydist.com. **Description:** Distributes and operates coin-operated vending machines and arcade games. **Office hours:** Monday – Friday, 8:00 a.m. – 5:00 p.m. **Corporate headquarters location:** This location. **Other U.S. locations:** Miami FL; Orlando FL; Memphis TN. **Number of employees nationwide:** 120.

CASHWELL APPLIANCE PARTS, INC.
P.O. Box 2549, Fayetteville NC 28302-2549. **Physical address:** 3485 Clinton Road, Fayetteville NC 28312-6147. 910/323-1111. **Toll-free phone:** 800/277-1220. **Fax:** 910/323-5067. **Toll-free fax:** 800/277-2877. **Contact:** Human Resources. **World Wide Web address:** http://www.cashwell-appl-parts.com. **Description:** Distributes bathroom fans, ceiling fans, dryers, electrical equipment parts, and washers. **NOTE:** Please visit website to see job listings. **Positions advertised include:** Warehouse Worker. **Other area locations:** Raleigh NC; Wilmington NC; Asheville NC; Charlotte NC; Greensboro NC. **Operations at this facility include:** This location is a distribution center,

L.R. GORRELL CO.
P.O. Box 33395. Raleigh NC 27636. 919/821-1161. **Physical address:** 544 Pylon Drive, Raleigh NC 27606. **Fax:** 919/832-1542. **Contact:** Employment. **E-mail address:** raleigh@lrgorrell.com. **World Wide Web address:** http://www.lrgorrell.com. **Description:** A distributor of parts for heating and cooling equipment. Founded in 1951. **NOTE:** Entry-level positions are offered. **Corporate headquarters location:** This location. **Other area locations:** Asheville NC; Greensboro NC; Charlotte NC; Wilmington NC. **Other U.S. locations:** Greenville SC; North Charleston SC. **Listed on:** Privately held. **President:** L.R. Gorrell.

GRAINGER
2533 North Chester Street, Gastonia NC 28052. 704/861-9239. 9235. **Fax:** 704/866-7054. **Contact:** Michael Kenney, Manager. **World Wide Web address:** http://www.grainger.com. **Description:** A national supplier of industrial equipment such as motors, pumps, and safety maintenance equipment. Grainger distributes a variety of equipment and components to the industrial, commercial, contracting, and institutional

markets. Products include equipment and components for motors, air tools, hydraulic products, refrigeration items, power and hand tools, office equipment, computer supplies, replacement parts, industrial products, safety items, cold weather clothing, and storage equipment. **Positions advertised include:** Outside Sales Account Manager; Branch Manager; Warehouse Associate; Customer Service Associate. **Office hours:** Monday – Friday, 8:00 a.m. – 5:00 p.m. **Corporate headquarters location:** Chicago IL. **Other area locations:** Statewide. **Other U.S. locations:** Nationwide. **International locations:** Worldwide. **Listed on:** New York Stock Exchange. **Stock exchange symbol:** GWW. **CEO:** Richard L. Keyser.

HONEYWELL SENSOTEC, INC.

1100 Airport Road, Shelby NC 28150. 704/482-9582. **Recorded jobline:** 614/850-6000 option 3. **Contact:** Human Resources. **E-mail address:** hrdepartment2@sensotec.com. **World Wide Web address:** http://www.sensotec.com. **Description:** Supplies components to the automotive, truck, appliance, heating, and aerospace industries. **NOTE:** Please visit http://honeywell.com/careers/index.html to search for jobs and apply online. Online applications are preferred. **Corporate headquarters location:** Columbus OH. **International locations:** Worldwide. **Parent company:** Honeywell.

SPEIZMAN INDUSTRIES, INC.

P.O. Box 242108, Charlotte NC 28224. 704/559-5777. **Physical address:** 701 Griffith Road, Charlotte NC 28217. **Fax:** 704/676-4222. **Contact:** Human Resources. **World Wide Web address:** http://www.speizman.com. **Description:** Distributes sock knitting machines manufactured by Lonati, S.P.A. in Brescia, Italy, which is one of the world's largest manufacturers of hosiery knitting equipment. It also distributes Lonati sock and sheer hosiery knitting machines in Canada. The company also sells dyeing and finishing equipment for the textile industry. **Corporate headquarters location:** This location. **Other U.S. locations:** Fort Payne AL. **International locations:** Montreal, Canada; Leicester, England. **Listed on:** NASDAQ. **Stock exchange symbol:** SPZN. **Number of employees at this location:** 70.

South Carolina

GRAINGER

730 Congaree Road, Greenville SC 29607. 864/288-0110. **Fax:** 864/297-1799. **Contact:** Human Resources. **World Wide Web address:** http://www.grainger.com. **Description:** A national supplier of industrial and commercial products to the industrial, commercial, contracting, and institutional markets. Products include equipment and components for motors, air tools, hydraulic products, refrigeration items, power and hand tools, office equipment, computer supplies, replacement parts, industrial products, safety items, cold weather clothing, and storage equipment. Founded in 1927. **Office hours:** 8:00 a.m. – 5:00 p.m. **Positions advertised include:** Customer Service Associate; Outside Sales

Territory Manager; Account Manager; Warehouse Associate; Distribution Associate; Project Manager. **Annual sales/revenues:** $5 billion.

IKON OFFICE SOLUTIONS
7 Technology Circle, Columbia SC 29203. 803/758-5555. **Contact:** Human Resources. **World Wide Web address:** http://www.ikon.com. **Description:** Distributes, sells, and repairs office equipment including photocopiers, fax machines, and printers. **Positions advertised include:** Account Executive. **Corporate headquarters location:** Malvern PA. **Other U.S. locations:** Nationwide. **International locations:** Worldwide. **Annual sales/revenues:** $5.3 billion. **Number of employees statewide:** 300. **Number of employees worldwide:** 37,000.

ORDERS DISTRIBUTING COMPANY, INC.
P.O. Box 17189, Greenville SC 29606. 864/288-4220. **Physical address:** 1 Whitlee Court, Greenville SC 29607. **Fax:** 864/458-7348. **Contact:** Mr. Wiley Johnson, Vice President of Human Resources. **World Wide Web address:** http://www.ordersdistributing.com. **Description:** A supplier of a broad range of floor coverings including hardwood, vinyl, carpet, and ceramic. Founded in 1955. **Corporate headquarters location:** This location. **Other locations:** Greensboro NC; Johnson City TN; Roanoke VA.

INDUSTRY ASSOCIATIONS

ACCOUNTING AND MANAGEMENT CONSULTING

AMERICAN ACCOUNTING ASSOCIATION
5717 Bessie Drive, Sarasota FL 34233-2399. 941/921-7747. **Fax:** 943/923-4093. **E-mail address:** Office@aaahq.org. **World Wide Web address:** http://aaahq.org. **Description:** A voluntary organization founded in 1916 to promote excellence in accounting education, research and practice.

AMERICAN INSTITUTE OF CERTIFIED PUBLIC ACCOUNTANTS
1211 Avenue of the Americas, New York NY 10036. 212/596-6200. **Toll-free phone:** 888/777-7077. **Fax:** 212/596-6213. **World Wide Web address:** http://www.aicpa.org. **Description:** A non-profit organization providing resources, information, and leadership to its members.

AMERICAN MANAGEMENT ASSOCIATION
1601 Broadway, New York NY 10019. 212/586-8100. **Fax:** 212/903-8168. **Toll-free phone:** 800/262-9699. **E-mail address:** info@amanet.org. **World Wide Web address:** http://www.amanet.org. **Description:** A non-profit association providing its members with management development and educational services.

ASSOCIATION OF GOVERNMENT ACCOUNTANTS
2208 Mount Vernon Avenue, Alexandria VA 22301. 703/684-6931. **Toll-free phone:** 800/AGA-7211. **Fax:** 703/548-9367. **World Wide Web address:** http://www.agacgfm.com. **Description:** A public financial management organization catering to the professional interests of financial managers at the local, state and federal governments and public accounting firms.

ASSOCIATION OF MANAGEMENT CONSULTING FIRMS
380 Lexington Avenue, Suite 1700, New York NY 10168. 212/551-7887. **Fax:** 212/551-7934. **E-mail address:** info@amcf.org. **World Wide Web address:** http://www.amcf.org. **Description:** Founded in 1929 to provide a forum for confronting common challenges; increasing the collective knowledge of members and their clients; and establishing a professional code conduct.

CONNECTICUT SOCIETY OF CERTIFIED PUBLIC ACCOUNTANTS
845 Brook Street, Building Two, Rocky Hill CT 06067-3405. 860/258-4800. **Fax:** 860/258-4859. **E-mail address:** info@cs-cpa.org. **World Wide Web address:** http://www.cs-cpa.org. **Description:** A statewide professional membership organization catering to CPAs.

INSTITUTE OF INTERNAL AUDITORS
247 Maitland Avenue, Altamonte Springs FL 32701-4201. 407-937-1100. **Fax:** 407-937-1101. **E-mail address:** iia@theiia.org. **World Wide Web address:** http://www.theiia.org. **Description:** Founded in 1941 to serves

members in internal auditing, governance and internal control, IT audit, education, and security worldwide.

INSTITUTE OF MANAGEMENT ACCOUNTANTS
10 Paragon Drive, Montvale NJ 07645-1718. 201/573-9000. **Fax:** 201/474-1600. **Toll-free phone:** 800/638-4427. **E-mail address**: ima@imanet.org. **World Wide Web address:** http://www.imanet.org. **Description:** Provides members personal and professional development opportunities in management accounting, financial management and information management through education and association with business professionals and certification in management accounting and financial management.

INSTITUTE OF MANAGEMENT CONSULTANTS
2025 M Street, NW, Suite 800, Washington DC 20036-3309. 202/367-1134. **Toll-free phone:** 800/221-2557. **Fax:** 202/367-2134. **E-mail address:** office@imcusa.org. **World Wide Web address:** http://www.imcusa.org. **Description** Founded in 1968 as the national professional association representing management consultants and awarding the CMC (Certified Management Consultant) certification mark.

NATIONAL ASSOCIATION OF TAX PROFESSIONALS
720 Association Drive, PO Box 8002, Appleton WI 54912-8002. 800/558/3402. **Fax:** 800/747-0001. **E-Mail address:** natp@natptax.com. **World Wide Web address:** http://www.natptax.com. **Description:** Founded in 1979 as a nonprofit professional association dedicated to excellence in taxation with a mission to serve professionals who work in all areas of tax practice.

NATIONAL SOCIETY OF PUBLIC ACCOUNTANTS
1010 North Fairfax Street, Alexandria VA 22314. 703/549-6400. **Toll-free phone:** 800/966-6679. **Fax:** 703/549-2984. **Email address:** members@nsacct.org. **World Wide Web address:** http://www.nsacct.org. **Description:** For more than 50 years, NSA has supported its members with resources and representation to protect their right to practice, build credibility and grow the profession. NSA protects the public by requiring its members to adhere to a strict Code of Ethics.

ADVERTISING, MARKETING, AND PUBLIC RELATIONS

ADVERTISING RESEARCH FOUNDATION
641 Lexington Avenue, New York NY 10022. 212/751-5656. **World Wide Web address:** http://www.thearf.com. **Description:** Founded in 1936 by the Association of National Advertisers and the American Association of Advertising Agencies, the Advertising Research Foundation (ARF) is a nonprofit corporate-membership association, which is today the preeminent professional organization in the field of advertising, marketing and media research. Its combined membership represents more than 400 advertisers, advertising agencies, research firms, media companies, educational institutions and international organizations.

AMERICAN ASSOCIATION OF ADVERTISING AGENCIES
405 Lexington Avenue, 18th Floor, New York NY 10174-1801. 212/682-2500. **Fax:** 212/682-8391. **World Wide Web address:** http://www.aaaa.org. **Description:** Founded in 1917 as the national trade association representing the advertising agency business in the United States.

AMERICAN MARKETING ASSOCIATION
311 South Wacker Drive, Suite 5800, Chicago IL 60606. 312/542-9000. **Fax:** 312/542-9001. **Toll-free phone:** 800/AMA-1150. **E-mail address:** info@ama.org. **World Wide Web address:** http://www.marketingpower.com. **Description:** A professional associations for marketers providing relevant marketing information that experienced marketers turn to everyday.

DIRECT MARKETING ASSOCIATION
1120 Avenue of the Americas, New York NY 10036-6700. 212/768-7277. **Fax:** 212/302-6714. **E-mail address:** info@the-dma.org. **World Wide Web address:** http://www.the-dma.org. **Description:** Founded in 1917 as a non-profit organization representing professionals working in all areas of direct marketing.

INTERNATIONAL ADVERTISING ASSOCIATION
521 Fifth Avenue, Suite 1807, New York NY 10175. 212/557-1133. **Fax:** 212/983-0455. **E-mail address:** iaa@iaaglobal.org. **World Wide Web address:** http://www.iaaglobla.org. **Description:** A strategic partnership that addresses the common interests of all the marketing communications disciplines ranging from advertisers to media companies to agencies to direct marketing firms to individual practitioners.

MARKETING RESEARCH ASSOCIATION
1344 Silas Deane Highway, Suite 306, PO Box 230, Rocky Hill CT 06067-0230. 860/257-4008. **Fax:** 860/257-3990. **E-mail address:** email@mra-net.org. **World Wide Web address:** http://www.mra-net.org. **Description:** MRA promotes excellence in the opinion and marketing

research industry by providing members with a variety of opportunities for advancing and expanding their marketing research and related business skills. To protect the marketing research environment, we will act as an advocate with appropriate government entities, other associations, and the public.

PUBLIC RELATIONS SOCIETY OF AMERICA
33 Maiden Lane, 11th Floor, New York NY 10038-5150. 212/460-1400. **Fax:** 212/995-0757. **E-mail address:** info@prsa.org. **World Wide Web address:** http://www.prsa.org. **Description:** A professional organization for public relations practitioners. Comprised of nearly 20,000 members organized into 116 Chapters represent business and industry, counseling firms, government, associations, hospitals, schools, professional services firms and nonprofit organizations.

AEROSPACE

AMERICAN INSTITUTE OF AERONAUTICS AND ASTRONAUTICS
1801 Alexander Bell Drive, Suite 500, Reston VA 20191-4344. 703/264-7500. **Toll-free phone:** 800/639-AIAA. **Fax:** 703/264-7551. **E-mail address:** info@aiaa.org. **World Wide Web address:** http://www.aiaa.org. **Description:** The principal society of the aerospace engineer and scientist.

NATIONAL AERONAUTIC ASSOCIATION OF USA
1815 N. Fort Myer Drive, Suite 500, Arlington VA 22209. 703/527-0226. **Fax:** 703/527-0229. **E-mail address:** naa@naa-usa.org. **World Wide Web address:** http://www.naa-usa.org. **Description:** A non-parochial, charitable organization serving all segments of American aviation whose membership encompass all areas of flight including skydiving, models, commercial airlines, and military fighters.

PROFESSIONAL AVIATION MAINTENANCE ASSOCIATION
717 Princess Street, Alexandria VA 22314. 703/683-3171. **Toll-free phone:** 866/865-PAMA. **Fax:** 703/683-0018. **E-mail address:** hq@pama.org. **World Wide Web address:** http://www.pama.org. **Description:** A non-profit organization concerned with promoting professionalism among aviation maintenance personnel; fostering and improving methods, skills, learning, and achievement in aviation maintenance. The association also conducts regular industry meetings and seminars.

APPAREL, FASHION, AND TEXTILES

AMERICAN APPAREL AND FOOTWEAR ASSOCIATION
1601 North Kent Street, Suite 1200, Arlington VA 22209. 703/524-1864. **Fax:** 703/522-6741. **World Wide Web address:** http://apparelandfootwear.org. **Description:** The national trade association representing apparel, footwear and other sewn products companies, and their suppliers. Promotes and enhances its members' competitiveness, productivity and profitability in the global market.

AMERICAN TEXTILE MANUFACTURERS INSTITUTE
1130 Connecticut Avenue, NW, Suite 1200, Washington DC 20036-3954. 202/862-0500. **Fax:** 202/862-0537. **ATMI FactsLine:** 202/862-0572. **World Wide Web address:** http://www.atmi.org. **Description:** The national trade association for the domestic textile industry with members operating in more than 30 states and the industry employs approximately 450,000 people.

THE FASHION GROUP
8 West 40th Street, 7th Floor, New York NY 10018. 212/301-5511. **Fax:** 212/302-5533. **E-mail address:** info@fgi.org. **World Wide Web address:** http://www.fgi.org. **Description:** A non-profit association representing all areas of the fashion, apparel, accessories, beauty and home industries.

INTERNATIONAL ASSOCIATION OF CLOTHING DESIGNERS AND EXECUTIVES
34 Thorton Ferry Road #1, Amherst NH 03031. 603/672-4065. **Fax:** 603/672-4064. **World Wide Web address:** http://www.iacde.com. **Description:** Founded in 1911, with the mission to serve as a global network for the sharing of information by its members on design direction and developments, fashion and fiber trends, and technical innovations affecting tailored apparel, designers, their suppliers, retailers, manufacturing executives and educational institutions for the purpose of enhancing their professional standing and interests.

ARCHITECTURE, CONSTRUCTION, AND ENGINEERING

AACE INTERNATIONAL: THE ASSOCIATION FOR TOTAL COST MANAGEMENT
209 Prairie Avenue, Suite 100, Morgantown WV 26501. 304/296-8444. **Fax:** 304/291-5728. **E-mail address:** info@aacei.org. **World Wide Web address:** http://www.aacei.org. **Description:** Founded 1956 to provide its approximately 5,500 worldwide members with the resources to enhance their performance and ensure continued growth and success. Members include cost management professionals: cost managers and engineers, project managers, planners and schedulers, estimators and bidders, and value engineers.

AMERICAN ASSOCIATION OF ENGINEERING SOCIETIES
1828 L Street, NW, Suite 906, Washington DC 20036. 202/296-2237. **Fax:** 202/296-1151. **World Wide Web address:** http://www.aaes.org. **Description:** A multidisciplinary organization of engineering societies dedicated to advancing the knowledge, understanding, and practice of engineering.

AMERICAN CONSULTING ENGINEERS COMPANIES
1015 15th Street, 8th Floor, NW, Washington DC, 20005-2605. 202/347-7474. **Fax:** 202/898-0068. **E-mail address:** acec@acec.org. **World Wide Web address:** http://www.acec.org. **Description:** Engaged in a wide range of engineering works that propel the nation's economy, and enhance and safeguard America's quality of life. These works allow Americans to drink clean water, enjoy a healthy life, take advantage of new technologies, and travel safely and efficiently. The Council's mission is to contribute to America's prosperity and welfare by advancing the business interests of member firms.

AMERICAN INSTITUTE OF ARCHITECTS
1735 New York Avenue, NW, Washington DC 20006. 202/626-7300. **Fax:** 202/626-7547. **Toll-free phone:** 800/AIA-3837. **E-mail address:** infocentral@aia.org. **World Wide Web address:** http://www.aia.org. **Description:** A non-profit organization for the architecture profession dedicated to: Serving its members, advancing their value, improving the quality of the built environment. Vision Statement: Through a culture of innovation, The American Institute of Architects empowers its members and inspires creation of a better-built environment.

AMERICAN INSTITUTE OF CONSTRUCTORS
466 94th Avenue North, St. Petersburg FL 33702. 727/578-0317. **Fax:** 727/578-9982. **E-mail address:** admin@aicenet.org. **World Wide Web address:** http://www.aicnet.org. **Description:** Founded to help individual construction practitioners achieve the professional status they deserve and serves as the national qualifying body of professional constructor. The Institute AIC membership identifies the individual as a true

professional. The Institute is the constructor's counterpart of professional organizations found in architecture, engineering, law and other fields.

AMERICAN SOCIETY FOR ENGINEERING EDUCATION
1818 N Street, NW, Suite 600, Washington DC, 20036-2479. 202/331-3500. **Fax:** 202/265-8504. **World Wide Web address:** http://www.asee.org. **Description:** A nonprofit member association, founded in 1893, dedicated to promoting and improving engineering and technology education.

AMERICAN SOCIETY OF CIVIL ENGINEERS
1801 Alexander Bell Drive, Reston VA 20191-4400. 703/295-6300. **Fax:** 703/295-6222. **Toll-free phone:** 800/548-2723. **World Wide Web address:** http://www.asce.org. **Description:** Founded to provide essential value to its members, their careers, partners and the public by developing leadership, advancing technology, advocating lifelong learning and promoting the profession.

AMERICAN SOCIETY OF HEATING, REFRIGERATION, AND AIR CONDITIONING ENGINEERS
1791 Tullie Circle, NE, Atlanta GA 30329. 404/636-8400. **Fax:** 404/321-5478. **Toll-free phone:** 800/527-4723. **E-mail address:** ashrae@ashrae.org. **World Wide Web address:** http://www.ashrae.org. **Description:** Founded with a mission to advance the arts and sciences of heating, ventilation, air conditioning, refrigeration and related human factors and to serve the evolving needs of the public and ASHRAE members.

AMERICAN SOCIETY OF MECHANICAL ENGINEERS
Three Park Avenue, New York, NY 10016-5990. 973-882-1167. **Toll-free phone:** 800/843-2763. **E-mail address:** infocentral@asme.org. **World Wide Web address:** http://www.asme.org. **Description:** Founded in 1880 as the American Society of Mechanical Engineers, today ASME International is a nonprofit educational and technical organization serving a worldwide membership of 125,000.

AMERICAN SOCIETY OF NAVAL ENGINEERS
1452 Duke Street, Alexandria VA 22314-3458. 703/836-6727. **Fax:** 703/836-7491. **E-mail address:** asnehq@navalengineers.org. **World Wide Web address:** http://www.navalengineers.org. **Description:** Mission is to advance the knowledge and practice of naval engineering in public and private applications and operations, to enhance the professionalism and well being of members, and to promote naval engineering as a career field.

AMERICAN SOCIETY OF PLUMBING ENGINEERS
8614 Catalpa Avenue, Suite 1007, Chicago IL 60656-1116. 773/693-2773. **Fax:** 773/695-9007. **E-mail address:** info@aspe.org. **World Wide Web address:** http://www.aspe.org. **Description:** The international organization for professionals skilled in the design, specification and inspection of plumbing systems. ASPE is dedicated to the advancement

of the science of plumbing engineering, to the professional growth and advancement of its members and the health, welfare and safety of the public.

AMERICAN SOCIETY OF SAFETY ENGINEERS
1800 E Oakton Street, Des Plaines IL 60018. 847/699-2929. **Fax:** 847/768-3434. **E-mail address:** customerservice@asse.org. **World Wide Web address:** http://www.asse.org. **Description:** A non-profit organization promoting the concerns of safety engineers.

ASSOCIATED BUILDERS AND CONTRACTORS
4250 N. Fairfax Drive, 9th Floor, Arlington VA 22203-1607. 703/812-2000. **E-mail address:** gotquestions@abc.org. **World Wide Web address:** http://www.abc.org. **Description:** A national trade association representing more than 23,000 merit shop contractors, subcontractors, material suppliers and related firms in 80 chapters across the United States. Membership represents all specialties within the U.S. construction industry and is comprised primarily of firms that perform work in the industrial and commercial sectors of the industry.

ASSOCIATED GENERAL CONTRACTORS OF AMERICA, INC.
333 John Carlyle Street, Suite 200, Alexandria VA 22314. 703/548-3118. **Fax:** 703/548-3119. **E-mail address:** info@agc.org. **World Wide Web address:** http://www.agc.org. **Description:** A construction trade association, founded in 1918 on a request by President Woodrow Wilson.

THE ENGINEERING CENTER (TEC)
One Walnut Street, Boston MA 02108-3616. 617/227-5551. **Fax:** 617/227-6783. **E-mail address:** tec@engineers.org. **World Wide Web address:** http://www.engineers.org. **Description:** Founded with a mission to increase public awareness of the value of the engineering profession; to provide current information affecting the profession; to offer administrative facilities and services to engineering organizations in New England; and to provide a forum for discussion and resolution of professional issues.

ILLUMINATING ENGINEERING SOCIETY OF NORTH AMERICA
120 Wall Street, Floor 17, New York NY 10005. 212/248-5000. **Fax:** 212/248-5017(18). **E-mail address:** iesna@iesna.org. **World Wide Web address:** http://www.iesna.org. **Description:** To advance knowledge and to disseminate information for the improvement of the lighted environment to the benefit of society.

JUNIOR ENGINEERING TECHNICAL SOCIETY
1420 King Street, Suite 405, Alexandria VA 22314. 703/548-5387. **Fax:** 703/548-0769. **E-mail address:** info@jets.org. **World Wide Web address:** http://www.jets.org. **Description:** JETS is a national non-profit education organization that has served the pre-college engineering community for over 50 years. Through competitions and programs, JETS

serves over 30,000 students and 2,000 teachers, and holds programs on 150 college campuses each year.

NATIONAL ACTION COUNCIL FOR MINORITIES IN ENGINEERING
440 Hamilton Avenue, Suite 302, White Plains NY 10601-1813. 914/539-4010. **Fax:** 914/539-4032. **E-mail address:** webmaster@nacme.org. **World Wide Web address:** http://www.nacme.org. **Description:** Founded in 1974 to provide leadership and support for the national effort to increase the representation of successful African American, American Indian and Latino women and men in engineering and technology, math- and science-based careers.

NATIONAL ASSOCIATION OF HOME BUILDERS
1201 15th Street, NW, Washington DC 20005. 202/266-8200. **Toll-free phone:** 800/368-5242. **World Wide Web address:** http://www.nahb.org. **Description:** Founded in 1942, NAHB has been serving its members, the housing industry, and the public at large. A trade association that promotes the policies that make housing a national priority.

NATIONAL ASSOCIATION OF MINORITY ENGINEERING PROGRAM ADMINISTRATORS
1133 West Morse Boulevard, Suite 201, Winter Park FL 32789. 407/647-8839. **Fax:** 407/629-2502. **E-mail address:** namepa@namepa.org **World Wide Web address:** http://www.namepa.org. **Description:** Provides services, information, and tools to produce a diverse group of engineers and scientists, and achieve equity and parity in the nation's workforce.

NATIONAL ELECTRICAL CONTRACTORS ASSOCIATION
3 Bethesda Metro Center, Suite 1100, Bethesda MD 20814. 301/657-3110. **Fax:** 301/215-4500. **World Wide Web address:** http://www.necanet.org. **Description:** Founded in 1901 as representative segment of the construction market comprised of over 70,000 electrical contracting firms.

NATIONAL ASSOCIATION OF BLACK ENGINEERS
1454 Duke Street, Alexandria VA 22314. 703/549-2207. **Fax:** 703/683-5312. **E-mail address:** info@nsbe.org. **World Wide Web address:** http://www.nsbe.org. **Description:** A non-profit organization dedicated to increasing the number of culturally responsible Black engineers who excel academically, succeed professionally and positively impact the community.

NATIONAL SOCIETY OF PROFESSIONAL ENGINEERS
1420 King Street, Alexandria VA 22314-2794. 703/684-2800. **Fax:** 703/836-4875. **World Wide Web address:** http://www.nspe.org. **Description:** An engineering society that represents engineering professionals and licensed engineers (PEs) across all disciplines. Founded in 1934 to promote engineering licensure and ethics, enhance the engineer image, advocate and protect legal rights, publish industry news, and provide continuing education.

SOCIETY OF FIRE PROTECTION ENGINEERS
7315 Wisconsin Avenue, Suite 620E, Bethesda MD 20814. 301/718-2910. **Fax:** 301/718-2242. **E-mail address:** sfpehqtrs@sfpe.org. **World Wide Web address:** http://www.sfpe.org. **Description:** Founded in 1950 and incorporated as in independent organization in 1971, the professional society represents professionals in the field of fire protection engineering. The Society has approximately 3500 members in the United States and abroad, and 51 regional chapters, 10 of which are outside the US.

ARTS, ENTERTAINMENT, SPORTS, AND RECREATION

AMERICAN ASSOCIATION OF MUSEUMS
1575 Eye Street NW, Suite 400, Washington DC 20005. 202/289-1818. **Fax:** 202/289-6578. **World Wide Web address:** http://www.aam-us.org. **Description:** Founded in 1906, the association promotes excellence within the museum community. Services include advocacy, professional education, information exchange, accreditation, and guidance on current professional standards of performance.

AMERICAN FEDERATION OF MUSICIANS
1501 Broadway, Suite 600, New York NY 10036. 212/869-1330. **Fax:** 212/764-6134. **World Wide Web address:** http://www.afm.org. **Description:** Represents the interests of professional musicians. Services include negotiating agreements, protecting ownership of recorded music, securing benefits such as health care and pension, or lobbying our legislators. The AFM is committed to raising industry standards and placing the professional musician in the foreground of the cultural landscape.

AMERICAN MUSIC CENTER
30 West 26th Street, Suite 1001, New York NY 10010. 212/366-5260. **Fax:** 212/366-5265. **World Wide Web address:** http://www.amc.net. **Description:** Dedicated to fostering and composition, production, publication, and distribution of contemporary (American) music.

AMERICAN SOCIETY OF COMPOSERS, AUTHORS, AND PUBLISHERS (ASCAP)
One Lincoln Plaza, New York NY 10023. 212/621-6000. **Fax:** 212/724-9064. **E-mail address:** info@ascap.com. **World Wide Web address:** http://www.ascap.com. **Description:** A membership based association comprised of composers, songwriters, lyricists, and music publishers across all genres of music.

AMERICAN SYMPHONY ORCHESTRA LEAGUE
33 West 60th Street, 5th Floor, New York NY 10023-7905. 212/262-5161. **Fax:** 212/262-5198. **E-mail address:** league@symphony.org. **World Wide Web address:** http://www.symphony.org. **Description:** Founded in 1942 to exchange information and ideas with other orchestra leaders. The league also publishes the bimonthly magazine.

AMERICAN ZOO AND AQUARIUM ASSOCIATION
8403 Colesville Road, Suite 710, Silver Spring MD 20910-3314. 301/562-0777. **Fax:** 301/562-0888. **World Wide Web address:** http://www.aza.org. **Description:** Dedicated to establishing and maintaining excellent professional standards in all AZA Institutions through its accreditation program; establishing and promoting high standards of animal care and welfare; promoting and facilitating collaborative conservation and research programs; advocating effective

governmental policies for our members; strengthening and promoting conservation education programs for our public and professional development for our members, and; raising awareness of the collective impact of its members and their programs.

ASSOCIATION OF INDEPENDENT VIDEO AND FILMMAKERS
304 Hudson Street, 6th floor, New York NY 10013. 212/807-1400. **Fax:** 212/463-8519. **E-mail address:** info@aivf.org. **World Wide Web address:** http://www.aivf.org. **Description:** A membership organization serving local and international film and videomakers including documentarians, experimental artists, and makers of narrative features.

NATIONAL ENDOWMENT FOR THE ARTS
1100 Pennsylvania Avenue, NW, Washington DC 20506. 202/682-5400. **E-mail address:** webmgr@arts.endow.com. **World Wide Web address:** http://www.nea.gov. **Description:** Founded in 1965 to foster, preserve, and promote excellence in the arts, to bring art to all Americans, and to provide leadership in arts education.

NATIONAL RECREATION AND PARK ASSOCIATION
22377 Belmont Ridge Road, Ashburn VA 20148-4150. 703/858-0784. **Fax:** 703/858-0794. **E-mail address:** info@nrpa.org. **World Wide Web address:** http://www.nrpa.org. **Description:** Works "to advance parks, recreation and environmental conservation efforts that enhance the quality of life for all people."

WOMEN'S CAUCUS FOR ART
P.O. Box 1498, Canal Street Station, New York NY 10013. 212/634-0007. **E-mail address:** info@nationalwca.com. **World Wide Web address:** http://www.nationalwca.com. **Description:** Founded in 1972 in connection with the College Art Association (CAA), as a national organization unique in its multi-disciplinary, multicultural membership of artists, art historians, students /educators, museum professionals and galleries in the visual arts.

AUTOMOTIVE

NATIONAL AUTOMOBILE DEALERS ASSOCIATION
8400 Westpark Drive, McLean VA 22102. 703/821-7000. **Toll-free phone:** 800/252-6232. **E-mail address:** nadainfo@nada.org. **World Wide Web address:** http://www.nada.org. **Description:** NADA represents America's franchised new-car and -truck dealers. Today there are more than 19,700 franchised new-car and -truck dealer members holding nearly 49,300 separate new-car and light-, medium-, and heavy-duty truck franchises, domestic and import. Founded in 1917.

NATIONAL INSTITUTE FOR AUTOMOTIVE SERVICE EXCELLENCE
101 Blue Seal Drive, SE, Suite 101, Leesburg VA 20175. 703/669-6600. **Toll-free phone:** 877/ASE-TECH. **World Wide Web address:** http://www.ase.com. **Description:** An independent, non-profit organization established in 1972 to improve the quality of vehicle repair and service through the testing and certification of repair and service professionals. More than 420,000 professionals hold current ASE credentials.

SOCIETY OF AUTOMOTIVE ENGINEERS
400 Commonwealth Drive, Warrendale PA 15096-0001. 724/776-4841. **E-mail address:** customerservice@sae.org. **World Wide Web address:** http://www.sae.org. **Description:** An organization with more than 84,000 members from 97 countries who share information and exchange ideas for advancing the engineering of mobility systems.

BANKING

AMERICA'S COMMUNITY BANKERS
900 Nineteenth Street, NW, Suite 400, Washington DC 20006. 202/857-3100. **Fax:** 202/296-8716. **World Wide Web address:** http://www.acbankers.org. **Description:** Represents the nation's community banks of all charter types and sizes providing a broad range of advocacy and service strategies to enhance their members' presence and contribution to the marketplace.

AMERICAN BANKERS ASSOCIATION
1120 Connecticut Avenue, NW, Washington DC 20036. 800/BANKERS. **World Wide Web address:** http://www.aba.com. **Description:** Founded in 1875 and represents banks on issues of national importance for financial institutions and their customers. Members include all categories of banking institutions, including community, regional and money center banks and holding companies, as well as savings associations, trust companies and savings banks.

BIOTECHNOLOGY, PHARMACEUTICALS, AND SCIENTIFIC R&D

AMERICAN ASSOCIATION FOR CLINICAL CHEMISTRY
2101 L Street, NW, Suite 202, Washington DC 20037-1558. 202/857-0717. **Fax:** 202/887-5093. **Toll-free phone:** 800/892-1400. **World Wide Web address:** http://www.aacc.org. **Description:** Founded in 1948 as an international scientific/medical society of clinical laboratory professionals, physicians, research scientists and other individuals involved with clinical chemistry and other clinical laboratory science-related disciplines. The society has 10,000 members.

AMERICAN ASSOCIATION OF COLLEGES OF PHARMACY
1426 Prince Street, Alexandria VA 22314. 703/739-2330. **Fax:** 703/836-8982. **E-mail address:** mail@aacp.org. **World Wide Web address:** http://www.aacp.org. **Description:** Founded in 1900 as the national organization representing the interests of pharmaceutical education and educators. Comprising all 89 U.S. pharmacy colleges and schools including more than 4,000 faculty, 36,000 students enrolled in professional programs, and 3,600 individuals pursuing graduate study, AACP is committed to excellence in pharmaceutical education.

AMERICAN ASSOCIATION OF PHARMACEUTICAL SCIENTISTS
2107 Wilson Boulevard, Suite 700, Arlington VA 22201-3042. 703/243-2800. **Fax:** 703/243-9650. **E-mail address:** aaps@aaps.org. **World Wide Web address:** http://www.aaps.org. **Description:** Founded in 1986 as professional, scientific society of more than 10,000 members employed in academia, industry, government and other research institutes worldwide. The association advances science through the open exchange of scientific knowledge; serves as an information resource; and contributes to human health through pharmaceutical research and development.

AMERICAN COLLEGE OF CLINICAL PHARMACY (ACCP)
3101 Broadway, Suite 650, Kansas City MO 64111. 816/531-2177. **Fax:** 816/531-4990. **E-mail address:** accp@accp.com **World Wide Web address:** http://www.accp.com. **Description:** A professional and scientific society providing leadership, education, advocacy, and resources enabling clinical pharmacists to achieve excellence in practice and research.

AMERICAN PHARMACISTS ASSOCIATION
2215 Constitution Avenue, NW, Washington DC 20037-2985. 202/628-4410. **Fax:** 202/783-2351. **E-mail address:** info@aphanet.org. **World Wide Web address:** http://www.aphanet.org. **Description:** Founded in 1852 as the national professional society of pharmacists. Members include practicing pharmacists, pharmaceutical scientists, pharmacy students, pharmacy technicians, and others interested in advancing the profession.

AMERICAN SOCIETY FOR BIOCHEMISTRY AND MOLECULAR BIOLOGY

9650 Rockville Pike, Bethesda MD 20814-3996. 301/634-7145. **Fax:** 301/634-7126. **E-mail address:** asbmb@asbmb.faseb.org. **World Wide Web address:** http://www.asbmb.org. **Description:** A nonprofit scientific and educational organization with over 11,900 members. Most members teach and conduct research at colleges and universities. Others conduct research in various government laboratories, nonprofit research institutions and industry. The Society's student members attend undergraduate or graduate institutions.

AMERICAN SOCIETY OF HEALTH-SYSTEM PHARMACISTS

7272 Wisconsin Avenue, Bethesda MD 20814. 301/657-3000. **Toll-free phone:** 866/279-0681. **World Wide Web address:** http://www.ashp.org. **Description:** A national professional association representing pharmacists who practice in hospitals, health maintenance organizations, long-term care facilities, home care, and other components of health care systems.

NATIONAL SPACE BIOMEDICAL RESEARCH INSTITUTE

One Baylor Plaza, NA-425, Houston TX 77030. 713/798-7412. **Fax:** 713/798-7413. **E-mail address:** info@www.nsbri.org. **World Wide Web address:** http://www.nsbri.org. **Description:** Conducts research into health concerns facing astronauts on long missions.

NATIONAL PHARMACEUTICAL COUNCIL

1894 Preston White Drive, Reston VA 20191-5433. 703/620-6390. **Fax:** 703/476-0904. **E-mail address:** main@npcnow.com. **World Wide Web address:** http://www.npcnow.org. **Description:** Conducts research and education programs geared towards demonstrating that the appropriate use of pharmaceuticals improves both patient treatment outcomes and the cost effective delivery of overall health care services.

BUSINESS SERVICES & NON-SCIENTIFIC RESEARCH

AMERICAN SOCIETY OF APPRAISERS
555 Herndon Parkway, Suite 125, Herndon VA 20170. 703/478-2228. **Fax:** 703/742-8471. **E-mail address:** asainfo@appraisers.org. **World Wide Web address:** http://www.appraisers.org. **Description:** Fosters professional excellence through education, accreditation, publication and other services. Its goal is to contribute to the growth of its membership and to the appraisal profession.

EQUIPMENT LEASING ASSOCIATION OF AMERICA
4301 North Fairfax Drive, Suite 550, Arlington VA 22203-1627. 703/527-8655. **Fax:** 703/527-2649. **World Wide Web address:** http://www.elaonline.com. **Description:** Promotes and serves the general interests of the equipment leasing and finance industry.

NATIONAL ASSOCIATION OF PERSONNEL SERVICES
The Village at Banner Elk, Suite 108, P.O. Box 2128, Banner Elk NC 28604. 828/898-4929. **Fax:** 828/898-8098. **World Wide Web address:** http://www.napsweb.org. **Description**: Serves, protects, informs, and represents all facets of the personnel services industry regarding federal legislation and regulatory issues by providing education, certification, and member services which enhance the ability to conduct business with integrity and competence.

CHARITIES AND SOCIAL SERVICES

AMERICAN COUNCIL FOR THE BLIND
1155 15th Street, NW, Suite 1004, Washington DC 20005. 202/467-5081. **Fax:** 202/467-5085. **Toll-free phone:** 800/424-8666. **World Wide Web address:** http://www.acb.org. **Description:** The nation's leading membership organization of blind and visually impaired people. It was founded in 1961.

CATHOLIC CHARITIES USA
1731 King Street, Alexandria VA 22314. 703/549-1390. **Fax:** 703/549-1656. **World Wide Web address:** http://www.catholiccharitiesusa.org. **Description:** A membership association of social service networks providing social services to people in need.

NATIONAL ASSOCIATION OF SOCIAL WORKERS
750 First Street, NE, Suite 700, Washington DC 20002-4241. 202/408-8600. **E-mail address:** membership@naswdc.org. **World Wide Web address:** http://www.naswdc.org. **Description:** A membership organization comprised of professional social workers working to enhance the professional growth and development of its members, to create and maintain professional standards, and to advance sound social policies.

NATIONAL COUNCIL ON FAMILY RELATIONS
3989 Central Avenue, NE, #550, Minneapolis MN 55421. 763/781-9331. **Fax:** 763/781-9348. **Toll-free phone:** 888/781-9331. **E-mail address:** info@ncfr.org. **World Wide Web address:** http://www.ncfr.org. **Description:** Provides a forum for family researchers, educators, and practitioners to share in the development and dissemination of knowledge about families and family relationships, establishes professional standards, and works to promote family well-being.

NATIONAL FEDERATION OF THE BLIND
1800 Johnson Street, Baltimore MD 21230-4998. 410/659-9314. **Fax:** 410/685-5653. **World Wide Web address:** http://www.nfb.org. **Description:** Founded in 1940, the National Federation of the Blind (NFB) is the nation's largest membership organization of blind persons. With fifty thousand members, the NFB has affiliates in all fifty states plus Washington D.C. and Puerto Rico, and over seven hundred local chapters. As a consumer and advocacy organization, the NFB is a leading force in the blindness field today.

NATIONAL MULTIPLE SCLEROSIS SOCIETY
733 Third Avenue, New York NY 10017. **Toll-free phone:** 800/344-4867. **World Wide Web address:** http://www.nmss.org. **Description:** Provides accurate, up-to-date information to individuals with MS, their families, and healthcare providers is central to our mission.

CHEMICALS, RUBBER, AND PLASTICS

AMERICAN CHEMICAL SOCIETY
1155 Sixteenth Street, NW, Washington DC 20036. 202/872-4600. **Fax:** 202/872-6067. **Toll-free phone:** 800/227-5558. **E-mail address:** help@acs.org. **World Wide Web address:** http://www.acs.org. **Description:** A self-governed individual membership organization consisting of more than 159,000 members at all degree levels and in all fields of chemistry. The organization provides a broad range of opportunities for peer interaction and career development, regardless of professional or scientific interests. The Society was founded in 1876.

AMERICAN INSTITUTE OF CHEMICAL ENGINEERS
3 Park Avenue, New York NY 10016-5991. 212/591-8100. **Toll-free phone:** 800/242-4363. **Fax:** 212/591-8888. **E-mail address:** xpress@aiche.org. **World Wide Web address:** http://www.aiche.org. **Description:** Founded in 1908 and provides leadership in advancing the chemical engineering profession; fosters and disseminates chemical engineering knowledge, supports the professional and personal growth of its members, and applies the expertise of its members to address societal needs throughout the world.

THE ELECTROCHEMICAL SOCIETY
65 South Main Street, Building D, Pennington NJ 08534-2839. 609/737-1902. **Fax:** 609/737-2743. **World Wide Web address:** http://www.electrochem.org. **Description:** Founded in 1902, The Electrochemical Society has become the leading society for solid-state and electrochemical science and technology. ECS has 8,000 scientists and engineers in over 75 countries worldwide who hold individual membership, as well as roughly 100 corporate members.

SOCIETY OF PLASTICS ENGINEERS
14 Fairfield Drive, PO Box 403, Brookfield CT 06804-0403. 203/775-0471. **Fax:** 203/775-8490. **E-mail address:** info@4spe.org. **World Wide Web address:** http://www.4spe.org. **Description:** A 25,000-member organization promoting scientific and engineering knowledge relating to plastics. Founded in 1942.

THE SOCIETY OF THE PLASTICS INDUSTRY, INC.
1801 K Street, NW, Suite 600, Washington DC 20006. 202/974-5200. **Fax:** 202/296-7005. **World Wide Web address:** http://www.socplas.org. **Description:** Founded in 1937, The Society of the Plastics Industry, Inc., is the trade association representing one of the largest manufacturing industries in the United States. SPI's members represent the entire plastics industry supply chain, including processors, machinery and equipment manufacturers and raw materials suppliers. The U.S. plastics industry employs 1.4 million workers and provides more than $310 billion in annual shipments.

COMMUNICATIONS:TELECOMMUNICATIONS AND BROADCASTING

ACADEMY OF TELEVISION ARTS & SCIENCES
5220 Lankershim Boulevard, North Hollywood CA 91601-3109. 818/754-2800. **Fax:** 818/761-2827. **World Wide Web address:** http://www.emmys.com. **Description:** Promotes creativity, diversity, innovation and excellence though recognition, education and leadership in the advancement of the telecommunications arts and sciences.

AMERICAN DISC JOCKEY ASSOCIATION
2000 Corporate Drive, #408, Ladera Ranch CA 92694. 888/723-5776. **World Wide Web address:** http://www.adja.org. **Description:** Promotes ethical behavior, industry standards and continuing education for its members.

AMERICAN WOMEN IN RADIO AND TELEVISION, INC.
8405 Greensboro Drive, Suite 800, McLean VA 22102. 703/506-3290. **Fax:** 703/506-3266. **E-mail address:** info@awrt.org. **World Wide Web address:** http://www.awrt.org. **Description:** A non-profit, professional organization of women and men who work in the electronic media and allied fields.

COMPTEL/ASCENT
1900 M Street, NW, Suite 800, Washington DC 20036. 202/296-6650. **Fax:** 202/296-7585. **World Wide Web address:** http://www.comptelascent.org. **Description:** An association representing competitive telecommunications companies in virtually every sector of the marketplace: competitive local exchange carriers, long-distance carriers of every size, wireless service providers, Internet service providers, equipment manufacturers, and software suppliers.

MEDIA COMMUNICATIONS ASSOCIATION-INTERNATIONAL
7600 Terrace Avenue, Suite 203, Middleton WI 53562. 608/827-5034. **Fax:** 608/831-5122. **E-mail address:** info@mca-i.org. **World Wide Web address:** http://www.itva.org. **Description:** A not-for-profit, member-driven organization that provides opportunities for networking, forums for education and the resources for information to media communications professionals.

NATIONAL ASSOCIATION OF BROADCASTERS
1771 N Street, NW, Washington DC 20036. 202/429-5300. **Fax:** 202/429-4199. **E-mail address:** nab@nab.org. **World Wide Web address:** http://www.nab.org. **Description:** A trade association that represents the interests of free, over-the-air radio and television broadcasters.

NATIONAL CABLE & TELECOMMUNICATIONS ASSOCIATION
1724 Massachusetts Avenue, NW, Washington DC 20036. 202/775-3550. **E-mail address:** webmaster@ncta.com. **World Wide Web**

address: http://www.ncta.com. **Description:** The National Cable and Telecommunications Association is the principal trade association of the cable and telecommunications industry. Founded in 1952, NCTA's primary mission is to provide its members with a strong national presence by providing a single, unified voice on issues affecting the cable and telecommunications industry.

PROMAX & BDA
9000 West Sunset Boulevard, Suite 900, Los Angeles CA 90069. 310/788-7600. **Fax:** 310/788-7616. **World Wide Web address:** http://www.promax.org. **Description:** A non-profit association dedicated to advancing the role and effectiveness of promotion, marketing, and broadcast design professionals in the electronic media.

U.S. TELECOM ASSOCIATION
1401 H Street, NW, Suite 600, Washington DC 20005-2164. 202/326-7300. **Fax:** 202/326-7333. **E-mail address:** membership@usta.org. **World Wide Web address:** http://www.usta.org. **Description:** A trade association representing service providers and suppliers for the telecom industry. Member companies offer a wide range of services, including local exchange, long distance, wireless, Internet and cable television service.

COMPUTER HARDWARE, SOFTWARE, AND SERVICES

ASSOCIATION FOR COMPUTING MACHINERY
1515 Broadway, New York NY, 10036. 212/626-0500. 212/626-0500. **Toll-free phone:** 800/342-6626. **World Wide Web address:** http://www.acm.org. **Description:** A 75-000-member organization founded in 1947 to advance the skills of information technology professionals and students worldwide.

ASSOCIATION FOR MULTIMEDIA COMMUNICATIONS
PO Box 10645, Chicago IL 60610. 773/276-9320. **E-mail address:** info@amcomm.org. **World Wide Web address:** http://www.amcomm.org. **Description:** A networking and professional organization for people who create New Media, including the Web, CD-ROMs and DVDs, interactive kiosks, streaming media, and other digital forms. The association promotes understanding of technology, e-learning, and e-business.

ASSOCIATION FOR WOMEN IN COMPUTING
41 Sutter Street, Suite 1006, San Francisco CA 94104. 415/905-4663. **Fax:** 415/358-4667. **E-mail address:** info@awc-hq.org. **World Wide Web address:** http://www.awc-hq.org. **Description:** A not-for-profit, professional organization for individuals with an interest in information technology. The association is dedicated to the advancement of women in the computing fields, in business, industry, science, education, government, and the military.

BLACK DATA PROCESSING ASSOCIATES
6301 Ivy Lane, Suite 700, Greenbelt MD 20770. 301/220-2180. **Fax:** 301/220-2185. **Toll-free phone:** 800/727-BDPA. **World Wide Web address:** http://www.bdpa.org. **Description:** A member-focused organization that positions its members at the forefront of the IT industry. BDPA is committed to delivering IT excellence to our members, strategic partners, and community.

INFORMATION TECHNOLOGY ASSOCIATION OF AMERICA
1401 Wilson Boulevard, Suite 1100, Arlington VA 22209. 703/522-5055. **Fax:** 703/525-2279. **Wide Web address:** http://www.itaa.org. **Description:** A trade association representing the U.S. IT industry and providing information about its issues, association programs, publications, meetings, and seminars.

INTERNATIONAL WEBMASTER'S ASSOCIATION- HTML WRITERS GUILD
119 E. Union Street, Suite F, Pasadena CA 91030. **World Wide Web address:** http://www.hwg.org. **Description:** Provides online web design training to individuals interested in web design and development.

NETWORK PROFESSIONAL ASSOCIATION
17 South High Street, Suite 200, Columbus OH 43215. 614/221-1900. **Fax:** 614/221-1989. **E-mail address:** npa@npa.org. **World Wide Web address:** http://www.npa.org. **Description:** A non-profit association for professionals in Network Computing.

SOCIETY FOR INFORMATION MANAGEMENT
401 North Michigan Avenue, Chicago IL 60611. 312/527-6734. **E-mail address:** sim@simnet.org **World Wide Web address:** http://www.simnet.org. **Description:** With 3,000 members, SIM is a network for IT leaders including CIOs, senior IT executives, prominent academicians, consultants, and others. SIM is a community of thought leaders who share experiences and knowledge, and who explore future IT direction. Founded in 1968.

SOCIETY FOR TECHNICAL COMMUNICATION
901 North Stuart Street, Suite 904, Arlington VA 22203-1822. Fax: 703/522-2075. **World Wide Web address:** http://www.stc.org. **Description:** A 25-000 member organization dedicated to advancing the arts and sciences of technical communication

SOFTWARE & INFORMATION INDUSTRY ASSOCIATION
1090 Vermont Avenue, NW, Sixth Floor, Washington DC 20005-4095. 202/289-7442. **Fax:** 202/289-7097. **World Wide Web address:** http://www.siia.net. **Description:** The SIIA is the principal trade association for the software and digital content industry. SIIA provides services in government relations, business development, corporate education and intellectual property protection to leading companies.

USENIX ASSOCIATION
2560 Ninth Street, Suite 215, Berkeley CA, 94710. 510/528-8649. **Fax:** 510/548-5738. **E-mail address:** office@usenix.org. **World Wide Web address:** http://www.usenix.org. **Description:** Founded in 1975 the association fosters technical excellence and innovation, supports and disseminates practical research, provides a neutral forum for discussion of technical issues, and encourages computing outreach to the community. USENIX brings together engineers, system administrators, scientists, and technicians working on the cutting edge of the computing world.

EDUCATIONAL SERVICES

AMERICAN ASSOCIATION OF SCHOOL ADMINISTRATORS
801 North Quincy Street, Suite 700, Arlington VA 22203-1730. 703/528-0700. **Fax:** 703/841-1543. **E-mail address:** info@aasa.org. **World Wide Web address:** http://www.aasa.org. **Description:** The professional organization for more than 14,000 educational leaders in the U.S. and other countries. The association supports and develops effective school system leaders who are dedicated to the highest quality public education for all children.

AMERICAN ASSOCIATION FOR HIGHER EDUCATION
One Dupont Circle, Suite 360, Washington DC 20036-1143. 202/293-6440. **Fax:** 202/293-0073. **E-mail address:** info@aahe.org. **World Wide Web address:** http://www.aahe.org. **Description:** An independent, membership-based, nonprofit organization dedicated to building human capital for higher education.

AMERICAN FEDERATION OF TEACHERS
555 New Jersey Avenue, NW, Washington DC 20001. 202/879-4400. **E-mail address:** online@aft.org. **World Wide Web address:** http://www.aft.org. **Description:** Improves the lives of its members and their families, gives voice to their professional, economic and social aspirations, brings together members to assist and support one another and to promote democracy, human rights and freedom.

COLLEGE AND UNIVERSITY PROFESSIONAL ASSOCIATION FOR HUMAN RESOURCES
Tyson Place, 2607 Kingston Pike, Suite 250, Knoxville TN 37919. 865/637-7673. **Fax:** 865/637-7674. **World Wide Web address:** http://www.cupa.org. **Description:** Promotes the effective management and development of human resources in higher education and offers many professional development opportunities.

NATIONAL ASSOCIATION FOR COLLEGE ADMISSION COUNSELING
1631 Prince Street, Alexandria VA 22314-2818. 703/836-2222. **Fax:** 703/836-8015. **World Wide Web address:** http://www.nacac.com. **Description:** Founded in 1937, NACAC is an organization of 8,000 professionals dedicated to serving students as they make choices about pursuing postsecondary education. NACAC supports and advances the work of college admission counseling professionals.

NATIONAL ASSOCIATION OF COLLEGE AND UNIVERSITY BUSINESS OFFICERS
2501 M Street, NW, Suite 400, Washington DC 20037. 202/861-2500. **Fax:** 202/861-2583. **World Wide Web address:** http://www.nacubo.org. **Description:** A nonprofit professional organization representing chief

administrative and financial officers at more than 2,100 colleges and universities across the country.

NATIONAL SCIENCE TEACHERS ASSOCIATION
1840 Wilson Boulevard, Arlington VA 22201-3000. 703/243-7100. **World Wide Web address:** http://www.nsta.org. **Description:** Promotes excellence and innovation in science teaching and learning.

ELECTRONIC/INDUSTRIAL ELECTRICAL EQUIPMENT AND COMPONENTS

AMERICAN CERAMIC SOCIETY
P.O. Box 6136, Westerville OH 43086-6136. 614/890-4700. **Fax:** 614/899-6109. **E-mail address:** info@ceramics.org. **World Wide Web address:** http://www.acers.org. **Description:** Provides technical, scientific and educational information to its members and others in the ceramics and related materials field, structures its services, staff and capabilities to meet the needs of the ceramics community, related fields, and the general public.

ELECTRONIC INDUSTRIES ALLIANCE
2500 Wilson Boulevard, Arlington VA 22201. 703/907-7500. **World Wide Web address:** http://www.eia.org. **Description:** A national trade organization including 2,500 U.S. manufacturers. The Alliance is a partnership of electronic and high-tech associations and companies whose mission is promoting the market development and competitiveness of the U.S. high-tech industry through domestic and international policy efforts.

ELECTRONICS TECHNICIANS ASSOCIATION, INTERNATIONAL
5 Depot Street, Greencastle IN 46135. **Fax:** 765/653-4287. **Toll-free phone:** 800/288-3824. **E-mail address:** eta@tds.net. **World Wide Web address:** http://www.eta-sda.org. **Description:** A not-for-profit, worldwide professional association founded by electronics technicians and servicing dealers in 1978. Provides professional credentials based on an individual's skills and knowledge in a particular area of study.

FABLESS SEMICONDUCTOR ASSOCIATION
Three Lincoln Center, 5430 LBJ Freeway, Suite 280, Dallas TX 75240. 972/866-7579. **Fax:** 972/239-2292. **World Wide Web address:** http://www.fsa.org. **Description:** An industry organization aimed at achieving an optimal balance between wafer supply and demand.

INSTITUTE OF ELECTRICAL AND ELECTRONICS ENGINEER (IEEE)
3 Park Avenue, 17th Floor, New York NY 10016-5997. 212/419-7900. **Fax:** 212/752-4929. **E-mail address:** ieeeusa@ieee.org. **World Wide Web address:** http://www.ieee.org. **Description:** Advances the theory and application of electrotechnology and allied sciences, serves as a catalyst for technological innovation and supports the needs of its members through a wide variety of programs and services.

INTERNATIONAL SOCIETY OF CERTIFIED ELECTRONICS TECHNICIANS
3608 Pershing Avenue, Fort Worth TX 76107-4527. 817/921-9101. **Fax:** 817/921-3741 **Toll-free phone:** 800/946-0201 **E-mail address:** info@iscet.org **World Wide Web address:** http://www.iscet.org. **Description:** Prepares and tests technicians in the electronics and

appliance service industry. Designed to measure the degree of theoretical knowledge and technical proficiency of practicing technicians.

NATIONAL ELECTRONICS SERVICE DEALERS ASSOCIATION
3608 Pershing Avenue, Fort Worth TX 76107-4527. 817/921-9061. **Fax:** 817/921-3741. **World Wide Web address:** http://www.nesda.com. **Description:** A trade organization for professionals in the business of repairing consumer electronic equipment, appliances, or computers

ENVIRONMENTAL & WASTE MANAGEMENT SERVICES

AIR & WASTE MANAGEMENT ASSOCIATION
One Gateway Center, 3rd Floor, 420 Fort Duquesne Boulevard, Pittsburgh PA 15222-1435. 412/232-3444. **Fax:** 412/232-3450. **E-mail address:** info@awma.org. **World Wide Web address:** http://www.awma.org. **Description:** A nonprofit, nonpartisan professional organization providing training, information, and networking opportunities to thousands of environmental professionals in 65 countries.

AMERICAN ACADEMY OF ENVIRONMENTAL ENGINEERS
130 Holiday Court, Suite 100, Annapolis MD 21401. 410/266-3311. **Fax:** 410/266-7653. **World Wide Web address:** http://www.aaee.net. **Description:** AAEE was founded in 1955 for the principal purpose of serving the public by improving the practice, elevating the standards, and advancing public recognition of environmental engineering through a program of specialty certification of qualified engineers.

NATIONAL SOLID WASTES MANAGEMENT ASSOCIATION
4301 Connecticut Avenue, NW, Suite 300, Washington DC 20008-2304. 202/244-4700. **Fax:** 202/364-3792. **Toll-free phone:** 800/424-2869. **World Wide Web address:** http://www.nswma.org. **Description:** A non-profit, trade association that represents the interests of the North American waste services industry.

INSTITUTE OF CLEAN AIR COMPANIES
1660 L Street, NW, Suite 1100, Washington DC 20036. 202/457-0911. **Fax:** 202/331-1388. **World Wide Web address:** http://www.icac.com. **Description:** The nonprofit national association of companies that supply air pollution monitoring and control systems, equipment, and services for stationary sources.

WATER ENVIRONMENT FEDERATION
601 Wythe Street, Alexandria VA 22314-1994. 703/684-2452. **Fax:** 703/684-2492. **Toll-free phone:** 800/666-0206. **World Wide Web address:** http://www.wef.org. **Description:** A not-for-profit technical and educational organization, founded in 1928, with members from varied disciplines. The federation's mission is to preserve and enhance the global water environment. The WEF network includes water quality professionals from 79 Member Associations in over 30 countries.

FABRICATED METAL PRODUCTS AND PRIMARY METALS

ASM INTERNATIONAL: THE MATERIALS INFORMATION SOCIETY

9639 Kinsman Road, Materials Park OH 44073-0002. 440/338-5151. **Fax:** 440/338-4634. **Toll-free phone:** 800/336-5152. **E-mail address:** cust-srv@asminternational.org. **World Wide Web address:** http://www.asm-intl.org. **Description:** An organization for materials engineers and scientists, dedicated to advancing industry, technology and applications of metals and materials.

AMERICAN FOUNDRYMEN'S SOCIETY

505 State Street, Des Plaines IL 60016-8399. 847/824-0181. **Fax:** 847/824-7848. **Toll-free phone:** 800/537-4237. **World Wide Web address:** http://www.afsinc.org. **Description:** An international organization dedicated to provide and promote knowledge and services that strengthen the metalcasting industry. AFS was founded in 1896 and has approximately 10,000 members in 47 countries.

AMERICAN WELDING SOCIETY

550 NW LeJeune Road, Miami FL 33126. 305/443-9353. **Toll-free phone:** 800/443-9353. **E-mail address:** info@aws.org. **World Wide Web address:** http://www.aws.org. **Description:** Founded in 1919 as a multifaceted, nonprofit organization with a goal to advance the science, technology and application of welding and related joining disciplines.

FINANCIAL SERVICES

FINANCIAL EXECUTIVES INSTITUTE
200 Campus Drive, PO Box 674, Florham Park NJ 07932-0674. 973/765-1000. **Fax:** 973/765-1018. **E-mail address:** conf@fei.org. **World Wide Web address:** http://www.fei.org. **Description:** An association for financial executives working to alert members to emerging issues, develop the professional and management skills of members, provide forums for peer networking, advocate the views of financial executives, and promote ethical conduct.

WOMEN'S INSTITUTE OF FINANCIAL EDUCATION
PO Box 910014, San Diego CA 92191. 760/736-1660. **E-mail address:** info@wife.org. **World Wide Web address:** http://www.wife.org. **Description:** A non-profit organization dedicated to providing financial education to women in their quest for financial independence.

NATIONAL ASSOCIATION FOR BUSINESS ECONOMICS
1233 20th Street, NW, #505, Washington DC 20036. 202/463-6223. **Fax:** 202/463-6239. **E-mail address:** nabe@nabe.com. **World Wide Web address:** http://www.nabe.com. **Description:** An association of professionals who have an interest in business economics and who want to use the latest economic data and trends to enhance their ability to make sound business decisions. Founded in 1959.

NATIONAL ASSOCIATION OF CREDIT MANAGEMENT
8840 Columbia 100 Parkway, Columbia MD 21045. 410/740-5560. **Fax:** 410/740-5574. **E-mail address:** nacm_info@nacm.org. **World Wide Web address:** http://www.nacm.org. **Description:** Founded in 1896 to promote good laws for sound credit, protect businesses against fraudulent debtors, improve the interchange of credit information, develop better credit practices and methods, and establish a code of ethics.

NATIONAL ASSOCIATION OF REAL ESTATE INVESTMENT TRUSTS
1875 Eye Street, NW, Washington DC 20006. 202/739-9400. **Fax:** 202/739-9401. **E-mail address:** info@nareit.org. **World Wide Web address:** http://www.nareit.com. **Description:** NAREIT is the national trade association for REITs and publicly traded real estate companies. Members are real estate investment trusts (REITs) and other businesses that own, operate and finance income-producing real estate, as well as those firms and individuals who advise, study and service these businesses.

THE BOND MARKET ASSOCIATION
360 Madison Avenue, New York NY 10017-7111. 646/637-9200. **Fax:** 646/637-9126. **World Wide Web address:** http://www.bondmarkets.com. **Description:** The trade association representing the largest securities markets in the world. The Association

speaks for the bond industry, advocating its positions and representing its interests in New York; Washington, D.C.; London; Frankfurt; Brussels and Tokyo; and with issuer and investor groups worldwide. The Association represents a diverse mix of securities firms and banks, whether they are large, multi-product firms or companies with special market niches.

SECURITIES INDUSTRY ASSOCIATION

120 Broadway, 35th Floor, New York NY 10271-0080. 212/608-1500. **Fax:** 212/968-0703. **E-mail address:** info@sia.com. **World Wide Web address:** http://www.sia.com. **Description:** The Securities Industry Association (SIA) was established in 1972 through the merger of the Association of Stock Exchange Firms (1913) and the Investment Banker's Association (1912). The Securities Industry Association brings together the shared interests of more than 600 securities firms to accomplish common goals. SIA member-firms (including investment banks, broker-dealers, and mutual fund companies) are active in all U.S. and foreign markets and in all phases of corporate and public finance.

FOOD AND BEVERAGES/AGRICULTURE

AMERICAN ASSOCIATION OF CEREAL CHEMISTS (AACC)
3340 Pilot Knob Road, St. Paul MN 55121-2097. 651/454-7250. **Fax:** 651/454-0766. **World Wide Web address:** http://www.aaccnet.org. **Description:** A non-profit international organization of nearly 4,000 members who are specialists in the use of cereal grains in foods. The association gathers and disseminates scientific and technical information to professionals in the grain-based foods industry worldwide for over 85 years.

CROPLIFE AMERICA
1156 15th Street, NW, Suite 400, Washington DC 20005. 202/296-1585. **Fax:** 202/463-0474. **World Wide Web address:** http://www.croplifeamerica.org. **Description:** Fosters the interests of the general public and member companies by promoting innovation and the environmentally sound manufacture, distribution, and use of crop protection and production technologies for safe, high-quality, affordable and abundant food, fiber and other crops.

AMERICAN FROZEN FOOD INSTITUTE
2000 Corporate Ridge, Suite 1000, McLean VA 22102. 703/821-0770. **Fax:** 703/821-1350. **E-mail address:** info@affi.com. **World Wide Web address:** http://www.affi.com. **Description:** A national trade association representing all aspects of the frozen food industry supply chain, from manufacturers to distributors to suppliers to packagers; the Institute is industry's voice on issues crucial to future growth and progress.

AMERICAN SOCIETY OF AGRICULTURAL ENGINEERS
2950 Niles Road, St. Joseph MI 49085. 269/429-0300. **Fax:** 269/429-3852. **World Wide Web address:** http://www.asae.org. **Description:** An educational and scientific organization dedicated to the advancement of engineering applicable to agricultural, food, and biological systems.

AMERICAN SOCIETY OF BREWING CHEMISTS
3340 Pilot Knob Road, St. Paul MN 55121-2097. 651/454-7250. **Fax:** 651/454-0766. **World Wide Web address:** http://www.asbcnet.org. **Description:** Founded in 1934 to improve and bring uniformity to the brewing industry on a technical level.

CIES – THE FOOD BUSINESS FORUM
8455 Colesville Road, Suite 705, Silver Spring MD 20910. 301/563-3383. **Fax:** 301/563-3386. **E-mail address:** us.office@ciesnet.com. **World Wide Web address:** http://www.ciesnet.com. **Description:** An independent global food business network. Membership in CIES is on a company basis and includes more than two thirds of the world's largest food retailers and their suppliers.

INTERNATIONAL DAIRY FOODS ASSOCIATION
1250 H Street, NW, Suite 900, Washington DC 20005. 202/737-4332.
Fax: 202/331-7820. **Description:** IDFA represents more than 500 dairy food manufacturers, marketers, distributors and industry suppliers in the U.S. and 20 other countries, and encourages the formation of favorable domestic and international dairy policies.

NATIONAL BEER WHOLESALERS' ASSOCIATION
1101 King Street, Suite 600, Alexandria VA 22314-2944. 703/683-4300.
Fax: 703/683-8965. **E-mail address:** info@nbwa.org. **World Wide Web address:** http://www.nbwa.org. **Description:** Founded in 1938 as a trade association for the nations' beer wholesalers. NBWA provides leadership which enhances the independent malt beverage wholesale industry; advocates before government and the public on behalf of its members; encourages the responsible consumption of beer; and provides programs and services that will enhance members' efficiency and effectiveness.

NATIONAL FOOD PROCESSORS ASSOCIATION
1350 I Street, NW, Suite 300, Washington DC 20005. 202/639.5900. **E-mail address:** nfpa@nfpa-food.org. **World Wide Web address:** http://www.nfpa-food.org. **Description:** NFPA is the voice of the $500 billion food processing industry on scientific and public policy issues involving food safety, nutrition, technical and regulatory matters and consumer affairs.

NATIONAL SOFT DRINK ASSOCIATION
1101 16th Street, NW, Washington DC 20036. 202/463-6732. **Fax:** 202/463-8277. **World Wide Web address:** http://www.nsda.org. **Description:** An association for America's non-alcoholic beverage industry, serving the public and its members for more than 75 years.

HEALTH CARE SERVICES, EQUIPMENT, AND PRODUCTS

ACCREDITING COMMISSION ON EDUCATION FOR HEALTH SERVICES ADMINISTRATION
2000 14th Street North, Arlington VA 22201. 703/894-0960. **Fax:** 703/894-0941. **World Wide Web address:** http://www.acehsa.org. **Description:** An association of educational, professional, clinical, and commercial organizations devoted to accountability and quality improvement in the education of health care management and administration professionals.

AMERICAN ACADEMY OF ALLERGY, ASTHMA, AND IMMUNOLOGY
611 East Wells Street, Milwaukee WI 53202-3823. 414/272-6071. **E-mail address:** info@aaaai.org. **World Wide Web address:** http://www.aaaai.org. **Description:** A professional medical specialty organization representing allergists, asthma specialists, clinical immunologists, allied health professionals, and other physicians with a special interest in allergy. Established in 1943.

AMERICAN ACADEMY OF FAMILY PHYSICIANS
11400 Tomahawk Creek Parkway, Leawood KS 66211-2672. 913/906-6000. **Toll-free phone:** 800/274-2237. **E-mail address:** fp@aafp.org. **World Wide Web address:** http://www.aafp.org. **Description:** Founded in 1947, the Academy represents family physicians, family practice residents and medical students nationwide. AAFP's mission is to preserve and promote the science and art of family medicine and to ensure high quality, cost-effective health care for patients of all ages.

AMERICAN ACADEMY OF PEDIATRIC DENTISTRY
211 East Chicago Avenue, Suite 700, Chicago IL 60611-2663. 312/337-2169. **Fax:** 312/337-6329. **World Wide Web address:** http://www.aapd.org. **Description:** A membership organization representing the specialty of pediatric dentistry.

AMERICAN ACADEMY OF PERIODONTOLOGY
737 North Michigan Avenue, Suite 800, Chicago IL 60611-2690. 312/787-5518. **Fax:** 312/787-3670. **World Wide Web address:** http://www.perio.org. **Description:** A 7,900-member association of dental professionals specializing in the prevention, diagnosis and treatment of diseases affecting the gums and supporting structures of the teeth and in the placement and maintenance of dental implants. The Academy's purpose is to advocate, educate, and set standards for advancing the periodontal and general health of the public and promoting excellence in the practice of periodontics.

AMERICAN ACADEMY OF PHYSICIANS ASSISTANTS
950 North Washington Street, Alexandria VA 22314-1552. 703/836-2272. **Fax:** 703/684-1924. **E-mail address:** aapa@aapa.org. **World**

Wide Web address: http://www.aapa.org. **Description:** Promotes quality, cost-effective, accessible health care, and the professional and personal development of physician assistants.

AMERICAN ASSOCIATION FOR CLINICAL CHEMISTRY

2101 L Street, NW, Suite 202, Washington DC 20037-1558. 202/857-0717. **Fax:** 202/887-5093. **Toll-free phone:** 800/892-1400. **World Wide Web address:** http://www.aacc.org. **Description:** Founded in 1948 as an international scientific/medical society of clinical laboratory professionals, physicians, research scientists and other individuals involved with clinical chemistry and other clinical laboratory science-related disciplines. The society has 10,000 members.

AMERICAN ASSOCIATION FOR ORAL AND MAXILLOFACIAL SURGEONS

9700 West Bryn Mawr Avenue, Rosemont IL 60018-5701. 847/678-6200. **E-mail address:** inquiries@aaoms.org. **World Wide Web address:** http://www.aaoms.org. **Description:** The American Association of Oral and Maxillofacial Surgeons (AAOMS), is a not-for-profit professional association serving the professional and public needs of the specialty of oral and maxillofacial surgery.

AMERICAN ASSOCIATION FOR RESPIRATORY CARE

9425 North MacArthur Boulevard, Suite 100, Irving TX 75063-4706. 972/243-2272. **Fax:** 972/484-2720. **E-mail address:** info@aarc.org. **World Wide Web address:** http://www.aarc.org. **Description:** Advances the science, technology, ethics, and art of respiratory care through research and education for its members and teaches the general public about pulmonary health and disease prevention.

AMERICAN ASSOCIATION OF COLLEGES OF OSTEOPATHIC MEDICINE

5550 Friendship Boulevard, Suite 310, Chevy Chase MD 20815-7231. 301/968-4100. **Fax:** 301/968-4101. **World Wide Web address:** http://www.aacom.org. **Description:** Promotes excellence in osteopathic medical education throughout the educational continuum, in research and in service; to enhance the strength and quality of the member colleges; and to improve the health of the American public.

AMERICAN ASSOCIATION OF COLLEGES OF PODIATRIC MEDICINE

15850 Crabbs Branch Way, Suite 320, Rockville MD 20855. **Fax:** 301/948-1928. **Toll-free phone:** 800/922-9266. **E-mail address:** aacpmas@aacpm.org. **World Wide Web address:** http://www.aacpm.org. **Description:** An organization advancing podiatric medicine and its education system.

AMERICAN DENTAL EDUCATION ASSOCIATION

1625 Massachusetts Avenue, NW, Suite 600, Washington DC 20036-2212. 202/667-9433. **Fax:** 202/667-0642. **World Wide Web address:** http://www.adea.org. **Description:** A national organization for dental education. Members include all U.S. and Canadian dental schools, advanced dental education programs, hospital dental education programs, allied dental education programs, corporations, faculty, and students.

AMERICAN ASSOCIATION OF HEALTHCARE CONSULTANTS
5938 North Drake Avenue, Chicago IL 60659. **Fax:** 773/463-3552. **Toll-free phone:** 888/350-2242. **E-mail address:** info@aahc.net. **World Wide Web address:** http://www.aahc.net. **Description:** Founded in 1949 as the professional membership society for leading healthcare consultants and consulting firms.

AMERICAN ASSOCIATION OF HOMES AND SERVICES FOR THE AGING
2519 Connecticut Avenue, NW, Washington DC 20008. 202/783.2242. **Fax:** 202/783-2255. **World Wide Web address:** http://www.aahsa.org. **Description:** The American Association of Homes and Services for the Aging (AAHSA) is committed to advancing the vision of healthy, affordable, ethical aging services for America. The association represents 5,600 not-for-profit nursing homes, continuing care retirement communities, assisted living and senior housing facilities, and home and community-based service providers.

AMERICAN ASSOCIATION OF MEDICAL ASSISTANTS
20 North Wacker Drive, Suite 1575, Chicago IL 60606. 312/899-1500. **World Wide Web address:** http://www.aama-ntl.org. **Description:** The mission of the American Association of Medical Assistants is to enable medical assisting professionals to enhance and demonstrate the knowledge, skills and professionalism required by employers and patients; protect medical assistants' right to practice; and promote effective, efficient health care delivery through optimal use of multiskilled Certified Medical Assistants (CMAs).

AMERICAN ASSOCIATION OF NURSE ANESTHETISTS
222 South Prospect Avenue, Park Ridge IL 60068. 847/692-7050. **World Wide Web address:** http://www.aana.com. **Description:** Founded in 1931 as the professional association representing more than 30,000 Certified Registered Nurse Anesthetists (CRNAs) nationwide. The AANA promulgates education, and practice standards and guidelines, and affords consultation to both private and governmental entities regarding nurse anesthetists and their practice.

AMERICAN CHIROPRACTIC ASSOCIATION
1701 Clarendon Boulevard, Arlington VA 22209. **Fax:** 703/243-2593. **Toll-free phone:** 800/986-4636. **E-mail address:** memberinfo@amerchiro.org. **World Wide Web address:** http://www.americhiro.org. **Description:** A professional association representing doctors of chiropractic that provides lobbying, public relations, professional and educational opportunities for doctors of chiropractic, funds research regarding chiropractic and health issues, and offers leadership for the advancement of the profession.

AMERICAN COLLEGE OF HEALTH CARE ADMINISTRATORS
300 North Lee Street, Suite 301, Alexandria VA 22314. 703/739-7900. **Fax:** 703/739-7901. **Toll-free phone:** 888/882-2422. **E-mail address:** membership@achca.org. **World Wide Web address:** http://www.achca.org. **Description:** A non-profit membership organization that provides educational programming, certification in a variety of positions, and career development for its members. Founded in 1962.

AMERICAN COLLEGE OF HEALTHCARE EXECUTIVES
One North Franklin Street, Suite 1700, Chicago IL 60606-4425. 312/424-2800. **Fax:** 312/424-0023. **World Wide Web address:** http://www.ache.org. **Description:** An international professional society of nearly 30,000 healthcare executives who lead our nation's hospitals, healthcare systems, and other healthcare organizations.

AMERICAN COLLEGE OF MEDICAL PRACTICE EXECUTIVES
104 Inverness Terrace East, Englewood CO 80112-5306. 303/799-1111. **Fax:** 303/643-4439. **Toll-free phone:** 877/275-6462. **E-mail address:** acmpe@mgma.com. **World Wide Web address:** http://www.mgma.com/acmpe. **Description:** Established in 1956, the ACMPE offers board certification, self-assessment and leadership development for medical practice executives.

AMERICAN COLLEGE OF OBSTETRICIANS AND GYNECOLOGISTS
409 12th Street, SW, PO Box 96920, Washington DC 20090-6920. **World Wide Web address:** http://www.acog.org. **Description:** Founded in 1951, the 46,000-member organization is the nation's leading group of professionals providing health care for women.

AMERICAN COLLEGE OF PHYSICIAN EXECUTIVES
4890 West Kennedy Boulevard, Suite 200, Tampa FL 33609. 813/287-2000. **Fax:** 813/287-8993. **Toll-free phone:** 800/562-8088. **E-mail address:** acpe@acpe.org. **World Wide Web address:** http://www.acpe.org. **Description:** A specialty society representing physicians in health care leadership. Provides educational and career development programs.

AMERICAN DENTAL ASSOCIATION
211 East Chicago Avenue, Chicago IL 60611-2678. 312/440-2500. **World Wide Web address:** http://www.ada.org. **Description:** A dental association serving both public and private physicians. Founded in 1859.

AMERICAN DENTAL HYGIENISTS ASSOCIATION
444 North Michigan Avenue, Suite 3400, Chicago IL 60611. 312/440-8900. **E-mail address:** mail@adha.net. **World Wide Web address:** http://www.adha.org. **Description:** Founded in 1923, the association develops communication and mutual cooperation among dental hygienists and represents the professional interests of the more than 120,000 registered dental hygienists (RDHs) in the United States.

AMERICAN HEALTH INFORMATION MANAGEMENT ASSOCIATION
233 North Michigan Avenue, Suite 2150, Chicago IL 60601-5800. 312/233-1100. **Fax:** 312/233-1090. **E-mail address:** info@ahima.org. **World Wide Web address:** http://www.ahima.org. **Description:** Represents more than 46,000 specially educated health information management professionals who work throughout the healthcare industry. Health information management professionals serve the healthcare industry and the public by managing, analyzing, and utilizing data vital for patient care -- and making it accessible to healthcare providers when it is needed most.

AMERICAN HOSPITAL ASSOCIATION
One North Franklin, Chicago IL 60606-3421. 312/422-3000. **Fax:** 312/422-4796. **World Wide Web address:** http://www.aha.org. **Description:** A national organization that represents and serves all types of hospitals, health care networks, and their patients and communities. Approximately 5,000 institutional, 600 associate, and 27,000 personal members belong to the AHA.

AMERICAN MEDICAL ASSOCIATION
515 North State Street, Chicago IL 60610. **Toll-free phone:** 800/621-8335. **World Wide Web address:** http://www.ama-assn.org. **Description:** American Medical Association speaks out on issues important to patients and the nation's health. AMA policy on such issues is decided through its democratic policy-making process, in the AMA House of Delegates, which meets twice a year.

AMERICAN MEDICAL INFORMATICS ASSOCIATION
4915 St. Elmo Avenue, Suite 401, Bethesda MD 20814. 301/657-1291. **Fax:** 301/657-1296. **World Wide Web address:** http://www.amia.org. **Description:** The American Medical Informatics Association is a nonprofit membership organization of individuals, institutions, and corporations dedicated to developing and using information technologies to improve health care. Founded in 1990.

AMERICAN MEDICAL TECHNOLOGISTS
710 Higgins Road, Park Ridge IL 60068. 847/823-5169. **Fax:** 847/823-0458. **Toll-free phone:** 800/275-1268. **World Wide Web address:** http://www.amt1.com. **Description:** A nonprofit certification agency and professional membership association representing nearly 27,000 individuals in allied health care. Provides allied health professionals with professional certification services and membership programs to enhance their professional and personal growth.

AMERICAN MEDICAL WOMEN'S ASSOCIATION
801 North Fairfax Street, Suite 400, Alexandria VA 22314. 703/838-0500. **Fax:** 703/549-3864. **E-mail address:** info@amwa-doc.org. **World Wide Web address:** http://www.amwa-doc.org. **Description:** An organization of 10,000 women physicians and medical students

dedicated to serving as the unique voice for women's health and the advancement of women in medicine.

AMERICAN NURSES ASSOCIATION
600 Maryland Avenue, SW, Suite 100 West, Washington DC 20024. 202/651-7000. **Fax:** 202/651-7001. **Toll-free phone:** 800/274-4ANA. **World Wide Web address:** http://www.nursingworld.org. **Description:** A professional organization representing the nation's 2.6 million Registered Nurses through its 54 constituent state associations and 13 organizational affiliate members. Fosters high standards of nursing practice, promotes the economic and general welfare of nurses in the workplace, projects a positive and realistic view of nursing, and by lobbies Congress and regulatory agencies on health care issues affecting nurses and the public.

AMERICAN OCCUPATIONAL THERAPY ASSOCIATION
4720 Montgomery Lane, PO Box 31220, Bethesda MD 20824-1220. 301/652-2682. **Fax:** 301/652-7711. **Toll-free phone:** 800/377- 8555. **World Wide Web address:** http://www.aota.org. **Description:** A professional association of approximately 40,000 occupational therapists, occupational therapy assistants, and students of occupational therapy.

AMERICAN OPTOMETRIC ASSOCIATION
243 North Lindbergh Boulevard, St. Louis MO 63141. 314/991-4100. **Fax:** 314/991-4101. **World Wide Web address:** http://www.aoanet.org. **Description:** The American Optometric Association is the acknowledged leader and recognized authority for primary eye and vision care in the world.

AMERICAN ORGANIZATION OF NURSE EXECUTIVES
325 Seventh Street, NW, Washington DC 20004. 202/626-2240. **Fax:** 202/638-5499. **E-mail address:** aone@aha.org. **World Wide Web address:** http://www.aone.org. **Description:** Founded in 1967, the American Organization of Nurse Executives (AONE), a subsidiary of the American Hospital Association, is a national organization of nearly 4,000 nurses who design, facilitate, and manage care. Its mission is to represent nurse leaders who improve healthcare.

AMERICAN ORTHOPEDIC ASSOCIATION
6300 North River Road, Suite 505, Rosemont IL 60018-4263. 847/318-7330. **Fax:** 847/318-7339. **E-mail address:** info@aoassn.org **World Wide Web address:** http://www.aoassn.org. **Description:** Founded in 1887, The American Orthopaedic Association is the oldest orthopaedic association in the world.

AMERICAN PHYSICAL THERAPY ASSOCIATION
1111 North Fairfax Street, Alexandria VA 22314-1488. 703/684-2782. **Fax:** 703/684-7343. **Toll-free phone:** 800/999-2782. **World Wide Web address:** http://www.apta.org. **Description:** The American Physical Therapy Association (APTA) is a national professional organization

representing more than 63,000 members. Its goal is to foster advancements in physical therapy practice, research, and education.

AMERICAN PODIATRIC MEDICAL ASSOCIATION
9312 Old Georgetown Road, Bethesda MD 20814. 301/571-9200. **Fax:** 301/530-2752. **Toll-free phone:** 800/ASK-APMA. **World Wide Web address:** http://www.apma.org. **Description:** The American Podiatric Medical Association is the premier professional organization representing the nation's Doctors of Podiatric Medicine (podiatrists). The APMA represents approximately 80 percent of the podiatrists in the country. APMA includes 53 component societies in states and other jurisdictions, as well as 22 affiliated and related societies.

AMERICAN PSYCHIATRIC ASSOCIATION
1000 Wilson Boulevard, Suite 1825, Arlington VA.22209-3901. 703/907-7300. **E-mail address:** apa@psych.org **World Wide Web address:** http://www.psych.org. **Description:** With 35,000 members, the American Psychiatric Association is a medical specialty society recognized worldwide.

AMERICAN PUBLIC HEALTH ASSOCIATION
800 I Street, NW, Washington DC 20001. 202/777-2742. **Fax:** 202/777-2534. **E-mail address:** comments@apha.org. **World Wide Web address:** http://www.apha.org. **Description:** The American Public Health Association (APHA) is the oldest and largest organization of public health professionals in the world, representing more than 50,000 members from over 50 occupations of public health.

AMERICAN SOCIETY OF ANESTHESIOLOGISTS
520 N. Northwest Highway, Park Ridge IL 60068-2573. 847/825-5586. **Fax:** 847/825-1692. **E-mail address:** mail@asahq.org. **World Wide Web address:** http://www.asahq.org. **Description:** An educational, research and scientific association of physicians organized to raise and maintain the standards of the medical practice of anesthesiology and improve the care of the patient. Founded in 1905.

AMERICAN SPEECH-LANGUAGE-HEARING ASSOCIATION
10801 Rockville Pike, Rockville MD 20852-3226. **Toll-free phone:** 800/638-8255. **E-mail address:** actioncenter@asha.org. **World Wide Web address:** http://www.asha.org. **Description:** The professional, scientific, and credentialing association for more than 110,000 audiologists, speech-language pathologists, and speech, language, and hearing scientists with a mission to ensure that all people with speech, language, and hearing disorders have access to quality services to help them communicate more effectively.

AMERICAN VETERINARY MEDICAL ASSOCIATION
1931 North Meacham Road, Suite 100, Schaumburg IL 60173. 847/925-8070. **Fax:** 847/925-1329. **E-mail address:** avmainfo@avma.org. **World Wide Web address:** http://www.avma.org. **Description:** A not-for-profit association founded in 1863 representing more than 69,000

veterinarians working in private and corporate practice, government, industry, academia, and uniformed services.

ASSOCIATION OF AMERICAN MEDICAL COLLEGES
2450 North Street, NW, Washington DC 20037-1126. 202/828-0400. **Fax:** 202/828-1125. **World Wide Web address:** http://www.aamc.org. **Description:** A non-profit association founded in 1876 to work for reform in medical education. The association represents the nation's 126 accredited medical schools, nearly 400 major teaching hospitals, more than 105,000 faculty in 96 academic and scientific societies, and the nation's 66,000 medical students and 97,000 residents.

ASSOCIATION OF UNIVERSITY PROGRAMS IN HEALTH ADMINISTRATION
2000 North 14th Street, Suite 780, Arlington VA 22201. 703/894-0940. **Fax:** 703/894-0941. **E-mail address:** aupha@aupha.org. **World Wide Web address:** http://www.aupha.org. **Description:** A not-for-profit association of university-based educational programs, faculty, practitioners, and provider organizations. Its members are dedicated to continuously improving the field of health management and practice. It is the only non-profit entity of its kind that works to improve the delivery of health services throughout the world - and thus the health of citizens - by educating professional managers.

HEALTH INFORMATION AND MANAGEMENT SYSTEMS SOCIETY
230 East Ohio Street, Suite 500, Chicago IL 60611-3269. 312/664-4467. **Fax:** 312/664-6143. **World Wide Web address:** http://www.himss.org. **Description:** Founded in 1961 and provides leadership for the optimal use of healthcare information technology and management systems for the betterment of human health.

HEALTHCARE FINANCIAL MANAGEMENT ASSOCIATION
2 Westbrook Corporate Center, Suite 700, Westchester IL 60154-5700. 708/531-9600. **Fax:** 708/531-0032. **Toll-free phone:** 800/252-4362. **World Wide Web address:** http://www.hfma.org. **Description:** A membership organization for healthcare financial management professionals with 32,000 members.

NATIONAL ASSOCIATION FOR CHIROPRACTIC MEDICINE
15427 Baybrook Drive, Houston TX 77062. 281/280-8262. **Fax:** 281/280-8262. **World Wide Web address:** http://www.chiromed.org. **Description:** A consumer advocacy association of chiropractors striving to make legitimate the utilization of professional manipulative procedures in mainstream health care delivery.

NATIONAL MEDICAL ASSOCIATION
1012 Tenth Street, NW, Washington DC 20001. 202/347-1895. **Fax:** 202/898-2510. **World Wide Web address:** http://www.nmanet.org. **Description:** Promotes the collective interests of physicians and patients of African descent with a mission to serve as the collective voice of

physicians of African descent and a leading force for parity in medicine, elimination of health disparities and promotion of optimal health.

HOTELS AND RESTAURANTS

AMERICAN HOTEL AND LODGING ASSOCIATION
1201 New York Avenue, NW, #600, Washington DC 20005-3931. 202/289-3100. **Fax:** 202/289-3199. **World Wide Web address:** http://www.ahla.org. **Description:** Provides its members with assistance in operations, education, and communications, and lobbies on Capitol Hill to provide a business climate in which the industry can continue to prosper. Individual state associations provide representation at the state level and offer many additional cost-saving benefits.

THE EDUCATIONAL FOUNDATION OF THE NATIONAL RESTAURANT ASSOCIATION
175 West Jackson Boulevard, Suite 1500, Chicago IL 60604-2702. 312/715-1010. **Toll-free phone:** 800/765-2122. **E-mail address:** info@nraef.org. **World Wide Web address:** http://www.nraef.org. **Description:** A not-for-profit organization dedicated to fulfilling the educational mission of the National Restaurant Association. Focusing on three key strategies of risk management, recruitment, and retention, the NRAEF is the premier provider of educational resources, materials, and programs, which address attracting, developing and retaining the industry's workforce.

NATIONAL RESTAURANT ASSOCIATION
1200 17th Street, NW, Washington DC 20036. 202/331-5900. 202/331-5900. **Fax:** 202/331-2429. **Toll-free phone:** 800/424-5156. **World Wide Web address:** http://www.restaurant.org. **Description:** Founded in 1919 as a business association for the restaurant industry with a mission to represent, educate and promote a rapidly growing industry that is comprised of 878,000 restaurant and foodservice outlets employing 12 million people.

INSURANCE

AMERICA'S HEALTH INSURANCE PLANS
601 Pennsylvania Avenue, NW, S0uth Building, Suite 500, Washington DC 20004. 202/778-3200. **Fax:** 202/331-7487. **World Wide Web address:** http://www.ahip.org. **Description:** A national association representing nearly 1,300 member companies providing health insurance coverage to more than 200 million Americans.

INSURANCE INFORMATION INSTITUTE
110 William Street, New York NY 10038. 212/346-5500. **World Wide Web address:** http://www.iii.org. **Description:** Provides definitive insurance information. Recognized by the media, governments, regulatory organizations, universities and the public as a primary source of information, analysis and referral concerning insurance.

NATIONAL ASSOCIATION OF PROFESSIONAL INSURANCE AGENTS
400 North Washington Street, Alexandria VA 22314. 703/836-9340. **Fax:** 703/836-1279. **E-mail address:** piaweb@pianet.org. **World Wide Web address:** http://www.pianet.com. **Description:** Represents independent agents in all 50 states, Puerto Rico and the District of Columbia. Founded in 1931.

PROPERTY CASUALTY INSURERS ASSOCIATION OF AMERICA
3025 Highland Parkway, Suite 800, Downers Grove IL 60515-1289. 630/724-2100. **Fax:** 630/724-2190. **World Wide Web address:** http://www.allianceai.org. **Description:** A property/casualty trade association representing more than 1,000 member companies, PCI advocates its members' public policy positions at the federal and state levels and to the public.

LEGAL SERVICES

AMERICAN BAR ASSOCIATION
750 North Clark Street, Chicago IL 60610. 312/988-5000. **E-mail address:** askaba@abanet.org. **World Wide Web address:** http://www.abanet.org. **Description:** A voluntary professional association with more than 400,000 members, the ABA provides law school accreditation, continuing legal education, information about the law, programs to assist lawyers and judges in their work, and initiatives to improve the legal system for the public.

FEDERAL BAR ASSOCIATION
2215 M Street, NW, Washington DC 20037. 202/785-1614. **Fax:** 202/785-1568. **E-mail address:** fba@fedbar.org. **World Wide Web address:** http://www.fedbar.org. **Description:** The professional organization for private and government lawyers and judges involved in federal practice.

NATIONAL ASSOCIATION OF LEGAL ASSISTANTS
1516 South Boston, #200, Tulsa OK 74119. 918/587-6828. **World Wide Web address:** http://www.nala.org. **Description:** A professional association for legal assistants and paralegals, providing continuing education and professional development programs. Founded in 1975.

NATIONAL FEDERATION OF PARALEGAL ASSOCIATIONS
2517 Eastlake Avenue East, Suite 200, Seattle WA 98102. 206/652-4120. **Fax:** 206/652-4122. **E-mail address:** info@paralegals.org. **World Wide Web address:** http://www.paralegals.org. **Description:** A non-profit professional organization representing more than 15,000 paralegals in the United States and Canada. NFPA is the national voice and the standard for excellence for the paralegal profession through its work on the issues of regulation, ethics and education.

MANUFACTURING: MISCELLANEOUS CONSUMER

ASSOCIATION FOR MANUFACTURING EXCELLENCE
380 Palantine Road West, Wheeling IL 60090-5863. 847/520-3282. **Fax:** 847/520-0163. **World Wide Web address:** http://www.ame.org. **Description:** A not-for-profit organization founded in 1985 consisting of 6000 executives, senior and middle managers who wish to improve the competitiveness of their organizations.

ASSOCIATION FOR MANUFACTURING TECHNOLOGY
7901 Westpark Drive, McLean VA 22102-4206. 703/893-2900. **Fax:** 703/893-1151. **Toll-free phone:** 703/893-2900. **World Wide Web address:** http://www.amtonline.org. **Description:** Supports and promotes American manufacturers of machine tools and manufacturing technology. Provides members with industry expertise and assistance on critical industry concerns.

ASSOCIATION OF HOME APPLIANCE MANUFACTURERS
1111 19th Street, NW, Suite 402, Washington DC 20036. 202/872-5955. **Fax:** 202/872-9354. **World Wide Web address:** http://www.aham.org. **Description:** Represents the manufacturers of household appliances and products/services associated with household appliances.

SOCIETY OF MANUFACTURING ENGINEERS
One SME Drive, Dearborn MI 48121. 313/271-1500. **Fax:** 313/425-3401. **Toll-free phone:** 800/733-4763. **World Wide Web address:** http://www.sme.org. **Description:** Promotes an increased awareness of manufacturing engineering and helps keep manufacturing professionals up to date on leading trends and technologies. Founded in 1932.

MANUFACTURING: MISCELLANEOUS INDUSTRIAL

ASSOCIATION FOR MANUFACTURING EXCELLENCE
380 Palantine Road West, Wheeling IL 60090-5863. 847/520-3282. **Fax:** 847/520-0163. **World Wide Web address:** http://www.ame.org. **Description:** A not-for-profit organization founded in 1985 consisting of 6000 executives, senior and middle managers who wish to improve the competitiveness of their organizations.

INSTITUTE OF INDUSTRIAL ENGINEERS
3577 Parkway Lane, Suite 200, Norcross GA 30092. 770/449-0460. **Fax:** 770/441-3295. **Toll-free phone:** 800/494-0460. **World Wide Web address:** http://www.iienet.org. **Description:** A non-profit professional society dedicated to the support of the industrial engineering profession and individuals involved with improving quality and productivity. Founded in 1948.

NATIONAL ASSOCIATION OF MANUFACTURERS
1331 Pennsylvania Avenue, NW, Washington DC 20004-1790. 202/637-3000. **Fax:** 202/637-3182. **E-mail address:** manufacturing@nam.org. **World Wide Web address:** http://www.nam.org. **Description:** With 14,000 members, NAM's mission is to enhance the competitiveness of manufacturers and to improve American living standards by shaping a legislative and regulatory environment conducive to U.S. economic growth, and to increase understanding among policymakers, the media and the public about the importance of manufacturing to America's economic strength.

NATIONAL TOOLING AND MACHINING ASSOCIATION
9300 Livingston Road, Fort Washington MD 20744-4998. 800/248-6862. **Fax:** 301/248-7104. **World Wide Web address:** http://www.ntma.org. **Description:** A trade organization representing the precision custom manufacturing industry throughout the United States.

SOCIETY OF MANUFACTURING ENGINEERS
One SME Drive, Dearborn MI 48121. 313/271-1500. **Fax:** 313/425-3401. **Toll-free phone:** 800/733-4763. **World Wide Web address:** http://www.sme.org. **Description:** Promotes an increased awareness of manufacturing engineering and helps keep manufacturing professionals up to date on leading trends and technologies. Founded in 1932.

MINING, GAS, PETROLEUM, ENERGY RELATED

AMERICAN ASSOCIATION OF PETROLEUM GEOLOGISTS
P.). Box 979, Tulsa OK 74101-0979. 918/584-2555. **Physical address:** 1444 South Boulder, Tulsa OK 74119. **Fax:** 918/560-2665. **Toll-free phone:** 800/364-2274. **E-mail address:** postmaster@aapg.org. **World Wide Web address:** http://www.aapg.org. **Description:** Founded in 1917, the AAPG's purpose is to foster scientific research, advance the science of geology, promote technology, and inspire high professional conduct. The AAPG has over 30,000 members.

AMERICAN GEOLOGICAL INSTITUTE
4220 King Street, Alexandria VA 22302-1502. 703/379-2480. **Fax:** 703/379-7563. **World Wide Web address:** http://www.agiweb.org. **Description:** A nonprofit federation of 42 geoscientific and professional associations that represents more than 100,000 geologists, geophysicists, and other earth scientists. Provides information services to geoscientists, serves as a voice of shared interests in the profession, plays a major role in strengthening geoscience education, and strives to increase public awareness of the vital role the geosciences play in society's use of resources and interaction with the environment.

AMERICAN NUCLEAR SOCIETY
555 North Kensington Avenue, La Grange Park IL 60526. 708/352-6611. **Fax:** 708/352-0499. **World Wide Web address:** http://www.ans.org. **Description:** A not-for-profit, international, scientific and educational organization with a membership of 10,500 engineers, scientists, administrators, and educators representing 1,600 corporations, educational institutions, and government agencies.

AMERICAN PETROLEUM INSTITUTE
1220 L Street, NW, Washington DC 20005-4070. 202/682-8000. **World Wide Web address:** http://www.api.org. **Description:** Functions to insure a strong, viable U.S. oil and natural gas industry capable of meeting the energy needs of our Nation in an efficient and environmentally responsible manner.

GEOLOGICAL SOCIETY OF AMERICA
3300 Penrose Place, P.O. Bos 9140, Boulder CO 80301. 303/447-2020. **Fax:** 303/357-1070. **Toll-free phone:** 888/443-4472. **E-mail address:** gsaservice@geosociety.org. **World Wide Web address:** http://www.geosociety.org. **Description:** The mission of GSA is to advance the geosciences, to enhance the professional growth of its members, and to promote the geosciences in the service of humankind.

SOCIETY FOR MINING, METALLURGY, AND EXPLORATION
8307 Shaffer Parkway, Littleton CO 80127-4102. 303/973-9550. **Fax:** 303/973-3845. **Toll-free phone:** 800/763-3132. **E-mail address:** sme@smenet.org. **World Wide Web address:** http://www.smenet.org.

Description: An international society of professionals in the mining and minerals industry.

SOCIETY OF PETROLEUM ENGINEERS
P.O. Box 833836, Richardson TX 75083-3836. 972/952-9393. **Physical address:** 222 palisades Creek Drive, Richardson TX 75080. **Fax:** 972/952-9435. **E-mail address:** spedal@spe.org. **World Wide Web address:** http://www.spe.org. **Description:** SPE is a professional association whose 60,000-plus members worldwide are engaged in energy resources development and production. SPE is a key resource for technical information related to oil and gas exploration and production and provides services through its publications, meetings, and online.

PAPER AND WOOD PRODUCTS

AMERICAN FOREST AND PAPER ASSOCIATION
1111 Nineteenth Street, NW, Suite 800, Washington DC 20036. **Toll-free phone:** 800/878-8878. **E-mail address:** info@afandpa.org. **World Wide Web address:** http://www.afandpa.org. **Description:** The national trade association of the forest, pulp, paper, paperboard and wood products industry.

FOREST PRODUCTS SOCIETY
2801 Marshall Court, Madison WI 53705-2295. 608/231-1361. **Fax:** 608/231-2152. **E-mail address:** info@forestprod.org. **World Wide Web address:** http://www.forestprod.org. **Description:** An international not-for-profit technical association founded in 1947 to provide an information network for all segments of the forest products industry.

NPTA ALLIANCE
500 Bi-County Boulevard, Suite 200E, Farmingdale NY 11735. 631/777-2223. **Fax:** 631/777-2224. **Toll-free phone:** 800/355-NPTA. **World Wide Web address:** http://www.gonpta.com. **Description:** An association for the $60 billion paper, packaging, and supplies distribution industry.

PAPERBOARD PACKAGING COUNCIL
201 North Union Street, Suite 220, Alexandria VA 22314. 703/836-3300. **Fax:** 703/836-3290. **E-mail address:** http://www.ppcnet.org. **World Wide Web address:** http://www.ppcnet.org. **Description:** A trade association representing the manufacturers of paperboard packaging in the United States.

TECHNICAL ASSOCIATION OF THE PULP AND PAPER INDUSTRY
15 Technology Parkway South, Norcross GA 30092. 770/446-1400. **Fax:** 770/446-6947. **Toll-free phone:** 800/332-8686. **World Wide Web address:** http://www.tappi.org. **Description:** The leading technical association for the worldwide pulp, paper, and converting industry.

PRINTING AND PUBLISHING

AMERICAN BOOKSELLERS ASSOCIATION
828 South Broadway, Tarrytown NY 10591. 914/591-2665. **Fax:** 914/591-2720. **Toll-free phone:** 800/637-0037. **E-mail address:** info@bookweb.org. **World Wide Web address:** http://www.bookweb.org. **Description:** A not-for-profit organization founded in 1900 devoted to meeting the needs of its core members of independently owned bookstores with retail storefront locations through advocacy, education, research, and information dissemination.

AMERICAN INSTITUTE OF GRAPHIC ARTS
164 Fifth Avenue, New York NY 10010. 212/807-1990. **Fax:** 212/807-1799. **E-mail address:** comments@aiga.org. **World Wide Web address:** http://www.aiga.org. **Description:** Furthers excellence in communication design as a broadly defined discipline, strategic tool for business and cultural force. AIGA is the place design professionals turn to first to exchange ideas and information, participate in critical analysis and research and advance education and ethical practice. Founded in 1914.

AMERICAN SOCIETY OF NEWSPAPER EDITORS
11690B Sunrise Valley Drive, Reston VA 20191-1409. 703/453-1122. **Fax:** 703/453-1133. **E-mail address:** asne@asne.org. **World Wide Web address:** http://www.asne.org. **Description:** A membership organization for daily newspaper editors, people who serve the editorial needs of daily newspapers and certain distinguished individuals who have worked on behalf of editors through the years.

ASSOCIATION OF AMERICAN PUBLISHERS, INC.
71 Fifth Avenue, 2nd Floor, New York NY 10003. 212/255-0200. **Fax:** 212/255-7007. **World Wide Web address:** http://www.publishers.org. **Description:** Representing publishers of all sizes and types located throughout the U.S., the AAP is the principal trade association of the book publishing industry.

ASSOCIATION OF GRAPHIC COMMUNICATIONS
320 Seventh Avenue, 9th Floor, New York NY 10001-5010. 212/279-2100. **Fax:** 212/279-5381. **E-mail address:** info@agcomm.org. **World Wide Web address:** http://www.agcomm.org. **Description:** The AGC serves as a network for industry information and idea exchange, provides graphic arts education and training, promotes and markets the industry, and advocates legislative and environmental issues.

BINDING INDUSTRIES OF AMERICA
100 Daingerfield Road, Alexandria VA 22314. 703/519-8137. **Fax:** 703/548-3227. **World Wide Web address:** http://www.bindingindustries.org. **Description:** A trade association representing Graphic Finishers, Loose-Leaf Manufacturers, and

suppliers to these industries throughout the United States, Canada, and Europe.

THE DOW JONES NEWSPAPER FUND
P.O.Box 300, Princeton NJ 08543-0300. 609/452-2820. **Fax:** 609/520-5804. **E-mail address:** newsfund@wsj.dowjones.com. **World Wide Web address:** http://djnewspaperfund.dowjones.com. **Description:** Founded in 1958 by editors of The Wall Street Journal to improve the quality of journalism education and the pool of applicants for jobs in the newspaper business. It provides internships and scholarships to college students, career literature, fellowships for high school journalism teachers and publications' advisers and training for college journalism instructors. The Fund is a nonprofit foundation supported by the Dow Jones Foundation, Dow Jones & Company, Inc. and other newspaper companies.

GRAPHIC ARTISTS GUILD
90 John Street, Suite 403, New York NY 10038-3202. 212/791-3400. **World Wide Web address:** http://www.gag.org. **Description:** A national union of illustrators, designers, web creators, production artists, surface designers and other creatives who have come together to pursue common goals, share their experience, raise industry standards, and improve the ability of visual creators to achieve satisfying and rewarding careers.

INTERNATIONAL GRAPHIC ARTS EDUCATION ASSOCIATION
1899 Preston White Drive, Reston VA 20191-4367. 703/758-0595. **World Wide Web address:** http://www.igaea.org. **Description:** An association of educators in partnership with industry, dedicated to sharing theories, principles, techniques and processes relating to graphic communications and imaging technology.

MAGAZINE PUBLISHERS OF AMERICA
810 Seventh Avenue, 24th Floor, New York NY 10019. 212/872-3746. **E-mail address:** infocenter@magazine.org. **World Wide Web address:** http://www.magazine.org. **Description:** An industry association for consumer magazines representing more than 240 domestic publishing companies with approximately 1,400 titles, more than 80 international companies and more than 100 associate members.

NATIONAL ASSOCIATION FOR PRINTING LEADERSHIP
75 West Century Road, Paramus NJ 07652-1408. 201/634-9600. **Fax:** 201/986-2976. **E-mail address:** information@napl.org. **World Wide Web address:** http://www.napl.org. **Description:** A not-for-profit trade association founded in 1933 for commercial printers and related members of the Graphic Arts Industry.

NATIONAL NEWSPAPER ASSOCIATION
P.O. Box 7540,, Columbia MO 65205-7540. 573/882-5800. **Fax:** 573/884-5490. **Toll-free phone:** 800/829-4662. **World Wide Web address:** http://www.nna.org. **Description:** A non-profit association promoting the common interests of newspapers.

NATIONAL PRESS CLUB
529 14th Street, NW, Washington DC 20045. 202/662-7500. **Fax:** 202/662-7512. **World Wide Web address:** http://npc.press.org. **Description:** Provides people who gather and disseminate news a center for the advancement of their professional standards and skills, the promotion of free expression, mutual support and social fellowship. Founded in 1908.

NEWSPAPER ASSOCIATION OF AMERICA
1921 Gallows Road, Suite 600, Vienna VA 22182-3900. 703/902-1600. **Fax:** 703/917-0636. **World Wide Web address:** http://www.naa.org. **Description:** A nonprofit organization representing the $55 billion newspaper industry.

THE NEWSPAPER GUILD
501 Third Street, NW, Suite 250, Washington DC 20001. 202/434-7177. **Fax:** 202/434-1472. **E-mail address:** guild@cwa-union.org. **World Wide Web address:** http://www.newsguild.org. **Description:** Founded as a print journalists' union, the Guild today is primarily a media union whose members are diverse in their occupations, but who share the view that the best working conditions are achieved by people who have a say in their workplace.

TECHNICAL ASSOCIATION OF THE GRAPHIC ARTS
68 Lomb Memorial Drive, Rochester NY 14623-5604. 585/475-7470. **Fax:** 585/475-2250. **E-mail address:** tagaofc@aol.com. **World Wide Web address:** http://www.taga.org. **Description:** A professional technical association founded in 1948 for the graphic arts industries.

WRITERS GUILD OF AMERICA WEST
7000 West Third Street, Los Angeles CA 90048. 323/951-4000. **Fax:** 323/782-4800. **Toll-free phone:** 800/548-4532. **E-mail address: World Wide Web address:** http://www.wga.org. **Description:** Represents writers in the motion picture, broadcast, cable and new technologies industries.

REAL ESTATE

INSTITUTE OF REAL ESTATE MANAGEMENT
430 North Michigan Avenue, Chicago IL 60611-4090. 312/329-6000. **Fax:** 800/338-4736. **Toll-free phone:** 800/837-0706. **E-mail address:** custserv@irem.org. **World Wide Web address:** http://www.irem.org. **Description:** IREM, an affiliate of the National Association of Realtors, is an association of professional property and asset managers who have met strict criteria in the areas of education, experience, and a commitment to a code of ethics.

INTERNATIONAL REAL ESTATE INSTITUTE
1224 North Nokomis, NE, Alexandria MN 56308. 320/763-4648. **Fax:** 320/763-9290. **E-mail address:** irei@iami.org. **World Wide Web address:** http://www.iami.org/irei. **Description:** A real estate association with members in more than 100 countries, providing media to communicate on an international basis.

NATIONAL ASSOCIATION OF REALTORS
30700 Russell Ranch Road, Westlake Village CA 91362. 805/557-2300. **Fax:** 805/557-2680. **World Wide Web address:** http://www.realtor.com. **Description:** An industry advocate of the right to own, use, and transfer real property; the acknowledged leader in developing standards for efficient, effective, and ethical real estate business practices; and valued by highly skilled real estate professionals and viewed by them as crucial to their success.

RETAIL

NATIONAL ASSOCIATION OF CHAIN DRUG STORES

413 North Lee Street, PO Box 1417-D49, Alexandria VA 22313-1480. 703/549-3001. **Fax:** 703/836-4869. **World Wide Web address:** http://www.nacds.org. **Description:** Represents the views and policy positions of member chain drug companies accomplished through the programs and services provided by the association.

INTERNATIONAL COUNCIL OF SHOPPING CENTERS

1221 Avenue of the Americas, 41st floor, New York NY 10020-1099. 646/728-3800. **Fax:** 212/589-5555. **E-mail address:** icsc@icsc.org. **World Wide Web address:** http://www.icsc.org. **Description:** A trade association of the shopping center industry founded in 1957.

NATIONAL RETAIL FEDERATION

325 7th Street, NW, Suite 1100, Washington DC 20004. 202/783-7971. **Fax:** 202/737-2849. **Toll-free phone:** 800/NRF-HOW2. **World Wide Web address:** http://www.nrf.com. **Description:** A retail trade association, with membership that comprises all retail formats and channels of distribution including department, specialty, discount, catalog, Internet and independent stores as well as the industry's key trading partners of retail goods and services. NRF represents an industry with more than 1.4 million U.S. retail establishments, more than 20 million employees - about one in five American workers - and 2003 sales of $3.8 trillion.

STONE, CLAY, GLASS, AND CONCRETE PRODUCTS

THE AMERICAN CERAMIC SOCIETY
PO Box 6136, Westerville OH 43086-6136. 614/890-4700. **Fax:** 614/899-6109. **E-mail address:** info@ceramics.org. **World Wide Web address:** http://www.acers.org. **Description:** An organization dedicated to the advancement of ceramics.

NATIONAL GLASS ASSOCIATION
8200 Greensboro Drive, Suite 302, McLean VA 22102-3881. 866/342-5642. **Fax:** 703/442-0630. **World Wide Web address:** http://www.glass.org. **Description:** A trade association founded in 1948 representing the flat (architectural and automotive) glass industry. The association represents nearly 5,000 member companies and locations, and produces the industry events and publications.

TRANSPORTATION AND TRAVEL

AIR TRANSPORT ASSOCIATION OF AMERICA
1301 Pennsylvania Avenue, NW, Suite 1100, Washington DC 20004-1707. 202/626-4000. **Fax:** 301/206-9789. **Toll-free phone:** 800/497-3326. **E-mail address:** ata@airlines.org. **World Wide Web address:** http://www.air-transport.org. **Description:** A trade organization for the principal U.S. airlines.

AMERICAN SOCIETY OF TRAVEL AGENTS
1101 King Street, Suite 200, Alexandria VA 22314. 703/739-2782. **Fax:** 703/684-8319. **World Wide Web address:** http://www.astanet.com. **Description:** An association of travel professionals whose members include travel agents and the companies whose products they sell such as tours, cruises, hotels, car rentals, etc.

AMERICAN TRUCKING ASSOCIATIONS
2200 Mill Road, Alexandria VA 22314. 703/838-1700. **Toll-free phone:** 888/333-1759. **World Wide Web address:** http://www.trucking.org. **Description:** Serves and represents the interests of the trucking industry with one united voice; positively influences Federal and State governmental actions; advances the trucking industry's image, efficiency, competitiveness, and profitability; provides educational programs and industry research; promotes highway and driver safety; and strives for a healthy business environment.

ASSOCIATION OF AMERICAN RAILROADS
50 F Street, NW, Washington DC 20001-1564. 202/639-2100. **World Wide Web address:** http://www.aar.org. **Description:** A trade associations representing the major freight railroads of the United States, Canada and Mexico.

INSTITUTE OF TRANSPORTATION ENGINEERS
1099 14th Street, NW, Suite 300 West, Washington DC 20005-3438. 202/289-0222. **Fax:** 202/289-7722. **E-mail address:** ite_staff@ite.org. **World Wide Web address:** http://www.ite.org. **Description:** An international individual member educational and scientific association whose members are traffic engineers, transportation planners and other professionals who are responsible for meeting society's needs for safe and efficient surface transportation through planning, designing, implementing, operating and maintaining surface transportation systems worldwide.

MARINE TECHNOLOGY SOCIETY
5565 Sterrett Place, Suite 108, Columbia MD 21044. 410/884-5330. **Fax:** 410/884-9060. **E-mail address:** mtsmbrship@erols.com. **World Wide Web address:** http://www.mtsociety.org. **Description:** A member-based society supporting all the components of the ocean community: marine sciences, engineering, academia, industry and government. The society

is dedicated to the development, sharing and education of information and ideas.

NATIONAL TANK TRUCK CARRIERS
2200 Mill Road, Alexandria VA 22314. 703/838-1960. **Fax:** 703/684-5753. **E-mail address:** inquiries@tanktruck.org. **World Wide Web address:** http://www.tanktruck.net. **Description:** A trade association founded in 1945 and composed of approximately 180 trucking companies, which specialize in the nationwide distribution of bulk liquids, industrial gases and dry products in cargo tank motor vehicles.

UTILITIES: ELECTRIC, GAS, AND WATER

AMERICAN PUBLIC GAS ASSOCIATION
11094-D Lee Highway, Suite 102, Fairfax VA 22030-5014. 703/352-3890. **Fax:** 703/352-1271. **E-mail address:** website@apga.org. **World Wide Web address:** http://www.apga.org. **Description:** A nonprofit trade organization representing publicly owned natural gas local distribution companies (LDCs). APGA represents the interests of public gas before Congress, federal agencies and other energy-related stakeholders by developing regulatory and legislative policies that further the goals of our members. In addition, APGA organizes meetings, seminars, and workshops with a specific goal to improve the reliability, operational efficiency, and regulatory environment in which public gas systems operate.

AMERICAN PUBLIC POWER ASSOCIATION (APPA)
2301 M Street, NW, Washington DC 20037-1484. 202/467-2900. **Fax:** 202/467-2910. **World Wide Web address:** http://www.appanet.org. **Description:** The service organization for the nation's more than 2,000 community-owned electric utilities that serve more than 40 million Americans. Its purpose is to advance the public policy interests of its members and their consumers, and provide member services to ensure adequate, reliable electricity at a reasonable price with the proper protection of the environment.

AMERICAN WATER WORKS ASSOCIATION
6666 West Quincy Avenue, Denver CO 80235. 303/794-7711. **Fax:** 303/347-0804. **Toll-free phone:** 800/926-7337. **World Wide Web address:** http://www.awwa.org. **Description:** A resource for knowledge, information, and advocacy to improve the quality and supply of drinking water in North America. The association advances public health, safety and welfare by uniting the efforts of the full spectrum of the drinking water community.

NATIONAL RURAL ELECTRIC COOPERATIVE ASSOCIATION
4301 Wilson Boulevard, Arlington VA 22203. 703/907-5500. **E-mail address:** nreca@nreca.coop. **World Wide Web address:** http://www.nreca.org. **Description:** A national organization representing the national interests of cooperative electric utilities and the consumers they serve. Founded in 1942.

MISCELLANEOUS WHOLESALING

NATIONAL ASSOCIATION OF WHOLESALER-DISTRIBUTORS (NAW)
1725 K Street, NW, Washington DC 20006-1419. 202/872-0885. **Fax:** 202/785-0586. **World Wide Web address:** http://www.naw.org. **Description:** A trade association that represents the wholesale distribution industry active in government relations and political action; research and education; and group purchasing.

INDEX OF PRIMARY EMPLOYERS

A

ABB Power T&D Company, Inc/140
ADC Engineering/73
A.G. Industries Inc./193
a4 Health Systems/112
AMT Datasouth /112
APAC/71
APAC-Barrus Construction Company/227
APAC-Coastal Carolina Division/227
APAC-Carolina, Inc./228
AVX Corporation/140
Acme Electric Corporation/135
Acme-McCrary Corporation/58
Actaris Metering Systems/141
Acterna/107
AdStreet Inc./53
AgFirst Farm Credit Bank/86
Aiken Standard/214
Ajilon Services Inc./112
Alabama Theatre/77
Alba-Waldensian, Inc./58
Alcatel USA Inc./107
ALCOA (Aluminum Company of America)/148
Allvac/146
Alpha Omega Health Inc./162
Altec Industries, Inc./193
American & Efird, Inc./58
American City Business Journals/211
American Fiber & Finishing/67
American General Finance/151
American Investment and Management
    Company (AIMCO)/219
American Red Cross/97
American Red Cross Blood Services/Carolina
    Blood Services Region/99
AMETEK, Inc./135
Analog Devices, Inc./135
Analysts International Corporation (AIC)/113
Anchor Sign/54
Anderson Area Medical Center/168
Anderson County School District 1/133
Appalachian State University/126
Arcadia Publishing /215
Asheboro City Schools/126
Atlantic Veneer Corporation/203

B

BASF Corporation/67, 101
BB&T Corporation/82
B/E Aerospace, Inc./55
BMW Manufacturing Corporation/80
BP Fabrics and Fibers/68
BSH Home Appliances/184
Babies 'R Us/225
Bank of America/83
Barnhill Contracting Company/227
Bassett Furniture Industries, Inc./184
Bausch & Lomb, Incorporated/168
Bayer Crop Science/89
Becton Dickinson and Company (BD)/168
Belk Stores Services Inc./221
BellSouth Advertising and Publishing
    Corporation/211
Berkeley Citizens/99
BI-LO, Inc./225
The Biltmore Company/
    Biltmore House/76
Blackbaud Inc./123
Blair Publishing/211
BLAST Software/113
Blockade Runner Hotel/174

Blue Cross and Blue Shield of North
    Carolina/177
Borg Warner Emissions/Thermal Systems/193
Boston Gear/194
Bowater Inc./207
Brady Distributing/233
Brevard College/126
Brooks, Pierce, McLendon, Humphrey &
    Leonard, L.L.P./181
Burke Mills, Inc./59
Burlington Industries/59

C

CB Richard Ellis/218
CCB Financial Corporation/83
CEM Corporation/136
Cii Associates, Inc./113
CSA Wireless/108
CVS/221
Caldwell County School District/127
Cambar Software, Inc./123
Canal Insurance Company/179
Caravelle Resort Inc./175
Carolina Farm Credit/83
Carolina Inn/174
Carolina Mirror Company/184
Carolina Turkeys/153
Carsons Inc./185
Cary, Town of/158
Case Farms, Inc./153
Cashwell Appliance Parts, Inc./233
Cato Corporation/221
Cedalion Corporation/113
Central Prison Hospital/162
CeramTec North America/149
Charleston County Government/161
Charleston Museum/77
Charlotte Marriott City Center/174
Charlotte Symphony Orchestra/76
Charlotte, City of/158
Charlotte-Mecklenburg School System/127
Chemetall Foote Mineral Company/201
Chemical Industry Institute of Toxicology
    (CIIT)/101
Ciber Information Services/113
Cisco Systems, Inc./114
Clayton Marcus/59
Club Group, Ltd./175
Coastal Carolina University/134
Coats North America/59
Coca-Cola Bottling Company
    Consolidated/153
Cogentrix Energy, Inc./201
Coleman Company, Inc./189
Collins & Aikman Corporation/80
Collins & Aikman Holdings Corporation/60
Colonial Life & Accident Insurance
    Company/179
Comcast Cablevision/110
Composites One LLC/229
ConAgra Specialty Snacks/154
Cone Mills Corporation/60
Cooper Bussmann Inc./136
Cooper Industries Inc./Cooper Tools
    Division/198
Cooperative Bankshares, Inc./83
Copeland Corporation/194
Cox Target Media/53
Crane Resistoflex Company/101
Cree Inc./137
Cross Creek Apparel Inc./60

Crown Holdings, Inc./199
Crowne Plaza Resort/175
Cummings Oil Company, Inc./232
Curtiss-Wright Corporation/55
Cutler-Hammer, Inc./141

D
DECI (Durham Exchange Club Industry,
    Inc.)/97
DP Connections, Inc./114
DP Solutions Inc./114
Dana Corporation/194
Datastream Systems, Inc./124
Davidson College/127
Davis Electrical Constructors, Inc./73
Davis Regional Medical Center/163
Elliot Davis & Company LLP/51
Dayco Products Inc./104
Defender Services/96
Deloitte & Touche/50
Delta Woodside Industries, Inc./68
Disabilities Board of Charleston County/161
Diversco Inc./96
R.R. Donnelley & Sons Company/215
RR Donnelley – Litho Industries/212
Douglas Battery Manufacturing Company/195
Drexel Heritage Furniture/185
Duke Energy Corporation/231
Duke University/128
Dunes Properties of Charleston, Inc./219
Durham Police Department/158
Durham Public Schools/128
Durham Regional Hospital/163

E
EDS (Electronic Data Systems
    Corporation)/114
EMC Corporation/115
East Carolina University/128
East Cooper Medical Center/169
Eaton Electrical/137
Electrolux Home Products/190
Ellett Brothers, Inc./190
Embrex Inc./89
Engelhard Corporation/105
ePlus Technology of North Carolina/115
Equifirst/84
Ericsson Inc./108
Ernst & Young LLP/50, 51
Evening Post Publishing Company/215

F
FFWD/53
FM Global/71
FMC Lithium/146
Family Dollar Stores, Inc./222
FarPoint Technologies, Inc./115
Fayetteville Observer Times/212
First Bancorp/First Bank/84
First Charter Corporation/First Charter
    National Bank/84
First Citizens Bancorporation of South
    Carolina, Inc./dba First Citizens Bank/87
First Citizens Bank & Trust/85
First Financial Holdings, Inc./87
First National Corporation/dba South Carolina
    Bank & Trust, N.A./87
Flambeau Products Corporation/102
Flowers Baking Company/154
Flowserve Pump Company/195
Fluor Corporation/74

Foam Design, Inc./103
Food Lion, Inc./222
Forsyth Technical Community College/129
Fountain Powerboat Industries Inc./185
Frey Media/216
Fujitsu Transactions Solutions/116
Futura Creative/212

G
GE Medical Systems/169
GMAC Insurance/177
Galey & Lord, Inc./61
General Engineering Laboratories, LLC/145
General Physics Corporation/96
Gilbarco/201
GlaxoSmithKline/94
Goerlich's Exhaust Systems/79
Gold Kist, Inc./157
Golden Corral Corporation/174
Good Hope Hospital/163
Goodrich Corporation/55
Goodyear Tire & Rubber Company/147
L.R. Gorrell Co./233
Grace Hospital/164
W.W. Grainger/234
Granite Knitwear, Inc./61
Greenville Hospital System/169
Greenville News/216
Greenwood Mills, Inc./68
Guardian Industries Corporation/229
Guilford Mills, Inc./61

H
HLM Design/71
Habitat for Humanity/Central South Carolina
    Habitat for Humanity/99
Hackney & Sons Inc./79
Hamilton Beach/
    Proctor-Silex, Inc./186
Hammary Furniture Company/186
Hampshire Designers, Inc./68
Hamrick's, Inc./225
Hanes Industries/61
Harris Teeter, Inc./222
Hatteras Yachts/230
Hawthorne Corporation/152
Haynsworth Sinkler Boyd, P.A./182
Henredon Furniture Industries, Inc./186
Hickory Chair Company/186
Hinshaw Music, Inc./212
Holt Hosiery/62
Holt Sublimation/62
Hon Industries/195
Honeywell Nylon Inc./195
Honeywell Sensotec/234
Honeywell/56, 62, 69
Hooker Furniture Corporation/187
Hunter Textbooks, Inc./212
Hydro Aluminum/149

I
IBM Corporation/116
iEntertainment Network/116
IKON Office Solutions/235
Indalex Inc./147
Ingles Markets, Inc./223
Insteel Industries, Inc./147
Intelicoat Technologies/102
International Employment Gazette/216
International Paper Company/203, 207
Intertape Polymer Group/190

Inveresk Research/90
Investors Title Insurance Company/178

J
J.C. Penney/223
JPS Industries/69
Jacobs Applied Technology/74
Jacobs Sirrine Engineers, Inc./75
Jacobsen/196
Jefferson-Pilot Communications/108
Jefferson-Pilot Financial/95
Jordan Lumber & Supply, Inc./204

K
KPMG/50, 52
Kaba Ilco Corporation/196
Kanawha Insurance Company, Inc./179
Kasho Gold Company, Inc./202
Kayser-Roth Corporation/62
Kearfott Guidance & Navigation
    Corporation/138
Kennametal Inc./199
Kennedy Covington Lobdell & Hickman/181
Kershaw County Medical Center/170
Kiawah Island Real Estate/219
Kidde Aerospace, Inc./56
Kimberly-Clark Corporation/63
King Hickory Furniture Company/187
King Pharmaceuticals, Inc./90
Kings Electronics Company Inc./141
Knowledge Systems Corporation/117
KoSa/63, 69
Kyrus Corporation/117

L
Laboratory Corporation of America
    (LabCorp)/90, 94
LANCE, Inc./155
Landstar Express America, Inc./230
La-Z-Boy Chair Company/187
Lea Industries/188
LEAD Technologies, Inc./117
Leatherwood Walker Todd & Mann P.C./182
Lee Industries/63
Level 8 Systems/117
Levolor Home Fashions/188
Lexington Home Brands/188
Lexington Medical Center/170
Liberty Corporation/110
Liberty Insurance Services Corporation/180
Lockheed Martin Aircraft and Logistics
    Center/56
Lockwood Greene Engineers, Inc./75
Long Agri-Business/196
Loris Healthcare Systems/Loris Community
    Hospital/170
Louis Rich Company/157
Lowe's Companies, Inc./223
Lowe's Foods/224
Lucent Technologies Inc./108

M
MCNC Research and Development
    Institute/117
Mack Trucks Inc./80
Management Information Systems Group,
    Inc./118
ManTech Environmental Technology, Inc./144
March of Dimes Birth Defects Foundation/99
Martin Color-Fi, Inc./105

McGladrey & Pullen, LLP/51
McKesson Information Solutions/118
McKinney & Silver/53
McLeod & Associates Incorporated/54
McNair Law Firm/182
MedCath Inc./164
Merchants Distributors Inc. (MDI)/155
Merck Manufacturing/91
Meredith College/129
Merrill Lynch & Co., Inc./152
Metro Productions/212
Michelin North America, Inc./105
Miller Desk Inc./188
Mission St. Joseph's Hospital/164
Misys, Inc./118
Modis IT Resource Management/124
Moog Components Group/138, 197
Moses Cone Health System/162
Motion Media/109
Murata Machinery USA/197
Muscular Dystrophy Association/100

N
Nan Ya Plastics Corporation, America/106
National Gypsum Company/228
National Institute of Environmental Health
    Sciences/91
National Spinning Company Inc./63
Nationwide Advertising Service Inc./54
Nestle USA/157
Network Controls International/138
Newark Electronics/142
News & Observer/213
News & Record/213
Nexsen Pruet Jacobs & Pollard, LLC/183
Nexus Software, Inc./119
Norcomp Limited Partnership/103
Nortel Networks/109
North Carolina A&T State University/129
North Carolina Biotechnology Center/97
North Carolina Central University/130
North Carolina Department of Agriculture &
    Consumer Services/159
North Carolina Department of Correction/159
North Carolina Department of
    Transportation/159
North Carolina Mutual Life Insurance
    Company/178
North Carolina School of the Arts/130
North Carolina State University/130
Northern Hospital/164
Nucor Corporation/148
Nucor Steel/149

O
Oakwood Homes/72
Office Depot/Business Services Division/224
Omega Performance Inc./130
One Price Clothing Stores/226
Onslow Memorial Hospital/165
Opsware, Inc./119
Opus One Graphic Design/213
Oracle Packaging/204
Oracle/119
Orangeburg Consolidated School District
    5/134
Orders Distributing Company, Inc./235
Oro Manufacturing Company/148
Owen Steel Company/149
Owens-Corning /229

P

PCA International, Inc./213
Palmetto Health/171
Paramount Paper/103
Margaret R. Pardee Memorial Hospital/165
Parker Hannifin Corporation/57
Parker Poe Adams & Bernstein/181
Perdue Farms, Inc./155
Perrigo Company/94
Perry, Perry & Perry/181
Piedmont Behavioral Health Care/98
Piedmont Natural Gas Co., Inc./231
Pirelli Cable Corporation/110
Pitt County Memorial Hospital/
    University Health Systems of Eastern
    Carolina/165
Powerware Corporation/138, 197
Premier Inc./166
Presidion Solutions, Inc./52
PricewaterhouseCoopers/51
Progress Energy/231
Progress Lighting, Inc./142
Progressive Computer Systems, Inc./119
Providence Hospitals/171
Prudential Carolinas Realty/218
Public Service Company of North Carolina,
    Inc./232

Q

Qualex, Inc./213
Quintiles Inc./92

R

RBC Centura/85
RF Micro Devices Inc./139
Raleigh, City of/159
Randolph Hospital/166
Rauch Industries, Inc./188
Red Hat Software, Inc./119
Regal Manufacturing Company/64
Reichhold Chemicals, Inc./103
Rental Service Corporation/95
Research Triangle Institute (RTI)/92
R.J. Reynolds Tobacco Holdings, Inc./156
Richland Memorial Hospital/171
Riverbanks Zoo & Garden/77
Rock Hill Telephone Company/111
Rocky Mount Cord Company/64
Royal & SunAlliance USA/178
Royal Home Fashions Inc./64
Ruddick Corporation/189
Rutherford County Schools/131
Ryan's Family Steak Houses, Inc./175

S

SAS Institute Inc./120
SPX Corporation/72
Saco Lowell, Inc./199
Saddle Creek Copak Corporation/54
Safety-Kleen Corporation/145
Saft America Inc./197
Salem College/Salem Academy/131
Salomon Smith Barney/152
Salvation Army/100
Sands Resorts/176
Sara Lee Hosiery/64
Sara Lee Intimate Apparel/64
ScanSource, Inc./142
Schlumberger Resource Management
    Services/202

Scotsman Ice Systems/200
Scott & Stringfellow, Inc./151
Sea Pines Associates, Inc./176
Sealy, Inc./189
Securitas/95
Security Finance Corporation/152
Seibels Bruce Group, Inc./180
Shadowline Inc./65
Shamrock Environmental Services/144
Shaw Group, Inc./dba B.F. Shaw, Inc./150
Simclar North America, Inc./120
Slickedit, Inc./120
Smithfield Packing Company, Inc./156
Smurfit-Stone Container Corporation/204, 208
M.J. Soffe Company, Inc./65
Solutience/124
Sonic Automotive Inc./224
Sonoco Products/200
Source Technologies, Inc./121
South Carolina Department of Agriculture/161
South Carolina Electric and Gas
    Company/232
South Carolina State Museum/77
South Coast Community Bank/88
South Trust/88
Southeastern Commercial Services/220
Southern Furniture Company/189
Southern Industrial Constructors, Inc./72
Span-America Medical Systems, Inc./172
Spartanburg Steel Products Inc./150
Speedway Motorsports, Inc./76
Speizman Industries, Inc./234
Spirax Sarco Inc./200
Springs Industries, Inc./191
Square D Company/142
St. Timothy Chair Company/189
Stanadyne Automotive Corporation/79
Standard Commercial Corporation/156
State Newspaper/217
Steinberg Law Firm/183
Sterling Healthcare/178
Strategic Technologies/121
Suitt Construction Company Inc./75
Sumitomo Electric Lightwave Corporation/109
Summus Limited/121
Superior Essex/143
Syngenta Biotechnology, Inc./93
Synnex Information Technologies, Inc./124
Synopsys, Inc./121

T

Tarheel Roller & Brayer/198
Tesa Tape, Inc/198
Textilease/96
Thales Computers/121
Thomas Built Buses, Inc./79
Thomasville Furniture/65
3M Company/191
Tietex International/69
Timken Company/81
TouchPoint Solutions/122
Transbotics Corporation/122
Triangle Transit Authority/230
Trico Engineering/75
Trion, Inc./139
Troxler Electronic Laboratories, Inc./139
Troy Group/122
Tuomey Healthcare System/172
Turner Padget Graham & Laney/183
Tyco Healthcare/dba Kendall Healthcare
    Company/173

Tyco Healthcare/Mallinckrodt/95, 103
Tyson Foods Inc./156

U
URS Corporation/144
U.S. Department of Agriculture Forest
    Service/Southern Research Station/160
U.S. Dept. of Veterans Affairs Durham
    Veterans Administration Medical
    Center/166
U.S. Environmental Protection Agency
    (EPA)/160
U.S. Federal Reserve Bank of Richmond/85
U.S. Foodservice/157
U.S. Postal Service/161
Ultimus/122
John Umstead Hospital/167
Underwriters Laboratories/73
Unifi, Inc./65
United Defense/81
University of North Carolina at Chapel Hill/131
University of North Carolina at Charlotte/132
University of North Carolina at
    Greensboro/132
University of North Carolina at Wilmington/132
University of North Carolina Center for Public
    Television/109
University of North Carolina Press/214
University of South Carolina/134

V
VF Corporation/66
Variety Wholesaler/224
Verbatim Corporation/122
Verizon Communications/109
Vishay Micro-Measurements/140
Vitafoam Inc./104
Vulcan Materials Company/228

W
Wachovia Corporation/85
Wachovia Corporation/First
    Union/Wachovia/88
Wake Forest University-Baptist Medical
    Center/167
Washington Mutual Home Loans/152
Waste Management, Inc./145
Watts Nursing School/133
Waverly Mills Incorporated/67
Wayne County Public Schools/133
Weavexx/198
Welcome Home, Inc./224
Weldon City School District/133
Western Carolina University/133
Westinghouse Electric Corporation/106
Westminster Homes/73, 218
Weyerhaeuser Company/205, 208
Williamsburg County School District/134
Wilson Sporting Goods Company/192
Wingfoot Commercial Tire Systems/104
Winston Hotels, Inc./175
Winston-Salem Industries for the Blind/98
Winston-Salem Journal/214
Winston-Salem, City of/160
Womble Carlyle Sandridge & Rice, PLLC/182
Women's Hospital of Greensboro/167
Woodlands Resort & Inn/78
Woven Electronics Corporation/143

X
Xerox/123

Y
Cale Yarborough Honda/Mazda/225

Z
Ziff Properties/220